[redacted]

LITURGY OF LIBERATION

A CHRISTIAN COMMENTARY ON SHANKARA'S
UPADEŚASĀHASRĪ

CHRISTIAN COMMENTARIES ON NON-CHRISTIAN SACRED TEXTS

The series "Christian Commentaries on Non-Christian Sacred Texts" provides a forum for Christian reflection on the meaning and importance of sacred texts (scriptures and religious classics) of other religious traditions for Christian faith and practice.

LITURGY OF LIBERATION

A CHRISTIAN COMMENTARY ON SHANKARA'S *UPADEŚASĀHASRĪ*

BY

REID B. LOCKLIN

PEETERS
LEUVEN – PARIS – WALPOLE, MA

WILLIAM B. EERDMANS PUBLISHING COMPANY
GRAND RAPIDS, MICHIGAN/CAMBRIDGE, U.K.

2011

Published jointly 2011
in Belgium by
Peeters Publishers
Bondgenotenlaan 153
3000 Leuven
and in the United States of America by
Wm. B. Eerdmans Publishing Company
2140 Oak Industrial Dr. N.E., Grand Rapids, Michigan 49505 /
P.O. Box 163 Cambridge CB3 9PU U.K.
www.eerdmans.com

Manufactured in Belgium

12 11 10 09 08 5 4 3 2 1

A catalogue record for this book is available from the Library of Congress.

Eerdmans ISBN 978-0-8028-6751-3
Peeters ISBN 978-90-429-2563-2
D/2011/0602/143

To My Teachers

vimathya vedodadhitaḥ samuddhṛtaṃ surairmahābdhestu yathā mahātmabhiḥ
tathā 'mṛtaṃ jñānamidaṃ hi yaiḥ purā namo gurubhyaḥ paramīkṣitaṃ ca yaḥ
Upadeśasāhasrī Padyabandha 19.28

TABLE OF CONTENTS

Dedication V

Abbreviations of Hindu Sources XI

Preface XIII

PART I:
ENCOUNTERING SHANKARA'S *UPADEŚASĀHASRĪ*

Chapter 1. Sacred Scripture, Sacred Scripts: The *Thousand Teachings* of Ādi Shankaracharya 3

I. The *Upadeśasāhasrī* as Portrait, Pedagogy and Practice 5
– *Myths of Ādi Shankaracharya* 7
– *"I Composed this Dialogue"* 12
– *The Boat of Knowledge* 15
– *Inter-Textuality and Orality* 20

II. Becoming an Interreligious Hearer of Shankara's *Upadeśasāhasrī* 23
– *Advaita Reception(s) of the* Upadeśasāhasrī 24
– *Hearing and Performing the Advaita Text* 30
– *Christian Commentary, Christian Saṃvāda* 35

Chapter 2. Traditions in Tension: USP 1 and the Christian Hearer 47

I. *Upadeśasāhasrī Padyabandha 1.1-2, 16-21a* 47

II. The Priority of Knowledge: Hearing USP 1 47
– *The End of the Vedas (USP 1.2-7)* 49
– *Objection and Reply (USP 1.8-14)* 54
– *The Superior Path (USP 1.15-21a)* 59
– *Rejection and Reconciliation (USP 1.21b-26)* 64

III. "I want you to understand this mystery": *Saṃvāda* and Reconciliation in the Commentarial Project 67

Part II:
Experiments in Dialogue

Chapter 3. A Scandalous Wisdom: Commentary on USP 2-7 .. 83

I. *Upadeśasāhasrī Padyabandha 5.1-5* 83

II. The Eternal Witness: Hearing USP 2-7 (Selections) 83
– *Self and Non-Self (USP 2.1 – 3.4)* 86
– *Why Do We Recoil? (USP 5.1-5)* 92
– *The Witness (USP 7.1-6)* 98

III. "God's foolishness is higher than human wisdom": A Christian *Saṃvāda* with USP 2-7 103

Chapter 4. Sowing the Word: Commentary on USG 1 113

I. *Upadeśasāhasrī Gadyabandha 1.1-3* 113

II. The Transmission of Knowledge: Hearing USG 1 (Selections) 113
– *Teacher and Student (USG 1.2-6a)* 115
– *Origin of the Body (USG 1.9-11, 16-21, 23a)* 121
– *The Primacy and Coherence of the Word (USG 1.39-43)* 131

III. "Not a human word, but God's word": A Christian *Saṃvāda* with USG 1 135

Chapter 5. Hearers of the Word: Commentary on USP 18 145

I. *Upadeśasāhasrī Padyabandha 18.29-30, 110* 145

II. *Tat-tvam-asi*: Hearing USP 18 (Selections) 145
– *A Question of Experience (USP 18.3-4, 9-10)* 147
– *Agreement and Difference (USP 18.96, 169-71, 188-90)* 152
– *The Reflection of the Self in the Mind (USP 18.26, 29-30, 109-10, 202-3)* 159

III. "It is God who is at work in you": A Christian *Saṃvāda* with USP 18 167

Chapter 6. Discernment and Communion: Commentary on USG 2 179

I. *Upadeśasāhasrī Gadyabandha 2.62-65* 179

II. Discerning the Self: Hearing USG 2 (Selections) 179
– *Mā-karṣīs-tarhi! (USG 2.51, 54a, 62-66, 69-70a, 71-73a)*... 182
– *Changeless and Changing Knowledge (2.73b-74a, 76-77, 102-3, 108b-111)*... 193

III. "Examine yourselves": A Christian *Saṃvāda* with USG 2..... 202

Chapter 7. A Pilgrim People: Commentary on USP 16........... 215

I. *Upadeśasāhasrī Padyabandha 16.65-69*.................................. 215

II. Steady on the Path of Knowledge: Hearing USP 16 (Selections) 215
– *Refuting the Other (USP 16.23-24, 30-32, 48-50, 61-62)*... 218
– *A Higher Renunciation (USP 16.17-18, 44, 64-69, 74)* 227

III. "Creation awaits the revealing of the children of God": A Christian *Saṃvāda* with USP 16 236

Chapter 8. *Anamnesis* and Liberation: Commentary on USG 3 249

I. *Upadeśasāhasrī Gadyabandha 3.115*...................................... 249

II. The Discipline of Recollection: Hearing USP 10 and USG 3 (Selections) 250
– *Rehearsing the Truth of the Self (USP 10.1-3, 7-8, 12-13)*.. 253
– *A Method of Repetition (USG 3.112, 114-15)* 260
– *A Vision of Transformation (USG 3.116)*........................... 268

III. "Lest you have come to believe in vain": A Christian *Saṃvāda* with USG 3 273

PART III:
THE LITURGY OF LIBERATION

Chapter 9. Conclusion: Shankara's *Upadeśasāhasrī* – All Things Reconciled? 289

I. "God was pleased to reconcile all things": Christ the Divine *Saṃvāda*.. 289

II. Therapy of Knowledge, Liturgy of Liberation: USP 19 After Commentary 297
– *Striving against Striving: The Means of Grace (USP 19.2-3)* 301

– *Telling the Truth: The Difficulty of Difference (USP 19.4-5)* 305
– *Interrupting the Intellect: A More and Other God (USP 19.6)* 309
– *Right Relations (USP 19.12)* 313

III. *Namaḥ*: The *Upadeśasāhasrī* and the Possibility of a Christian Salutation 318

Index of Scriptural Citations 323

Index of Names 325

ABBREVIATIONS OF HINDU SOURCES

AUBh	Shankara, *Aitareya-Upaniṣad-Bhāṣya*
BG	*Bhagavad-Gītā*
BGBh	Shankara, *Bhagavad-Gītā-Bhāṣya*
BSBh	Shankara, *Brahma-Sūtra-Bhāṣya*
BU	*Bṛhadāraṇyaka Upaniṣad*
BUBh	Shankara, *Bṛhadāraṇyaka-Upaniṣad-Bhāṣya*
CU	*Chāndogya Upaniṣad*
CUBh	Shankara, *Chāndogya-Upaniṣad-Bhāṣya*
GKBh	Shankara, *Gauḍapādīya-Kārikā-Bhāṣya*
IU	*Iśa Upaniṣad*
IUBh	Shankara, *Iśa-Upaniṣad-Bhāṣya*
KaU	*Kaṭha Upaniṣad*
KaUBh	Shankara, *Kaṭha-Upaniṣad-Bhāṣya*
KeUBh	Shankara, *Kena-Upaniṣad-Bhāṣya*
Manu	*Law of Manu*
MaUBh	Shankara, *Māṇḍūkya-Upaniṣad-Bhāṣya*
MuU	*Muṇḍaka Upaniṣad*
MuUBh	Shankara, *Muṇḍaka-Upaniṣad-Bhāṣya*
NS	Sureśvara, *Naiṣkarmya-Siddhi*
TU	*Taittirīya Upaniṣad*
USG	Shankara, *Upadeśasāhasrī Gadyabandha*
USP	Shankara, *Upadeśasāhasrī Padyabandha*

PREFACE

For six days in late July and early August 2009, hundreds of devotees streamed from throughout Canada and the world to a hotel and conference center in the western suburbs of Toronto. They gathered to honor the 16th anniversary of the passing of Swami Chinmayananda, a modern teacher in the non-dualist Hindu tradition of Advaita Vedanta and founder of the international Chinmaya Mission. At the Mahasamadhi Family Camp, as it was called, adults and children honored this auspicious date by embarking on rigorous, parallel programs of meditation, chanting, cultural performances, and lectures and discussions with prominent acharyas – authorized teachers of the Chinmaya movement. At the center of this program: a series of discourses by the spiritual head of the Chinmaya Mission, His Holiness Swami Tejomayananda, focused on one of the great classics of Hindu devotional piety, the *Bhagavata Purāṇa*. A spirit of devotion was palpable throughout the event, with every transition marked by the chanting of sacred mantras and, in the afternoons, more formal worship in a common rite known as *arati*. On the final day, in a grand "*Mahasamadhi Puja*," devotees arranged themselves in neat lines and, led by Swami Tejomayananda and other acharyas on a raised platform, offered flower petals and hymns to stylized icons of the great guru's holy sandals.

Few contemporary Christians, Hindus or other religious persons would be especially surprised to discover that an event like the Mahasamadhi Family Camp was punctuated by ritual worship. Slightly less familiar or expected might be the firm conviction that the Camp as a whole and especially its discourses might also be seen to constitute a form of ritual worship on the analogy of Vedic sacrifice – a *jñāna-yajña*, or "sacrifice of knowledge," as Swami Chinmayananda and the Chinmaya Mission came to describe the movement's signature week-long teaching programs on the Bhagavad-Gita and the sacred Upanishads. The goal of such sacrifice? A transformed life, in the wider world. A young woman from Maryland captured it nicely one morning of the Camp, in a testimonial witness to Swami Chinmayananda's popular book, *A Manual of Self-Unfoldment*: "It really helps me to further [my] spiritual practice. I thought the only way to grow spiritually was to meditate at great length; but this book reveals how [we] can grow spiritually through [our] everyday lives as students and professionals and mothers." True spirituality, this devotee argued, pertains to the everyday: with the guidance of the right teacher and teaching tradition, any act can be transformed into authentic spiritual discipline. In this sense, the teaching itself becomes the highest possible rite and the central form of spiritual practice, and thus it is appropriate to refer to it as a *yajña*, as a carefully scripted and meticulously executed ritual sacrifice.

The close association between teaching, on the one hand, and transformative spiritual practice, on the other, lies at the heart of this commentarial project. As one volume in the Peeters series, "Christian Commentaries on Non-Christian Sacred Texts," this book offers a close reading and Christian theological commentary on a sacred text of the Advaita tradition of Hinduism: the *Upadeśasāhasrī*, or *Thousand Teachings*, of the great eighth-century CE teacher and commentator Ādi Shankaracharya. At one level, this ancient Sanskrit text bears only the most tenuous relationship to the modern scene described above. In form, it offers a combination of poetic verses and prose sections, of first-person address and third-person accounts, of meditative repetition and fierce, polemic debate. It certainly does not envision "students and professionals and mothers" as its idealized hearers and disciples, and it invokes the idiom of Vedic ritual only to reject it in the strongest terms possible. Yet, the *Upadeśasāhasrī* also bears within itself not only the same fundamental message – *tat-tvam-asi,* "you are that," "you are the divine Self of all beings" – but also a fundamentally similar character as scripted dialogue and ritualized practice. In the light of the broader teaching tradition, I shall argue, a text like the *Upadeśasāharī* emerges as something distinct from a theological treatise, a philosophical exposition or a guidebook to mystical experience and inquiry, though it is also explicable on each of these levels. What it offers is both less and more: a series of scripted dialogues and discursive practices that aim to transform every aspect of its disciples' lives and thus to render them ever more transparent to the eternally released, divine Self of all. It offers what I term, only somewhat playfully, a "liturgy of liberation."

I first read the *Upadeśasāharī* in graduate school at Boston College, and it was there that I decided that it would be, along with the *De catechizandis rudibus* of St. Augustine of Hippo, the focus of my doctoral dissertation. But I would say that I first *encountered* this work as a sacred text of the Hindu tradition when I studied it in India, under the guidance of an Advaita acharya. It is not that I discovered how sacred the *Upadeśasāharī* itself was in the lives of most devotees: though it is the only non-commentarial text accepted by most historical scholars as the work of Ādi Shankaracharya, its extremely terse and technical prose has meant that contemporary teachers often prefer to teach from other scriptural sources or more popular treatises. Indeed, at one point in our study of the *Upadeśasāharī*'s second prose chapter,[1] my teacher pointed to a particularly difficult text and exclaimed, "Students would run!"

Rather, as I became ever more familiar with the rhythm of the text, it began to resonate strongly with the rhythms of receiving individual instruction, of attending public discourses, of chanting the mantras to sanctify Advaita study, of witnessing the occasional *pūjā* to the teaching tradition. And these resonances expanded, as I studied, to force me to re-encounter my own Christian tradition in a new way.[2] Above all, this text has underscored and more fully revealed to me the close, mutually informing relationship between word and table, scriptural text and ritual practice and, more broadly, liturgical performance and the life of faith. I have often been surprised at how this ostensibly anti-ritualist, intellectualist text and tradition continually turn me back to reflect upon the profound sacramentality and Eucharistic character of all embodied existence, as we wait in hope for its glorious consummation. I have come to see Christ ever more fully revealed in the full range of human experience, I believe, precisely because I have encountered Christ in dialogue with this Hindu teaching tradition.

Stated differently, the sacred character of this text became manifest as a lens through which to encounter the sacred tradition of Advaita Vedanta – and also to re-encounter the sacred traditions of the Christian churches – in its fullest, living expression. These traditions and their sacred words are persistently and at some level necessarily oral in character, continually re-created in and through a shared practice of teaching, learning and assiduous self-cultivation.[3] To write a commentary on the *Upadeśasāhasrī* is, therefore, to attempt a still greater task: namely, to write a commentary on that sacred tradition that the text itself presumes, implies and models for its hearers. To write a *Christian* commentary on this text is to judge this sacred tradition in the light of Christ, to be sure;

[1] See chapter 6, below, for further discussion.

[2] I have reflected on this experience in more detail in my short apologia *Spiritual but Not Religious? An Oarstroke Closer to the Farther Shore* (Collegeville, MN: Liturgical Press, 2005).

[3] The oral, fluid character of scripture in Hindu (and other traditions) is brought out particularly well in Harold COWARD, *Scripture in the World Religions: A Short Introduction* (Oxford: Oneworld, 1988, 2000), and Leela PRASAD, *Poetics of Conduct: Oral Narrative and Moral Being in a South Indian Town* (New York: Columbia University Press, 2007).

but it is also, no less importantly, an opportunity to encounter this same Christ anew, in the self-illuminating light of Advaita.

To the degree that I have succeeded in this task, the credit is certainly not due to me alone. I have dedicated this commentary to all of the teachers from whom I have been privileged to learn these many years, and so it is appropriate to begin by thanking my most significant gurus: the priest and scholar Fr. Francis X. Clooney, S.J. and the Advaita acharya Swami Paramarthananda Saraswati. Both have been extraordinary mentors to me, albeit in very different ways, and their unflagging support has compensated for many of my own defects. I live in hope that I may yet come to reflect some fraction of the grace I have discovered in them.

I have been privileged, too, to conduct my research and writing with the support of various teaching and learning communities. Of these, the first is of course the community of disciples that is the Christian Church, particularly as so beautifully embodied by the Jesuits, women religious and lay Catholics associated with Aikiya Alayam and the Institute for Dialogue with Cultures and Religions in Chennai, India. St. Michael's College, the Catholic college of the University of Toronto, has also provided an extremely enriching environment for my work. I am deeply grateful for the support of students and colleagues at St. Mike's and the Centre for the Study of Religion, and to the University itself for providing me a much-needed study leave in the spring of 2008 to complete a first draft of the manuscript. Work on chapters 5, 6 and 7 was supported by a 2007 Lilly Endowment grant from the Wabash Center for Teaching and Learning in Theology and Religion, and portions of chapters 6 and 8 have been presented and discussed with participants in the Conference on the Study of the Religions of India in 2009 and 2010. The manuscript was brought into its final form during a short but invaluable writing retreat at St. John's University, in Collegeville, Minnesota, in the summer of 2010 and during my appointment as a Senior Fellow at the Martin Marty Center for the Advanced Study of Religion at the University of Chicago in the academic year 2010-2011. My work is far richer from my discussions and companionship in all of these communities.

Liturgy of Liberation was not merely written *in* community; it is in an important sense the work *of* a community, of which I am only one member. I offer heartfelt thanks to the following colleagues, who read the manuscript in part or in whole, and who made many helpful suggestions: Francis X. Clooney, Jennifer A. Harris, Grace Ji-Sun Kim, Julia Lauwers, Michael McLaughlin, Laurie Patton, Balkaran Raj, Colleen Shantz,

Michael Stoeber, and some ten anonymous reviewers from both manuscript and tenure review processes. Julia Lauwers and Michael O'Connor deserve special mention for the hours they invested helping me to articulate a number of key concepts and offering important guidance in the revision process, as does Lisa Gasson for her assistance with the index. I began my study of Shankara with Hugh Nicholson, and he has continued to accompany me along the way, as he commented on my drafts and I commented on drafts of his important monograph, *Comparative Theology and the Problem of Religious Rivalry* (Oxford University Press, 2011). This work would look very different – and much weaker – without Hugh's contribution. I also owe a debt of gratitude to Peeters Press and especially to the series editor, Catherine Cornille, who patiently bore with many delays in the course of writing and revising the manuscript and whose suggestions significantly strengthened the final work. Finally, my wife Jolie Chrisman not only read this work carefully and supported me in a hundred different ways as I struggled to bring it to term, but also suffered graciously as I read most of it aloud, usually in multiple successive versions. To the extent that I have captured any aspect of the oral character of the tradition in my prose, I am sure that I have Jolie to thank for it.

One aspect of this commentary is perhaps worth noting at the outset, before moving to explore the historical background and rough texture of the *Upadeśasāhasrī* in chapter 1. With regard to gendered pronouns, I have attempted to recognize both Shankara's own ancient tradition, which was certainly gender-exclusive in describing those qualified to receive the teaching, and the creative extension of this tradition to a much wider and more diverse community of disciples by contemporary teachers like Swami Chinmayananda and modern movements like the Chinmaya Mission, among many others. I therefore use the masculine pronoun to describe the disciple who is explicitly identified in the *Upadeśasāhasrī*'s prose portion and the feminine pronoun to describe the disciple who is implied in the verse portion of the text. For the prose sections and verses selected for direct comment, I have – with some, small modifications – followed the translation by Sengaku Mayeda.[4] I am very grateful to the State University of New York Press for granting permission to reprint these selections here; the copyright, of course, remains with its owner.

[4] Sengaku MAYEDA (trans.), *A Thousand Teachings: The Upadeśasāhasrī of Śaṅkara* (Albany: State University of New York Press, 1992).

In reflecting on the life and works of Ādi Shankaracharya, the great Indologist Daniel H.H. Ingalls offered the following reflection about the Indian commentarial tradition:

> In the West we think of commentators as dull creatures, lacking in imagination, who take some one else's text to furnish themselves with ideas... But the Indian tradition is different. The most original and imaginative products of the Indian intellect are given us in the form of commentaries. The Indian authors may try to hide their originality, borrowing from tradition as much as they can, attributing even their new ideas to some ancient sage, but the originality is still there. Often it may be as great in a pious Sanskrit commentary as in a professedly revolutionary tract written in English or in German. The Indians are not less original; they are simply more anonymous.[5]

The present work attempts to stand in the commentarial tradition Ingalls describes. It does so, first, because it attempts to understand the *Upadeśasāhasrī* within the Advaita tradition, including not only the commentaries on this work, but also the broader teaching traditions to which it is so closely related. At the same time, it aspires to emulate the wisdom of the commentarial tradition by, insofar as possible, letting the ancient voices – Hindu and Christian alike – speak directly and intelligibly to those who may be hearing some of these teachings for the first time. I am nevertheless hopeful that the result may turn out to be an original and helpful contribution to the discipline of comparative theology and to the broader pursuit of interreligious dialogue and collaboration, particularly between those Christians and Hindus who so deeply value the diverse texts and traditions that inform this study.

Śivarātri
March 2011
Chicago, Illinois

[5] Daniel H.H. INGALLS, "The Study of Śaṃkarācārya," *Annals of the Bhandarkar Oriental Research Institute* 33 (1952): p. 3.

PART I:

ENCOUNTERING SHANKARA'S *UPADEŚASĀHASRĪ*

CHAPTER 1

SACRED SCRIPTURE, SACRED SCRIPTS: THE *THOUSAND TEACHINGS* OF ĀDI SHANKARACHARYA

"A compendium of the essential meaning of all the *Upanishads*."[1]

Thus the commentator Śri Ānandagiri Acharya, writing in the mid-thirteenth century CE, characterizes the *Upadeśasāhasrī* (*A Thousand Teachings*) of Ādi Shankaracharya. This assessment would be echoed by another commentator, Śri Rāmatīrtha, some four hundred years later.[2] So also we, in turn, might begin this Christian commentary on the *Upadeśasāhasrī* by reflecting briefly on Ānandagiri's terse précis.

First of all, a "compendium of the *Upanishads*" is, by definition, *not* identical with the *Upanishads* themselves. These scriptures, the final major portion of the Vedic corpus, hold a place in the highest tier of sacred authority in Hindu orthodoxy. They are classified as *śruti*, "what is heard," revelation in the proper sense of the word. The *Upadeśasāhasrī*, on the other hand, is just what its title suggests: a compilation or assortment of Shankara's teachings, perhaps more appropriately described as *smṛti*, "what is remembered," subordinate to "what is heard." The Vedas are generally understood as *a-pauruṣeya*, "authorless," beyond and above any human intention, beyond and above the created world, even beyond and above those many deities whose images adorn temples in India and abroad.[3] The *Upadeśasāhasrī* is, by contrast, importantly

[1] In Sanskrit: *sarva-upaniṣad-artha-sāra-saṃgrāhikā upadeśasāhasrī.*

[2] See ĀNANDAGIRI's comment in S. SUBRAHMANYA SASTRI (ed.), *Shri Shankarabhagavatpada's Upadeshasahasri with the Tika of Shri Anandagiri Acharya*, Advaita Grantha Ratna Manjushi Ratna 15 (Varanasi: Mahesh Research Institute, 1978), p. 121 (line 11), and RĀMATĪRTHA's in D. GOKHALE (ed.), *Shri Shankarāchārya's Upadeśasāhasrī with the Gloss Padayôjanīkā by Shrī Rāmatīrtha* (Bombay: Gujurati Printing Press, 1917), p. 1.

[3] See Purusottama BILIMORIA, "The Idea of Authorless Revelation (*Apauruṣeya*)," in R. PERRETT (ed.), *Indian Philosophy of Religion*, ed. (Dordrecht: Kluwer Academic Publishers, 1989), pp. 143-66; Francis X. CLOONEY, S.J., "Why the Veda Has No Author:

pauruṣeya, written by a particular person at a particular place and time in Indian history.

Nevertheless, it is not to the *Upanishads* but to the *Upadeśasāhasrī* that the commentators encourage us to look for the "essential meaning" of Vedic revelation.

This ambivalent character of the *Upadeśasāhasrī* as both *pauruṣeya* and "essential meaning," both historically-conditioned exposition and quintessential distillation of an eternal truth, makes it a peculiar kind of sacred text. From a Christian perspective, it may seem strange to call it *sacred* at all, even if we prescind from asking theological questions about the elements of truth and holiness it may (or may not) contain. "Tradition" would seem a better label. The *Upadeśasāhasrī* would then be regarded as comparable to the decrees of the Council of Nicaea or John Calvin's *Institutes of the Christian Religion*. Worthy of comment, perhaps, but certainly not a "sacred text" on a par with the Hebrew Bible, the New Testament or even a more well-known Hindu *smṛti* like the *Bhagavad-Gītā*.[4]

On one level, such reservations are well taken. But "sacred text" and "sacred tradition" are not so easily separated in the Hindu tradition of Advaita Vedanta from which it comes and for which it possesses its highest status. Here, final authority resides – to borrow a phrase often employed by Shankara and his successors – in "scripture and the teacher" (*śāstra-ācārya*), and neither apart from the other. Though the *Upadeśasāhasrī* may be *pauruṣeya*, moreover, the *puruṣa* who composed it is regarded by many as a living embodiment of the Vedic revelation and, thus, of whatever we might mean by "sacred" itself.

In this introductory chapter, I attempt a first exploration of the *Upadeśasāhasrī* as both sacred text and sacred tradition, a compilation of teachings whose revelatory power is located less in the words themselves than in their scripted performance by teachers and students from Shankara's time to our own. The burden of this interpretation is borne primarily by the first section, in which I offer successive portraits of Ādi Shankaracharya, the *Upadeśasāhasrī* and the teaching tradition it both

Language as Ritual in Early Mīmāṃsā and Post-Modern Theology," *Journal of the American Academy of Religion* 55 (1988): pp. 677-78; and Wilhelm HALBFASS, *Tradition and Reflection* (Albany: State University of New York Press, 1991), pp. 144-51. For a critical evaluation of this claim in Advaita tradition, see K. Satchidananda MURTY, *Revelation and Reason in Advaita Vedānta* (Waltair: Andhra University, 1959).

[4] See, for example, C. CORNILLE (ed.), *Song Divine: Christian Commentaries on the Bhagavad Gītā* (Leuven, Paris, and Dudley, MA: Peeters and W.B. Eerdmans, 2006).

presumes and models for its hearers. Then, in the second section, I attempt to develop an initial vision of what the distinctive character of this sacred text requires of its Christian commentator. To comment on this text, I suggest, one must be willing to *hear* it, to become a participant in the scripts it provides, and to enter into what Shankara upholds as the religious practice *par excellence*: *saṃvāda*, or "dialogue." The Christian commentator who enters into dialogue with the *Upadeśasāhasrī* continues a dialogue initiated in the text itself, and this dialogue is in turn constitutive of its status as a sacred text of the Advaita tradition.

I.

THE *UPADEŚASĀHASRĪ* AS PORTRAIT, PEDAGOGY AND PRACTICE

Any encounter with the *Upadeśasāharī* must begin by giving some account of the extraordinary individual whom traditional teachers and historical scholars agree lies behind its pages: Ādi Shankaracharya. Such a task is more easily said than done, as it turns out, for Shankara tells us very little about himself. The majority of his writings are commentarial in form, making it difficult to discern the 'true' or 'authentic' personality behind them. Shankara, not unlike the ideal wise person he describes in one of his commentaries, seems to have acted "without his actions being known, pursuing his *dharma* privately...' and 'With no outward signs or ostentatious behaviour'"[5] – or, at least, this is how it seems from a vantage some 1200 or 1300 years removed from his own.

Despite the paucity of direct evidence, it is not difficult to establish a few basic parameters. One can, first of all, securely assert that Shankara has emerged over the course of time as one of the most prominent advocates for the Hindu teaching tradition of Advaita Vedanta, as well as becoming one of the most influential figures in the intellectual and religious history of India. Even those Hindu disputants who later disagree vehemently with Shankara's teaching do so largely on terms he set for them. Most significantly, this great teacher produced the earliest extant commentary on the so-called *Brahma-* or *Vedānta-Sūtras*, a collection of highly compact sentences and phrases probably committed to writing in the early centuries of the Common Era. Shankara's own dates are

[5] BSBh 3.4.50, quoted in J.G. SUTHREN HIRST, *Śaṃkara's Advaita Vedānta: A Way of Teaching*, RoutledgeCurzon Hindu Studies Series (London and New York: RoutledgeCurzon, 2005), p. 17.

disputed, but an emerging consensus locates his life and work in the early to middle eighth century CE, with a fairly broad margin of error on either side.[6]

More secure, perhaps, is the content of Shankara's thought. The Shankara scholar Bradley Malkovsky offers the following thumbnail sketch:

> The essence of Advaitic teaching is frequently summarized according to the following verse: *"Brahman is real, the world is an illusory appearance; the individual soul is Brahman alone, none other."* Though this statement does not originate with Śaṃkara, it expresses well the common interpretation of *advaita* or nonduality as a form of monism. Accordingly, though we experience ourselves as belonging to a world of multiplicity and change, there is really only one reality, *brahman*, the changeless and eternal ground of being; all else is but a passing appearance that vanishes in the higher intuition of oneness. From the perspective of highest truth or standpoint (*paramārtha-avasthā*), only *brahman* is.[7]

As it turns out, Malkovsky actually distances himself from this traditional interpretation, especially its alleged "illusionism" or "monism."[8] Others have gone further, questioning the very project of treating Shankara's "doctrines" apart from the methods he employed to communicate them.[9] In the midst of such quibbles (in which I will also indulge in these pages), Shankara's fundamental teaching nevertheless rings clear: namely, that what we conventionally call "self" (*Ātman*) and what we conventionally call "divine reality" or "God" (*Brahman*) cannot be separated one from the other – or, perhaps better, it is our conventional labels alone which falsely divide what is one divine reality. Hence

[6] Hajime NAKAMURA proposed 700-750 CE, and these dates have been widely accepted. Tilmann VETTER argues for a somewhat broader range, suggesting that it is impossible to settle on any precise date between 650 and 800 CE. See Hajime NAKAMURA, *A History of Early Vedānta Philosophy: Part One*, T. LEGGETT, S. MAYEDA, T. UNNO, and others (trans.), Religions of Asia Series 1 (Delhi: Motilal Banarsidass, 1983), pp. 48-89; Tilmann VETTER, *Studien zur Lehre und Entwicklung Śaṅkaras* (Wien: Institut für Indologie der Universität Wien, 1979), pp. 11-12; and the discussion in SUTHREN HIRST, *Śaṃkara's Advaita Vedānta*, pp. 25-26.

[7] Bradley MALKOVSKY, "Advaita Vedānta and Christian Faith," *Journal of Ecumenical Studies* 36 (1999): pp. 400-401.

[8] Ibid, pp. 410-15, as well as Bradley MALKOVSKY, "The Personhood of Śaṃkara's *Para Brahman*," *The Journal of Religion* 77 (1997): pp. 541-62.

[9] Notably SUTHREN HIRST, *Śaṃkara's Advaita Vedānta*; Francis X. CLOONEY, S.J., *Theology after Vedānta: An Experiment in Comparative Theology* (Albany: State University of New York Press, 1993); and Michael COMANS, *The Method of Advaita Vedānta: A Study of Gauḍapāda, Śaṅkara, Sureśvara and Padmapāda* (Delhi: Motilal Banarsidass, 2000).

the term used to identify the tradition in Sanskrit is *a-dvaita*, "non-difference" or "non-duality."

Beyond these few certainties about Shankara and his fundamental message, we also have a considerable body of writing attributed to him, as well as what Jonathan Bader has called "myths" of Shankara: legendary narratives and speculative reconstructions of his life and development.[10] As "myths," these portraits do not capture "the *real* Shankara." Yet they do, Bader argues, create "a sense of order in the face of the contradictions inherent in Śaṅkara's life and work."[11] Each casts a different light on this mercurial persona and, by so doing, more fully illumines the *Upadeśasāhasrī* as a sacred text of the tradition.[12]

Myths of Ādi Shankaracharya

The first myth we must contend with is that of Shankara as a divine conqueror, a powerful *avatāra* – very loosely, "incarnation" – of the god Shiva who, in his short mortal span, traveled throughout India defeating opponents in debate, re-establishing the ancient *dharma* of Hindu orthodoxy and, by so doing, dramatically transforming the face of India. This portrait emerges very clearly in the so-called *vijaya*s, a body of hagiographical literature dating from about the fourteenth century CE onwards. The most prominent of these, *Shankara's Conquest of the Quarters* (*Śaṅkara-dig-vijaya*), attributed to a figure named Mādhava, represents a compilation and synthesis of prior accounts that seems to have been brought into its final form sometime between 1650 and 1740.[13]

[10] See Jonathan BADER, *Meditation in Śaṅkara's Vedānta* (New Delhi: Aditya Prkashan, 1990), pp. 15-24.

[11] Ibid, p. 23.

[12] Other helpful treatments include John GRIMES, "Śaṅkara and the *Vivekacūḍāmaṇi*," in S. RAO and G. MISHRA (eds.), *Paramparā: Essays in Honour of R. Balasubrahmanian* (New Delhi: Indian Council of Philosophical Research, 2003), esp. pp. 73-78; and Jacqueline SUTHREN HIRST, "Images of Śaṃkara: Understanding the Other," *International Journal of Hindu Studies* 8 (2004): pp. 157-81.

[13] MĀDHAVA's *Śaṅkara-dig-vijaya* is available in two English translations: Swami TAPASYANANDA, trans., *Sankara-Dig-Vijaya: the Traditional Life of Sri Sankaracarya, by Madhava Vidyaranya* (Madras: Sri Ramakrishna Math, 1978), and K. PADMANABAN, trans., *Srimad Sankara Digvijayam by Vidyaranya*, 2 vols. (Madras: K. Padmanaban, 1985-86), which includes both Sanskrit text and English translation. The dating of the text is by no means certain. Following the textual critical analysis of W.D. ANTARKAR, Jonathan BADER assigns such a late date to the *Śaṅkara-dig-vijaya* due to its apparent literary dependence upon three other hagiographies. See his full argument in *The Conquest of the Four Quarters: Traditional Accounts of the Life of Śaṅkara* (New Delhi: Aditya Prakashan, 2000), pp. 17-70, as well as the further discussion in Matthew CLARK, *The*

The hagiographies serve a clear devotional purpose, exalting the Advaita tradition by styling one of its foremost proponents as a conquering king.[14] It is unlikely that their authors would have aspired to be regarded as historians in any modern sense, notwithstanding claims later made on their behalf.[15] Nevertheless, one method of historical reconstruction involves stripping the hagiographies of their most legendary features and treating whatever remains as reliable data. David Lorenzen, for example, distills out the following portrait:

> The facts we can accept with confidence are that [Shankara] was born in a Brāhman family from the Kerala region but left home at an early age to become a wandering ascetic (*saṃnyāsin*); that he became a student of a teacher named Govinda, a pupil of Gauḍapāda; that he wrote various philosophical and devotional works including commentaries on the Upaniṣads, Bhagavad Gītā, and Brahma-sūtra; and that he travelled throughout India with his own disciples defeating rival theologians. It is probable though not at all certain... that his father died while he was still a young child; that he later performed the funeral rites of his widowed mother over the objections of his kinsmen; that one of his most important debating triumphs was over a man named Maṇḍana Miśra, a mīmāṃsā follower of Kumārila; that his most important disciples were named Ānandagiri, Padmapāda (Sanadana), Sureśvara (doubtfully identified with Maṇḍana Miśra and Viśvarūpa), Hastāmalaka, and Toṭakācārya; that he established various religious centers especially at Śṛṅgerī in the South, at

Daśanāmī-Saṃnyāsīs: The Integration of Ascetic Lineages into an Order, Brill's Indological Library 25 (Leiden and Boston: Brill, 2006), pp. 148-51. Vidyasankar SUNDARESAN has, in turn, challenged these textual criteria in "Conflicting Hagiographies and History: The Place of Śaṅkaravijaya Texts in Advaita Tradition," *International Journal of Hindu Studies* 4 (2000): pp. 109-84. If accepted, Sundaresan's arguments could push the work's date back as far as the fourteenth century, though this still post-dates Śaṅkara by at least six centuries.

14 Such a narrative strategy was by no means unique to Advaita tradition. Many hagiographies of the period transposed the *dig-vijayas* of legendary kings to the similarly legendary accounts of the great renouncers from a wide range of teaching lineages, including those in explicit conflict with Advaita. See especially SAX, "Conquering the Quarters," and Phyllis GRANOFF, "Holy Warriors: A Preliminary Study of Some Biographies of Saints and Kings in the Classical Indian Tradition," *Journal of Indian Philosophy* 12 (1984): pp. 291-303.

15 Even for the modern Shankaracharyas, the claims made on behalf of the *Śaṅkara-dig-vijaya* are not strictly historical. See the following statement of the Shankaracharya of Śṛṅgerī, quoted in BADER, *Conquest*, 334: "These *vijayas* are of the nature of *kāvya* not history... Although it is based in actual history, in *kāvya*, the author has the freedom to embellish his work. For example, in enumerating the various opponents encountered by Śaṅkara, additional adversaries [who may not have been contemporaries of Śaṅkara] might be cited by the author. These *vijayas* are not intended to be authoritative (*pramāṇa*)."

> Purī in the East, Dvārakā in the West, and Badarikāśrama in the North; and that he died at a young age, thirty-two according to most accounts, at either Badarikāśrama, Kāñcī or somewhere in Kerala.[16]

This portrait is compact and accessible, even with what may be quite a number of unfamiliar names. It offers an attractive account of a life that was both thoroughly human and thoroughly extraordinary, bounded by the ordinary exigencies of birth and familial obligation yet open to the transformation of the sub-continent. At the same time, with the exception of Shankara's extant works and those of his immediate disciples, few if any of these details can be verified from any source outside the *vijaya* literature itself.[17]

With such cautions in mind, a cadre of modern scholars has attempted to generate another, quite different portrait of the great teacher, based exclusively upon the internal evidence of his extant writings. Some have endeavored to illustrate the inner consistency and penetrating insight of "Shankara the philosopher" or, more contentiously, "Shankara the theologian" from these writings. Notable examples include Paul Deussen's *Das System des Vedāntas* at the turn of the previous century, followed by a string of comparable works by Eliot Deutsch, Richard DeSmet, Anantanand Rambachan, and Jacqueline G. Suthren Hirst, among others, from the mid-twentieth century up to the present day.[18]

[16] LORENZEN, "Life of Śaṅkarācārya," p. 88. See also the similar summaries in Surendranath DASGUPTA, *A History of Indian Philosophy*, vol. I (Cambridge: Cambridge University Press, 1957), pp. 432-37; and Sengaku MAYEDA (trans.), *A Thousand Teachings: The Upadeśasāhasrī of Śaṅkara* (Albany: State University of New York Press, 1992), pp. 3-10. For more extensive historical reconstructions based on the hagiographical materials, see Mariasusai DHAVAMONY, "Śaṅkara and Rāmānuja as Hindu Reformers," *Studia Missionalia* 34 (1985): pp. 119-30; Natalia ISAYEVA, *Shankara and Indian Philosophy* (Albany: State University of New York Press, 1993), pp. 69-83; Govind Chandra PANDE, *Life and Thought of Śaṅkarācārya* (Delhi: Motilal Banarsidass, 1994); and S. SANKARANARAYANAN, *Śri Śaṅkara: His Life, Philosophy and Relevance to Man in Modern Times*, Adyar Library General Series 14 (Madras: The Adyar Library and Research Centre, 1995).

[17] See, e.g., Karl H. POTTER, "Śaṃkarācārya: The Myth and the Man," *Journal of the American Academy of Religion Thematic Studies* 48/3-4 (1982), pp. 111-25, as well as the discussion in SUTHREN HIRST, *Śaṃkara's Advaita Vedānta*, pp. 13-16.

[18] Paul DEUSSEN, *The System of The Vedānta according to Bādarāyana's Brahma-Sūtras and Śaṅkara's Commentary Thereon Set Forth as a Compendium of the Dogmatics of Brāhmanism from the Standpoint of Śaṅkara*, C. JOHNSTON (trans.) (New York: Dover Publications, [1973; German original, 1906]); R.V. DE SMET, "The Theological Method of Śaṃkara," Ph.D. Thesis, Pontifical Gregorian University, Rome, 1953; Eliot DEUTSCH, *Advaita Vedānta: A Philosophical Reconstruction* (Honolulu: East-West Center Press, 1968); Anantanand RAMBACHAN, *Accomplishing the Accomplished: The Vedas as a Source*

A related line of inquiry attempts to distinguish Shankara's authentic thought from prior and subsequent developments in Advaita tradition and even from many writings attributed – erroneously, it seems – to Shankara's own hand. Though this work was pioneered by a traditional Advaitin teacher named Swami Satchidanandendra, the decisive blow was struck in a 1950 article by the German Indologist Paul Hacker.[19] Discerning the most characteristic terminology and emphases of Shankara's *Brahma-Sūtra* commentary, Hacker proposed a flexible set of criteria to test the authenticity of other works. As the range of texts attributed to Shankara narrowed, moreover, confidence in their internal consistency also began to wane. And this, in turn, provoked various theories about Shankara's intellectual development and maturation. Hacker himself suggested that the great teacher only slowly overcame the twin influences of Yoga and Buddhism, which dominate his earlier writings,[20] and this proposal has been developed further by Tilmann Vetter and, albeit along quite different lines, Madeleine Biardeau.[21]

There is good reason to question the viability of such theories. Hacker and Vetter's proposals, for example, depend upon accepting a disputed text as authentic.[22] Even setting aside such questions, the enterprise is

of Valid Knowledge in Śaṅkara, Monographs of the Society for Asian and Comparative Philosophy 10 (Honolulu: University of Hawaii Press, 1991); J.G. SUTHREN HIRST, "The Place of Teaching Techniques in Śaṃkara's Theology," *Journal of Indian Philosophy* 18 (1990): pp. 113-50; and SUTHREN HIRST, *Śaṃkara's Advaita Vedānta.*

[19] Paul HACKER, "Eigentümlichkeiten der Lehre und Terminologie Śaṅkaras," *Zeitschrift der Deutschen Morgenländischen Gesellschaft* 100 (1950), pp. 246-86. This article is available in English translation in Wilhelm HALBFASS (ed.), *Philology and Confrontation: Paul Hacker on Traditional and Modern Vedānta* (Albany: State University of New York Press, 1995), pp. 57-100. Further background is available in BADER, *Meditation*, pp. 7-9, and SUTHREN HIRST, *Śaṃkara's Advaita Vedānta*, pp. 4-5, 22-25, as well as Daniel H.H. INGALLS's seminal essay, "The Study of Śaṃkarācārya," *Annals of the Bhandarkar Oriental Research Institute* 33 (1952): pp. 1-14.

[20] Paul HACKER, "Śaṅkara der Yogin und Śaṅkara der Advaitin. Einige Beobachtungen," *Wiener Zeitschrift für die Kunde Süd- und Ostasiens* 12-13 (1968-69): pp. 119-48. English translation in HALBFASS, *Philology and Confrontation,* pp. 101-34.

[21] VETTER, *Studien*, esp. pp. 16-19 and passim; and Madeleine BIARDEAU, "Quelques Réflections sur L'Apophatisme de Śaṅkara," *Indo-Iranian Journal* 3 (1959): pp. 81-101.

[22] See, e.g., T.S. RUKMANI, "The Problem of the Authorship of the *Yogasūtrabhāṣyavivaraṇam*," *Journal of Indian Philosophy* 20 (1992): pp. 419-23; T.S. RUKMANI, "Śaṅkara's Views on Yoga in the *Brahmasūtrabhāṣya* in the Light of the Authorship of the *Yogasūtrabhāṣyavivaraṇa*," *Journal of Indian Philosophy* 21 (1993): pp. 395-404; and T.S. RUKMANI, "The *Yogasūtrabhāṣyavivaraṇa* is Not a Work of Śaṅkarācārya the Author of the *Brahmasutrabhāṣya*," *Journal of Indian Philosophy* 26 (1998): pp. 263-74; as well as HALBFASS, *Tradition and Reflection*, pp. 205-42.

weakened by what Wilhelm Halbfass refers to as its "inevitably hypothetical"[23] and circular method, as each historian constructs a framework from variations in Shankara's authentic texts and then uses that framework to interpret the very same variations from which it was constructed in the first place. We can, finally, draw attention to a rather suspect notion implicit in many reconstructions of Shankara as a unique, originating *auctor:* namely, the distinctively modern presumption that individual expression represents the only, or the best, key to authenticity. Invariably, the scales are tipped in favor of autonomy and novelty as requisite qualities of "genius." That Shankara was a unique and extraordinary individual seems certain. Nonetheless, based on the repeated invocations of tradition and teaching lineage throughout these very writings, it seems far more probable that, for Shankara as for many of his contemporaries, true authenticity lies in one's faithfulness to the teaching tradition, rather than in one's distinctiveness from it.

At the end of the day, in fact, it may be the myth of Shankara as a teacher of liberation in a long tradition of such teachers – and in a world of many rival teachers and traditions – that we find our most reliable baseline for interpreting a text like the *Upadeśasāhasrī*. For example, after surveying the major episodes of the *Śaṅkara-dig-vijaya,* Suthren Hirst reaches the following conclusion:

> The aetiological and polemical functions of this portrait are clear. However, they reflect a Southern Advaitin claim to derive inspiration from a teacher who stood within the correct tradition of interpretation yet towered above it, whose confidence was in scripture and reason, whose own model of the teacher was scripturally based and compassionate and who worked within yet transcended the (purported) religious norms of his day. This is not just a stereotype of any Indian *guru*, but reflects emphases in the Advaita tradition, which for all their later modes of expression, are in accordance with Shankara's own concerns.[24]

This sketch cuts through both questions about the *vijayas*' historical accuracy and the "inevitably hypothetical" nature of reconstructions from Shankara's authentic texts. According to the best evidence we have, whatever activities this great teacher did in fact undertake in his lifetime – traveling, debating, writing commentaries and other works – he undertook in order to communicate a liberating truth, not for any other purpose. In so doing, he stood squarely within a tradition that

[23] HALBFASS, *Tradition and Reflection*, p. 144.
[24] SUTHREN HIRST, *Śaṃkara's Advaita Vedānta*, pp. 16-17.

both preceded and followed him, even if his own position in this tradition would eventually prove to be decisive.[25] This is what we discover in the *vijaya* literature, as well as in Shankara's commentaries on the *Upanishads*, the *Bhagavad-Gīta* and Badarāyaṇa's *Brahma-Sūtras*. And it is also, most importantly for our purposes, what we discover as we turn from the various portraits of Ādi Shankaracharya to the pages of his *Upadeśasāhasrī*.

"I Composed this Dialogue"

As we shift our attention from teacher to text, we immediately encounter a bit of a paradox. On the one hand, the authority of the *Upadeśasāhasrī* depends almost entirely upon the stature of Ādi Shankaracharya. On the other, as the sole non-commentarial text whose authenticity remains undisputed by most historical critics, it has also become a very important resource for seeking out Shankara himself. At some level, any portrait of the great teacher stands or falls on evidence in the *Upadeśasāhasrī*;[26] and the text, in turn, explicitly addresses itself to the formation of ideal teachers in the tradition. Across its pages, we might say, the line between text and teacher begins to blur.

Here too, however, the evidence is not all of one piece. Unlike the very popular Advaita treatise *Vivekacūḍāmaṇi* – "The Crest-Jewel of Discrimination" – no single dominant theme emerges from this compilation of "a thousand teachings," and there is no over-arching narrative to bind it into a single whole. The work consists of two major components: a "verse portion" (*padya-bandha*, hereafter USP) of nineteen chapters, and a "prose portion" (*gadya-bandha*, hereafter USG) of three chapters.

[25] This approach closely mirrors that of CLOONEY, but it gives more weight to the social dynamic of teacher and student, rather than focusing narrowly upon exegetical and commentarial practice. As COMANS (*Method of Early Advaita Vedānta*, pp. 182-83) puts the issue, "The regular compounding of the word 'scripture' along with 'teacher' (*ācārya*) should make it clear that Advaita is not just a matter of a serious, solitary, engagement with the Text. At some point it is a matter of the committed seeker seriously engaging the Text under the guidance of a competent teacher (a guru)." See also William CENKNER, *A Tradition of Teachers: Śaṅkara and the Jagadgurus Today* (Delhi: Motilal Banarsidass, 1983, 1995 [reprint]), esp. pp. 29-59.

[26] This is Sengaku MAYEDA's contention in "Ādi-Śaṅkarācārya's Teaching on the Means to Mokṣa: Jñāna and Karman," *Journal of Oriental Research* 34-35 (1966): pp. 66-67. The central importance MAYEDA ascribes to the *Upadeśasāhasrī* is challenged in Bradley J. MALKOVSKY, *The Role of Divine Grace in the Soteriology of Śaṃkarācārya*, Numen Studies in the History of Religions 91 (Leiden: Brill, 2001), pp. 393-96; and in Roger MARCAURELLE, *Freedom through Inner Renunciation: Śaṅkara's Philosophy in a New Light* (Albany: State University of New York Press, 2000), pp. 32-40.

Each of these 22 chapters reveals evidence of independent composition. This is manifest in the case of the verse chapters, but – as we shall see – a good case can be made that the prose chapters should also be so regarded. In the text's final form, the three prose chapters follow a clear logical sequence, whereas seventeen of the nineteen verse chapters are arranged in order of increasing length. The exceptions are the first and last verse chapters, which thereby lend coherence to the verse portion and perhaps also to the *Upadeśasāhasrī* as a whole.[27]

The strong impression given by the *Upadeśasāhasrī* is that of a loose collection of writings, likely composed on different occasions and for a variety of purposes, but eventually gathered together into a single work by a later disciple or possibly by Shankara himself. Especially in its verse portion, the effect of the piece is cumulative rather than strictly logical and progressive; indeed, as I will argue more fully below, the work may be best approached not as "writings" at all, but as performative "scripts" arising from and oriented to a variety of teaching situations. If so, then it is not necessary to read the *Upadeśasāhasrī* like a novel, from beginning to end. One may be better advised simply to choose an appropriate place in the text and dive in.

Diving in is precisely what we shall do, then, to gain an initial impression of the *Upadeśasāhasrī* in its final form. We enter at USP 8, traditionally entitled "The Dissolution of the Mind."[28] The chapter begins with a kind of protest made by the true self, *Ātman*, against the mind and personality with which it is so persistently confused:

> O my mind, my true nature is pure consciousness, connection with taste and other objects of physical experience is due to your delusion. No result whatever accrues to me from your activities as I am free from all distinctions. (USP 8.1)

The next three verses develop this idea, first enjoining the mind to overcome its vain striving and ceaseless activities (8.2a) and then expounding the true nature of the "I" (*aham*) as none other than highest *Brahman*, ever-present in all beings yet entirely free from action, impurity and any

[27] Cf. Sengaku MAYEDA (ed.), *Śaṅkara's Upadeśasāhasrī, Critically Edited with Introduction and Indices* (Tokyo: Hokuseido Press, 1973), pp. 65-68.

[28] In Sanskrit: *mati-vilāpanam*. Citations from USP 8 follow the translation in A.J. ALSTON (trans.), *The Thousand Teachings (Upadeśa Sāhasrī) of Śrī Śaṃkarācārya* (London: Shanti Sadan, 1990), pp. 123-25, with small modifications. Some manuscript traditions do not use this title, simply identifying the chapter by its first word in the Sanskrit text. See MAYEDA, *Śaṅkara's Upadeśasāhasrī*, p. 223.

form of relationship (8.2b-4). "Therefore," *Ātman* declares, "there is nothing that you can do for me, since I am without a second" (8.4b).

The themes introduced in this short account clearly echo the traditional interpretation of Shankara's teaching presented above, setting out the ultimate non-difference of *Ātman* and *Brahman* and inveighing against identification with such phenomenal realities as the individual mind or personality. What makes the present chapter stand out is its rhetorical point of view – speaking in the "voice" of *Ātman* – as well as its final two stanzas, in which a yet another authorial voice provides a brief gloss on this distinctive literary form:

> Noticing that the people are excessively attached to the domain of cause and effect, I have written this dialogue to liberate them from this attachment. It will cause enlightenment as to the nature of final reality. (8.5)
> If a man reflects over this dialogue he will be liberated from the onset of the great dangers that arise from ignorance. Ever free from desire, he will roam the earth free from grief, a knower of the self, happy. (8.6)

In this gloss, we encounter the first of what will be quite a number of social restrictions on the teaching: though it is "people" in general who are deluded, it is presumed that only a male person, a "man," will hear and ponder the verses of this chapter.[29] More importantly for our present purpose, Shankara also speaks directly to the hearer about his intention in composing these verses in the first place. Having observed people in bondage, he says, he has devised a helpful instrument to be used in seeking release from it. What *sort* of instrument is likely to accomplish this goal? This too is specified, and even emphasized by repetition: only a *saṃvāda*, a "dialogue" or "conversation," fits the bill.

The dialogue represented in USP 8 is, of course, one that could never actually occur in ordinary life. According to Advaita teaching, the speaker, *Ātman*, is "one without a second," beyond the slightest trace of distinction or relation with any other reality. Yet Shankara depicts *Ātman* engaging in conversation at various points throughout the *Upadeśasāhasrī* – as he does, for example, in the previous verse chapter (USP 7), in the practice of repetition in the prose portion (USG 3), and especially in the dialogue which concludes the verse portion (USP 19). The ultimate reality that pervades and grounds all our experience is, it turns out, rather chatty.

If we expand the term "dialogue" to include any form of conversation or debate, moreover, it emerges as a very prominent feature of the whole

[29] In Sanskrit, these two terms are *jana* and *nara*, respectively.

Upadeśasāhasrī. The first two prose chapters can be described as *saṃvādas* in a very literal sense. In each, a student approaches a teacher to inquire about liberation, and a lively debate ensues. And, throughout the verse chapters, Shankara's voice is merely one of many voices debating issues of bondage and liberation. At one point in the middle of USP 1, Shankara dismisses the position represented in preceding verses with the phrase, "thus some people think," before launching into an extended refutation (1.11).[30] In another place, after a series of verses presenting Buddhist arguments, he exclaims, "Tell me to whom final release... belongs, if everything perishes?" (16.30).[31] Sometimes it is difficult to discern the precise boundaries between Shankara's own verses and those offering the positions of adversaries.[32]

Less difficult to discern is the central importance given by Shankara to such dialogue itself. Freedom from bondage, the text implies in all its parts, necessarily involves something more than "inquiry" or "study" as conventionally understood, at least in the West. It involves vibrant interactions, conversations and debates on a number of related levels – between student and teacher, between the teachers of this tradition and rival teachers, even between the true self and the ultimately unreal mind and personality of the seeker. Hence, it may not introduce too great a distortion to see in the final verses of USP 8 a good characterization of the whole *Upadeśasāhasrī*. It is a *saṃvāda*, an extended and variegated "conversation" or "dialogue," composed to help both seekers and teachers in the ongoing communication of a liberating truth.

The Boat of Knowledge

If we take "dialogue" as our point of entry into the *Upadeśasāhasrī*, we immediately face a tension internal to this same text. For this "dialogue" is also something that "has been composed" (USP 8.5).[33] On the one hand,

[30] Trans. MAYEDA, *A Thousand Teachings*, p. 104.

[31] Ibid, p. 150.

[32] KING brings out these elements of fluidity, debate and the complex negotiation of competing claims well in his *Indian Philosophy: An Introduction to Hindu and Buddhist Thought* (Edinburgh: Edinburgh University Press, 1999), esp. pp. xiii-xv, and pp. 130-37, though I believe he somewhat overstates the "public framework" of these debates. As with the parallel disputations in the second major section of the *Brahma-Sūtra* commentary, it seems safe to presume that the "opposing" view is usually constructed to a greater or lesser degree by the rhetorical and apologetic purposes of Shankara and the other commentators. On this point, see especially the arguments in CLOONEY, *Theology after Vedānta*, pp. 102-13; and Hugh NICHOLSON, "Two Apologetic Moment's in Śaṅkara's Concept of Brahman," *Journal of Religion* 87 (2007): pp. 528-55.

[33] In Sanskrit: *praklptavant*.

it seems highly likely that the preserved writing has its roots in actual verbal exchanges. On the other hand, in the process of composition and compilation, these living conversations have been scripted in a fixed form – or, better, a fair variety of fixed forms, now bound together, set in order, and thus organized into a kind of curriculum in liberation. The text does not stand alone as an independent composition; instead, its various scripted teachings draw our attention to an ongoing network of pedagogical situations, re-enacted and re-invented each time a new conversation begins.

Perhaps the best example of such scripting can be found in the *Upadeśasāhasrī*'s prose portion. As already mentioned, all three prose chapters could stand as independent compositions. In the first, for example, Shankara presents what he describes as a "method of instruction," an idealized narrative in which a Brahmin disciple who has already taken up the life of a wandering ascetic approaches an anonymous teacher, and is examined, found fit to receive instruction, and immediately trained in the important Upanishadic sentences which establish the unity of *Ātman* and *Brahman* (USG 1.1-8). The subsequent discussion takes these scriptural texts as its point of departure, and the teacher reminds the student of them at key points.

Such scriptural citations are notably absent in the second prose chapter. In the place of USP 1's "disciple" (*śiṣya*) and "teacher" (*ācārya*), it begins with a "life-long student" (*brahmacārin*) approaching a "knower of *Brahman*" (*brāhmaṇa*) later identified with the term *guru*,[34] and this is followed by a highly technical question about the experience of pain (USG 2.45-46), all narrated in the past tense. In the third prose chapter, the teacher himself falls away, leaving only a sole "seeker after liberation" (*mumukṣu*) and a "method of repetition" (*parisaṃkhyāna*) to bring this seeker to his goal (USG 3.112). None of these chapters makes direct reference to the others. Each has a unique narrative structure, a definite beginning and a definite conclusion. At the end of USG 2, in fact, the disciple is declared to be liberated, there and then (USG 2.110). What further need of the meditative practice prescribed in USG 3?

One can easily imagine that these three chapters had their origins in different teaching situations, with different students, and even possibly

[34] In general, *guru* represents the teacher in a more personal relationship with the student than does the more formal title *ācārya*. See Minoru HARA, "Hindu Concepts of Teacher, Sanskrit *Guru* and *Ācārya*," in M. NAGATOMI, B. MATILAL, J. MASSON, and E. DIMOCK, Jr. (eds.), *Sanskrit and Indian Studies: Essays in Honor of Daniel H.H. Ingalls* (Dordrecht, Holland: D. Reidel Publishing Company, 1980), pp. 93-118.

in different phases of Shankara's development.[35] Nevertheless, once joined together into a single script, they come to embody a canonical three-fold vision of Advaita study: "hearing" of the Vedic scriptures (*śravaṇa*), disciplined "reflection" on their content (*manana*), and sustained practice of "contemplation" (*nididhyāsana*).[36] The continuous numbering of all three chapters in the manuscript, as well as textual cues such as "now" (*atha*) to mark the beginning of the script (USG 1.1) and repetition of its final word to punctuate its final section (USG 3.116), merely ratify a more basic insight into its essential coherence as different moments or dimensions of one Advaita teaching practice.

A second, rather different example of such scripting can be found in the seventeenth verse chapter of the *Upadeśasāhasrī*. Again, there are good reasons to regard this chapter as having its own integrity, even among the nineteen chapters of the verse portion. First of all, as already noted, chapters 2-18 of this portion are not arranged in any logical order, but only by length: USP 17 stands where it does simply because it is longer than USP 16 and shorter than USP 18. Moreover, like USP 18 but unlike any of the other verse chapters, the seventeenth chapter is bounded by opening and closing salutations (USP 17.1-3, 87-88 [88-89]).[37] This mirrors the introduction and conclusion of the verse portion itself (USP 1.1, 19.28), and thus offers another cue to suggest that the chapter can be read entirely on its own. We might even hypothesize that USP 17, as a self-contained unit within the *Upadeśasāhasrī*, offers a kind of microcosm or précis of the verse portion and possibly even of the whole Advaita teaching.

[35] See VETTER, *Studien*, pp. 75-78, 89-91, 139-42.

[36] BADER (*Meditation*, p. 13) observes that, "it is well recognised within the Advaita tradition that the work's three chapters have been intentionally arranged so as to correspond to the threefold process of *śravaṇa-manana-nididhyāsana*. Whether Śaṅkara actually composed the three *prakaraṇa*-s with this in mind, or whether the arrangement was the later work of his disciples, it is clear that the USG can stand as a unified text." For further discussion of the threefold method, see CENKNER, *Tradition of Teachers*, pp. 21-26; RAMBACHAN, *Accomplishing the Accomplished*, pp. 97-116; and Jaqueline SUTHREN HIRST, "Strategies of Interpretation: Śaṃkara's Commentary on Bṛhadāraṇyakopaniṣad," *Journal of the American Oriental Society* 116 (1996): pp. 59-66.

[37] For this chapter, there are some variants in the manuscript traditions, resulting in different verse numberings. For the sake of consistency, the citations in the body of my text follow verse numberings of the critical edition in MAYEDA, *Śaṅkara's Upadeśasāhasrī*, pp. 131-45. For the translations of USP 17, however, I have generally followed Swāmi JAGADĀNANDA (trans.), *A Thousand Teachings in Two Parts – Prose and Poetry – of Srī Sankarāchārya* (Madras: Sri Ramakrishna Math, [1941]), pp. 191-217, with some modifications. The verse numberings in brackets refer to the numberings in JAGADĀNANDA'S text.

This hypothesis receives some support from the traditional title of the chapter, "Right Knowledge,"[38] as well as from the sheer scope of the scripted discourse it provides. The following outline gives a general sense of this script:

USP 17

<u>1-6 General Introduction</u>

1-3	Salutations to *Ātman*, to the teaching lineage, and to the individual teacher
4-6	The "definite conclusion" about *Brahman* as life's highest attainment

<u>7-13 Causes of Bondage and Liberation</u>

7	Fundamental idea: ignorance is bondage, knowledge brings it to an end
8-9	Knowledge: the single aim of the Vedas
10-13	Responses to various objections

<u>14-30 That Which Is To Be Rejected: Empirical Causes and Effects</u>

14-20	Consciousness as the source of perception; analogies of dream and a jewel
21-22a	Knowledge: taught in the scriptures and revealed in the pure mind
22b-23	Means for purifying the mind
24-27	Ignorance as the seed of experience; analogy of reflected light
28-30	Analogy of the magician and magical illusion

<u>31-49 Supreme and Pure Truth: the Divine Self (*Ātman*)</u>

31	The nature of *Ātman* revealed in the *Upanishads*
32-41	*Ātman* as self-evident and self-revealing, confirmed in the *Upanishads*
42-49	Freedom through renunciation of caste, actions, and false notions of self

<u>50-57 The Attainment of Knowledge</u>

50-52	Seeker, teacher, and the boat of knowledge
53-55	The one consciousness and the diversity of appearance
56-57	Renunciation, attaining *Brahman*, crossing the ocean of ignorance

<u>58-80 Knowers of *Brahman*</u>

58-60	Freedom from rebirth; analogy of ghee separated from milk
61-63	Scriptural themes: freedom from fear, freedom from the results of action
64-73	The content of firm conviction

[38] In Sanskrit: *samyaṅ-mati*.

74	Contrast: those who are "pitiable" versus those who are their own masters
75-80	Meditation on *Ātman* as *oṃ*, as free from impurity, and as world-source

81-88 General Conclusion

81	Summary of the teaching and its results
82-84	Right knowledge: truth of *Ātman*, secret of the Vedas, cause of freedom
85-86	The importance of testing the student
87-88	Salutations to *Ātman* and to the teaching lineage

Whereas the three chapters of the prose portion depict various moments or aspects of the traditional teaching practice, USP 17 renders this same practice into a tightly organized treatise, with a preliminary introduction (vv. 4-6), a thesis statement (v. 7), an account of what must be rejected (vv. 14-31) and what must be accepted (vv. 32-49) in the pursuit of "right knowledge," a practical description of the concrete means to undertake such pursuit (vv. 50-57), a vivid portrait of the transformation such knowledge brings (vv. 58-80), and a final summary and conclusion (vv. 81-84). Along the way, Shankara also offers a grab-bag of analogies and explanatory devices, some of which we will encounter again in the pages that follow: analysis of the three experiential states of waking, dream and deep sleep (vv. 14-15, 17-19, 25, 27, 38, 65-66); separation of clarified butter from milk as an image of liberation (v. 61); and various pedagogical strategies to explain our experience of the created world, such as the appearance of objects in a clear jewel (vv. 16), reflections of sun or moon on the surface of water (v. 26-27, 33-34, 55), magician and magical illusion (vv. 28-30), and the stationary magnet that draws or repels other objects by its mere presence (v. 80). Each of these images sheds light on one or another aspect of the Advaita teaching, and each thus finds a place in the structured argument of USP 17.

If one wanted to understand Advaita as a system of thought, this verse chapter would be a good place to start. For all its comprehensiveness and organization, however, it is no more than yet another script. It is not to be confused with the living conversations and dialogues it undoubtedly both reflects and intends further to generate. Indeed, at the climax of his argument in this chapter, Shankara points beyond its verses to a more primary, extra-textual reality:

> The seeker after truth should withdraw into the self the love for external things. For this love, secondary to that of the self, is inconstant and entails pain. [This seeker] should then take refuge in a teacher, a knower

> of *Brahman* who is tranquil, free, bereft of actions, and established in *Brahman*, as the *śruti* and *smṛti* say, "One who has a teacher knows" and "Know that" (USP 17.50-51 [51-52]).
> That teacher should immediately take the disciple... in the boat of knowledge of *Brahman* across the great ocean of darkness within (17.52 [53]).[39]

This image of the "boat of knowledge" also appears at USG 1.3 and thereby frames the dialogues of the first prose chapter and indeed of the entire prose portion, at least in its final form. Through this shared image, these two scripts – one depicting a series of external and internal dialogues, the other mapping and structuring the content of such dialogues in poetic form – begin to overlap, interpenetrate and qualify one another. Like the various illustrations of USP 17 itself, neither of these scripts offers a complete picture. Bound together and juxtaposed in the *Upadeśasāhasrī*'s final form, they each illumine one or another aspect of what should surely be regarded as a single "boat of knowledge," a teaching tradition and instructional method designed to carry disciples across an ocean of ignorance to a farther shore. The boat of knowledge can be identified, in a certain sense, as nothing other than *saṃvāda*, fixed in various scripts like those of the *Upadeśasāhasrī*, only to be unfixed again in a living and continuous oral performance.

Inter-Textuality and Orality

The kind of textual inter-connection we witness in USG 1.3 and USP 17.50-52, both drawing on the same scriptures and offering the same basic image in different literary contexts, is certainly striking. But it is by no means unique. We might say that such inter-textuality represents yet another persistent feature of the *Upadeśasāhasrī* in its final form.

We discover overlapping themes and connections among the *Upadeśasāhasrī*'s various teaching scripts first and foremost in what appears to be a well-traveled fund of explanatory devices, many of which reappear not only in the *Upadeśasāhasrī* but throughout Advaita tradition.[40] This includes such illustrations as the clear jewel that appears to be red in the presence of a red flower, to which we have already alluded in our treatment of USP 17, as well as the ubiquitous piece of rope mistaken for a snake, which we will encounter repeatedly in this commentary. Beyond such recurring examples, a smaller set of shared themes and

[39] JAGADĀNANDA, *A Thousand Teachings*, pp. 206-7 (modified). The scriptural citations are from CU 6.14.2 and BG 4.34, respectively.

[40] See SUTHREN HIRST, "Teaching Techniques," pp. 116-27.

tropes can establish resonances between otherwise disparate texts. Sometimes the connection between two passages is so strong that one suspects borrowing, such as when a particular grammatical argument about "knowing" and the status of "knowledge" in *Ātman* is employed by the model teacher in USG 2.76-77 and by Shankara himself in USP 18.53-54. In at least one case, inter-textuality shades into identity, when the same line of Sanskrit verse appears verbatim in two different stanzas of two different chapters (USP 7.1a; 18.94a). The trope, used to address two different points of interpretation, acquires a different meaning in each context, but the words and rhythm of the Sanskrit verse are essentially the same.

Determining the priority of one or another occurrence of a shared image, argument or line of verse would, in most cases, be a nearly impossible feat. The first prose chapter may offer the only exception. Here, concluding an argument about the proper locus of pain, the teacher states:

> The memory-image of the pain must evidently have the same locus as the pain. And the feeling of aversion for the pain and its cause must have the same locus as the memory-image, as it is only perceived with the memory of the latter. Thus it has been said, 'Feelings such as attachment, aversion, fear and the like, have the same seat as the impressions derived from the perception of forms which bring such feelings into being. The mind is perceived as the common locus of all of them. Therefore the true knower is ever beyond fear and danger' (USG 1.35).[41]

At one level, this is just a technical argument about pain, memory and perception, the nuances of which would surely be lost on many readers. More important than the content of the account, however, is the specific manner in which it is resolved: that is, by quoting a stanza from elsewhere in the *Upadeśasāhasrī* with the marker, "it has been said" (USP 15.13). Given the preponderance of scriptural citations in the first prose chapter, we may be tempted to imagine that this citation of the *Upadeśasāhasrī* lends credibility to its status as a "sacred text." In a fascinating moment of self-reference, the model teacher of USG 1 might then be enlisted as the earliest witness to the sacred authority of the very text in which he plays a leading role.

A more cautious assessment might, following Paul Hacker's student Sengaku Mayeda – the foremost historical critic of the *Upadeśasāhasrī* – simply take the citation as evidence that the verse portion, or at least

[41] Trans. ALSTON, *The Thousand Teachings*, p. 35.

USP 15, probably existed in textual form by the time Shankara composed USG 1, such that one of its stanzas could be quoted with the words, "it has been said."[42] But this, in turn, presumes a model of authorship that ill suits the *Upadeśasāhasrī*. If, as I have suggested, this text can be regarded as a complex tapestry of teaching scripts, then we can imagine that many of its teachings may have been in wide use in discourse and debate before ever being committed to writing. The *Upadeśasāhasrī*, in other words, may well have been brought into written form at a relatively late moment in its "composition."

It has long been recognized that ancient Indian texts such as the Vedic scriptures and the *sūtra* literature are primarily oral in character.[43] Paul Griffiths has extended such observations into the medieval period, noting that many so-called "texts" were preserved in memory long before and, in some cases, long after they were written down.[44] Shankara himself identifies a powerful memory as one of the requisite characteristics of the ideal teacher (USG 1.6). It thus seems reasonable to suppose that the inter-textuality of the *Upadeśasāhasrī* is rooted in a deeper orality, by which a common repertoire of images and examples, along with certain highly effective lines of argument and of verse, might have been memorized and deployed in a variety of ways and contexts.[45] When the teacher of USG 1 quotes one of the verse chapters in conversation with a student, he may not so much cite an authoritative "text" as rehearse an alternative "script" drawn from this repertoire. We can well imagine that the stanza quoted by the teacher pre-dates the composition of the first prose chapter; but the kind of dialogue depicted therein pre-dates both texts, and can therefore claim a deeper kind of priority. The inter-textuality of the *Upadeśasāhasrī*, in other words, becomes another pointer to that broader,

[42] See MAYEDA, *Śaṅkara's Upadeśasāhasrī*, p. 67.

[43] See FLOOD, *Hinduism*, pp. 35-36; Michael WITZEL, "Vedas and Upaniṣads," in G. FLOOD (ed.), *The Blackwell Companion to Hinduism* (Oxford and Malden: Blackwell Publishing, 2003), pp. 68-71; and Patrick OLIVELLE (trans.), *The Early Upaniṣads: Annotated Text and Translation*, South Asia Research Series (New York and Oxford: Oxford University Press, 1998), pp. 8-10.

[44] Paul J. GRIFFITHS, *Religious Reading: The Place of Reading and the Practice of Religion* (New York and Oxford: Oxford University Press, 1999), esp. pp. 22-59.

[45] A good introduction to orality and patterns of oral literature, including the ground-breaking studies of Milman Parry, Albert Lord and Jack Goody, is available Walter J. ONG, *Orality and Literacy: The Technologizing of the Word* (London and New York: Methuen, 1982). See also the impassioned defense of orality as a significant entry point for considering not only Hindu scriptures, but the very understanding of "scripture" itself in Harold COWARD, *Scripture in the World Religions: A Short Introduction* (Oxford: Oneworld, 1988, 2000), esp. pp. 111-22, 159-89.

predominantly oral teaching tradition we have already identified as the "boat of knowledge."

There is no doubt that the *Upadeśasāhasrī* is the product of a highly literate social world. The mere preservation of the manuscript traditions, depending as they did upon continual re-copying, bears this out.[46] Shankara himself almost certainly emerged from and was comfortable in this culture. It seems likely that he produced many of his writings as continuous, literate compositions: his major commentaries read like such compositions, and this is also how he is depicted in the *Śaṅkara-dig-vijaya* and other hagiographies. Nevertheless, the *Upadeśasāhasrī* is a teaching text, the fruit of what were probably innumerable lived conversations and debates. Its teachings seem designed more to be heard than to be read, to be concretely enacted in the dynamic process they themselves reflect and, especially in the prose portion, explicitly model.

The 22 chapters and two major portions of the *Upadeśasāhasrī* may thus be said to enshrine a kind of oral textuality or textualized orality, whose full expression lies outside and beyond the pages of the text. It thus interrupts familiar literate notions of how a sacred text like the *Upadeśasāhasrī* might be intended to function. To read this text well, one must be ready to *hear* it, and to imagine it squarely within that extra-textual, social and inextricably performative reality from which its "thousand teachings" undoubtedly spring.

II.

Becoming an Interreligious Hearer of Shankara's *Upadeśasāhasrī*

I began this introductory chapter by observing that the *Upadeśasāhasrī* represents a distinctive kind of sacred text. Now, having discerned an initial image of Shankara the teacher and the rough contours of the *Upadeśasāhasrī*, we may be ready to imagine ourselves as a unique class of hearers of this distinctive text. We are interreligious hearers, those who enter the dialogues and conversations it models and extend this dialogue beyond the boundaries of the Hindu fold – specifically, for this

[46] Mayeda (*Śaṅkara's Upadeśasāhasrī*, pp. 1-14) examines 42 extant manuscripts, classified into two major recensions, to construct his critical edition, though he counts 70 complete and incomplete manuscripts worldwide. Of those he surveys, the oldest is dated 1733.

commentary project, across the boundaries of Hinduism and Christianity. In the remainder of this chapter, I offer some reflections on the specific character of this interreligious hearing, at least as it is attempted in the pages and chapters that follow.

It is important, first, to recognize that interreligious hearers are not the first or primary hearers of this sacred text, nor indeed the first to attempt a commentary on the teaching scripts it offers. To enter the scripted dialogues of the *Upadeśasāhasrī* aright, we are well advised to enter the company of those other disciples who heard its scripts before us and who responded with still further Advaita scripts, taking up their performance and bringing them forward from Shankara's era into our own. Though our hearing will of course be different from these other disciples' hearings in important ways, it can emulate them, draw warrants from them and even style itself as a continuation of fundamental dynamics inherent in the Advaita tradition itself.

Advaita Reception(s) of the *Upadeśasāhasrī*

There are several Sanskrit words employed in Advaita Vedanta to give breadth and depth to the living, oral tradition emulated in the *Upadeśasāhasrī*. *Paraṃparā* – literally, "one after another" – recognizes the central importance of succession from one generation of wise teachers to the next, whereas another term, *sampradāya*, "what is passed on," emphasizes the content, practices or traditional methods that are so transmitted. The *Bṛhadāraṇyaka Upanishad* uses the image of a bamboo shoot to describe the teaching lineage, with each successive ring of the bamboo representing the next generation of teachers.[47] Each of these terms recognizes a plurality of teachers through time, while also underscoring a more basic continuity of the teaching these teachers both receive and constitute.

Advaita tradition has long maintained that Shankara received his teaching from his own guru, named Govinda, and that Govinda's guru was Gauḍapāda, author of a commentary and exposition on the *Māṇḍūkya Upanishad* called the *Māṇḍūkya-kārikās,* on which Shankara would, in turn, write one of his most important commentaries. Reverence for prior teachers in the tradition is also evident in the scripts of the *Upadeśasāhasrī.* In USP 17, for example, Shankara begins his exposition of "right knowledge" with reverent salutations to the lineage of teachers and his own teacher (vv. 2-3) and concludes with further salutation to "the

[47] See BU 2.6; 4.6; 6.5; Sanskrit text and English translation in Olivelle, *Early Upaniṣads*, pp. 74-75, 130-33, 162-65.

all-knowing teachers who have, by imparting knowledge, carried us across the great ocean of births and deaths, filled with ignorance" (v. 88 [89]).[48] If Shankara's teachings are illuminating and effective, such salutations imply, it is only because Shankara too had a teacher... and this teacher had a still more impressive teacher of his own.

This flow of wisdom does not stop with Shankara or the *Upadeśasāhasrī*. Shankara's immediate disciples similarly render homage to their shared teacher, comparing him to the god Shiva, his speech to an axe that destroys the "opinions of logicians," and his compassion to yet another great ocean.[49] The salutations by which his prolific disciple Sureśvara concludes his *Naiṣkarmya-siddhi* (*Realization of the Absolute*) may be taken as exemplary in this regard:

> Having worshiped with devotion Śaṅkara who is all-knowing, established in *Brahman*, accompanied by a host of sages, I obtained, from [him] who is treasure of the most excellent virtues, knowledge – like the Ganges and illumined by the Vedāntas – that follows the feet of Viṣṇu and that, while destroying all existences, Śaṅkara had attained through *Yoga*; and from compassion, I have set it forth for sufferers to annihilate the stream of birth and death.
>
> Divine knowledge, imbedded in the Vedāntas, shining and devoid of dust, destroys the darkness of our intellects and nowhere contradicts even the supersensible object. Salutations to this venerable Guru of gurus who, driving away darkness which is the seed of all transmigratory existences with his stick of reasoning, revealed to us divine knowledge.[50]

The language used to describe Shankara here is formulaic and communicates very little useful biographical information.[51] What it does instead is to provide a further, illuminating image for the teaching lineage itself. Knowledge, Sureśvara suggests, can be compared to a sacred river like the Ganges. By means of teachers such as Shankara and Sureśvara himself, this knowledge flows downward and outward into the world, purifying everything in its path. Both the river itself and the sacred lineage by which it is transmitted are therefore worthy of deep reverence.

[48] Trans. JAGADĀNANDA, *A Thousand Teachings*, pp. 191, 217 (modified).

[49] See SUTHREN HIRST, *Śaṃkara's Advaita Vedānta*, pp. 11-13.

[50] *Naiṣkarmya-siddhi* 4.76-77, translated by MAYEDA in *Śaṅkara's Upadeśasāhasrī*, pp. 48-49 (slightly modified). The Sanskrit text and an alternate English translation are available in A.J. ALSTON (trans.), *The Realization of the Absolute: The 'Naiṣkarmya Siddhi' of Śrī Sureśvara* (London: Shanti Sadan, 1959, 1971), pp. 268-69. Hereafter, the *Naiṣkarmya Siddhi* is abbreviated as *NS*.

[51] See SUTHREN HIRST, *Śaṃkara's Advaita Vedānta*, p. 13.

Such reverence for the tradition represents more than a point of academic interest for the Christian commentator. For, in the *Naiṣkarmyasiddhi,* Sureśvara does not merely offer salutations to his "venerable Guru of gurus." He also cites Shankara in support of his own position, and thus represents the earliest Advaita reception of the *Upadeśasāhasrī* as a sacred, authoritative text. For, after his own exposition, Sureśvara writes:

> So we conclude our summary of the teachings of the three previous books. Now this well-known Vedānta doctrine we have expounded, though it has to be learned from the authoritative texts with the help and grace of a teacher, by no means depends on the presence of the texts and the grace of a teacher, but exists and asserts itself as true in its own right. Nevertheless there exist some pious people who cannot accept anything unless it is made dependent on some authority or another, and as a concession to them we subjoin some quotations from a recognized authority.
> What we are saying has all been clearly stated by the holy [teacher] of worshipful feet, the one who was devoted to the welfare of every creature.[52]

In the remainder of the work, Sureśvara makes good on his promise, offering over 50 citations from the *Upanishads*, the *Bhagavad Gītā* and other authoritative sources of Advaita teaching. Significantly, over a third of these references are taken from Shankara's *Upadeśasāhasrī*. The *Upadeśasāhasrī* is, in fact, cited more frequently than any other single text.[53]

The high status Sureśvara accords his teacher's work is, by itself, worthy of notice. It is also revealing to observe the manner by which the *Upadeśasāhasrī* is concretely employed. Sureśvara draws all of his citations from the verse portion of the text: the teachings of the prose portion are conspicuously absent. In one place, he quotes a single verse, USP 15.16, to illustrate the relation of the "'I'-notion" to the self.[54] A bit earlier, he cites the first four verses of USP 6 as a unit, albeit in a revised order.[55] The vast majority of such citations, however, come from USP 18, the longest verse chapter of the *Upadeśasāhasrī* and the one whose arguments and strategies most strongly influence Sureśvara. The verses are quoted in whole or in part, and sometimes it is difficult to distinguish the quoted verse from Sureśvara's gloss. Finally, though these verses are drawn selectively from throughout USP 18 and interspersed among other quotations, they do appear in numerical order.[56] USP 18 thus seems intended to

[52] *NS* 4.18-19, in ALSTON, *Realization of the Absolute*, pp. 242-43.

[53] See MAYEDA, *Śaṅkara's Upadeśasāhasrī*, pp. 44-45.

[54] *NS* 4.30, in ALSTON, *Realization of the Absolute*, p. 248.

[55] *NS* 4.26-29, in Ibid, pp. 247-48.

[56] See MAYEDA, *Śaṅkara's Upadeśasāhasrī*, pp. 46-47.

frame the whole exposition in this section of the treatise. Other selections from the *Upadeśasāhasrī*, from Gauḍapāda and even from the *Bṛhadāraṇyaka Upanishad* are strung on the basic structure it provides.

In the case of Sureśvara, a direct disciple of Shankara, we can discern a continuation of the very same inter-textual patterns we already observed in the *Upadeśasāhasrī*. In a much later work like the *Jīvan-Mukti-Viveka* (*Discerning Liberation While Living*) of the renowned fourteenth-century teacher and administrator Vidyāraṇya, we encounter much greater fragmentation of this text, as well as a further witness to its authoritative status. Vidyāraṇya's work is self-consciously synthetic, drawing various traditions together into what one scholar has termed a distinctive kind of "Yogic Advaita."[57] Hence, when the *Upadeśasāhasrī*'s verse portion is quoted, as it is in four places in the *Jīvan-Mukti-Viveka*, such quotations invariably appear in combination with other sources, including selections from such diverse authorities as the *Upanishads*, the *Bhagavad-Gītā*, various *purāṇas* or legendary histories, the *Yoga-Sūtras* of Patañjali, and other writings of Shankara, Sureśvara and other prominent voices in the tradition.[58] On only one occasion does Vidyāraṇya cite three verses in sequence (USP 10.1-3); generally, single verses stand alone. Such a synthetic approach can also be found in other works from this later period, such as the *Pañcadaśī*, also attributed to Vidyāraṇya, and the fifteenth- or sixteenth-century *Vedāntasāra* of Sadānanda.[59] In these works, moreover, citations from the *Upadeśasāhasrī* are not always identified. Sometimes, they are simply marked with "[it] has been said" or, in the *Pañcadaśī*, incorporated seamlessly into the author's own exposition.[60] This may offer a further indication of the fundamentally oral character of the tradition, continuing well into the early modern period.

[57] See Andrew O. FORT, "Liberation While Living in the *Jīvanmuktiviveka*: Vidyāraṇya's 'Yogic Advaita,'" in A. FORT and P. MUMME (eds.), *Living Liberation in Hindu Thought* (Albany: State University of New York Press, 1996), pp. 135-55.

[58] Sanskrit text and English translation in Swami MOKṢADĀNANDA, trans., *Jīvan-Mukti-Viveka of Swami Vidyāraṇya* (Kolkata: Advaita Ashrama, 1996), pp. 17-19, 61-64, 152-54, 214-17.

[59] MAYEDA, *Śaṅkara's Upadeśasāhasrī*, pp. 51-54. Few scholars regard the *Jīvan-Mukti-Viveka* and the *Pañcadaśī* as works of the same author. T.M.P. MAHADEVAN suggested the possibility of two figures at Śṛṅgerī who shared the name "Vidyāraṇya": Mādhava-Vidyāraṇya, who authored the *Jīvan-Mukti-Viveka*, and his older contemporary Bhāratītīrtha-Vidyāraṇya, who composed the *Pañcadaśī*. See T.M.P. MAHADEVAN, *The Philosophy of Advaita, with Special Reference to Bhāratītīrtha-Vidyāraṇya*, 4th ed. (New Delhi: Arnold-Heinemann, 1976), pp. 1-8.

[60] MAYEDA, *Śaṅkara's Upadeśasāhasrī*, pp. 52-53.

At the other extreme from such strategies of fragmentation and incorporation, the *Upadeśasāhasrī* has also generated a modest, highly literate commentarial tradition. Mayeda identifies four major commentaries.[61] Of these, Bodhanidhi, in the twelfth century, and Akhaṇḍadhāman, in the fourteenth, comment on only the verse or prose portion, respectively, and make no reference at all to the other portion. Ānandagiri (c. thirteenth century) and Rāmatīrtha (c. seventeenth century), to whom we referred at the beginning of this chapter, both comment on the entire *Upadeśasāhasrī*, but according to different ordering principles. Ānandagiri appears to judge that Shankara wrote the verse portion first, whereas Rāmatīrtha gives priority to the prose portion of the text.[62] Ānandagiri is quite terse, clarifying obscure points with infuriating efficiency. Rāmatīrtha, on the other hand, comments at greater leisure and length, expanding on important points and often supplying implied questions or context. Both attend to the *Upadeśasāhasrī* in its literary integrity, taking its teachings up chapter by chapter and verse by verse, as they appear in the work's final form.[63]

This commentarial tradition did not end with Ānandagiri and Rāmatīrtha, but continued in various forms up to the present day. For one contemporary example, we can turn to an annual series of oral discourses given by Swami Paramarthananda Saraswati beginning in the 1990s.[64] Paramarthananda, a teacher whose lineage includes Swami Chinmayananda and other prominent Advaitins in the modern era, offered these lectures as components of an early summer retreat programme at an ashram in the mountains of Rishikesh, India. Speaking in English, Paramarthananda initiates his series very simply, explaining that the *Upadeśasāhasrī* is an important Advaita text by Ādi Shankaracharya and cautioning his hearers not to confuse it with the *Upadeśasāra* of the popular 20th-century mystic Ramana Maharshi. The *Upadeśasāhasrī* is famous, he further explains, because of its comprehensive scope and particularly because it

[61] Ibid, pp. 1-2, 54-55.

[62] Ibid, p. 3.

[63] V. NARASIMHAN provides an English translation of the *Upadeśasāhasrī* along with a synthesis of the commentaries of RĀMATĪRTHA and ĀNANDAGIRI in his *Upadeśa Sāhasri: A Thousand Teachings of Ādi Śankara* (Bombay: Bharatiya Vidya Bhavan, 1996). In the present volume, I have depended heavily upon NARASIMHAN, both as a useful reference in its own right and as a guide to locate salient points in the original commentaries.

[64] Swami PARAMARTHANANDA Saraswati, *UPADEŚA SĀHASRĪ*, audio cassettes, Vedānta Vidyārthi Sangha, n.d. At the time of writing, I had access to the cassettes for only USP 1-15 and 18.

includes a renowned exposition of the great saying *tat-tvam-asi*, "you are that" in its eighteenth verse chapter. He also points out that it has two major portions. Paramarthananda's discourses focus exclusively on the verse portion, leaving the prose portion to the side.[65]

In the discourses themselves, Paramarthananda generally follows the model set by the commentators, moving slowly through each chapter, verse by verse, analyzing the Sanskrit text into its component parts and offering extended explanations. Over the course of several summer retreats, he moves systematically through the first fifteen chapters, then jumps to USP 18, and eventually returns to pick up where he left off, at USP 16. His explanations are, throughout, interspersed with quotations from the *Upanishads* and Shankara's other writings, with jokes and maxims in English and Tamil, and with a wide variety of illustrations drawn from tradition and from contemporary experience.

On the one hand, Paramarthananda self-consciously inscribes himself firmly within the teaching tradition. At one point, referring to the commentary of Rāmatīrtha, Paramarthananda self-effacingly refers to his own discourses as "borrowed wisdom."[66] Elsewhere, he comments that it is impossible to make "heads or tails" of these very obscure verses without the help of the commentarial tradition.[67] On the other hand, his teaching is also recognizably modern, not only because of the examples he employs, but also due to the composition of his audience. In his regular teaching venues in Chennai, and also at these retreats, Paramarthananda teaches mainly to middle-class Indian laypersons, including both women and men. Consistent with his *paraṃparā*, Paramarthananda does not restrict his teaching to the upper-caste renunciant males envisioned in the pages of the *Upadeśasāhasrī*.[68] Simultaneously traditional

[65] Ibid, cassette #1-1. Though PARAMARTHANANDA does not lecture on the prose portion, he does encourage its study. My commentaries on USG 1-3 in chapters 4, 6, and 8 of this volume, as well as on USP 16 and 19 in chapters 7 and 9, also depend in part upon private instruction I received from Swami PARAMARTHANANDA in Chennai between October 1999 and March 2000.

[66] PARAMARTHANANDA, *UPADEŚA SĀHASRĪ*, cassette #4-2.

[67] Ibid, cassette #18-1.

[68] See, e.g., the explanation given by PARAMARTHANANDA's guru Swami DAYANANDA Saraswati in B. THORNTON (ed.), *Introduction to Vedānta: Understanding the Fundamental Problem* (New Delhi, Bombay and Hyderabad: Vision Books, 1989, 1997), pp. 24-27. For a more critical demographic and ideological analysis of the contemporary movement to which Paramarthananda belongs, see C.J. FULLER and John HARRISS, "Globalizing Hinduism: A 'Traditional' Guru and Modern Businessmen in Chennai," in J. ASSAYAG and C. FULLER (eds.), *Globalizing India: Perspectives from Below* (London: Anthem Press, 2005), pp. 211-36.

and innovative, Paramarthananda embodies the fundamental orality of the Advaita teaching tradition, bringing the scripts of Shankara's text alive in the experience of a quite different set of hearers.

Hearing and Practicing the Advaita Text

The contemporary Christian hearer of the *Upadeśasāhasrī*, reading and writing at some remove not only from Vidyāraṇya's *pīṭha* in the medieval village of Śṛṅgerī but also from a setting like Paramarthananda's early summer retreats, can draw upon this history of reception in at least three ways. First of all, both those teachers who incorporate the *Upadeśasāhasrī* into their own works, like Sureśvara and Vidyāraṇya, and those who comment upon it, such as Ānandagiri, Rāmatīrtha and Paramarthananda, provide a rich reservoir of wisdom upon which to draw in understanding the text in its Advaita context. We will find ourselves referring frequently, if selectively, to these sources in order to amplify and clarify important points.

Secondly, and perhaps more importantly, in their variety these traditional receptions of the *Upadeśasāhasrī* also provide important sign-posts and a certain degree of license for further re-interpretation. It is clear, for example, that the verse portion is considered primary, the prose portion secondary, and that the two can be variously situated relative to one another.[69] Only three commentators explicitly take up the prose portion, and two of them differ about whether it should be treated first or second in the course of exposition. With regard to the verse portion, the commentators preserve the chapters in their present order. Paramarthananda, however, feels free to re-order them in his exposition, and Sureśvara and Vidyāraṇya draw very selectively from within the chapters themselves. For them, the basic unit of the *Upadeśasāhasrī* appears to be the individual stanza, or cluster of such stanzas, which can stand largely on their own.

When we bring these observations together with our previous discussion of the *Upadeśasāhasrī* as scripted dialogue, fundamentally oral in character, we might grant ourselves even greater freedom in our deployment of these scripts. This, at least, is what I have done in selecting sections and verses for comment in this volume. My key interpretative judgment, informed by the Advaita history of reception, has been to give

[69] The primacy of the verse portion is also supported by the surviving manuscript traditions. MAYEDA (*Śaṅkara's Upadeśasāhasrī*, p. 1) draws on 27 manuscripts of the verse portion and only 11 manuscripts of the prose portion as the basis for his critical edition.

the verse portion textual priority and then to inscribe the prose portion within it. Where a deliberate ordering principle can be discerned in the actual content of the scripts, I have tried to honor this order, at least in a general way. Thus, we encounter USP 1 first, USP 19 last, and the three chapters of the prose portion in sequence, albeit with verse chapters interspersed between them. My hope is that this arrangement will preserve the logical development of the prose portion, while also allowing its extended script to come into a more direct relation with the various, closely related scripts of the verse portion. Necessity dictated that, for most chapters, I have chosen a representative sample of sections or verses for comment. Only USP 1-3, 5, and 7 appear in full. Mayeda's excellent translation of the *Upadeśasāhasrī* forms the basis of the commentary proper.[70]

My primary concern in making these selections and ordering them this way has been to provide a sense of the sacred tradition itself, as this tradition is fixed, given a distinctive shape and imaginatively enacted in these teaching scripts. In so doing, I attempt to invite readers into a genuine hearing of the *Upadeśasāhasrī*, one which not only clarifies its various scripts by recourse to the tradition, but also allows these same scripts to interact and overlap so as to display – insofar as possible in a printed volume – the complex, layered reality of the tradition.

And this, in turn, suggests a third insight to be drawn from the various receptions of the *Upadeśasāhasrī,* insofar as they reveal, even in their variety, a continuation of the fundamentally practical and performative sensibility of the Advaita teaching tradition. This is manifest in the case of the work of a contemporary guru like Swami Paramarthananda, in which every discourse begins and concludes with a sequence of prayerful recitation and the teaching itself proceeds through regular, scripted intervals of discourse and *satsang*, or open discussion, in the carefully orchestrated space of the lecture hall. Though it would certainly be

[70] Except where otherwise noted, all translations from this point forward are taken from MAYEDA, *A Thousand Teachings*, and references to the original come from the romanized Sanskrit text in MAYEDA, *Śaṅkara's Upadeśasāhasrī*. I have made only the following emendations in MAYEDA's translation: 1) When Shankara cites a verse or phrase from the *Upanishads*, I have generally not filled in the remainder of the text, as MAYEDA does, but have only included the portion that is explicitly cited; 2) in a few cases, and where it does not distort the Sanskrit text, I have rendered some expressions in gender-inclusive language. Though Shankara undoubtedly envisioned only male students, a number of contemporary Advaita *sampradāyas* have recognized the universal appeal of the teaching and lifting this restriction. Hence, the use of an inclusive idiom seems appropriate.

inappropriate simply to project such practices back into the social and religious worlds of a Rāmatīrtha, a Vidyāraṇya or a Sureśvara, both the model provided by the *Upadeśasāhasrī* and evidence from their own texts suggest that the subsequent interpretations of these teachers, too, emerged along with and out of reverent, disciplined and continuous practices of oral performance.

For the Christian hearer, this Advaita emphasis on performative practice in the reception of these sacred scripts would seem to invite a response akin to contemplative recitation, chastened and empowered by what the liturgical theologian E. Byron Anderson has described as a distinctive "pattern or complex of patterns ever forming, transforming, and emerging through regular participation in the 'means of grace.'"[71] To borrow and extend Anderson's phrase, a fruitful Christian hearing of this Advaita text invites the fullest possible engagement in that "pattern or complex of patterns" emerging through participation in the Advaita teaching tradition and the means of liberation it prescribes. Most Christians would, of course, stop short of actually gathering firewood and placing themselves at the feet of a self-realized guru to achieve such an interpretive perspective. Yet, any Christian can interpret the *Upadeśasāhasrī* with an eye to the ways that such interpretation can model, rehearse and thus approximate these distinctively Advaita patterns. We can imaginatively enter the world of these scripts, seeking the deep understanding that emerges not through a purely notional apprehension of a handful of leading concepts, but also – and far more importantly, from the point of view of the tradition – through repeated practice and habituation.

We can, in short, aspire not merely to read the *Upadeśasāhasrī* as a sacred text, but to participate in its scripts as a privileged, sacred practice closely akin to liturgical performance: a *liturgy of liberation*, enacted through oral performance and oriented toward final release, an efficacious sign and liberating instrument of *Ātman* the divine self.

This may seem to push too far, and in some ways it does. On the Advaita side, however, we can draw support from the work of Francis X. Clooney on Advaita Vedanta as the "later" (*uttara*) Mīmāṃsā. For Clooney has convincingly demonstrated how Shankara and other leading Advaita interpreters, as successors to the "earlier" (*pūrva*) Mīmāṃsā tradition of Vedic ritual exegesis, consistently mounted their arguments within a Pūrva Mīmāṃsā paradigm, a pattern that would continue at

[71] E. Byron ANDERSON, *Worship and Christian Identity: Practicing Ourselves*, Virgil Michel Series (Collegeville: Liturgical Press, 2003), p. 6.

least through the later Vedanta of Rāmānuja.[72] This paradigm shaped Advaita exegetical practices first and foremost, substituting the Upanishadic wisdom rather than Vedic ritual as the primary object of interpretation; yet, implicit in this shift from one object of inquiry to another – as we shall see especially in the next chapter – is a strong claim about the relative value of exegetical and ritual practices themselves. Teaching and learning from the *Upanishads*, as scripted in the Advaita tradition, come to replace Vedic ritual practice and are thus invested with a status and character analogous to ritual performance.

On the Christian side, we can observe that the semantic valence of *leitourgia* or "liturgy" need not and in some senses cannot be restricted to worship in church settings. The bishops of the Second Vatican Council of the Catholic Church, as just one example, described the Eucharistic liturgy as "source and summit" of the broader practice of Christian discipleship, which Aloysius Pieris refers to as the "liturgy of life" and others have labeled as *lex vivendi* or *lex agendi*, the Christian "law of living" and/or "law of ethical action."[73] Reaching back to the *Rule* of Benedict of Nursia, the influential anthropologist Talal Asad has also problematized any too-sharp distinction between liturgical performances of the Divine Office and other practices of monastic life, such as manual labor or contemplative study. Despite the important differences among such activities, all represent roughly analogous disciplines intended to shape monks into new, Christian selves.[74] He writes:

> It is striking that in the *Rule*, the proper performance of the liturgy is regarded not only as integral to the ascetic life but also as one of the 'instruments'

[72] See especially CLOONEY, *Theology after Vedānta*, pp. 23-30; and Francis X. CLOONEY, "*Devatādhikaraṇa*: A Theological Debate in the Mīmāṃsā-Vedānta Tradition," *Journal of Indian Philosophy* 16 (1988): pp. 277-98.

[73] Aloysius PIERIS, S.J., *An Asian Theology of Liberation*, Faith Meets Faith (Maryknoll: Orbis Books, 1988), pp. 4-7; ANDERSON, *Worship and Christian Identity*, pp. 27-28, 192-94 (drawing on the work of Kevin Irwin and Don Saliers); and *Sacrosantum Concilium* no. 10, in Norman P. TANNER, S.J. (ed.), *Decrees of the Ecumenical Councils, Volume Two: Trent to Vatican II* (London: Sheed and Ward, and Washington, DC: Georgetown University Press, 1990), p. 823. See also the insightful discussion of the connection between Eucharistic and other Christian cultures of faith and practice in Terrence TILLEY, *Inventing Catholic Tradition* (Maryknoll: Orbis Books, 2000), pp. 67-75.

[74] See Talal ASAD, "Toward a Genealogy of the Concept of Ritual," in *Genealogies of Religion: Discipline and Reasons of Power in Christianity and Islam* (Baltimore and London: Johns Hopkins University Press, 1993), pp. 62-65; ASAD, "On Discipline and Humility in Medieval Christian Monasticism," in *Genealogies of Religion*, pp. 125-67; and the further discussion in Nathan D. MITCHELL, *Liturgy and the Social Sciences* (Collegeville: Liturgical Press, 1999), pp. 71-80.

> of the monk's 'spiritual craft,' which he must acquire by practice... The liturgy is not a species of enacted symbolism to be classified separately from activities defined as technical but is a practice among others essential to the acquisition of Christian virtues. In other words, the liturgy can be isolated only conceptually, for pedagogic reasons, not in practice, from the entire monastic program.[75]

This principle extends even to such apparently quotidian activities as copying manuscripts by hand, which monks seamlessly compared to fasting and prayer. "In this sense," Asad concludes, "the technical art of calligraphy was, like the liturgy, one part of a monastic program and therefore expressive, like divine service; a rite, like any act of penance."[76]

To say that calligraphy is *like* public prayer or penance is not quite the same thing as pronouncing complete equivalence: analogy is not identity. The liturgy is not just one additional discipline for practicing and shaping the Christian self, even for an interpreter like Asad. It is, instead, a discipline *par excellence* of monastic life, which gives other activities their distinctive meanings and ideal shape. In the case of Shankara's Advaita, such a privileged sphere of human action and experience does not consist of Vedic rites, devotional *pūjā,* celebration of the Eucharist or even singing the Divine Office, though it shares with the latter its essential character as embodied speech. Indeed, as I have argued at some length in this chapter, the teaching tradition might be aptly characterized as, borrowing from Asad, an essentially oral and"dialogic process by which the self makes (or fails to make) itself in a disciplined way."[77]

The *Upadeśasāhasrī* offers an array of scripted dialogues to Advaita teachers and students for their self-conscious imitation, reflection and creative appropriation. Shankara insists that it is only through *this* kind of practice, and no other, that the potential hearer can gain enlightenment and become "liberated from the onset of the great dangers that arise from ignorance," as we have already heard in USP 8. "Ever free from desire," the great teacher contends, such a well-scripted disciple of *Brahma-vidyā* will eventually come to "roam the earth free from grief, a knower of the self, happy" (USP 8.6). Such a person will, through assiduous practice, be re-made as a new, liberated, Advaitin self. And, though there will of course be limits, interreligious hearers of *Upadeśasāhasrī* do well to undertake an analogous discipline of self-transformation through

75 ASAD, "Toward a Genealogy of the Concept of Ritual," pp. 62-63.
76 Ibid., p. 64.
77 ASAD, "On Discipline and Humility in Medieval Christian Monasticism," p. 144.

assiduous performance not only of its teaching scripts themselves, but also of the discursive practice at their core: precisely *saṃvāda*, dialogue or conversation.

Christian Commentary, Christian Saṃvāda

So far, in drawing insights from the ongoing Advaita reception of the *Upadeśasāhasrī* and – more specifically – in suggesting a broadly liturgical hearing of its scripted dialogues, we have not yet broached the question of what makes this particular practice of commentary and dialogue with the Advaita text a distinctively *Christian* one. It is one thing to employ recognizably Christian terms like "liturgy" to hear and interpret this sacred text; it is quite another to offer an interpretation that stands both inside the Advaita tradition and outside of it at one and the same moment of hearing and interpretation, and that attempts to articulate distinctively Christian insights from its no less distinctively Advaita teaching scripts.

As a first approximation, we can observe that it was by no means unknown for teachers to comment on texts outside their own traditions in the Indian scholastic world from which Shankara and the *Upadeśasāhasrī* emerge. Shankara is sometimes credited with a commentary on the *Yoga-Sūtras* of Patañjali, and this text is also incorporated into the *Jīvan-Mukti-Viveka* of Vidyāraṇya, discussed above.[78] In some cases, such as when the medieval Kashmiri Abhināvagupta offered a Śaiva re-interpretation of Vaiṣṇava texts or when Shankara's younger contemporary Bhāskara adopted the great teacher's *Brahma-Sūtra-Bhāṣya* as the basis of his own rival exposition of Vedanta in terms of *bheda-a-bheda*, "identity-and-difference," such commentaries across traditions served apologetic and polemical purposes.[79] In other cases, such as the elucidations

[78] On the latter, see especially Andrew O. FORT, "On Destroying the Mind: The *Yogasūtras* in Vidyāraṇya's *Jīvanmuktiviveka*, " *Journal of Indian Philosophy* 27 (1999): pp. 377-95.

[79] See Surendranath DASGUPTA, *A History of Indian Philosophy*, vol. 3 (Cambridge: Cambridge University Press, 1968), pp. 1-11; Daniel H.H. INGALLS, "Bhāskara the Vedāntin," *Philosophy East and West* 17 (1967): pp. 61-69; and Klaus RÜPING, *Studien zur Frühgeschichte der Vedānta-Philosophie, Teil I: Philologische Untersuchungen zu den Brahmasūtra-Kommentaren des Śaṅkara und des Bhāskara*, Alt- und Neu-Indische Studien herausgegeben vom Seminar für Kultur und Geschichte Indiens and der Universität Hamburg 17 (Wiesbaden: Franz Steiner Verlag, 1977), esp. pp. 65-68. RÜPING contests the earlier proposal, advanced by Daniel INGALLS ("Śaṃkara's Arguments," pp. 291-95), that the close affinity between Shankara and Bhāskara can be traced to an earlier "Proto-Commentator" on which both equally depend. In RÜPING's view, the previous "*sūtra*

of Nyāya, Mīmaṃsā and Advaita teachings by the famous ninth-century polymath Vācaspati Miśra, it is far more difficult to discern a polemical intent.[80] In light of such precedents, it seems but a short step to attempt a commentary from a tradition further outside the Hindu fold. Apologetics and refutation cannot be excluded from such an endeavor. But it is also possible to imagine other possibilities, in which diverse positions come to be held in fruitful tension or even, ultimately, to foster transformation of those positions themselves.

Indeed, one might go so far as to say that the transformation of persons and positions is intrinsic to the very notion of dialogue as a disciplined practice. This, at least, is the case made by Laurie L. Patton and Chakravarthi Ram-Prasad in an important article entitled, "Hinduism with Others."[81] Alluding to many of the Indian scholastic traditions also discussed in this chapter, Patton and Ram-Prasad defend a broad interpretation of *saṃvāda* as "interlogue," marked less by a conversation across binary opposites (*dia-logos*) – scholar and adherent, Hindu and non-Hindu, and so on – than by a more open-ended "engagement between people in various, multiple, complex and changing historical circumstances."[82] They write:

> In all its complexity in the Sanskrit tradition, *samvada* conveys the idea of transformation through conversation. In the *samvadas* of early and classical India, there might be two or more speakers, but the participants were many – witnesses, audiences, praisers, and detractors. And all acknowledged the social transformation that takes place in the *samvada*.[83]

Patton and Ram-Prasad go on to articulate a number of fundamental principles or "metavalues" necessary for such *saṃvāda* to function as a virtue in the modern liberal academy. First and foremost, these metavalues include scholarly commitments to interpreting texts in their literary and historical contexts, learning incrementally from lower to higher stages of study, and cultivating self-reflexivity and a capacity for self-correction.[84]

commentator" (*sūtra-bhāṣya-kāra*) to which Bhāskara refers in his commentary is none other than Shankara himself.

80 See KING, *Indian Philosophy*, pp. 60, 64.

81 Laurie L. PATTON and Chakravarthi RAM-PRASAD, with Kala ACHARYA, "Hinduism with Others: Interlogue," in J. HAWLEY and V. NARAYANAN (eds.), *The Life of Hinduism* (Berkeley, Los Angeles and London: University of California Press, 2006), pp. 288-99.

82 Ibid., 289.

83 Ibid.

84 Ibid., pp. 295-298.

Though it is surely to be hoped that these values mark all of the work in the pages that follow, two further principles possess particular relevance for this commentary: namely, "multiplicity" and "building commonality". According to the former principle, rooted in Indian traditions as early as the fifth century BCE, the authentic *saṃvādin* emerges as the one who can maintain uncompromising advocacy of a particular tradition or school of interpretation while simultaneously recognizing and even valuing the plurality of such traditions, such that "even in debate we join together in learning from texts and ceremonies that surround ideas and practices we all hold in reverence."[85] According to the latter principle, on the other hand, it is also critically important to choose battles carefully and to identify those common ideas or core values that ground the debate, bind the opposing sides together and, for precisely that reason, may risk being lost in the fray. For Krishna in the *Bhagavad-Gītā,* Patton and Ram-Prasad suggest, such commonality can be found in "the larger cause of peace"; for they themselves as modern scholars, it is preserving "the study of Hinduism at the university level."[86] For this volume, and for the Hindu and Christian traditions it purports to address, the primary commonality that grounds interreligious conversation is a shared desire to re-discover and re-make ourselves in the divine likeness, as well as a conviction that such transformation can be effected, at least in part, through discursive practices of teaching, hearing and *saṃvāda.*

The *saṃvāda* described by Patton and Ram-Prasad could and does, of course, take many different forms; in this particular case, it takes the form of commentary. Just as this volume is not the first commentary on the *Upadeśasāhasrī,* moreover, neither is it the first attempt to enter this interreligious conversation through the disciplined practice of Christian commentary on a Hindu text. The first volume in the present series of Christian Commentaries on Non-Christian Sacred Texts offered a diverse selection of Christian commentaries on the *Bhagavad-Gītā,* and its purpose was outlined by series editor Catherine Cornille as follows:

> Broadly speaking, a Christian commentary on the sacred text of another religion may be seen to involve a deliberate assumption of the Christian worldview and faith tradition as the hermeneutical lens through which a particular text is understood and interpreted. It attempts to elucidate the meaning and importance of a particular sacred text for a Christian

[85] Ibid., p. 295.
[86] Ibid., p. 297.

> readership and to point to the way in which the reading of the text may come to deepen Christian self-understanding... A Christian reading of the *Bhagavad-Gītā* can no more consist in merely superimposing Christian beliefs and presuppositions on a non-Christian text, than it can involve simply taking that text wholesale into the Christian tradition. It rather involves a real dialogue in an atmosphere of respect for the radical irreducibility of the 'other' text.[87]

There is, obviously, a strong resonance between Cornille's account and the ideal of *saṃvāda* advanced by Patton and Ram-Prasad. And such resonance gains breadth and depth when we turn from this first essay collection to the more sustained commentarial projects that immediately followed: Daniel P. Sheridan's *Loving God: Kṛṣṇa and Christ* and Francis X. Clooney's *The Truth, the Way, the Life*.[88]

At one level, Sheridan and Clooney's volumes complement each other very nicely. Both take up sacred texts from the broad stream of Vaiṣṇava devotionalism: the tenth or eleventh century CE *Nārada Sūtras* in one case, and the Śrīvaiṣṇava Tiru Mantra, Dvaya Mantra and Carama Śloka in the other. Both also, appropriately, focus their respective discussions on devotion, on the transformation of our affections and on both the need for and authentic possibility of personal surrender to a personal God. Finally, and most importantly for our purposes, both develop these themes through sustained dialogue between their primary, Hindu texts and other traditions drawn from Christian scripture, from the Church Fathers, and from spiritual writers that run the gamut from Hadewijch of Antwerp to Raimundo Panikkar, Bede Griffiths to Pope Benedict XVI.

The two volumes are, nevertheless, different in important ways. In Cornille's terms, Clooney gives relatively greater privilege to the "radical irreducibility of the 'other' text," devoting the great majority of his text to the reception of the three mantras by the great Śrīvaiṣṇava commentator Vedānta Deśika and reserving his explicitly Christian commentary to the margins of the study, in short reflections interspersed throughout and in the brief, concluding portions of each major chapter and the book as a whole. The emphasis remains solidly on the mantras themselves and their

87 CORNILLE, *Song Divine*, pp. 5-6.

88 Daniel P. SHERIDAN, *Loving God: Kṛṣṇa and Christ: A Christian Commentary on the* Nārada Sūtras, Christian Commentaries on Non-Christian Sacred Texts (Leuven, Paris and Dudley, MA: Peeters and W.B. Eerdmans, 2007); Francis X. CLOONEY, S.J., *The Truth, the Way, the Life: Christian Commentaries on the Three Holy Mantras of the Śrīvaiṣṇava Hindus*, Christian Commentaries on Non-Christian Sacred Texts (Leuven, Paris and Dudley, MA: Peeters and W.B. Eerdmans, 2008).

power to transform the Christian reader. Nevertheless, particularly through the creative juxtaposition of such core mantras as "I approach for refuge the feet of Nārāyaṇa with Śrī, obeisance to Nārāyaṇa with Śrī" and "Father, into Thy hands, I commend my spirit," one can discern theological "insights," "openings" and "concerns" for further inquiry, deep resonances with Christian devotional practice, and even the real if limited possibility of Christian prayer and surrender to "Nārāyaṇa with Śrī."[89]

Sheridan, by contrast, gives much greater privilege to the "Christian worldview and faith tradition" in his commentary, offering a full, substantive "Catholic Reflection" on each of the *Nārada Sūtras* in turn. For Sheridan, dialogue between Hindu and Christian traditions proceeds by means of "homologies" between texts and traditions, by which the Hindu *bhakti* and Christian *caritas* are compared as "two different realities which have a similar role in each system."[90] The study of this Hindu text does not so much highlight the transformation of Christian theology and practice as turn its readers – primarily though not exclusively its Catholic readers – back to their own traditions in a renewed way. It functions, in Sheridan's terms, as an "external catalytic partner" in a dialogue "internal" to the Christian tradition.[91] "The aim of this book," he writes, "is to comment on the *Nārada Sūtras on Loving God* in such a way that it will serve as an effective catalyst for Catholic readers both to reexamine their own tradition of Catholic reflection on the love of God and to renew their own love of God."[92]

In content, the present volume represents a significant departure from both Clooney and Sheridan's commentaries, for in it we are turning our attention away from the *bhakti* devotional tradition to one of its most serious rivals. For Śrīvaiṣṇavas like Vedānta Deśika and other Hindu critics, as we shall see, Shankara's tradition represented something far closer to the Buddhist traditions which have been the subject of more recent contributions to this series[93] than to the *Nārada Sūtras,* the Three

[89] See, e.g., Clooney, *The Truth, the Way, the Life*, pp. 139-45, 175-93.

[90] SHERIDAN, *Loving God*, p. 9.

[91] Ibid.

[92] Ibid., p. 2.

[93] Leo D. LEFEBURE and Peter FELDMEIER, *The Path of Wisdom: A Christian Commentary on the Dhammapada,* Christian Commentaries on Non-Christian Sacred Texts (Leuven, Paris and Dudley, MA: Peeters and W.B. Eerdmans, 2010); J.P. KEENAN and L.K. KEENAN, *I Am/No Self: A Christian Commentary on the Heart Sutra*, Christian Commentaries on Non-Christian Sacred Texts (Leuven, Paris and Dudley, MA: Peeters and W.B. Eerdmans, 2011).

Holy Mantras or indeed anything such interlocutors would identify as orthodox Hindu faith and practice. The present volume is nevertheless deeply indebted to both Clooney and Sheridan in form and structure. I aspire to take something like a mediating position, somewhere between Clooney's interest in full immersion in the Hindu text and deployment of limited, controlled juxtapositions, on the one hand, and Sheridan's more eclectic use of "homologies" from throughout the Christian tradition and his sharper focus on the renewal of Christian theology and practice, on the other.

What follows, then, is an exposition, commentary and Christian *saṃvāda* with 150 selected verses and sections of Shankara's *Upadeśasāhasrī,* structured both to highlight its most significant teaching scripts and to trace the path of self-cultivation and transformation these scripts aim to foster on the part of its hearers. Chapter 2 continues this introduction and begins our commentary with the *Upadeśasāhasrī*'s own general introduction: the first verse chapter (USP 1). In these verses, Shankara sets out major themes of the Advaita teaching tradition and reflects on its primary, internal relation to Pūrva Mīmāṃsā and Vedic ritualism. In so doing, I will argue, Shankara also establishes a basic pattern of "mutual priority and reconciliation," which echoes a similar dynamic at the heart of Christian origins and Christian faith. The interpretative category of reconciliation is then explored at somewhat greater length, as a useful heuristic for that hearer who wishes to set the *Upadeśasāhasrī* and the tradition it embodies into critical *saṃvāda* with the Christian tradition and its own sacred scripts.

The next six chapters attempt to apply this heuristic in a series of "experiments in dialogue," each of which moves us a bit further into both the Advaita teaching tradition and a Christian engagement with it. Chapter 3 addresses the question of scandal, paradox and challenge as key aspects of this teaching, focusing especially on Advaita claims about *jīvan-mukti*, "liberation in life," as presented in several short chapters toward the beginning of the verse portion. Chapters 4 and 5 focus on the communication and reception of this scandalous message in, respectively, the dialogues of the first prose chapter and Shankara's extended reflection on *tat-tvam-asi*, "you are that," in USP 18. In both chapters, we witness how the word of the scriptures, specific social contexts and pedagogical practices, and the very constitution of the human person become privileged means by which Advaita disciples literally re-cognize their identity with the self and become ever more transparent to its liberating, divine presence.

The consequences of such re-cognition for human relationships and the transformation of human living will occupy us in the last three "experiments" in this section of the commentary. Related questions of spiritual communion and interpersonal community dominate our treatment in chapters 6 and 7, as the highly technical debates of the second prose chapter are mapped onto a broader social canvas in USP 16. The identity of teacher and student alike as the self of all beings dissolves all those distinctions that separate us from one another. Yet, this highest unity is concretely actualized by a well-defined group of "seekers on the path," sharply distinguished from rival teachings and traditions. Finally, in chapter 8, we treat USP 10 and USG 3 together in terms of *anamnesis*, exploring how the disciplined practice of recollection can serve as a vehicle for transformed vision and, potentially, transformed action in the world.

To a certain extent, this hearing of the *Upadeśasāhasrī* already represents a kind of *saṃvāda* between the Advaita scripts and their Christian hearers. That is, the selection, deployment and interpretation of these scripts already reflect distinctively Christian concerns even as they are interpreted with almost exclusive reference to their primary, Advaita context. Nevertheless, if the structure of the whole work establishes a very broad commonality or bridge to Christian faith through its liturgical hearing of these scripts, the structure of individual commentary chapters is intended to draw each particular script into immediate dialogue with specific themes and texts from Christian tradition, so as to exhibit convergences and divergences, commonality and multiplicity, in incremental stages. Each chapter begins with a short selection from the primary text, without comment. This is followed, in section II, by a more ample selection from the particular prose or verse chapter(s) of the *Upadeśasāhasrī*, accompanied by exposition and also – following the model provided by Clooney – occasional, marginal Christian reflections that highlight individual points of similarity or difference, invite further considerations, and set a trajectory for deeper engagement.

It is in the third and final section of each chapter that dialogical engagement emerges as the central object of inquiry. Following the particular model of comparative theology so strongly advocated by Clooney, both in his commentary on the Three Holy Mantras and in other works,[94] such dialogue is in each case facilitated by the creative intersection

[94] See, e.g., Francis X. CLOONEY, S.J., *Comparative Theology: Deep Learning Across Religious Borders* (Chichester, West Sussex, U.K.: Wiley-Blackwell, 2010); Reid B. LOCKLIN,

and juxtaposition of the *Upadeśasāhasrī*'s teaching scripts with specific, comparable scripts drawn from the Christian tradition. These Christian scripts begin in every case with the apostle Paul, but then extend to include such later teachers as Irenaeus of Lyons, Augustine of Hippo, Peter Lombard, Mary Ward and the bishops of the Second Vatican Council. Here commentary takes the shape of comparison, albeit a comparison intended not so much to produce a general theory of religious pedagogy or liturgical practice as to "see the other [tradition] in light of our own, and our own in light of the other."[95] As texts and traditions are set side by side and read together, previously settled meanings become unsettled, reconfigured and perhaps even reaffirmed in new ways, in and out of their mutual juxtaposition.

Clooney has described this style of comparison as a "necessarily arbitrary and intuitive practice" and commends an approach that proceeds "by intuitive leaps, according to instinct," rather than according to some grand design or theoretical project.[96] Sheridan too reflects on the necessarily "subjective" and "ahistorical" nature of the Catholic interlocutors selected in his commentary, and he defends such subjectivity by insisting that "there is an experiential and hermeneutical continuity in the history of the Christian and Catholic tradition of loving God that allows me to range over the centuries in order to find viewpoints that shed light on loving God for the twenty-first century."[97] So also here, my selection of scripts for dialogue in each of the following chapters will likely seem more than a little arbitrary and subjective, governed by my own personal interest in returning to Paul after a number of years of working with the *Upadeśasāhasrī* in dialogue with other sources, by a modestly idiosyncratic commitment to chronological sequence in identifying those texts that extend Paul's insights into later Christian tradition from one chapter to the next, and by a generous dose of instinct.

Having granted this point, it is nevertheless also true that the selection of these intersecting scripts has not been purely arbitrary; in each case,

"Interreligious *Prudentia*: Wisdom from Peter Lombard for the Post-Conciliar Church," in W. MADGES (ed.), *Vatican II: Forty Years Later*, Annual Publication of the College Theology Society 51 (Maryknoll: Orbis, 2006), pp. 283-307; Hugh NICHOLSON, "Comparative Theology after Liberalism" *Modern Theology* 23 (2007): pp. 229-51; and Reid B. LOCKLIN and Hugh NICHOLSON, "The Return of Comparative Theology," *Journal of the American Academy of Religion* 78 (2010): pp. 477-514.

[95] CLOONEY, *Comparative Theology*, p. 11.

[96] Ibid., pp. 11, 96.

[97] SHERIDAN, *Loving God*, p. 13.

it will also emerge from our hearing of the *Upadeśasāhasrī* itself. The epistles of Paul, specifically, commend themselves as ideal sources for facilitating engaged dialogue between Advaita and Christian traditions for several reasons beyond instinct or personal interest. They represent the earliest authoritative sources of Christian faith and practice, for one thing, in their actual composition and in the subsequent processes of circulation and canonization. As James D.G. Dunn argues in his magisterial work, *The Theology of Paul the Apostle*, Paul can be recognized as the "first Christian theologian," both in the sense of his temporal priority among all those Christians "who have seen it as part of their calling to articulate their faith in writing and to instruct others in their common faith" and in the sense of his preeminence as a member of a uniquely creative and formative generation of Christian disciples, as a "second founder" of Christianity and as, at least arguably, the "*greatest* Christian theologian of all time."[98] "It is important," Dunn contends, "for each generation of Christian theology to reflect afresh on Paul's theology."[99] Insofar as this is true for Christian theology in general, it is true *a fortiori* of a Christian theology that aspires to enter into dialogue with a tradition like Advaita Vedanta. If one goal of dialogue is creative transformation, then it does well to attend to this voice, which was so decisive in the creative transformation of the earliest Jesus movement into what we now recognize as Christianity.

There is at least one further reason to select Paul as a suitable interlocutor for the various teaching scripts of the *Upadeśasāhasrī*: namely, the fundamental character of his entire corpus as scripted dialogue and conversation. Dialogue is intrinsic not only to the rhetorical form of Paul's epistles, most if not all of which were dictated orally and read aloud to their recipients, but also to the content of Paul's theology. As Dunn explains:

> With Paul's letters... it is impossible to escape their character as *letters*, communications from a *known* author to *specific* people in *particular* circumstances... [T]he theological force of Paul's letters is again and again inextricably related to their character as dialogue with their recipients, indeed, as one side of a sequence of specific dialogues whose terms in large part at least have been determined by the situations addressed.[100]

[98] Paul D.G. Dunn, *The Theology of Paul the Apostle* (Grand Rapids and Cambridge: William B. Eerdmans Publishing Company, 1998), pp. 2-3.
[99] Ibid., p. 4.
[100] Ibid., p. 11.

For Dunn himself, such dialogue does not pertain merely to understanding Paul's rhetorical patterns and historical contexts; for the theme of dialogue also extends, in his interpretation, to Paul's own "dialogue with himself" and the continuing dialogue that invariably results as subsequent interpreters and theologians "bring our own questions and traditions to our scrutiny of what Paul has said."[101] To this list we can add engagement between rival traditions of faith and practice, as evidenced in a special way by Paul's agonized reflections on the future of historic Israel in God's plan.[102] To engage Paul's thought is to engage in dialogue; ergo, it seems only natural to facilitate our experiments dialogue with recourse to his epistles.

Ultimately, of course, the most important dialogue is not that which obtains between Shankara and Paul, or between the *Upadeśasāhasrī* and the teaching texts of Peter Lombard or any other Christian interpreter. It is the dialogue that results as Christian hearers become personally implicated in this sacred text and the sacred tradition it models for its hearers. This most important *saṃvāda* is one that truly occurs only after commentary and beyond the printed page, in the lives of those who have become Christian hearers of these sacred scripts. As one such hearer, however, I have also attempted in chapter 9 to engage the *Upadeśasāhasrī* more directly, by advancing a series of synthetic propositions in freer dialogue with USP 19. In this chapter, a commentary *after* commentary, the carefully delimited experiments in dialogue attempted in the previous chapters open into a broader reflection on Christ as the divine *saṃvāda*, whose reconciling work is both reflected and advanced by the more limited acts of dialogue, debate and reconciliation with a sacred text like the *Upadeśasāhasrī*. In the disciplined practice of *saṃvāda*, the Christian hearer may re-discover a divine likeness that reconfigures all our relations with one another and with the God of Jesus Christ. Such a rediscovery carries consequences for such hearers' practice of Christian discipleship, for our apprehension of the means of grace, and for that cultivated vulnerability that is newly revealed and also fruitfully concealed in the scripted dialogues of Shankara's *Upadeśasāhasrī*. This chapter concludes with a brief meditation on *namaḥ*, the reverence and reverent salutations for the Advaita teaching tradition that may (or may not) follow, in and out of a transforming encounter with the liturgy of liberation it prescribes.

[101] Ibid., p. 24.

[102] See below, ch. 2, pp. 67-72.

To arrive at judgment on this question, prior to an encounter with the sacred scripts themselves, would be premature. So, to continue this introductory treatment and to begin the commentary proper, we turn to Shankara's own introduction to the *Upadeśasāhasrī* verse portion and, arguably, to the Advaita tradition as a whole – a sustained *saṃvāda* of the Advaita teaching with its nearest relation, elder sibling and foremost rival: the Pūrva Mīmāṃsā.

Chapter 2

TRADITIONS IN TENSION: USP 1 AND THE CHRISTIAN HEARER

I.

Upadeśasāhasrī Padyabandha 1.1-2, 16-21a

Salutation to the all-knowing Pure Consciousness which pervades all, is all, abides in the hearts of all beings, and is beyond all objects.

Having completed all the rituals, preceded by the marriage ceremony and the ceremony of installing the sacred fire, the *Veda* has now begun to utter knowledge of *Brahman.*

It is the innate assumption of people that *Ātman* is not distinct from the body and the like. This arises from nescience. So long [as they have it], the Vedic injunction to perform actions would be [valid].

[The *Śruti* passage,] 'Not thus! Not so!' (BU 2.3.6), excluding the body and the like, leaves *Ātman* unexcluded so that [one] may know *Ātman* free from distinction. Thereby nescience is removed.

Once nescience has been removed through the right means of knowledge, how can it arise again, since it does not exist in the one alone, the inner *Ātman* free from distinction?

If nescience cannot arise again, how can there be the notions, '[I am] an agent, [I am] an experiencer,' when there is the knowledge, 'I am the Existent'? Therefore knowledge has no helper.

Renunciation is therefore said by the *Śruti* to 'be superior' to the actions [there enumerated, beginning with truth and] ending with mental activity. '[Only] this much,' says the Vājins' *Śruti*,

'[is, verily, the means to] immortality.' Therefore action should be abandoned by seekers after final release.

II.

The Priority of Knowledge: Hearing USP 1

We begin our hearing of Shankara's *Upadeśasāhasrī* where the great teacher himself begins in the first verse chapter. That is, we begin with reverent salutations:

> Salutation to the all-knowing Pure Consciousness which pervades all, is all, abides in the hearts of all beings, and is beyond all objects (USP 1.1).

Salutations such as this serve as important literary devices, marking beginnings and endings, as well as setting out major themes of the works in which they occur. At the beginnings of many of his commentaries, for example, Shankara will quote verses of praise to Lord Vishnu, invoke the blessings of lesser Vedic deities like Indra, or offer salutations to the Advaita teaching lineage or his own teacher. Here, in order to introduce the *Upadeśasāhasrī*'s first verse chapter, Shankara offers salutations to the primary subject and object of the teaching: the One who knows or witnesses all things as their innermost self. Reading forward in the Sanskrit original, the verse begins with the familiar reality of "awareness" (*caitanya*), as experienced by each and every conscious being, and then advances a series of startling claims on its behalf. Such awareness pervades, witnesses, resides in, transcends, and yet *is* the true reality of all existence. What is an appropriate response? Reverence... indeed, that highest reverence we might customarily reserve for divine beings like Indra, or for teachers, or for the Lord. Though not explicitly named as such, it is clear that this Pure Consciousness to whom Shankara offers reverent salutation is none other than the highest *Brahman*, which we may tentatively name "God."[1]

> **Initial Reflection:** The Christian hearer of this text will, quite properly, be moved to ask: can we say with any confidence that this is the *same* God to whom we too offer reverent worship, or is it a different, alien god? Though this is a central question of this commentarial project, it may be important at this early point in our hearing to remember that the deepest truths about God according to Christian faith – above all, the Trinity – would not and cannot be truly known except through participation in the economy of salvation, as this economy unfolds in history, in Scripture and in Christian practice. So also we should expect that we cannot answer the question of "the god of Advaita" except through participation in the economy it prescribes. And, as it happens, the central focus of USP 1, and by extension the *Upadeśasāhasrī* as a whole, is precisely to delimit and define the authentic economy of liberation.

[1] See Arvind SHARMA, "The Vedāntic Concept of God," in *Perspectives on Vedānta: Essays in Honor or Professor P.T. Raju*, ed. S.S. Rama Rao PAPPU (Leiden: E.J. Brill, 1988), pp. 114-31; Bradley MALKOVSKY, "The Personhood of Śaṃkara's *Para Brahman*," *The Journal of Religion* 77 (1997), pp. 541-62; and Michael COMANS, *The Method of Early Advaita Vedānta: A Study of Gauḍapāda, Śaṅkara, Sureśvara and Padmapāda* (Delhi: Motilal Banarsidass Publishers, 2000), pp. 225-31. For a broad treatment of Advaita theism, also see A.G. Krishna WARRIER, *God in Advaita* (Simla: Indian Institute of Advanced Study, 1977).

The End of the Vedas (USP 1.2-7)

For convenience, I have divided USP 1 into four major sections. In this first section, we follow Shankara as he situates the Advaita teaching in relation to its predecessor and primary rival: the ritualistic tradition of Pūrva Mīmāṃsā. Vedanta is often called the "later" (*uttara*) Mīmāṃsā, as distinct from the "earlier" (*pūrva*) Mīmāṃsā from which it emerged and with which it remained closely joined through its employment of Mīmāṃsā modes of reasoning and scriptural exegesis.[2] Though there are many aspects of this relationship that could occupy our attention, it is perhaps most important at this point to note that the relation between the two traditions was simultaneously *social* and *textual*, and neither apart from the other. The two groups shared a fundamental text – the *Vedas*, including its ritual portions and at least the earliest *Upanishads* – as well as similar exegetical strategies. Though Shankara excludes a Mīmāṃsā background as a *sine qua non* of Vedantic study, he nevertheless generally presumes it on the part of his students.[3] The task of the Vedantin teacher thus necessarily involves some defense of the scope, necessity and benefits of Vedanta, as such, against a presumed ritualist background. Shankara must argue that his tradition truly represents the "end of the *Veda*s," the pursuit of which both concludes and fulfills the requirements of Vedic ritual.

Who is eligible to receive the teaching? Why would anyone bother? And, most importantly, how is this tradition, based as it is on the final "knowledge portion" (*jñāna-kāṇḍa*) of the *Vedas* – that is, the *Upanishads* – related to the "ritual portion" (*karma-kāṇḍa*) which precedes it? Anticipating such questions, Shankara writes:

> Having completed all the rituals, preceded by the marriage ceremony and the ceremony of installing the sacred fire, the *Veda* has now begun to utter knowledge of *Brahman* (USP 1.2).

[2] CLOONEY, *Theology after Vedānta*, pp. 23-26, 129-35. Contemporary Buddhist and Hindu witnesses consistently recognized the close link between the two Mīmāṃsās; in the *Arthaśāstra* attributed to the statesman Kauṭilya, in fact, Pūrva Mīmāṃsā and Vedanta are classified together as *trayī* – Vedic study or "theology" – distinct from the "philosophy" (*ānvīkṣikī*) of Sāṃkhya, Yoga and Lokāyata materialism. See the discussion in Hajime NAKAMURA, *A History of Early Vedānta Philosophy: Part One*, T. LEGGETT, S. MAYEDA, T. UNNO, and others (trans.), Religions of Asia Series 1 (Delhi: Motilal Banarsidass, 1983), pp. 182-84, 319-22, 409-13.

[3] See especially Francis X. CLOONEY, S.J., *Theology after Vedānta: An Experiment in Comparative Theology* (Albany: State University of New York Press, 1993), pp. 129-41; Sengaku MAYEDA, "Adi-Śaṅkarācārya's Teaching on the Means to Mokāa: Jñāna and Karman," *Journal of Oriental Research* 34-35 (1966): pp. 66-75; and NAKAMURA, *History*, pp. 409-14.

The second line of this verse includes *atha-idānīṃ*, "thereafter now," possibly signaling a transition from one object or activity to another. The first of the *Brahma-Sūtras* of Bādarāyaṇa, the core text for all of the schools of Vedanta, also begins with the particle *atha*, "then," "thence," or "thereafter," and thus may be read to invite the question: after *what*? In his *Brahma-Sūtra* commentary, Shankara responds by specifying a set of personal predispositions which qualify the aspirant for inquiry into *Brahman*: 1) discrimination between what is eternal and what is non-eternal; 2) detachment from worldly and heavenly goods; 3) acquisition of personal virtues such as mental restraint; and 4) a strong desire for freedom from the bonds of continued rebirth.[4] Here in the *Upadeśasāhasrī*, on the other hand, Shankara highlights various social requirements, including marriage, procreation and those ritual and ethical obligations set down for householders in the *Vedas*, as well as in legal codes such as *Manu*.[5]

Patrick Olivelle offers the following thumbnail sketch of this householder ideal:

> A twice-born man,[6] following his vedic initiation, studies the Vedas at the house of his teacher; after returning home he marries a suitable wife and establishes his sacred fires;[7] he begets offspring, especially sons, by his legitimate wife; and during his entire life offers sacrifices, recites the Veda, offers food and water to his deceased ancestors, gives food to guests and mendicants, and offers food oblations to all creatures.[8]

[4] See BSBh 1.1.1, in Swami GAMBHIRANANDA (trans.), *Brahma-Sūtra-Bhāṣya of Śrī Śaṅkarācārya* (Calcutta: Advaita Ashrama, 1965, 1972), p. 9, as well as the discussion in Anantanand RAMBACHAN, *Accomplishing the Accomplished: The Vedas as a Source of Valid Knowledge in Śaṅkara*, Monographs of the Society for Asian and Comparative Philosophy 10 (Honolulu: University of Hawaii Press, 1991), pp. 85-92, and J.G. SUTHREN HIRST, *Śaṃkara's Advaita Vedānta: A Way of Teaching*, RoutledgeCurzon Hindu Studies Series (London and New York: RoutledgeCurzon, 2005), pp. 41-42.

[5] See Patrick OLIVELLE (trans.), *The Law Code of Manu*, Oxford World's Classics (Oxford and New York: Oxford University Press, 2004), pp. 48-64; Gavin FLOOD, *An Introduction to Hinduism* (Cambridge, New York and Melbourne: Cambridge University Press, 1996), pp. 40-44; and T.N. MADAN, "The Householder Tradition in Hindu Society," in G. FLOOD (ed.), *The Blackwell Companion to Hinduism* (Oxford and Malden: Blackwell Publishing, 2003), esp. pp. 290-95.

[6] That is, a male from the Brahmin (priestly), Kṣatriya (warrior/princely) or Vaiśya (trade/agricultural) classes of Vedic society.

[7] Three such fires would have been installed at the time of marriage, kept continuously burning throughout the householder's life, and employed in all sacrifices performed or sponsored by that householder. See Fritz STAAL, *AGNI: The Vedic Ritual of the Fire Altar*, vol. 1 (Berkeley: Asian Humanities Press, 1983), pp. 41-44.

[8] Patrick OLIVELLE, *The Āśrama System: History and Hermeneutics of a Religious Institution* (New York: Oxford University Press, 1993), p. 55.

We can presume that it is to this vision, or something like it, that Shankara alludes by mentioning those "rituals" or "works" preceded by marriage and instalment of the three domestic fires. It is also, not incidentally, the pattern of life upheld as the primary religious ideal by such Pūrva Mīmāṃsākas as Jaimini, Śabara and Kumārila Bhaṭṭa.[9] Though Shankara upholds the importance of ritual life, he clearly describes it as something belonging to the past. *Now,* after such a life has been concluded, the *Veda* begins to teach the knowledge of *Brahman.*

But why, one might ask, should ritual life give way to the discipline of knowledge at all? Shankara answers by offering a brief summary of *saṃsāra,* the cycle of rebirth:

> Actions[10] produce association with a body. When there is association with a body, pleasant and unpleasant things are inevitable. From these result passion and aversion [and] from them actions (1.3).
> [From actions] merit and demerit result [and] from merit and demerit there results an ignorant person's association with a body in the same manner again. Thus this transmigratory existence rolls onward powerfully forever like a wheel (1.4).

Shankara here places a distinct and deliberate emphasis upon the centrality of "action" (*karma*) in the cycle of rebirth. In the context of the previous verse, the primary referent of the term *karma* here is almost certainly Vedic ritual, though one cannot exclude ethical obligations, as well as such practices as meditative recitation (*japa*) or Temple worship (*pūjā*) – all of which have tended in Hindu tradition to be assimilated to the logic of Vedic sacrifice.[11] The key axiom underlying this logic is that ritual, if performed correctly and with confidence or faith in its efficacy, secures some desired benefit, from worldly success to a heavenly reward. Such actions thus both result *from* a desire for benefits and result *in* the perpetuation of embodied existence until these benefits actually come to pass. The same logic applies to actions that are unethical or performed incorrectly, though in these cases with negative results.

So far, so good. The problem with this scheme is that the cycle is self-perpetuating: actions generate a pool of "merit and demerit," not all

[9] See Ibid, pp. 238-42, and Karl H. POTTER, "Introduction to the Philosophy of Advaita Vedānta," in K. POTTER (ed.), *Encyclopedia of Indian Philosophies: Advaita Vedānta up to Śaṃkara and His Pupils* (Delhi, Varanasi and Patna: Motilal Banarsidass, 1981), pp. 38-40.

[10] MAYEDA leaves this untranslated as "*Karmans.*"

[11] See OLIVELLE, *The Āśrama System*, pp. 53-55, and Klaus K. KLOSTERMAIER, *A Survey of Hinduism*, 2d ed. (Albany: State University of New York Press, 1994), pp. 155-69.

of which take effect in the present life; unexpended "merit and demerit" thus produce further "association with a body" in some form of earthly, heavenly or even hellish embodiment; continued embodiment, in turn, leads to the experiencing of those "pleasant and unpleasant things" that inevitably produce "passion and aversion" in the person experiencing them; finally, such "passion and aversion" leads to further actions, as one attempts to pursue objects of passion and avoid objects of fear or aversion. And so on. And so on. And so on. Shankara invokes the image of a wheel to illustrate how this cycle of *saṃsāra* turns powerfully forward, with no end in sight.

In this dismal situation, is there room for hope? No and yes. On the one hand, it seems evident that *karma* itself offers no solution. According to Shankara's account, it is the lynch-pin of the whole cycle. Actions provide the fuel that keeps the pistons pumping, inexorably generating future births. On the other hand, also hidden in this description is an important caveat: namely, that this wheel of *saṃsāra* continues to turn only for the "ignorant person" (*ajña*) still bound by it. This opens a window, which Shankara goes on to explain more fully:

> Since the root cause of this transmigratory existence is ignorance, its destruction is desired. Knowledge of *Brahman* therefore is entered on. Final beatitude results from this knowledge (1.5).

We recall that, in verse 2, Shankara stated that the *Vedas* begin teaching *Brahma-vidyā* after concluding the ritual life of the householder, and we asked the question, "why?" In this verse, Shankara gives a straightforward reply: because such knowledge brings about "final beatitude" (*niḥśreyasa*), release from this eternally grinding wheel of actions and results. This follows, he further explains, from the simple fact that ignorance lies at the root of the cycle. Uproot ignorance, and *saṃsāra* comes to an end.

More could obviously be said about ignorance, knowledge and liberation; indeed, the *Upadeśasāhasrī* consists in the main of explorations and defenses of this deceptively uncomplicated claim. Before engaging in any such further discussion, however, Shankara needs to lay an obvious alternative to rest:

> Only knowledge can destroy ignorance; action cannot, since [action] is not incompatible [with ignorance]. Unless ignorance is destroyed, passion and aversion will not be destroyed (1.6).
>
> Unless passion and aversion are destroyed, action arises inevitably from [those] faults. Therefore, for the sake of final beatitude, only knowledge is set forth here (1.7).

A key expression appears in at the beginning of verse 6 and the end of verse 7: "knowledge alone" (*vidyā-eva*). Having established – or, at least, asserted – in the previous verse that knowledge *can* bring about final release, Shankara now insists that continued performance of *karma*, upheld by prominent Mīmāṃsākas as the way to liberation, does *not* possess the requisite characteristics to achieve this end.[12]

Shankara advances two main arguments to support this contention. First of all, he notes that ignorance can only be removed by what is naturally opposed to it, just as darkness can only be removed by light. And what is naturally opposed to ignorance? Only knowledge fits the bill. The second argument flows more directly from the account of *saṃsāra* provided in vv. 3-4. Since action, including especially ritual action, is invariably motivated by such "faults" as "passion and aversion," it is inextricably bound up with the cycle of rebirth. If one persists in such practices, it simply proves that one is still ignorant, tossed to and fro by the storms of desire and doomed to continued rebirth. "Knowledge alone" can remove this ignorance; hence, the practice of "knowledge alone" is prescribed here for the sake of liberation.

Ritual life is preserved as remote preparation for this teaching, but excluded as a means of liberation in itself. Just as the ritual portions of the *Vedas* end in the *Upanishads*, so also ritual life ends with the pursuit of *Brahma-vidyā*. The baton has, by implication, passed from Pūrva-Mīmāṃsā to its natural successor and true end: the Vedanta.

A Christian Reflection: Several features of this account were (and are) widely shared in the South Asian religious milieu, accepted in broad detail by other Vedantins, by the exponents of rival Hindu traditions like Pūrva-Mīmāṃsā and especially by Buddhists and Jains. Such shared features include, perhaps above all, Shankara's teaching on the cycle of rebirth. Though there have been exceptions throughout its history, most forms of Christianity have regarded this teaching as incompatible with Christian faith. This is a significant point of disagreement, on the level of both metaphysics and soteriology. At the same time, those Christians who object

[12] See WARRIER, *Concept of Mukti*, pp. 183-209; Surendranath DASGUPTA, *A History of Indian Philosophy*, vol. 1 (London and New York: Cambridge University Press, 1969), pp. 399-403; and Ganganatha JHA, *Pūrva-Mīmāṃsā in Its Sources*, 2d ed., ed. S. Radhakrishnan (Varanasi: Banaras Hindu University, 1964), pp. 31-34. For a more detailed comparison between Pūrva-Mīmāṃsā and Uttara-Mīmāṃsā on the path to liberation, see two consecutive articles by Chakravarthi RAM-PRASAD: "Knowledge and Action I: Means to the Human End in Bhaṭṭa Mīmāṃsā and Advaita Vedānta," *Journal of Indian Philosophy* 28 (2000): pp. 1-24, and "Knowledge and Action II: Attaining Liberation in Bhaṭṭa Mīmāṃsā and Advaita Vedānta," *Journal of Indian Philosophy* 28 (2000): pp. 25-41.

to this teaching on the grounds that it construes liberation as a kind of metaphysical "progress through the ranks" may, paradoxically, find themselves standing with Shankara against his Pūrva Mīmāṃsāka rivals. Liberation should not and cannot be viewed as an achievement in any ordinary sense of that term; according to Shankara, true liberation completely overturns the calculus of effort, achievement and reward, particularly as applied to ritual. But therein, in turn, may lie a deeper rub.

Objection and Reply (USP 1.8-15)

In vv. 2-7, we have encountered a tension between two ideals of religious life, one with its center of gravity in Vedic ritual and the other centered in *Brahma-vidyā*. Elsewhere, Shankara will refer to these ideals using the broad categories "steadfastness in action" (*karma-niṣṭhā*) and "steadfastness in knowledge" (*jñāna-niṣṭhā*).[13] He insists that only the latter can provide liberation, but he does not diminish the value of Vedic ritualism in its own sphere.

In vv. 8-15, an objection is raised from a third point of view, which asks, "Why this obsessive need to choose between ritual action and knowledge, between one portion of the *Veda*s and another? Retain both!" This position is known as the "combination of knowledge and action" (*jñāna-karma-samuccaya*), and in Advaita tradition it is sometimes associated with Shankara's older contemporary Maṇḍana Miśra and a more obscure seventh-century Vedantin named Brahmadatta.[14] We will return to some of Maṇḍana Miśra's leading ideas in chapter 5. For now, it is sufficient to note that Maṇḍana, as both Pūrva-Mīmāṃsāka and Advaitin, upheld the priority of knowledge in achieving liberation while also insisting upon a permanent supporting role for meditation and ritual performance.[15] At first glance, such a proposal seems like an attractive *via media*, preserving key values of both religious ideals.

[13] On these two competing ideals, see especially Roger MARCAURELLE, *Freedom through Inner Renunciation: Śaṅkara's Philosophy in a New Light* (Albany: State University of New York Press, 2000), pp. 83-104.

[14] On the latter, see M. HIRIYANNA, "Brahmadatta: An Old Vedāntin," *Journal of Oriental Research* 2 (1928): pp. 1-9. Maṇḍana Miśra is by far the more significant of the two figures for the study of Shankara. See the excellent analysis in Allen Wright THRASHER, "The Dates of Maṇḍana Miśra and Śaṅkara," *Wiener Zeitschrift für die Kunde Südasiens und Archiv für indische Philosophie* 23 (1979), pp. 117-39, as well as POTTER, "Introduction," pp. 14-17.

[15] See POTTER, "Introduction," pp. 42-44; MARCAURELLE, *Freedom through Inner Renunciation,* p. 23; and John GRIMES, *A Concise Dictionary of Indian Philosophy: Sanskrit Terms Defined in English,* rev. ed. (Albany: State University of New York Press, 1996), p. 151.

Its existence also suggests that the distinction between Pūrva-Mīmāṃsā and the Vedanta, as Uttara-Mīmāṃsā, may not have been evident to many of Shankara's contemporaries. Yet, perhaps in part for this reason, Shankara will reject this *via media* in no uncertain terms. In so doing, he further heightens the tension between the two portions of the *Vedas*, as well as between those patterns of life associated with one or the other division of this shared text.

Shankara begins his critique of the *jñāna-karma-samuccaya* position by introducing a *pūrva-pakṣin,* or adversarial voice, to advocate on its behalf:

> [Objection:] 'Should not action too always be performed while life lasts? For this, being concomitant with knowledge, leads to final release (USP 1.8).
> 'Action, like knowledge, [should be adhered to], since [both of them] are equally enjoined [by the *Śrutis*]. As the *Smṛti* also [lays it down that] transgression [results from the neglect of action, so] action should be performed by seekers after final release (1.9).

The *pūrva-pakṣin* contends that, contrary to Shankara's reading of *Brahma-vidyā* as succeeding and displacing Vedic ritual, both receive equal emphasis in the *Vedas* themselves. Both should therefore be maintained. More specifically, such laying aside of prescribed ritual and ethical obligations would seem to incur a sin of omission, as described in the *Law of Manu*: "When a man fails to carry out prescribed acts, performs disapproved acts, and is attached to the sensory objects, he is subject to a penance" (*Manu* 11.44).[16] Beyond being scripturally mandated, the *pūrva-pakṣin* adds, continued performance of these obligations might also be understood as a secondary cause of liberating knowledge, without compromising the priority of *Brahma-vidyā* as the sole means of liberation itself.

The *pūrva-pakṣin* anticipates an objection to this schema:

> '[If you say that] as knowledge [of *Brahman*] has permanent fruit, and so does not depend upon anything else, [we reply:] Not so! Just as the *Agniṣṭoma* sacrifice, though it has permanent fruit, depends upon things other than itself, // so, though knowledge has permanent fruit, it always depends upon action' (1.10-11a).

The *Agniṣṭoma* rite mentioned here functions as the basis of several Vedic sacrifices, all of which involve ritual pressing of a somewhat mysterious

[16] In OLIVELLE, *Law of Manu,* p. 193.

plant called *Soma*. From the *pūrva-pakṣin*'s point of view, two aspects of this rite are of central importance. First, the *Agniṣṭoma* and related rituals are believed to achieve "permanent fruit," rebirth in a heavenly realm. Second, they are assisted in this by a number of supporting rites, including consecration of the ritual patron and *Soma* veneration in the days leading up to the *Agniṣṭoma* rite.[17] None of these auxiliary rituals is capable of achieving the heavenly realm by themselves. Nevertheless, the *Agniṣṭoma* cannot achieve its intended result without their performance. So also, by analogy, the "permanent fruit" generated by *Brahma-vidyā* can be said to depend upon continued ritual practice.

This argument relies in part upon Pūrva-Mīmāṃsāka exegetical methods. Shankara will eventually recognise the validity of these methods, at least in their own sphere (see v. 23, below). But first he attempts to strike at the root of the *jñāna-karma-samuccaya* claim:

> Thus some people think. [Reply:] Not so, because action is incompatible [with knowledge] (1.11b).
> In fact, action is incompatible with knowledge, since [it] is associated with misconception. And knowledge is declared here to be the view that *Ātman* is changeless (1.12).
> [From the notion,] 'I am an agent; this is mine' arises action. Knowledge depends upon the real, [whereas] the Vedic injunction depends upon an agent (1.13).

Shankara leads with a short statement of his position in the second half of verse 11. It is not possible to combine ritual action and *Brahma-vidyā*, he contends, for a simple reason: they are fundamentally incompatible with and even opposed to one another.

In verses 12 and 13, Shankara demonstrates the incompatibility of knowledge and action by offering an analysis of their respective psychologies. Actions are invariably performed to achieve results, he observes, and thus depend upon "misconception" or mistaken self-assertion, including most importantly a sense of oneself as an "agent" (*kartṛ*) capable of action and possession. Later in this chapter (v. 24), Shankara will refer to this sense of identity and agency by the term *ahaṃ-kāra*, the "I-notion"

[17] RĀMATĪRTHA mentions a cluster of more general 'accessories' that would also accompany the ritual, such as the singing of the *Sāma Veda* by a priest called the Udgātṛ and mere knowledge of the heavenly beings (*devatās*) to whom the sacrifice is offered. See the full comment in D. GOKHALE (ed.), *Shri Shankarāchārya's Upadeśasāhasrī with the Gloss Padayôjanīkā by Shrī Rāmatīrtha* (Bombay: Gujurati Printing Press, 1917), p. 10.

or ego. To undertake a ritual, one is faced with various questions for deliberation and choice: will I perform this ritual or not? When and how will I perform it? What do I intend to accomplish? These kinds of deliberation presume the *ahaṃ-kāra* for their operation, and necessarily include presumptions of duality and change. Continued insistence on ritual performance for the purpose of achieving liberation is therefore rather like attempting to give up smoking by having another cigarette. The action reinforces the very habit of thought that the Advaita teaching tradition endeavors to reverse.

Even setting aside such distinctively Advaita claims about human psychology and the force of habit, knowledge and action still differ essentially. Vedic ritual originates in deliberation and choice, as we have seen. Knowledge does not. It originates in and thus depends uniquely upon the "reality" (*vastu*) one is attempting to know.[18] Stated another way, choice enters into the question of the concrete acquisition of knowledge – that is, whether or not one pursues this knowledge, or the various instruments or methods one uses to do so. Yet, the known object alone determines the content of this knowledge. In his commentary on this verse, Swami Paramarthananda offers a helpful illustration: one can choose to get a blood-test, or not, but the results of the test, as such, do not depend upon this choice. Presuming the test is accurate, the results depend upon the content of one's blood, and that alone.[19] Or to offer another analogy: the actual shape of planet earth does not now and never has depended upon what people knew about it. It was spherical even when many people may have thought it was flat. Such "dependence-upon-its object" (*vastu-adhīna*, v. 13) differentiates all knowledge from all action, and this contrast is even more pronounced when the object of inquiry is one's innermost self.

Shankara continues:

> Knowledge destroys the factors of action[20] as [it destroys] the notion that there is water in the salt desert. After accepting this true view, [how] would one decide to perform action? (1.14).

[18] See MARCAURELLE, *Freedom through Inner Renunciation,* pp. 23-24.

[19] Swami PARAMARTHANANDA Saraswati, *UPADEŚA SĀHASRĪ*, audio cassettes, Vedānta Vidyārthi Sangha, n.d., cassette #1-4.

[20] In this context, "factor of action" (*kāraka*) likely functions as a short hand for the self-identity and "I-notion," along with the sense of duality that arises with them, as discussed in the previous two verses. See Sengaku MAYEDA (trans.), *A Thousand Teachings: The Upadeśasāhasrī of Śaṅkara* (Albany: State University of New York Press, 1992), p. 106, n11.

> Because of the incompatibility [of knowledge with action] a person who knows thus, being possessed of this knowledge, cannot perform action. For this reason action should be renounced by a seeker after final release (USP 1.15).

In verse 14, Shankara introduces one of his favorite tropes to illustrate the acquisition of knowledge: the image of the desert mirage. In the case of such a mirage, knowledge does not destroy any actual water, but only destroys a false perception of it; so also the truth of *Brahma-vidyā* aims to eliminate those mistaken notions of agency and identity that sustain ritual practice. Deliberately persisting in such practice would be like taking a long drink of sand even after one has determined to see the truth behind the mirage.

What makes better sense? This is specified in verse 15: rejection of all ritual obligations and the taking up of ascetic life. From the metaphysical and psychological incompatibility of knowledge and action, Shankara thus advances the further claim that liberating knowledge has social consequences. The self-knower simply cannot perform action, and the seeker after liberation is enjoined to renounce it. There is no middle way.

> **A Christian Reflection:** In its fierce rejection of the combination of knowledge and action, Shankara's teaching script may be heard to advocate one or another kind of antinomianism, perhaps echoing those radical reformers who have at different points in Christian history rejected even baptism and the Lord's Supper in favor of a pure spiritual faith completely untainted by ritualistic "works." There is no doubt that such radicalism represents a permanent possibility for the Advaitin no less than for the Christian. Nevertheless, as we argued in the previous chapter, both traditions also privilege participation in certain forms of scripted – we might even say *ritualized* – performative practice.[21] Both traditions invariably become implicated in the deeper and more tangled project of defending the performance of such ritualized practices against the purported "ritualism" of their opponents. For most Christian traditions, this involves nuanced arguments about faith, discipleship and the means of grace; for Shankara, it involves a no less nuanced account of renunciation, ascetic life and the means of knowledge, to which we now turn.

[21] For the theorist Catherine BELL, "ritualization" describes a strategic practice that differentiates and sets apart the activity of the ritual agents from ordinary activities in a specific cultural context so as to invest it with a privileged status. See her *Ritual Theory, Ritual Practice* (New York and Oxford: Oxford University Press, 1992), pp. 88-93, and *Ritual: Perspectives and Dimensions* (New York and Oxford: Oxford University Press, 1997), pp. 81-82. Interpreted through this lens, Shankara's polemic against Vedic ritual and the requirements of ordinary, householder life functions to distinguish, to privilege and thus to "ritualize" the alternative practices he prescribes.

The Superior Path (USP 1.16-21a)

The previous section concluded, as we have just seen, with an injunction to give up ritual actions and their results. Elsewhere, in the prose portion of the *Upadeśasāhasrī*, Shankara will be more specific, closely associating his teaching tradition with a readily identifiable social group: an order of ascetics called *paramahaṃsa*, whose members abandon their ritual fires, break their sacrificial thread,[22] remove their topknot,[23] and carry either a single staff or no staff at all.[24] By Shankara's era, such institutions of renunciant life, or *saṃnyāsa*, represented an enduring alternative and challenge to the householder religious ideal. Though some legal codes attempted to accommodate *saṃnyāsa* by incorporating it as the last of four "stages of life" (*āśrama*), recent scholarship suggests that this neat scheme may have been honored more in the breach than in the observance. Shankara, for one, seems to have held that male members of the Brahmin caste, and they alone, could take up *saṃnyāsa* – but that they could do so at any point in their lives, regardless of their stage of life, precisely in order to pursue *Brahma-vidyā*.

The literature related to Shankara's teaching on *saṃnyāsa* is immense, in no small part because this teaching has occasioned controversy, both in its interpretation and in its social consequences. The full scope of this controversy need not delay us here.[25] It is sufficient to note that, as Shankara continues his refutation of the *jñāna-karma-samuccaya* position, he also defends *saṃnyāsa* as the natural result and privileged means of liberation.

He begins this defense by clarifying the fundamental nature of bondage:

> It is the innate assumption of people that *Ātman* is not distinct from the body and the like. This arises from nescience. So long [as they have it], the Vedic injunction to perform actions would be [valid] (1.16).

[22] So-called "twice-born" or upper caste men are invested with this sacred thread between the ages of eight and twenty-four, traditionally prior to taking up student life with a teacher. See FLOOD, *Introduction to Hinduism*, 204-205.

[23] See Patrick OLIVELLE, *Renunciation in Hinduism: A Medieval Debate: Volume One: The Debate and the Advaita Argument* (Vienna: Institut für Indologie der Universität Wien, 1986), p. 30: "The topknot [*śikhā*] consisted of several locks of hair that were left uncut on the head. The early literature indicates that family customs regulated the wearing of the topknot. Some kept the topknot on the right side of the head, others on both sides, and yet others shaved their heads completely.... In time the topknot, just as the sacrificial cord, was considered obligatory on all."

[24] See OLIVELLE, *Āśrama System*, pp. 170-73, and OLIVELLE, *Renunciation*, pp. 33-34, 52-54.

[25] MARCAURELLE surveys the relevant literature in *Freedom through Inner Renunciation*, pp. 3-13. Also see Kapil N. TIWARI, *Dimensions of Renunciation in Advaita Vedānta* (Delhi: Motilal Banarsidass, 1977).

> [The *Śruti* passage,] 'Not thus! Not so!' (BU 2.3.6), excluding the body and the like, leaves *Ātman* unexcluded so that [one] may know *Ātman* free from distinction. Thereby nescience is removed (1.17).

In these verses Shankara introduces one of the central categories of his teaching: "nescience" or "fundamental ignorance" (*avidyā*), a rough synonym of the more general "ignorance" (*ajñānam*) that appeared as root cause of *saṃsāra* in vv. 5-7. We might tend to think of such ignorance as resulting from some prior misperception. Shankara here reverses such expectations, asserting that *avidyā* is more properly conceived as the fundamental *cause* of error rather than as its result.

What is the specific error caused by *avidyā*? It is what Shankara will elsewhere name "superimposition" (*adhyāsa*), described in verse 16 as the natural and spontaneous assumption that we are defined and delimited by our bodies, senses, minds, personalities and all those properties that differentiate us from other persons and the created order.[26] This error, Shankara suggests, is exposed as such by such Vedic texts as *Bṛhadāraṇyaka Upanishad* 2.3.6 and its parallels,[27] which describe our true, innermost self with the negative construction *na-iti, na-iti*, translated above as "Not thus! Not so!" We are called by these scriptures to shift our most basic self-identification from these limiting properties to that One who remains after they have been systematically excluded. By removing the error, we also remove its fundamental cause.

Various aspects of this account of bondage and its removal will occupy us in future chapters. In the present context, the account functions primarily to sort out different types of persons, to whom different rules apply.[28] Those persons who retain the "innate assumption" or misidentification with their "body and the like" remain subject to Vedic ritual and ethical obligations. But the same *Veda*s also offer an alternative pattern of existence:

> Once nescience has been removed through the right means of knowledge,[29] how can it arise again, since it does not exist in the one alone, the inner *Ātman* free from distinction? (1.18).

[26] In USG 2, Shankara approaches the question differently, simply defining *avidyā* in terms of superimposition. See the further discussion in chapter 6 of this commentary, as well as MAYEDA, *A Thousand Teachings*, pp. 76-79.

[27] BU 3.9.26; 4.2.4; 4.4.22; 4.5.15.

[28] PARAMARTHANANDA, *UPADEŚA SĀHASRĪ*, cassette #1-6.

[29] That is, from the *Śruti*, which Śaṅkara regards as the sole authentic *pramāṇa* or means of knowledge for knowing the self. See especially RAMBACHAN, *Accomplishing the Accomplished*, pp. 31-54; Anantanand RAMBACHAN, "Where Words Can Set Free: The

> If nescience cannot arise again, how can there be the notions, '[I am] an agent, [I am] an experiencer,' when there is the knowledge, 'I am the Existent'? Therefore knowledge has no helper (1.19).

Shankara continues the chain of reasoning from the immediately preceding verses and draws it together with his earlier discussion of ignorance and personal agency in verses 12-13. Knowledge, once achieved, is permanent. Freed by the word of the scriptures from *avidyā* and the error that proceeds from it, the hearer no longer understands herself as the subject of action and experience. Instead, she identifies exclusively with that innermost "Existent" which remains unexcluded by the Upanishadic *na-iti, na-iti,* "Not thus! Not so!" Liberation does not exactly result from such a correction; rather, the firm identification, "I am that sole Existent," *is* liberation, since that Existent is not now nor ever has been bound by suffering or ignorance.[30]

Shankara's concluding remark – that "knowledge has no helper" – again allows us to differentiate among different persons and patterns of life. Persons with this knowledge are *not like* persons who persist in error, and they need not follow the same rules. To be more specific:

> Renunciation is therefore said by the *Śruti* to 'be superior' to the actions [there enumerated, beginning with truth and] ending with mental activity. '[Only] this much,' says the Vājins' *Śruti*,[31] // '[is, verily, the means to] immortality' (BU 4.5.15). Therefore action should be abandoned by seekers after final release (1.20-21a).

For some hearers, the repeated "therefore" in these verses may strike an odd chord. How exactly does an injunction to renounce follow from the previous arguments?

We can trace some of the steps of Shankara's reasoning by turning to one of the scriptures he cites to support this conclusion: *Bṛhadāraṇyaka*

Liberating Potency of Vedic Words in the Hermeneutics of Śaṅkara," in J.R. TIMM (ed.), *Texts in Context: Traditional Hermeneutics in South Asia* (Albany: State University of New York Press, 1992), pp. 35-42; and Anantanand RAMBACHAN, "Śaṅkara's Rationale for *Śruti* as the Definitive Source of *Brahmajñāna*: A Refutation of Some Contemporary Views," *Philosophy East and West* 36 (1986), pp. 25-40. Also see the further discussion of this issue in chapters 4 and 5 of this commentary.

[30] See MAYEDA, *A Thousand Teachings*, pp. 74-75; POTTER, "Introduction,", 32-33; and especially Thomas A. FORSTHOEFEL, *Knowing Beyond Knowledge: Epistemologies of Religious Experience in Classical and Modern Advaita*, Ashgate World Philosophies (Hants and Burlington: Ashgate Publishing, 2002), pp. 46-52.

[31] MAYEDA identifies "Vājin" with "Vājasaneyin," a Vedic tradition closely associated with the *Bṛhadāraṇyaka Upanishad* (*A Thousand Teachings*, p. 106n13).

Upanishad 4.5.15, one of the *loci classici* of Advaita teachings on formal renunciation. In his commentary on this passage in its original context, Shankara makes the argument that such renunciant life follows from liberating self-knowledge, the knowledge thematized in USP 1.19 as, "I am that Existent." "Inasmuch as self-knowledge destroys the cause of all action," he writes in *BUBh* 5.5.15, "at the dawn of knowledge action will come to an end."[32] Elsewhere he will describe this as the renunciation that arises "naturally" or even "spontaneously" from self-knowledge, regardless of one's previous state of life.[33] It represents, we might say, the most appropriate social expression of the self-knower's non-dual awareness, which no longer differentiates among castes or stages of life nor desires to benefit by performing any action whatever.

In his comment on the *Bṛhadāraṇyaka Upanishad*, having begun by insisting upon renunciation as a consequence of self-knowledge, Shankara immediately extends its scope:

> ... renunciation belongs to enlightened persons simply because of their knowledge of the self. So also it is proved that the one who desires the truth *can also renounce the world*, as evidenced by the passage, 'aspiring after this world [i.e. the *Ātman*] alone, the ascetics renounce all worldly attachment' [BU 4.4.22].... It is well-known in all the scriptures that activities springing up from desire are impediments to knowledge. Therefore, in the case of one who is dispassionate and who is desirous of liberation, the injunction, 'he should renounce and go from the stage of a celibate itself,' etc., is but reasonable, even though he is without knowledge.[34]

Shankara's reasoning here is both scriptural and pragmatic. If liberating self-knowledge naturally conduces to *saṃnyāsa*, it stands to reason that *saṃnyāsa* would also naturally conduce to the acquisition of such knowledge. Hence, it can be prescribed for those seeking self-knowledge, as well as those who already have it.[35] The authentic desire for liberation

[32] In PANOLI, *Upanishads*, vol. 4, p. 1123 (modified).

[33] The text is the AUBh introduction, and the Sanskrit term is *artha-prāpta*. Sankrit text and English translation in V. PANOLI (trans.), *Upanishads in Śaṅkara's Own Words*, vol. 2, rev. ed. (Calicut: Mathubhumi Printing and Publishing Company, 1996), esp. pp. 444-49. See also the discussion in MARCAURELLE, *Freedom through Inner Renunciation*, pp. 131-42, and Karl H. POTTER, "Śaṃkarācārya: The Myth and the Man," *Journal of the American Academy of Religion Thematic Studies* 48/3-4 (1982): pp. 115-18.

[34] In PANOLI, *Upanishads*, vol. 4, pp. 1127-29 (modified, with italics added). Cf. MARCAURELLE, *Freedom through Inner Renunciation*, pp. 142-48.

[35] Later Advaita tradition would further specify and formalise Shankara's implicit distinction between these two kinds of *saṃnyāsa*, differentiating the renunciant who gives up action as a result of knowledge (*vidvat-saṃnyāsin*) from the one who renounces for

shifts its subject into a new social and religious world, a world shaped by the distinctively Advaita teaching on self-knowledge. Renunciation naturally pertains to such persons, just as ritual injunctions pertain to those who persist in ignorance. In each case, interior disposition and exterior state of life fall into perfect alignment.[36]

Though these two patterns of life may be appropriate to differently qualified persons, they are decidedly not parallel. To demonstrate this, Shankara alludes to another scriptural text, the so-called *Mahā Nārāyaṇa Upaniṣad*.[37] This Upanishad, after listing a series of spiritual disciplines, extols renunciation as superior to all of them. For Shankara, such praise applies to the Advaita tradition as a whole, from which renunciant life takes its specific shape and for which all other disciplines function as prelude or preparation. Vedic ritualism is again preserved, albeit in an inferior role that its advocates could scarcely have recognized.

the purpose of knowledge (*vivideṣa-saṃnyāsin*). For further discussion, see CLOONEY, *Theology after Vedānta*, pp. 147-49, and POTTER, "Introduction," pp. 34-36.

[36] By implication, of course, particularly if one follows Shankara's narrow insistence that only male members of the Brahmin caste are actually eligible for the prescribed renunciation, the Advaita tradition appears here to fly its true colors, to reveal itself as the exclusive province of a small cadre of social elite. See especially Lance E. NELSON, "Theism for the Masses, Non-Dualism for the Monastic Elite: A Fresh Look at Śaṃkara's Trans-Theistic Spirituality," in W. SHEA (ed.), *The Struggle over the Past: Fundamentalism in the Modern World*, (Lanham: University Press of America, 1993), pp. 61-77. As it happens, Shankara reveals greater interpretive flexibility than we might initially expect, and he does find ways to accommodate significant variations on such highly restrictive norms, notably including the legendary sage-king Janaka. See TIWARI, *Dimensions of Renunciation*, pp. 115-20; Comans, *Method of Early Advaita Vedānta*, 325-26; Yoshitsugu Sawai, *The Faith of Ascetics and Lay Smārtas: A Study of the Śaṅkaran Tradition of Śṛṅgerī*, Publications of the De Nobili Research Library 19 (Vienna: Institut für Indologie der Universitat Wien, 1992), pp. 129-30; Reid B. LOCKLIN, "Integral *Saṃnyāsa*? Adi Shankaracharya and Liberation Hermeneutics," *Journal of Hindu-Christian Studies* 20 (2007): pp. 43-51; and especially two further essays by Roger MARCAURELLE: "The Basic Types of Renunciation in Hinduism: with Special Reference to Śaṅkara's *Gītā-Bhāṣya*," in K. YOUNG (ed.), *Hermeneutical Paths to the Sacred Worlds of India: Essays in Honour of Robert W. Stevenson* (Atlanta: Scholars Press, 1994), pp. 104-22, and "Śaṅkara's Hermeneutics of Renunciation in the *Gītā*," in A. SHARMA (ed.), *New Essays in the Bhagavadgītā: Philosophical, Methodological, and Cultural Approaches* (New Delhi: Books and Books, 1987), pp. 98-126.

[37] This work is sometimes appended to the *Taittirīya Upanishad* as the tenth book of the *Taittiriya Āraṇyaka* (TU consisting of books 7-9). The text exists in three different manuscript traditions. In the critical edition and French translation prepared by Jean VARENNE, the relevant text occurs at *Mahā Nārāyaṇa Upanishad* 505-17, with the quotation at 516: Jean VARENNE, *La Mahā Nārāyaṇa Upaniṣad: Édition Critique, avec Une Traduction Française, Une Étude, des Notes et, en Annexe, La Praṇāgnihotra Upaniṣad*, Publications de L'Institut de Civilisation Indienne 8/11 & 8/13 (Paris: Éditions E. de Boccard, 1960), vol. 1, pp. 130-31.

A Christian Reflection: At the outset of this chapter, we noted that the question of "the god of Advaita" would be, for the Christian hearer, irresolvable except in and through the economy of liberation prescribed by the tradition. But this economy, it turns out, is twofold, incorporating Vedic ritualism and the householder ideal at one level and the far superior path of renunciation and the discipline of knowledge at another. As the "later" (*uttara*) Mīmāṃsā, the tradition of Advaita Vedanta both emerges from the "earlier" (*pūrva*) and older Mīmāṃsā and is as different from it as day from night. Thus, this teaching script may be heard to echo not only Christian arguments about celibacy and ascetic life, but also – much more – the relationship of the New Covenant to the Old Covenant that preceded it. The temptation, for Advaita and Christian hearer alike, may be to reject, to dismiss, to leave the older tradition and perhaps even its "lower, alien god" permanently behind. This is a trajectory of interpretation followed by Marcion of Pontus, by many Gnostic Christians and by the Manichees in the early history of the Church, but it is not the course followed by Christian orthodoxy. Nor, interestingly, is it the course followed by Ādi Shankaracharya – at least not quite.

Rejection and Reconciliation (USP 1.21b-26)

In the previous three sections, we have heard Shankara situate the Advaita teaching in a tense but definite relation with Pūrva Mīmāṃsā and the householder religious ideal. We might at this point characterize this relation as one of *mutual priority*. On the one hand, the "ritual portion" of the *Veda*s and the religious life that flows from it possess a kind of temporal priority: they precede the "knowledge portion" of the *Veda*s, function as remote preparation for it, and are largely presumed as the dominant religious worldview of prospective students. Textually and existentially, the ritual life of the householder ordinarily comes before the pursuit of knowledge. This priority, moreover, possesses its own distinctive stability and permanence. Vedic injunctions retain their full force, here and now, in the case of those ignorant persons who have yet to conceive an authentic desire for liberation.

On the other hand, as this last qualifying phrase well reveals, Shankara clearly gives a far more significant priority to knowledge. Knowledge alone conduces to "final beatitude" (vv. 2-7), is fundamentally incompatible with continued ritual performance (vv. 8-15), and is thus embodied in an entirely different mode of life (vv. 16-21a). In and of itself, the life of action represents a coherent religious ideal. In the light of *Brahma-vidyā*, it simply melts away. Thus, in addition to speaking in terms of "earlier" and "later," Shankara will also speak of "higher" and "lower," "superior" and "inferior," and even "true" and "false" when comparing his tradition to those otherwise legitimate patterns of Vedic religious observance that precede it.

The basic parameters of this argument are already firmly in place. A few questions, however, may yet linger. Shankara takes up these lingering issues and consolidates his position in the final section of the chapter, beginning with the aforementioned *Agniṣṭoma* rite:

> [You] said that, as with the *Agniṣṭoma* sacrifice, [knowledge depends upon action]. To this the following reply is given (USP 1.21cd):
> Because action has to be accomplished through various factors of action and varies in its result, knowledge is the opposite of it. Therefore the example is not applicable (1.22).
> Since the *Agniṣṭoma* sacrifice, like agriculture, etc., has as its object a result, it requires support from other actions. But what else does knowledge depend upon? (1.23).

In vv. 10-11, we may recall, the *pūrva-pakṣin* suggested an analogy: just as the *Agniṣṭoma* draws on other supports to achieve a heavenly realm, so also might knowledge draw on ritual performance as a secondary cause of liberation. If so, then knowledge and ritual action should be pursued together.

Shankara has already rejected the "combination of knowledge and action" (*jñāna-karma-sumuccaya*) theory on logical grounds. Here he simply points out that, in light of everything that has been said thus far, the proposed analogy between the acquisition of knowledge and the *Agniṣṭoma* fails. Knowledge, as we have heard especially in verse 13, depends exclusively upon its object. Like the examples of the blood-test or the shape of the earth, self-knowledge gives invariable results and depends entirely upon its object. Careful and attentive ritual practice is not without value. It simply pertains to a lesser sphere of existence from which *Brahma-vidyā*, those possessed of it, and even those engaged in its sincere pursuit, stand intrinsically exempt.

The next verse makes this more explicit:

> The transgression [resulting from neglect of action] is imputed only to one who has 'I'-notion. A knower of *Ātman* has neither 'I'-notion nor desire for the result [of action] (1.24).

This verse applies Shankara's general principle to the specific example of the "sin of omission" invoked by the *pūrva-pakṣin* in verse 9, above. If the presence or absence of the *ahaṃkāra,* or "I-notion," determines whether one is bound by *any* Vedic injunctions, this also *ipso facto* covers those specific injunctions that mandate life-long ritual performance.

Such obligations again retain their full effectiveness within their proper sphere; but the practice of the discipline of knowledge belongs to a different, higher sphere of human life and activity.

Having now addressed all of the objections posed by the *pūrva-pakṣin*, Shankara can draw the chapter to a conclusion.

> Therefore, in order to destroy ignorance, end transmigratory existence, and set forth knowledge of *Brahman*, this Upaniṣad has been commenced (1.25). And the word 'Upaniṣad' may be derived from the verbal root '*sad*' preceded by the prefix '*upa*' and '*ni*' and followed by the suffix '*kvip*,'[38] since it diminishes and destroys birth and the like (1.26).

In these final two verses of USP 1, Shankara sets out the purpose and scope of the *Upadeśasāhasrī* by defining it as an "*Upaniṣad.*" This may initially seem an odd choice of terms. Normally, in this commentary and in common usage, we have referred to the *Upanishads* as a group of sacred scriptures that compose the fourth and final section of the *Vedas*. To defend the ascription of the same exalted label to his own teaching, here and elsewhere Shankara provides a distinctive grammatical derivation of the term in terms of its constituent particles (v. 26).[39] According to this derivation, the word "*Upaniṣad*" comes to denote not merely a particular canon of scriptural writings, but any teaching which weakens the wheel of *saṃsāra* by destroying the ignorance at its root.

In his *Kaṭha-Upanishad* commentary, Shankara offers a fuller explanation:

> ... to shatter the cause of *saṃsāra* such as *avidyā* and the like, as borne by the meaning of the root *sad*, is impossible by means of a mere book, but is possible by means of knowledge... Therefore, the word Upanishad primarily denotes knowledge, but is used in a figurative sense to denote a book.[40]

[38] According to Pāṇini's grammar, this suffix disappears in combination with a root and prefixes, as it does here. It converts the verbal root into an agent noun: "that which X" or "the one who X." See MAYEDA, *A Thousand Teachings*, p. 17n17; ALSTON, *The Thousand Teachings*, p. 106n1; and PARAMARTHANANDA, *UPADEŚA SĀHASRĪ*, cassette #1-7.

[39] Shankara's derivation has not won wide acceptance among modern scholars. A commonly accepted definition is "to sit close by [the teacher] devotedly" (GRIMES, *Concise Dictionary*, p. 329), but OLIVELLE follows L. RENOU and others in suggesting that the term was originally used in the sense of "connection" or "equivalence." See Patrick OLIVELLE, *The Early Upaniṣads: Annotated Text and Translation*, South Asia Research Series (New York and Oxford: Oxford University Press, 1998), p. 24.

[40] KaUBh introduction. Sanskrit text and English translation in V. PANOLI (trans.), *The Upanishads in Śaṅkara's Own Words*, vol. 2, rev. ed. (Calicut: Mathrubhumi Printing and Publishing Co. Ltd., 1995), p. 154 (modified).

Following this rule, Shankara can refer to his own treatise as an *Upaniṣad* in a figurative sense, as in fact the *Upanishads* of the *Vedas* are also figuratively so described. Behind such extended usages stands *Brahma-vidyā* as the primary and proper meaning of the term.

Just as with the initial salutation, so also this grammatical derivation at the conclusion of USP 1 offers a précis of the essential teaching. There, in the chapter's first stanza, we were given a brief introduction to the One whom we seek to know, all-pervading and all-transcending, abiding in the hearts of all. Here, we learn the benefits of knowing this innermost self: the destruction of ignorance, an end to the wheel of rebirth, ultimate freedom. At one level, things are very simple. At another, as the intervening verses amply reveal, Shankara's chapter also bears witness to a highly contested religious context. Acceptance of this teaching necessarily involves its disciples in debate, argument and a delicate negotiation of conflicting claims.

True self-knowers may well attain a state of total freedom. The Advaita tradition constituted by such knowers, however, remains inextricably joined to prior traditions of practice and belief by virtue of the Vedic scriptures that they share. USP 1 reflects this tension and models a sophisticated strategy of dialogue, rejection and reconciliation, setting aside Pūrva Mīmāṃsā and the householder religious ideal without conclusively setting itself against them. Non-dualist though he may be, Shankara introduces his *Upaniṣad* in explicit dialogue with a social and religious other who is, like *Ātman* the divine self, not really "other" at all.

III.

"I WANT YOU TO UNDERSTAND THIS MYSTERY": *SAṂVĀDA* AND RECONCILIATION IN THE COMMENTARIAL PROJECT

> So that you may not claim to be wiser than you are, brothers and sisters, I want you to understand this mystery: a hardening has come upon part of Israel, until the full number of the Gentiles has come in. And so all Israel will be saved; as it is written,
>
> 'Out of Zion will come the Deliverer;
> he will banish ungodliness from Jacob.'
> 'And this is my covenant with them,
> when I take away their sins.'
>
> As regards the gospel they are enemies of God for your sake; but as regards election they are beloved, for the sake of their ancestors; for the gifts and

> the calling of God are irrevocable. Just as you were once disobedient to God but have now received mercy because of their disobedience, so they have now been disobedient in order that, by the mercy shown to you, they too might now receive mercy. For God has imprisoned all in disobedience so that he may be merciful to all (Romans 11:25-32).

On first hearing, the cool back-and-forth of USP 1 may seem to have little to offer the Christian hearer, who may not have ever heard of the *Vedas*, who will probably never perform a rite like the *Agniṣṭoma*, and who almost certainly does not share the commitment to these scriptures and their ritual practice that grounds the entire debate. Such hearers can, nevertheless, appreciate what has been accomplished in 26 short verses. Through the stanzas of this teaching script, prospective students receive a concise introduction to the essential scope, benefits and necessity of the Advaita teaching tradition as a whole. What does the tradition purport to communicate? *Brahma-vidyā*, divine knowledge, which is also knowledge of one's own innermost self. What is the benefit of this teaching? Freedom from the cycle of rebirth. Why is this teaching necessary? Since ignorance lies at the root of my sense of agency, of my identification with limited body, mind and personality, and of the relentless wheel of *saṃsāra*, knowledge alone can bring these to an end. Hence, an alternative pattern of living, a life that flows spontaneously from *Brahma-vidyā*, is opened for those who conceive the requisite desire.

Shankara also takes on one more, quite central task in this chapter: that is, he defines this Vedanta teaching in self-conscious relation with its Pūrva Mīmaṃsā predecessor, a relation I have labeled *mutual priority*. Vedic ritualism and the householder life come *prior* to the pursuit of knowledge, in the Vedic scriptures themselves and presumably in the lives of most Advaita students, and they represent a coherent religious ideal. Rituals yield real results and, when performed in conjunction with an ethical life and the proper disposition, may even attain heavenly realms. It is only in the specific perspective offered by *Brahma-vidyā* that this ideal suddenly appears to stand in contradiction to the sole authentic and truly final liberation, which cannot be identified with any or all such heavenly realms. For the person possessed of this liberating *vidyā*, as well as the person desirous of it, the higher priority of knowledge has come dramatically to light; for others, the ethical and ritual injunctions of the *Veda*s have a permanent, even irrevocable, character. The two clusters of practices and patterns of life purportedly have nothing whatever to do with one another… yet, as the sometimes convoluted argument of USP 1 itself well reveals, these two nevertheless remain bound together in their own distinctive form of *saṃvāda* – a sustained, ongoing and mutually defining dialogue and debate.

Encountering such arguments for what may be the first time, the Christian hearer certainly finds herself on foreign ground. At the same time, this narrative of two distinct interpretative traditions, rising from the same scriptural sources, sharing many theological commitments and exegetical methods, and thereby bound together in a close relation of mutual priority, mutual tension and mutual dialogue, also strikes a chord in the deep reservoir of Christian memory. For we can discern a comparable dynamic, of no less central significance for the tradition, in the preaching of the apostle Paul on God's irrevocable gifts and calling of the Jewish people, to which we have alluded in the brief selection from Romans, quoted above.

This selection arises near the conclusion of an extended meditation on the place of historic Israel in God's plan of salvation, which Paul develops across three chapters of what many scholars would consider the most important source of his thought: his letter to the Christian community in Rome (Romans 9-11). In these chapters, Paul addresses a series of related questions, above all that most pressing, anguished demand, "has God rejected his people?" (Rom 11:1). Paul's answer is forceful and clear: "By no means!" To defend this position, he offers, first, a creative "retelling of the story of Israel" that re-affirms the status of Christian believers as the true heirs of God's promise even in the face of widespread Jewish rejection of the gospel (9:6 – 10:21), and, second, an argument "from basic principles that God still intends to save ethnic Jews" (11:1-36).[41] Despite the hardening of "part of Israel" and their opposition as "enemies of God" in the present time, Paul asserts, it is still possible to proclaim that "all Israel will be saved" (11:25-26, 28).

The precise meaning of "all Israel" in this passage has been the subject of controversy. For many centuries, motivated by a supersessionist or replacement theology, Christian interpreters have assumed that Paul must be referring here to the church or perhaps to that small Jewish remnant joined to it through Christian faith.[42] If God's promises definitively

[41] N.T. WRIGHT, "The Letter to the Romans," in *The New Interpreter's Bible*, vol. 10 (Nashville: Abingdon Press, 2002), pp. 622-23.

[42] See Eugene J. FISHER, "Covenant Theology and Jewish-Christian Dialogue," *American Journal of Theology and Philosophy* 9 (1988), pp. 6-9, and Mark REASONER, *Romans in Full Circle: A History of Interpretation* (Louisville: Westminster John Knox Press, 2005), pp. 121-28.

passed from Judaism to its Christian successor with the death and resurrection of Jesus the Christ, then Paul could not possibly hold out hope for the salvation of those who had no less definitively rejected this same Christ. For Catholics and many others, however, a new context was created by the teaching of the Second Vatican Council, especially in its "Declaration on the Relationship of the Church to Non-Christian Religions" (*Nostra Aetate*), which strongly affirmed with Paul that the Jewish people "should not be represented as rejected by God or accursed" (no. 4).[43] *Nostra Aetate* cleared the ground for a series of pastoral initiatives in Jewish-Christian dialogue, as well as for Christian re-assessments of Judaism, of covenantal history and even of Christianity itself.[44]

In the field of New Testament studies, such re-assessments also drew strength from another important development: the "new perspective on Paul," pioneered by E.P. Sanders' 1977 book *Paul and Palestinian Judaism*. In this and subsequent works, Sanders offers a compelling portrait of a very Jewish Paul, along with a first-century Judaism rich with convictions about God's mercy and grace. Paul's key insight and radical departure from most of his Jewish contemporaries, according to Sanders, was not that salvation is a free gift from God rather than something to be earned through human effort; it was, instead, that this free gift comes, not through the Mosaic covenant, but through participation, by faith, in the death and resurrection of Christ. Paul redefined the terms by which Jews and Gentiles alike share in the promises given to Israel, rather than repudiating Judaism as such.[45] Thus, it seems reasonable to

[43] Latin text and English translation available in Norman TANNER, S.J. (ed.), *Decrees of the Ecumenical Councils, Volume Two: From Trent to Vatican II* (London: Sheed & Ward; Washington: Georgetown University Press, 1990), pp. 968-71. Useful discussions of this document's teaching on Jews and Judaism, including its historical background and development, can be found in Stephen SCHLOESSER, S.J., "Against Forgetting: Memory, History, Vatican II," *Theological Studies* (2006), pp. 289-97; Elena PROCARIO-FOLEY, "Heir or Orphan? Theological Evolution and Devolution before and after *Nostra Aetate*," in W. MADGES (ed.), *Vatican II: Forty Years Later*, Annual Publication of the College Theology Society 51 (Maryknoll: Orbis Books, 2006), pp. 308-17; and Edward Idris Cardinal CASSIDY, *Ecumenism and Interreligious Dialogue: Unitatis Redintegratio and Nostra Aetate*, Rediscovering Vatican II (New York/Mahwah: Paulist Press, 2005), pp. 125-31.

[44] See, e.g., CASSIDY, *Ecumenism and Interreligious Dialogue*, pp. 160-224; PROCARIO-FOLEY, "Heir or Orphan?" pp. 315-31; and Michael S. KOGAN, "Into Another Intensity: Christian-Jewish Dialogue Moves Forward" *Journal of Ecumenical Studies* 41 (2004): pp. 1-17.

[45] E.P. SANDERS, *Paul and Palestinian Judaism: A Comparison of Patterns of Religion* (Philadelphia: Fortress Press, 1977), esp. pp. 422-23 and 511-15. Cf. E.P. SANDERS, *Paul, the Law, and the Jewish People* (Philadelphia: Fortress Press, 1983); E.P. SANDERS,

venture that when Paul says "all Israel" will be saved, he intends precisely those persons he also refers to as his "kindred according to the flesh" (Rom 9:3): that is, historic Israel. The fact that it is difficult to hold such a conclusion together with other key Pauline convictions about salvation in Christ, Sanders claims, merely highlights the relatively "non-systematic" character of Paul's thought.[46]

These two late 20th century developments did not arise in mutual isolation. The teaching of *Nostra Aetate* draws heavily on a new interpretation of Romans 9-11, and the "new perspective on Paul" emerged out of the new ecumenical climate created in the wake of Vatican II.[47] Together they have opened still greater possibilities with regard to Christian understandings of the apostle Paul and of the Judaism he never renounced – at least, not completely.

This may appear to be an esoteric point of biblical interpretation, and in some ways it is. But the very existence of a debate about the interpretation of Paul raises important questions about interpretive perspective itself: Paul's own perspective, as well as that of any subsequent Christian engaged in interreligious study or dialogue – including, of course, the Christian hearer of a sacred text like the *Upadeśasāhasrī*. In addressing this central question, some scholars have suggested that Christians can speak of a unique dispensation for Israel, entirely apart from the new covenant given in Christ.[48] Others demur.[49] In *The Theology of Paul the Apostle*, James Dunn advances a kind of mediating view, speaking of the "divided 'I' of Israel": Israel of the old covenant, presently hardened by

Paul, Past Masters (Oxford and New York: Oxford University Press, 1991); and the further development and clarification of these themes in James D.G. DUNN, *The New Perspective on Paul: Collected Essays* (Tübingen: Mohr Siebeck, 2005). Donald HAGNER contests some aspects of this account, arguing that one can indeed speak of "anti-Judaism," but not "anti-Semitism" in Paul's preaching. See his "Paul's Quarrel with Judaism," in C. EVANS and D. HAGNER (eds.), *Anti-Semitism and Early Christianity: Issues of Polemic and Faith*, (Minneapolis: Fortress Press, 1993), pp. 128-50.

[46] See especially SANDERS, *Paul*, pp. 117-28, and SANDERS, *Paul, the Law, and the Jewish People*, pp. 144-48, 192-99.

[47] See FISHER, "Covenant Theology," pp. 20-22, and James D.G. DUNN, *The Theology of Paul the Apostle* (Grand Rapids and Cambridge: William B. Eerdmans Publishing Company, 1998), pp. 335-40.

[48] See the discussion in Joseph A. FITZMYER, S.J., "The Letter to the Romans," in R. BROWN, J. FITZMYER, and R. MURPHY (eds.), *The New Jerome Biblical Commentary* (Englewood Cliffs: Prentice Hall, 1990), pp. 861-62 [51:110] and FISHER, "Covenant Theology," pp. 25-34.

[49] E.g., SANDERS, *Paul, the Law, and the Jewish People*, p. 194; HAGNER, "Paul's Quarrel," pp. 146-48; and WRIGHT, "Romans," esp. pp. 624-26, 683-90, 693.

God to reject the gospel, and Israel of the new covenant, Jews and Gentiles together, already experiencing God's grace by faith. The latter does not eclipse the former. Instead, Paul holds the two "Israels" in deliberate tension, a tension that will not be resolved until the end of time.[50]

We might see a similar tension in a parallel discussion of "righteousness" in Romans 10 and its parallels. Sanders, for example, offers the following summary:

> ... [Paul] distinguishes between two righteousnesses, Jewish righteousness, which is by the law, and God's righteousness, which is by faith. That is also the formulation of Philippians 3:6 and 3:9; 'righteousness by the law', which Paul as an obedient Jew once had, is contrasted to 'righteousness based on faith in Christ'. The truth finally comes out: there is such a thing as righteousness by the law. Further, it is not wicked. *In and of itself* it is 'gain' (Phil. 3:9). It *becomes wrong* only because God has revealed another one.[51]

Whether we are speaking of the "divided 'I' of Israel" or of "two righteousnesses," these scholars suggest that Paul maintains a kind of double vision. Historic Israel and "righteousness by the law" have their own proper integrity: the law is good, and those who follow it remain beloved of God, the recipients of an irrevocable call, and destined for salvation... at least when treated on their own terms. But the revelation of Jesus the Christ also radically transforms this vision and transposes all of its various parts. From the perspective of faith in the risen Christ – and *only* from this perspective – the whole schema has shifted.

Of course, this is not merely a "perspective," either for Paul or for subsequent Christian tradition. It is revealed truth. Still, Paul does not do what so many later Christians *would* do. He does not attempt to resolve the tension embodied in this truth by speaking in terms of "replacement," "supersession," or even "two parallel covenants." He speaks of a "mystery" (*mysterion*), an unveiling that begins with Christ's resurrection and looks forward to his return.[52] Until God's final resolution of history, the apostle seems to imply, "righteousness" remains in tension with "righteousness," and "Israel" with "Israel."

I am not setting out in these reflections to offer some new theological assessment of Christianity and Judaism. The various Jewish-Christian

[50] DUNN, *Theology of Paul*, esp. pp. 472-77, 508-9, 521-24, 526-27.

[51] SANDERS, *Paul*, p. 122 (emphasis added). Cf. DUNN, *Theology of Paul*, pp. 515-18.

[52] On this eschatological sense of "mystery," see especially Joseph A. FITZMYER, S.J., "Pauline Theology," in BROWN, FITZMYER, and MURPHY, *New Jerome*, p. 1389 [82:33-34] and FISHER, "Covenant Theology," pp. 34-39.

initiatives in the years since *Nostra Aetate* have extended the boundaries of this conversation well beyond mere interpretation of the apostle Paul, important as that may still be.[53] For the purposes of this chapter, it is not so much Paul's position on Judaism that attracts our interest, but the *way* he articulates this position. Writing in the mid-to-late 50s CE, Israelite by birth and believer in Christ by revelation, Paul draws our attention to a deep tension both inside and – in no small part through his own evangelizing efforts – outside the boundaries of the Jewish scriptures and Jewish tradition he holds so dear. And this, in turn, creates an important interpretative space for the Christian hearer of USP 1. For, in this text, Shankara too draws our attention to two distinct traditions in tension with one another and with a scriptural foundation both claim as their own.

Obviously, the terms of Paul's discussion and those of Shankara are specifically different, with consequences that reach far beyond the narrow interpretation of Romans 9-11 and USP 1. Particularly in comparison with the attractive "combination of knowledge and action" (*jñāna-karma-samuccaya*) position, for example, Shankara's rejection of Vedic ritual may seem to shade his teachings in a supersessionist direction. His distinctively Hindu strategy of ascribing higher and lower paths to differently qualified persons is not, moreover, a strategy pursued by the apostle Paul, though it might resonate with some developments of his thought in the direction of covenantal pluralism.[54] Paul's own framework, as we will continue to explore in future chapters, is primarily eschatological. "Higher" and "lower" is not, at the end of the day, precisely the same as "already-not yet."

Even in the face of such important differences, we can still adduce a critical correlation between these two arguments, in their respective contexts.[55] We can, in other words, discern sufficient resonance to draw

[53] See CASSIDY, *Ecumenism and Interreligious Dialogue*, pp. 241-63; Peter C. PHAN, "Jesus as the Universal Savior: God's Eternal Covenant with the Jewish People," in *Being Religious Interreligiously* (Maryknoll: Orbis Books, 2004), pp. 137-46; and Jacques DUPUIS, S.J., *Christianity and the Religions: From Confrontation to Dialogue* (Maryknoll: Orbis Books, 2001), pp. 96-113.

[54] See, for example, the proposals advanced in R. Kendall SOULEN, *The God of Israel and Christian Theology* (Minneapolis: Fortress Press, 1996); and Michael S. KOGAN, *Opening the Covenant: A Jewish Theology of Christianity* (New York and Oxford: Oxford University Press, 2008).

[55] See Hugh NICHOLSON, "A Correlational Model of Comparative Theology," *Journal of Religion* 85 (2005): pp. 191-213. Along similar lines, Daniel P. SHERIDAN prefers the language of "homology" to that of analogy, emphasizing the similar function of

them into a new relation of *saṃvāda* – critical, creative and mutually transformative dialogue.

Above all, it is important to note that the relation that joins each of these paired traditions together even while it defines their distinct identities is, in both cases, simultaneously textual and social in character. So Shankara, for example, in addition to presenting the content of the teaching, must also defend an internal, mutual priority of the "ritual portion" and "knowledge portion" of the *Vedas* themselves. To make this case in USP 1, Shankara argues primarily from the higher perspective of *Brahma-vidyā*, showing how certain scriptures such as the Vedic account of *Agniṣṭoma* or *Manu-Smṛti's* proscription against giving up ritual performance do not apply in this special case. To underscore this exemption more forcefully, he also alludes briefly to the "Not thus! Not so!" of the *Bṛhadāraṇyaka Upanishad*, as well as to a few other texts that provide sanction for the life of *saṃnyāsa*. Later, in USG 1, we will encounter a more explicit strategy of interpreting and reconciling the claims of apparently discordant scriptural texts.

Each of these strategies deserves attention in its own right. If we attempt to hear USP 1 as a teaching script and as a defining entry to the myriad scripts of the *Upadeśasāhasrī*, however, we should first note the centrality of such reconciliation itself in the practice these scripts model for their hearers. The scripted dialogue of USP 1 is, in an important if strictly hermeneutical sense, precisely a dialogue of reconciliation. The voices of the Pūrva Mīmāṃsāka and of alternative perspectives like the *jñāna-karma-samuccaya-vādin* are refuted in this script, to be sure, and their religious ideals definitively renounced. But these voices are also preserved in the actual performance of the script and therefore made intrinsic to the practice of *Brahma-vidyā*. To be an Advaitin is to remain in continuous and permanent dialogue with a Vedic text that ends in the *Upanishads* and a social and ritual order that has been renounced with the commencement of the teaching. Paradoxically, one attains the liberating knowledge of *Brahman* by assiduously working to reconcile those other teachings, texts and traditions that appear, from the perspective that such knowledge provides – and only from that perspective – to perpetuate bondage rather than resolving it. The practice of *Brahma-vidyā* is a practice of reconciliation.

different realities in their respective systems rather than introducing false generalizations or mere assertions of common ground. See his *Loving God: Kṛṣṇa and Christ: A Christian Commentary on the Nārada Sūtras* (Leuven, Paris and Dudley, MA: Peeters and W.B. Eerdmans, 2008), 9-12.

The question for the Christian hearer, then, is this: what does the dialogue modeled in this teaching script reveal about our own dialogue with those teachings, texts and traditions that may appear, from the perspective of faith in the risen Christ, – and only from this perspective – to stand in tension with and even opposition to God's plan of salvation? For the Christian who has become a hearer of USP 1, this may now include not only historic Israel, but also Shankara and the *Upadeśasāhasrī*. What might a Christian dialogue of reconciliation look like, when faced with teachings, traditions and indeed an entire economy of liberation that appears to diverge significantly from the economy revealed in Christ?

We can gain some clarity on this point by turning to yet another parallel discussion which both draws upon and brings forward the fundamental insights of Romans 9-11: a 2001 document of the Pontifical Biblical Commission (PBC) entitled "The Jewish People and their Sacred Scriptures in the Christian Bible."[56] The genesis of this document owed much to the new Jewish-Catholic initiatives following *Nostra Aetate*,[57] and it does indeed deal in its third major chapter with specific portrayals of the Jewish people in the Christian New Testament, including the letters of the apostle Paul (see esp. nos. 79-81). In the first two chapters, however, the PBC addresses the even more basic internal relationship between the scriptural texts themselves, taking up first the integral place of the Jewish scriptures in the Christian Bible and juxtaposing several "fundamental themes" of these scriptures with their reception in the light of Christ.

Of particular interest is section II.A of the document, entitled "Christian Understanding of the Relationship between the Old and New Testaments." This section begins with a fundamental affirmation of this relationship:

> By 'Old Testament' the Christian Church has no wish to suggest that the Jewish scriptures are outdated or surpassed. On the contrary, it has always affirmed that the Old Testament and the New Testament are inseparable.... This relationship is also reciprocal: on the one hand, the New Testament demands to be read in light of the Old, but it also invites "re-reading" of the Old in light of Jesus Christ (cf. Luke 24:45). How is this "re-reading"

[56] PONTIFICAL BIBLICAL COMMISSION, "The Jewish People and Their Sacred Scriptures in the Christian Bible," *The Holy See*, <http://www.vatican.va/roman_curia/congregations/cfaith/pcb_documents/rc_con_cfaith_doc_20020212_popolo-ebraico_en.html>, accessed 26 May 2005. Hereafter cited by section number in the text.

[57] See CASSIDY, *Ecumenism and Interreligious Dialogue*, pp. 212-13.

> to be done? It extends to "all the Scriptures" (Lk 24:27) to "everything written in the Law of Moses, the Prophets and the Psalms" (24:44), but the New Testament only offers a limited number of examples, not a methodology (no. 19).

The authors of the document next walk through a series of such Christian re-readings, beginning with Paul and the other NT authors, moving through allegorical interpretations and the eventual re-assertion of scripture's "literal sense" in the medieval period, and then taking up the difficult question of prophecy and fulfillment (nos. 19-21). The PBC concludes:

> The Old Testament in itself has great value as the Word of God. To read the Old Testament as Christians then does not mean wishing to find everywhere direct reference to Jesus and to Christian realities. True, for Christians, all the Old Testament economy is in movement towards Christ; if then the Old Testament is read in the light of Christ, one can, retrospectively, perceive something of this movement. But since it is a movement, a slow and difficult progression throughout the course of history, each event and each text is situated at a particular point along the way, at a greater or lesser distance from the end. Retrospective re-readings through Christian eyes mean perceiving both the movement toward Christ and the distance from Christ, prefiguration and dissimilarity. Conversely, the New Testament cannot be fully understood except in light of the Old Testament (no. 21).

Following this recommendation, the section concludes with an appreciative treatment of Jewish interpretations of the Bible. Both Christian and Jewish readings, the PBC asserts, "are irreducible," and each might have something to learn from the other (no. 22).

In this section of "The Jewish People and their Sacred Scriptures in the Christian Bible," we witness a careful reflection on the precise issue of interpretive strategy in a situation of mutual priority. The PBC models its approach on the Christian re-readings of Jewish scriptures by the apostle Paul and other NT authors. By so doing, we can now see, it also echoes key elements of Shankara's account in the *Upadeśasāhasrī*'s first verse chapter. The authors of this contemporary text, moreover, also add distinctions and nuance we have not seen in either Paul or Shankara, at least not yet. Thus the PBC commends a creative "re-reading" of the Jewish scriptures in light of Christian faith, but it also recognizes the legitimacy of an alternate "Jewish reading" of those same scriptures, certainly including the Old Testament but potentially including the New Testament as well. It upholds a Christian conviction that the Jewish scriptures do intend and point in the direction of Christ, but it also recognizes that this movement can only be seen "in retrospect," and only in part. Each individual piece of the scriptures should first be taken on its own terms, albeit with an eye to both "prefiguration and dissimilarity" in relation to the revelation of Christ. And all this should be executed with the firm conviction that the "New Testament cannot be fully understood except in light of the Old Testament." The Jewish scriptures retain their own integrity and priority over the New Testament scriptures, even as they are also re-read in light of Christ.

This account of the PBC adds depth and texture to a dynamic we've encountered in both Shankara and Paul. The connection is, of course, manifest in the case of Paul. Once a correlative dynamic has been recognized in the *Upadeśasāhasrī*, however, the Christian hearer may also discern an invitation to undertake a comparable Christian re-reading of this Hindu text, informed by both the PBC and by USP 1. The members of the PBC, recognizing the tension between the church and historic Israel so powerfully witnessed by Paul, recommend a creative re-reading of the Old Testament attuned to this tension and to patterns of "prefiguration and dissimilarity" in the light of Christ. For his part, Shankara conclusively rejects Vedic ritual performance as a means of liberation while also reconciling the ritualists' teaching to his own in terms we have already seen: preparation and fulfilment (vv. 2-7), incompatible spheres of existence and frames of discourse (vv. 8-15, vv. 21b-24), and the different ways of life pertaining to these spheres (vv. 16-21a). In either case, precisely because of the relationship of mutual priority that binds these different traditions together even as it separates them, the tension between them cannot be written out or excluded from the home tradition. It must, instead, be actively engaged, in a dynamic process of dialogue, debate and hermeneutical reconciliation.

Such a strategy of dialogue and reconciliation is, in rough outline, what will be attempted in chapters 3-8 of this volume, which I have collectively labeled "experiments in dialogue."

Before taking up the first of these experiments, we should note an important *pūrva-pakṣa:* that is, an adversarial voice and possible objection to the proposed analogy and the dialogical strategy that follows from it. For some Christian hearers will at this point wish to observe that, by drawing a parallel from Paul and the PBC document to this commentary, we may seem – *mutatis mutandis* – to recognize in Advaita or in the *Upadeśasāhasrī* a privileged, revelatory status comparable to that of the Jewish Scriptures. Certainly, one can adduce theological arguments that draw just such a parallel between the Hebrew revelation and God's revealing activity in other religious traditions.[58] Yet, one can also find authoritative statements that challenge any such claim, or at least qualify it severely.[59]

The difficulty is not unique to the present endeavor. In the first volume of this series of Christian Commentaries on Non-Christian Sacred Texts, series editor Catherine Cornille offers the following reflections:

> Reacting to the perceived threats of relativism and pluralism, the Magisterium of the Roman Catholic Church has come to reserve the designation "inspired texts" for the canonical Christian scriptures, while recognizing the presence of "seeds" or "rays of Truth," or words inspired by God in the sacred texts of other [religions]. Theological presuppositions such as these of course determine the way in which one engages the truth of the sacred texts of other [religions]. Though Christians might not approach the *Bhagavad Gītā* with the same degree of devotion and reverence as they would their own scriptures, the text may still be regarded... as a source of revelation which may come to inspire and enrich the Christian tradition, perhaps even awakening it to insights hitherto unsuspected.[60]

For the purposes of this Christian commentary, a resolution on the question is not vital, at least not at the front end. We can note, for example, that the theological and political forces that shaped the Vatican II declaration *Nostra Aetate* were complex. The document began as a declaration devoted exclusively to Jews and Judaism, but eventually widened to include Islam, Hinduism, Buddhism and other religious paths. This suggests that, even if the Jewish revelation cannot be equated with the "seeds" and "rays" of truth in other traditions, the church's relation with Judaism can nevertheless open broader questions about other traditions and suggest specific strategies for reading other sacred texts.[61] Insofar as

[58] See especially DUPUIS, *Christianity and the Religions*, pp. 114-37, as well as the fuller treatment in DUPUIS, Jacques, S.J., *Toward a Christian Theology of Religious Pluralism* (Maryknoll: Orbis Books, 1997), pp. 235-53.

[59] One of the strongest recent statements to this effect is no doubt the CONGREGATION FOR THE DOCTRINE OF THE FAITH, "'*Dominus Iesus*': On the Unicity and Salvific Universality of Jesus Christ and the Church," esp. nos. 5-8, in S. POPE and C. HEFLING (eds.), *Sic et Non: Encountering Dominus Iesus* (Maryknoll: Orbis Books, 2002), pp. 6-9.

[60] Catherine CORNILLE, "Introduction," in C. CORNILLE (ed.), *Song Divine: Christian Commentaries on the Bhagavad Gītā* (Leuven, Paris, and Dudley, MA: Peeters and W.B. Eerdmans, 2006), p. 5. In this quotation, CORNILLE is drawing upon "Dominus Iesus," no. 8, and *Nostra Aetate*, no. 5.

[61] See especially Michael BARNES, S.J., *Theology and the Dialogue of Religions*, Cambridge Studies in Christian Doctrine 8 (Cambridge: Cambridge University Press, 2002), pp. 29-64.

the *Upadeśasāhasrī* can be recognized as such a sacred text for Christians, this will emerge only in and through the concrete process of listening to its message, engaging in sustained reflection and dialogue with it in light of Christian sources, and then, subsequently, presenting the results to Christ in prayer and meditation.[62] Christian hearers may therefore feel justified in forging ahead and listening further in this script, inscribing ourselves into its distinctive vision of bondage and liberation even as we do our best to place its teachings into a creative, critical and mutually defining relation with our own.

Such hearers may also, at the outset of this commentarial project, draw additional support from the fact that we have already encountered in the verses of USP 1 something that Christianity shares with Advaita Vedanta, but not with Judaism – nor, at least presumably, with Pūrva Mīmāṃsā or many other religious traditions of the world: namely, *a primary, inextricable and internal relationship with a religious other.*[63] Shankara advances the claims of his tradition in specific and self-conscious tension with a tradition that is both other and not-other than his own. So also, in very different contexts, do the apostle Paul and the members of the Pontifical Biblical Commission. And so also, perhaps, may we.

[62] This process, as I have described it, deliberately echoes the threefold method of the Vedanta, discussed briefly in the previous chapter and more fully in chapter 8.

[63] On this significant point of asymmetry in the Jewish-Christian relationship, see Ruth LANGER, "Jewish Understandings of the Religious Other," *Theological Studies* 84 (2003): pp. 274-75n55. This statement should not be read to imply that Judaism cannot also be viewed in close relation to Canaanite religion and other antecedents, as has been suggested by much recent historical scholarship. I believe it is fair to say, however, that such historical relationships have never been as prominent a feature of Jewish self-understanding as the Christian relationship to ancient Judaism.

PART II:

EXPERIMENTS IN DIALOGUE

CHAPTER 3

A SCANDALOUS WISDOM: COMMENTARY ON USP 2-7

I.

UPADEŚASĀHASRĪ PADYABANDHA 5.1-5

Just as the sage Udaṅka did not accept the nectar, thinking that it was urine, so people do not accept the knowledge of *Ātman* out of fear that action will be destroyed.

Ātman, abiding in the intellect, is seen as it were moving and meditating. The mistake about transmigratory existence is like that of a person in a [moving] boat who thinks that it is the trees [along the shore which are moving].

Just as to a person in the boat the trees [appear to] move in the opposite direction, so does *Ātman* [appear to] transmigrate, since the *Śruti* reads, 'appearing to think.'

Intellect being pervaded by the reflection of Pure Consciousness, knowledge arises in it; and so sound and other [objects] appear. By this people are deluded.

The 'I'-notion appears to be as it were Pure Consciousness and exists for Its sake. And it does not do so, when the 'this'-portion has been destroyed. [So] this Pure Experience is the Highest.

II.

THE ETERNAL WITNESS: HEARING USP 2-7 (SELECTIONS)

Few doctrines have more deeply troubled critics of Advaita Vedanta than its distinctive teaching on "liberation-in-life" (*jīvan-mukti*): the notion that release from bondage and suffering can be attained here and now, without awaiting either the death of the body or some final transformation of history.[1] Shankara's view on this issue is nuanced, but

[1] Perhaps most notably, Shankara's position on this issue was decisively rejected in the "qualified non-dualist" (*viśiṣṭādvaita*) Vedanta of Rāmānuja in the thirteenth century

uncompromising. In the *Upadeśasāhasrī*'s fourth verse chapter, for example, he teaches:

> A person who has knowledge of *Ātman*, which negates the notion that the body is *Ātman* and is as [firm] as [ordinary people's] notion that the body is *Ātman*, is released even without wishing (USP 4.5).

This terse formula echoes key aspects of our hearing of USP 1, above, especially in its insistence that liberation, as the result of knowledge alone, does not depend upon choice or will. It depends upon what is already the true nature of each and every conscious being, and that alone. Lance Nelson explains: "Ontologically speaking, we are always liberated... To speak of attaining liberation is... figurative – accurate only from the epistemological point of view. The human experience of bondage – our sense of not being liberated – is a problem of our not being aware of what we already have."[2] Once the student of the teaching truly knows herself – identifying with *Ātman* as naturally as ordinary persons identify with their bodies, minds and personalities – liberation follows without delay.

This ideal of immediate liberation is central to Advaita teaching, central enough that the fourteenth-century sage Vidyāraṇya singled out this short verse as an apt distillation of the "scope" or "conclusion" of the whole teaching.[3] The ideal is also highly paradoxical, forcing its hearers to view all persons, from the liberated sage to the ignorant masses, within opposed frames of liberation and bondage simultaneously. To address this point of tension, some teachers in the tradition have explained that even liberated self-knowers continue to bear a trace or faint impression of ignorance until their natural death. Drawing upon such analogies as the potter's wheel, which continues to turn even after the potter has ceased to spin it, or the arrow which, once loosed, must continue to its target, Shankara and his successors elaborated theories of "ripened" (*prārabdha-* or

CE. See Kim SKOOG, "Is the *Jīvanmukti* State Really Possible? Rāmānuja's Perspective," in A. FORT and P. MUMME (eds.), *Living Liberation in Hindu Thought* (Albany: State University of New York Press, 1996), pp. 63-90.

[2] Lance E. NELSON, "Living Liberation in Śaṅkara and Classical Advaita: Sharing the Holy Waiting of God," in FORT and MUMME, *Living Liberation*, p. 19.

[3] Sanskrit text and English translation in Swāmī MOKṢADĀNANDA (trans.), *Jīvanmukti-Viveka of Swāmī Vidyāraṇya* (Kolkata: Advaita Ashrama, 1996), p. 18. The verse is also incorporated into *Pañcadaśī* 7.20; Sanskrit text and English translation in Swāmī SWĀHĀNANDA (trans.), *Pañcadaśī of Śrī Vidyāraṇya* (Madras: Sri Ramakrishna Math, [1967]), p. 241.

ārabdha-) karma to explain the persistence of the *jīvan-mukta*'s body, mind and personality after the dawn of knowledge.[4]

For Shankara, however, such theorizing represents the exception rather than the rule. More characteristically, and for our purposes far more importantly, the great teacher emphasizes the paradoxical force of the claim itself, sharply juxtaposing bondage and liberation and thereby pushing students toward a kind of crisis in which they shift their self-identification from one frame of reference to the other.[5] The great Hindu teacher does not, in other words, defend *jīvan-mukti* as an abstract idea; he simply re-describes embodied experience in such a way that identification with the ever-liberated *Ātman* follows as a matter of course. It becomes as instinctively natural to the hearer of the teaching, he suggests in USP 4.5, as her former identification with the limited body, mind and personality.

Such a pedagogical strategy of redescription emerges not only in USP 4.5, but also in several of the other teaching scripts that occupy the first few pages of the *Upadeśasāhasrī*'s verse portion. Of these initial treatments, four recommend themselves for special attention: chapters 2-3, chapter 5, and chapter 7. In these chapters, Shankara leads the hearer through a scripted practice of discriminating self-inquiry, whereby she ever more clearly differentiates herself from all that is non-self and identified instead with the eternal "witness" (*sākṣin*) at the base of all possible experience. Along the way, the Hindu teacher also recognises the difficulty of this teaching on bondage and liberation, and even its tendency to provoke fear, disgust and rejection on the part of prospective hearers.

> **An Initial Reflection:** In Christian terms, the Advaita teaching on *jīvan-mukti* can be regarded as a kind of *skandalon*, a "stumbling block" which upsets conventional assumptions and values on the way toward final liberation. As such, it invites a creative re-reading in light of the *skandalon* of the cross. But it will also be important to keep in mind that these two stumbling blocks are specifically different. One is an historical claim about

[4] See especially NELSON, "Living Liberation," pp. 31-38; A.G. Krishna WARRIER, *The Concept of Mukti in Advaita Vedānta*, Madras University Philosophical Series 9 (Madras: University of Madras, 1961), pp. 469-528; and Yoshitsugu SAWAI, "Śaṅkara's Theory of Saṃnyāsa," *Journal of Indian Philosophy* 14 (1986): pp. 378-79.

[5] See Sengaku MAYEDA, "Adi-Śaṅkarācārya's Teaching on the Means to Mokṣa: Jñāna and Karman," *Journal of Oriental Research* 34-35 (1966), pp. 73-74; as well as, more broadly, John A. TABER, *Transformative Philosophy: A Study of Śaṅkara, Fichte, and Heidegger* (Honolulu: University of Hawaii Press, 1983); and B.R. Shantha KUMARI, "Tansformative Metaphysics: Advaita as Model," in R. BALASUBRAHMANIAN (ed.), *The Tradition of Advaita* (New Delhi: Munshiram Manoharlal, 1994), pp. 178-200.

God's gracious act of salvation in the life, death and resurrection of Jesus the Christ, and its consequences for the whole created order. The other is an epistemological claim about the human constitution itself, with consequences for our apprehension of the entire created order. For Christian hearers, then, the central question is not whether the Advaita teaching on *jīvan-mukti* can be equated with the scandal of Christ crucified. The central question is whether a Christian hearing of this teaching, as unfolded in the scripted dialogues of these verse chapters, may function to reawaken us to this scandalous claim and to drive us, in a renewed way, to the foot of the cross.

Self and Non-Self (USP 2.1 – 3.4)

Though they explore different topics and may have been composed at different times, the second and third verse chapters of the *Upadeśasāhasrī* form a natural pair. Both are extremely terse, and each models the kind of discriminating knowledge required for fruitful reception of the Advaita message. Chapter two, simply entitled "negation" (*pratiṣedha*) after the first word of its Sanskrit text, asks how *Ātman* can emerge through mere negation of all that is alien to it, including especially the limited body, mind and personality of the student. Chapter three, entitled "the Lord" (*īśvara*), makes a further claim about what *does* pertain to this same *Ātman*: *Brahman* the divine self. Behind the entire discussion, Shankara presumes a broad scriptural context provided by the Vedic scriptures, especially such Upanishadic "great sayings" as "*ahaṃ brahma-asmi*": "I am *Brahman*" (BU 1.4.10).

Reduced to its most basic terms, a statement like *ahaṃ brahma-asmi* can be parsed into two distinct, but related issues: "who am I?" and "who is *Brahman*, the Lord?" These are precisely the questions taken up by Shankara in verse chapters 2 and 3, respectively. He initiates the discussion by advancing a fundamental thesis:

> As [*Ātman*] cannot be negated, [It] is left unnegated [by the *Śruti*,] 'Not thus! Not so!' [BU 2.3.6]. One attains [It] in some such way as 'I am not this. I am not this.' (2.1)

In USP 1.17, we recall, Shankara defined *Ātman* as that which remains after all attributes and false identifications have been removed by the negative construction "Not thus! Not so!" Here, this definition has been transposed into a kind of method for attaining self-knowledge. Precisely by saying, "I am not this, I am not this," Shankara suggests, the seeker arrives at self-knowledge.

Shankara does not specify what he means by "this" (*idam*), but the commentators fill this gap precisely as we might expect. Beginning with the physical body and extending to features of the so-called "subtle body" of mind, senses and vital forces – including everything with which most persons, including the most fervent idealist, would ordinarily identify themselves – each defining characteristic of embodied existence should be systematically excluded as "not-me" (*na-aham*).[6] That which *cannot* be negated in such a process of self-inquiry, the "I" who is conscious of things such as a body and mind, alone emerges as the true *Ātman* of the enquirer.

But both the possibility and the desirability of such a method are, on the face of it, far from obvious. How precisely does one distinguish self from non-self in this process of discriminating inquiry? And how can one be sure that, after repeatedly affirming "I am not this, I am not this," any *Ātman* will yet remain? In response to such concerns, Shankara writes:

> The notion '[I am] this' arises from the *ātman* [which is identified with] 'this' and is within the range of a verbal handle.[7] As it has its origin in the negated *ātman*, it could not become [accepted as] a right notion again. (2.2)
> Without negating a previous notion, a following view does not arise. The Seeing is one alone, self-established. As It is the result,[8] It is not negated. (2.3)

This highly condensed argument can be clarified by starting with its key assertion, in verse 3, that the true self, described here as "Seeing" (*dṛśi*),

[6] Swāmi JAGADĀNANDA (trans.), *A Thousand Teachings in Two Parts – Prose and Poetry – of Srī Sankarāchārya* (Madras: Sri Ramakrishna Math, [1941]), p. 6n1, ĀNANDAGIRI, *Upadeśasāhasrī*, p. 7 (lines 12-13), and RĀMATĪRTHA, *Upadeshasahasri*, p. 124.

[7] *Vāca-ārambhaṇa-gocara*, translated by A.J. ALSTON as "within the sphere of the activity of speech," in *The Thousand Teachings (Upadeśa Sāhasrī) of Śrī Śaṃkarācārya* (London: Shanti Sadan, 1990), p. 107. The reference here is to Uddālaka Āruṇi's teaching of his son Śvetaketu in CU 6.1.4: "It's like this, son. By means of just one lump of clay one would perceive everything made of clay – the transformation is a verbal handle [*vāca-ārambhaṇa*], a name – while the reality is just this: 'It's clay,'" following the translation in Patrick OLIVELLE, *The Early Upaniṣads: Annotated Text and Translation*, South Asia Research Series (New York and Oxford: Oxford University Press, 1998), pp. 246-47. In 6.1.5-6, Aruni extends the same analysis to everything made of copper and iron, respectively. In each case, the differentiations between individual objects are sharply subordinated to the more fundamental reality of their material substrate. So too, in this verse, Shankara is suggesting that the individuating features of embodied life can be sharply subordinated to the more fundamental self to which they are predicated. See also the more extended discussion of the *vāca-ārambhaṇa* in BSBh 2.1.14-20, in Swami GAMBHIRANANDA (trans.), *Brahma-Sūtra-Bhāṣya of Śrī Śaṅkarācārya* (Calcutta: Advaita Ashrama, 1965, 1972), pp. 326-46.

[8] MAYEDA and JAGADĀNANDA interpret *phalatvat,* "as it is the result," as a reference to the means of knowledge (*pramāṇas*) by which knowledge is established; ALSTON and NARASIMHAN interpret the same term as a reference to the self-evident and self-validating nature of the self. I have followed the latter interpretation in my comment.

is "one only" and "self-established." Such a statement may seem esoteric, but in fact it proceeds from a commonsense observation about the acquisition of knowledge: namely, that any act of knowing presumes some conscious knower. In the absence of a subject capable of perception and learning, knowledge does not and cannot take place. Such a subject precedes and serves as a necessary condition for any particular conclusions this same subject might reach in the course of inquiry. She cannot, as such, "be negated" by any such conclusion, no matter what it may lead her to believe – even about herself. "One may say in a paradox," Paul Hacker reflects, "that the self is unknowable because it cannot become an object of knowledge, but it is at the same time better known than any object inasmuch as no object can be cognized save in light of the self."[9]

The difficulty, according to Shankara, is that the self-established *Ātman* is always presented to our experience in combination with much that is not intrinsic to it – here described, confusingly enough, as *idam-ātman,* "this-self." Swami Paramarthananda draws a helpful analogy to the perception of objects like furniture and other persons in a lighted room.[10] On the one hand, we become aware of such objects only by means of the light; on the other, we also ordinarily become aware of the light only by means of these same illuminated objects, which reflect the light back to us. "Light," as such, is accessible in and through the objects it illuminates, but it is not thereby reducible to them. Similarly, we become aware of *Ātman* in and through various phenomena, which come and go in the presence of this same self.

Included among such passing phenomena is every limiting characteristic of embodied existence. Thus, Shankara claims, anything which we can objectify, saying "this [is the] self," is by that very act of identification exposed as "non-self" (*an-ātman*), intrinsically different from the perceiving subject in whose presence alone any such identification can occur. Just as we can distinguish light from the objects illumined by it, so also we can distinguish the self-established "Seeing" from every and all such experiences as we apprehend them.

But why on earth would we want to? Shankara borrows an allegory from the *Upanishads* to encourage our continued interest:

[9] Paul HACKER, "Śaṅkara's Conception of Man," in W. HALBFASS (ed.), *Philology and Confrontation: Paul Hacker on Traditional and Modern Vedānta* (Albany: State University of New York Press, 1995), pp. 182-83.

[10] Swami PARAMARTHANANDA Saraswati, *UPADEŚA SĀHASRĪ,* audio cassettes, Vedānta Vidyārthi Sangha, n.d., cassette #2-1.

> When one has traversed the forest of 'this' which is contaminated with anxiety, delusion, and so on, one arrives at one's own *Ātman*, just as the person from the land of Gandhāra [arrived at Gandhāra] through the forest. (2.4)

In the *Chāndogya Upanishad*, the great sage Uddalāka Āruṇi tells his son Śvetaketu a tale of abduction to illustrate what would become one of the most important *mahā-vākya*s of Advaita tradition: *tat-tvam-asi*, "you are that." The story goes as follows:

> Take, for example, son, a person who is brought here blindfolded from the land of Gandhāra and then left in a deserted region. As he was brought blindfolded and left there blindfolded, he would drift about there toward the east, or the north, or the south. Now, if someone were to free him from his blindfold and tell him, 'Go that way; the land of Gandhāra is in that direction,' being a learned and wise person, he would go from village to village asking for directions and finally arrive in the land of Gandhāra. In exactly the same way in this world when a person has a teacher, he knows: 'There is delay for me here only until I am freed; but then I will arrive!' (CU 6.14.1-2).[11]

This is one of Shankara's favorite illustrations, and he employs it in a variety of ways.[12] Here the narrative serves mainly to emphasize the benefit of the kind of discrimination modeled in USP 2. Such self-inquiry is not a useless exercise, Shankara claims, because it promises to bring us safely home. There is no question, of course, of literally arriving at a new place or state of existence: the "home" in this case is our own, ever-liberated *Ātman*.

With this allegory and the promise it implies, Shankara concludes the second verse chapter. In the next chapter, however, he immediately picks up the other side of the equation:

> If the Lord is non-*Ātman*, one ought not to dwell upon [the knowledge] 'I am He.' If He is *Ātman*, the knowledge 'I am the Lord' destroys the other [knowledge]. (3.1)

In the four verses of USP 2, Shankara has described what does *not* pertain to the self, according to a simple rule: if we can say, "this [is the] self,"

[11] Sanskrit text and English translation in OLIVELLE, *Early Upaniṣads*, pp. 256-57 (slightly modified).

[12] See J.G. SUTHREN HIRST, "The Place of Teaching Techniques in Śaṃkara's Theology," *Journal of Indian Philosophy* 18 (1990): p. 128, as well as J.G. SUTHREN HIRST, *Śaṃkara's Advaita Vedānta: A Way of Teaching*, RoutledgeCurzon Hindu Studies Series (London and New York: RoutledgeCurzon, 2005), pp. 60, 80-81.

then our categorical language invalidates the very statement we have made. If, on the other hand, we say, "I am not this, I am not this," we – like the person abducted from Gandhāra – can arrive back at our own, innermost *Ātman*. In the present verse, Shankara considerably extends the scope of this analysis, suggesting that this same *Ātman* is also none other than "the Lord" (*īśvara*).

In this verse, Shankara speaks hypothetically: "*If* the Lord is *Ātman*...." How can we know for sure that this hypothesis holds true? The words of scripture provide the key:

> If, being different from *Ātman*, [the Lord] is taken to have characteristics such as 'not coarse,' what is the use of them when He is not an object of knowledge? If He is *Ātman*, the notion of difference is destroyed. (3.2) Understand, therefore, that [the predication of qualities] such as 'not coarse' are meant to negate false superimposition. If [they] were meant to negate [false superimposition] upon something other [than *Ātman*], this would indeed be a description of emptiness.[13] (3.3)

In the *Bṛhadāraṇyaka Upanishad*, the "imperishable" is, like the *Ātman* with which it is ultimately identified, described by a process of negation: "neither coarse nor fine," "neither short nor long," and so on (see BU 3.8.8).[14] Reading such a list of negations, Shankara suggests, we face two possibilities. First of all, they may lead nowhere at all: like peeling an onion, we may find ourselves pulling away layer after layer of description only to discover that *Brahman* is, at best, an impenetrable mystery of no practical use to the enquirer (v. 2) or, at worst, devoid of any reality at all (v. 3). Both of these options are, according to Shankara, ruled out by the scriptures, which speak clearly of *Brahman* as a reality to be known. So, in the only other possibility, *Brahman* may emerge as both real and knowable, but inaccessible through categorical description. This would require that the Lord be self-evident, available for knowledge prior to and independent of all those characterizations that the *Upanishad* strips away.

From the four verses of verse chapter 2, we know that only one reality fits this bill: that "Seeing" which is "one only" and "self-established" (USP 2.3) – namely, the innermost *Ātman*. Hence, this self stands revealed

[13] *Śūnyatā*, "emptiness" is a central element of Madhyamika Buddhism, and it is likely that Shankara employs the term here with both polemical and apologetic intent, to distinguish the content of his teaching from that of the Buddhists. See MAYEDA, *A Thousand Teachings*, p. 111n5, and Surendranath DASGUPTA, *A History of Indian Philosophy*, vol. 2 (Cambridge: Cambridge University Press, 1965), pp. vol. 2, pp. 3-8, as well as the discussion below, ch. 7, pp. 218-23.

[14] In OLIVELLE, *Early Upaniṣads*, pp. 90-91.

as none other than the Lord. In negating characteristics such as "coarse" or "long," the scriptures merely remove those qualities we falsely superimpose upon Lord and self alike.

To strengthen the force of the claim, Shankara introduces one more piece of evidence:

> And if it is thought [that they are meant to negate false superimposition] upon something other than the inner *Ātman* of a person who wishes to know, the words, '... without breath, without mind, pure' [MuU 2.1.2] would also be meaningless. (3.4)

This is, again, an allusion to the words of scripture, this time from the *Muṇḍaka Upanishad*:

> That Person, indeed, is divine, he has no visible form;
> He is both within and without, unborn, without breath or mind;
> He is radiant, and farther than the farthest imperishable (MuU 2.1.2).[15]

As before, we encounter negative characterizations of the divine, in this case applied to that primordial "Person" (*puruṣa*) from whom springs the whole creation. But these negations are of a very peculiar sort. Why, for example, describe the Lord as unborn, unless someone might assume the opposite? Why, more importantly, negate "mind" or "breath" in God? Taken by themselves, such negations are puzzling – who ever assumed that the divine Person needed to breathe? They become meaningful only in relation to some reality for which most persons would spontaneously presume birth, mind and breath. In other words, such descriptions really only make sense if they are taken to negate qualities commonly associated with bodies and minds, which we so often and so easily mistake for our true selves.

It is important, moreover, that Shankara does not refer here to the "inner *Ātman*" of some generic human being: he speaks instead of the self of "the one who desires to know" or more literally "the one who wishes to awaken" (*bubhutsu*), presumably referring to the Advaitin student. We thus receive a cue that Shankara's intent, throughout these scripts, remains thoroughly practical. Distinguishing between self and non-self is not an exercise in speculative philosophy. It is a kind of guided apprenticeship, reversing many long-standing habits by leading students along a path of self-discovery. From one verse to the next, such students are brought to the edge of a startling, seemingly absurd kind of

[15] Ibid, pp. 442-43.

claim: that I, here and now, listening to these verses, am none other than the Lord.

> **A Christian Reflection:** The second-century Christian polemicist Tertullian famously declared, "I believe because it is absurd," and some Christians throughout history have, with him, insisted that the revelation of Christ implies a suspension or radical rejection of natural reason. This is not a conclusion embraced by mainstream Christianity or even by Tertullian himself in his willingness to generate an entire technical vocabulary for later Christian doctrines of the Trinity and the Incarnation. So too, Shankara does not ask the Advaitin student to accept the message "I am the Lord" because it is absurd; he asks such a student to discover this as the inevitable conclusion if one follows both the demands of reason and the word of the scriptures to their furthest, logical extent. But this, if anything, only intensifies the offense such a message poses to our conventional assumptions – including, perhaps, our assumptions about reason and the scriptures themselves.

Why Do We Recoil? (USP 5.1-5)

Taken only thus far, the strange claim of Advaita may remain just that: strange. But strange is not enough for Shankara. The great Advaitin teacher wants to demonstrate that *Brahma-vidyā* is more than an interesting piece of scriptural trivia. This wisdom, he proclaims, is truly good news – indeed, the best possible news – for those few with the wherewithal to accept it. For others, this same word of salvation can appear dangerous, even offensive, because it reverses many assumptions of ordinary human existence. Far from representing some megalomaniacal fantasy or arrogant solipsism, the assertion "I am the Lord" radically de-centers everything about myself that I have heretofore held dear. In the course of genuine self-inquiry, whatever I previously meant by "self" undergoes a complete transformation.

The fifth verse chapter of the *Upadeśasāhasrī* further develops the terms of this transformation and the challenge it implies. The chapter begins with a vivid illustration:

> Just as the sage Udaṅka did not accept the nectar, thinking that it was urine, so people do not accept the knowledge of *Ātman* out of fear that action will be destroyed. (5.1)

Shankara refers here to a story embedded in one of the great Hindu epics, the *Mahābhārata.*[16] In this episode, Vishnu grants the great sage

[16] See Kisari Mohan GANGULI (trans.), *The Mahabharata of Krishna-Dwaipayana Vyasa*, vol. 4 (New Delhi: Munshiram Manoharlal Publishers, 2004), *Aswamedha Parva*, pp. 97-99.

Udaṅka a boon, promising to provide water whenever the sage concentrates on Vishnu with firm devotion. When Udaṅka wanders into a desert, he follows Vishnu's instructions and awaits some cool refreshment. He instead receives an unclean and unkempt hunter, surrounded by hounds, bristling with weapons and discharging large amounts of urine. Offered this urine to slake his thirst, Udaṅka vehemently refuses. Later, he learns that the hunter was actually Vishnu's emissary, the god Indra in disguise, and that what appeared to be urine was actually *amṛta*, the nectar of immortality. The sage's offence is perfectly understandable. Who would not balk at drinking urine? Nevertheless, Udaṅka's resistance deprives him of a heavenly benefit.

The story offers candid recognition that Advaita teaching might be dismissed, as well as conveying some sense of the sheer revulsion such a critic might feel for it. This no doubt reflects aspects of Shankara's historical situation. And, indeed, the teaching of Advaita was rejected in no uncertain terms by many of Shankara's contemporaries. Daniel H.H. Ingalls, for example, characterizes the position of the rival Vedantin Bhāskara as follows:

> ... if a Vedantī is capable of hatred, Bhāskara truly hated Śaṃkara's philosophy. In one place, after quoting from Śaṃkara he says, 'No one but a man in his drunkenness could put forth such an argument.' And after describing Śaṃkara's concept of final release he says 'Some of us would rather be jackals in a forest than have your kind of release.'[17]

Why such vehemence? Obviously, Bhāskara could provide his own reasons for criticizing Advaita doctrine.[18] From Shankara's point of view, however, the rationale behind this and any such rejection can be reduced to one simple motive: "fear."

Fear of what? In this verse, Shankara describes it as "fear that action will be destroyed." In a parallel discussion from his commentary on the *Māṇḍūkya-Kārikā* of Gauḍapāda, he speaks of those who, "on account of fear, are wont to see their own destruction."[19] At first glance,

[17] Daniel H.H. INGALLS, "The Study of Śaṅkarācārya," *Annals of the Bhandarkar Oriental Research Institute* 33 (1952), p. 8.

[18] See Daniel H.H. INGALLS, "Bhāskara the Vedantin," *Philosophy East and West* 17 (1967), esp. pp. 65-66; and the more extensive discussion in Klaus RÜPING, *Studien zur Frühgeschichte der Vedānta-Philosophie, Teil I: Philologische Untersuchungen zu den Brahmasūtra-Kommentaren des Śaṅkara und des Bhāskara*, Alt- und Neu-Indische Studien herausgegeben vom Seminar für Kultur und Geschichte Indiens and der Universität Hamburg 17 (Wiesbaden: Franz Steiner Verlag, 1977).

[19] GKBh 3.39; Sankskrit text and English translation in V. PANOLI (trans.), *Upanishads in Sankara's Own Words,* vol. 1, rev. ed. (Calicut: Mathrubhumi Printing and

"destruction of action" (*karma-nāśa*) and "self-destruction" (*ātma-nāśa*) may seem very different, but for Shankara they represent two sides of the same coin. According to the vision of *saṃsāra* sketched in USP 1, this limited body, mind and personality is nothing but the result of previous actions in this birth or in previous births. Further actions can also, by the same token, be viewed as unique expressions of this same body, mind and personality. Individuality and action thus go hand-in-hand. Invalidate action, and you invalidate those accomplishments, failures, relationships and goals by which we conventionally define ourselves. Relativize individual identity, and you remove the sole basis for future striving. For those seeking a future for this body, mind or personality, some continued embodiment or perduring individuality, Shankara offers a sharp challenge, even a rebuke. There is, in other words, good reason to fear.

But, we might ask, what is the basis of the attachment that gives rise to such fear? Why do we hold so firmly to this limited, embodied existence? This is specified in verses 2-3:

> *Ātman*, abiding in the intellect, is seen as it were moving and meditating. The mistake about transmigratory existence is like that of a person in a [moving] boat who thinks that it is the trees [along the shore which are moving]. (5.2)
> Just as to a person in the boat the trees [appear to] move in the opposite direction,[20] so does *Ātman* [appear to] transmigrate, since the *Śruti* reads, 'appearing to think' [BU 4.3.7]. (5.3)

In these two verses and the one that follows, Shankara introduces an idea which he will further develop in the eighteenth verse chapter of the *Upadeśasāhasrī*: the reflection of the self in the mind.[21] According to Shankara, the word "I" (*aham*) has at least three distinct referents: 1) the

Publishing Co., 1995), pp. 450-51. For the broader context of this assertion, see the helpful discussion in Michael COMANS, *The Method of Advaita Vedānta: A Study of Gauḍapāda, Śaṅkara, Sureśvara and Padmapāda* (Delhi: Motilal Banarsidass, 2000), pp. 130-50.

[20] Mayeda's original translation reads, "in a direction opposite...."

[21] USP 5.4 uses the term *pratibimba*, while *ābhāsa* is the more common term in USP 18, below. *Ābhāsa* can also mean "appearance," and it is used this way by some later Vedantins (such as Sureśvara), in distinction from the use of "reflection" (*pratibimba*) by others (such as Padmapāda) to explain the relation between the self and the embodied individual. But MAYEDA argues that, for Shankara, the two terms are often used interchangeably (*A Thousand Teachings*, pp. 36-37). See also Pulasth Soobah ROODURMAN, *Bhāmatī and Vivaraṇa Schools of Advaita Vedānta: A Critical Approach*, K. RAM (ed.) (Delhi: Motilal Banarsidass Publishers, 2002), pp. 133-39.

buddhi, translated above as "intellect," which is the discriminative faculty of the "inner organ" or mind; 2) the self-established and self-revealing *Ātman*; and 3) the "reflection" of this *Ātman* in this same intellect. In the context of USP 18, as we shall see in chapter five of this commentary, this reflection plays a key role in facilitating reception of the teaching. Here, on the contrary, emphasis falls upon how it contributes to the fundamental problem. We habitually mistake reflection for reality. Because the individual *buddhi* acts, thinks, meditates, dies and is reborn, we mistakenly associate these activities with the *Ātman* reflected in it.

Shankara provides an analogy to illustrate such misperception: the illusion of a moving shore as seen from a moving boat. Swami Paramarthananda suggests another: the apparent movement of the sun across the sky.[22] At least since Copernicus and Galileo, we have known that it is not the sun that moves relative to the earth, but the earth that moves relative to the sun. Yet we persist in speaking of the sun's rising and setting at the beginning and end of each day, as well as its seasonal movement higher or lower in the sky. So also, Shankara suggests, we say, "I think," "I meditate," and "I die and will be reborn," when in fact it is not truly "I" but only the reflection of this "I" in an ephemeral intellect that appears to do these things.

The next verse continues along the same trajectory:

> Intellect being pervaded by the reflection of Pure Consciousness, knowledge arises in it; and so sound and other [objects] appear. By this people are deluded. (5.4)

Here we encounter the technical expression "reflection of Pure Consciousness" (*caitanya-pratibimba*) for the first time, but the present verse continues along the same lines as the preceding ones. The root of confusion for "people" or, perhaps better, for "the world" (*jagat*), is the false superimposition of the qualities of empirical perception and categorical knowledge, which belong to the individual intellect, onto that "Pure Consciousness" or *Ātman* which, as we have seen, is free of all such limiting characteristics. Since this consciousness pervades the intellect and is reflected in it, we never experience one without the other, at least not so long as the intellect itself persists. It is therefore only natural that we confuse what belongs to one with what belongs to the other.

If so, then where can we find a solution? What ultimately distinguishes the ordinary, ignorant soul who refuses this teaching from the

[22] PARAMARTHANANDA, *UPADEŚA SĀHASRĪ*, cassette #5-2.

jīvan-mukta who has been set free by it? To such queries, Shankara offers an initial, oblique reply:

> The 'I'-notion[23] appears to be as it were Pure Consciousness and exists for Its sake.[24] And it does not do so, when the 'this'-portion has been destroyed. [So] this Pure Experience is the highest. (5.5)

Shankara concludes the fifth verse chapter by offering a brief sketch of final release. He opens with the 'I'-notion, or sense of individual identity. This only *appears* identical with the true "I," the *Ātman*, he teaches, because both invariably arise together in our awareness, just as – to draw on an earlier example – we commonly perceive light in connection with those objects illumined by it. Since this perceived identity is a matter of appearance rather than reality, it can be reversed. How? Through the discriminating inquiry modeled in USP 2, by which the "this-portion" of one's identity is systematically negated by setting aside anything and everything about which one can say "this [is the] self."

The result of such a process of negation is *anubhava*, translated above as "Pure Experience." This may suggest to some that Shankara equates *jīvan-mukti* with a unique mystical insight or elevated meditative state.[25] Against this widespread view, the Advaitin scholar Anantanand Rambachan has insisted that Shankara gives "no special significance" to *anubhava* as some kind of privileged mystical experience of *Brahman*, placing his emphasis instead upon the word of the Vedic

[23] Here simply *aham*, though Shankara seems to be using the term as a rough synonym of the *ahaṃ-kāra* of USP 1.24. See MAYEDA, *A Thousand Teachings*, pp. 39-40.

[24] In Sanskrit: *tad-ārthya*. The 'I'-notion does not possess its own existence, but exists only in dependence upon and, thus, "for the sake of" the *Ātman*, here identified as "pure consciousness." Here "for the sake of" does not presume some need on the part of the *Ātman*, which would reverse this order of dependence; a better, if considerably more awkward translation might be to say that the I-notion "exists for the purpose of That [Pure Consciousness]" or even, more loosely, that it "exists in relation to That." This idea is taken up and developed in USG 2, which we treat in chapter 6 of this commentary.

[25] See, for example, Paul HACKER, "The Idea of the Person in the Thinking of Vedānta Philosophers," in HALBFASS (ed.), *Philology and Confrontation*, esp. pp. 160-64, and Rudolf OTTO, *Mysticism East and West: A Comparative Analysis of the Nature of Mysticism*, B. BRACEY and R. PAYNE (trans.) (New York: MacMillan Company, 1960 [1932]), esp. pp. 97-104, as well as the broader surveys of views in Anantanand RAMBACHAN, *Accomplishing the Accomplished: The Vedas as a Source of Valid Knowledge in Śaṅkara*, Monographs of the Society for Asian and Comparative Philosophy 10 (Honolulu: University of Hawaii Press, 1991), pp. 1-14, and Wilhem HALBFASS, *India and Europe: An Essay in Understanding* (Albany: State University of New York Press, 1988), pp. 378-87.

scriptures as the sole, necessary and sufficient means of self-knowledge and liberation.[26]

In the present context, the issue is partially resolved by interpreting "the highest" (*para*) as a substantive epithet of *Brahman*, rather than as an adjective modifying *anubhava*.[27] Then we can say, following Thomas Forsthoefel, that there is no question of an elevated experience *of Brahman*; there is, instead, a more fundamental "experience which *is* Brahman."[28] Since this *Brahman* is none other than one's own self-established and self-revealing *Ātman*, this cannot be a new experience. It can only be a new *recognition* of that sole reality which pervades all of our experience all of the time and is the condition for the possibility of any experience at all.[29] If so, then liberation-in-life (*jīvan-mukti*) consists, not in some new experiential state, but in a new, fundamental and irreversible orientation toward that transcendent *Ātman* which profoundly relativizes each and every aspect of our categorical awareness.

The urine, in other words, has not somehow been transformed into sweet nectar. It was *always* nectar; and it *still* looks and smells like urine. The *jīvan-mukta* is simply that person who, having discerned the truth within and beyond all such appearances, no longer fears to drink.

[26] RAMBACHAN, *Accomplishing the Accomplished*, p. 114. See also Anantanand RAMBACHAN, "Where Words Can Set Free: The Liberating Potency of Vedic Words in the Hermeneutics of Śaṅkara," in J. TIMM (ed.), *Texts in Context: Traditional Hermeneutics in South Asia* (Albany: State University of New York Press, 1992), pp. 33-46, and especially Anantanand RAMBACHAN, "Śaṅkara's Rationale for *Śruti* as the Definitive Source of *Brahmajñāna*: A Refutation of Some Contemporary Views," *Philosophy East and West* 36 (1986), pp. 25-40.

[27] This interpretation is supported by ALSTON (*The Thousand Teachings*, p. 116), JAGADĀNANDA (*A Thousand Teachings*, p. 97), and the commentators, as well as by the parallel usage in USP 7.2 and 7.6, below. Cf. V. NARASIMHAN, *Upadeśa Sāhasrī: A Thousand Teachings of Adi Śaṅkara* (Bombay: Bharatiya Vidya Bhavan, 1996), p. 23, and MAYEDA, *A Thousand Teachings*, p. 115, n. 5.

[28] Thomas A. FORSTHOEFEL, *Knowing Beyond Knowledge: Epistemologies of Religious Experience in Classical and Modern Advaita*, Ashgate World Philosophies (Hants and Burlington: Ashgate Publishing, 2002), p. 48.

[29] This interpretation also coheres with the judgment of COMANS, *Method of Early Advaita Vedānta*, pp. 309-11. SUTHREN HIRST appears to ascribe a kind of asymptotic quality to this *anubhava*; in *Saṃkara's Advaita Vedānta*, p. 68, for example, she writes: "*Anubhava* is the non-dual realization gained from the scripture so interpreted. It, as knowledge of *brahman*, is identical with that self which is to be known as witness, not as object… Any term we retain [to describe this] bears the scent of difference: experience, intuition, realization, just as much as knowing. The advantage of the last is that it always keeps in focus the nature of the Advaitin enterprise, as a textually based quest for that which transcends even itself."

A Christian Reflection: It would be quite natural for the Christian hearer of this script to evade the challenge it poses by focusing on *anubhava* as a particular thematization of mystical experience or an extraordinary disposition cultivated by the seeker after liberation. Indeed, such a phenomenological domestication of the Advaita message may ultimately prove inevitable, effectively removing this message to a sphere or dimension of human living penultimate to the core proclamation of the Christian gospel – just as we heard Shankara remove the practice of Vedic ritual to a sphere penultimate to formal renunciation and the practice of *Brahma-vidyā*, in the previous chapter. It is, however, important to defer such a strategic move as long as possible, even indefinitely. To try to explain *anubhava* in terms of mystical experience, personal disposition or even the reception of the teaching itself is to revert our attention, once again, from the innermost *Ātman* to its reflection in the embodied intellect. So Christian hearers may be better advised to press forward in our hearing of these scripts, to allow the Advaita message of *jīvanmukti* to stand and, thereby, to allow ourselves to be thoroughly scandalized.

The Witness (USP 7.1-6)

USP 2 and 3 bring prospective students, through a disciplined practice of analysis and self-inquiry, to one of the most central claims of Advaita teaching: "I am *Brahman*, the Lord." USP 5 lingers on a kind of precipice created by this claim, exploring the innate resistance of many hearers to this teaching on both existential and metaphysical levels. For all their differences in approach, however, each of these three scripts squarely confronts such hearers with the concrete possibility of liberation in this life itself. Whether by identification with a lost soul from Gandhāra, mental negation of such unlikely attributes as "breath" and "birth" from the Lord, or an explanatory device like the reflection of Pure Consciousness in the mind, these verses encourage hearers to re-imagine themselves in a new, paradoxical light as already liberated, at this very moment, in this very limited body, mind and personality.

Thus far, however, our analysis has focused nearly exclusively on a single experiential fact: the mind and consciousness of that implied student who hears the teaching and undertakes its journey of self-discovery. The whole "world" may well be subject to delusion, but *Ātman* reveals itself in and through the intellect of the individual hearer. This leaves some key aspects of embodied life as yet unexamined. What, for starters, about all those other conscious beings, similarly endowed with intellect, whom I encounter every day? What about the sheer variety of experiences that passes through my awareness in the course of a lifetime, a week, or even a single day? If I am identical with the Lord, already liberated and ever-free, do all these phenomena somehow dissolve?

Shankara takes up these questions in the seventh verse chapter through an extended reflection on *Ātman* as the hidden "witness" (*sākṣin*), who beholds and pervades this diversity without thereby becoming bound to it. To press his challenge, he adopts a new idiom, speaking in the person of this very *sākṣin:*

> Everything located in the intellect is always seen by Me in every case. Therefore, I am the highest *Brahman*; I am all-knowing and all-pervading. (USP 7.1)

This verse re-states and draws out the consequences of several ideas that have already occupied us in these pages. The verse's second line, in fact, offers a précis of the teaching's essential message, "I am the highest *Brahman*," albeit with two additional qualifiers we have not thus far encountered: "all-knowing" and "all-pervading."

These qualifiers raise a serious difficulty when attributed to the "I." In what sense am *I* all-knowing, when so much in the world lies outside of my experience? One kind of answer is given in the verse's first line. "I" am all-knowing because "I" am the one who witnesses all those things that happen to be "located" or "seated" in my intellect at any given point. Swami Paramarthananda again provides a very helpful analogy to illustrate this idea: an old-fashioned film projector.[30] Before the advent of digital technology, when I used go to the theater to take in the latest feature, the images I saw on the screen could be traced to at least two distinct causes. First of all, the film reel contained a rapid succession of individual frames – about 24 per second – which traced the narrative of the film. Secondly, and perhaps more importantly, the projector's arc-light, mounted behind these frames, cast these images on a screen and made them available for viewing. The frames changed rapidly; the light remained the same.

When the projector analogy is applied to this verse, of course, it is the intellect which constitutes the various, ever-changing frames, while their 'projection' depends upon the light of the *Ātman*. Since the *Ātman* illumines each and every experience of this intellect, it both knows and pervades them. Thus "I" can be described, in a sense, as both all-knowing and all-pervading; I know and pervade all things presented to me in my own experience.

This may seem to be a singularly unambitious "all." So Shankara continues:

[30] PARAMARTHANANDA, *UPADEŚA SĀHASRĪ*, cassette #7-1.

> Just as [I] am the Witness of the movements in My own intellect, so am I [also the Witness of the movements] in others' [intellects]. I can be neither rejected nor accepted. Therefore, I am indeed the highest. (7.2)
> There is no change in the *Ātman*, nor impurity, nor materiality, and because It is the Witness of all intellects, there is no limitation of its knowledge, as there is in the case of knowledge of intellect. (7.3)

In these two verses, Shankara introduces the theme of *sākṣin*, "witness," to characterize *Ātman*. He affirms, first, that this witness does not present itself to me as an object to be accepted or rejected; instead, as we have already seen in USP 2, "it" is actually the self-evident "I," the sole basis of any deliberation or inquiry. It is also necessarily different from the intellect whose movements it continuously perceives, by virtue of that very fact of perception itself.[31] Finally, precisely as different, the witnessing *Ātman* does not share the intellect's intrinsic limitations.

The upshot of this analysis is a deeper understanding of what it means to say that "I" am all-knowing. If "I" indicates my intellect, this is clearly nonsense: this individual, embodied intellect is limited by language, culture, historical location and its considerable propensity to error. But if the "I" refers to the consciousness that pervades and is reflected in this mind, then it becomes clear that this same property can be identified in each and every conscious being. So "I," the witness behind this intellect, am also the witness behind every other intellect, as well. To extend the previous metaphor, the frames – indeed, even the movies – that pass through the film projector may be many and various, but all are pervaded and projected by the one light.

A further metaphor underscores the point:

> Just as in a jewel the forms such as red color are manifested in the sunshine, so in my presence everything becomes visible [in the intellect]. Therefore through Me [everything becomes visible] as through sunshine. (7.4)
> The object of knowledge in the intellect exists when the intellect exists; otherwise it does not exist. Since the Seer is always seer, duality does not exist. (7.5)

[31] It is one of Shankara's fundamental axioms that, in any act of perception, the perceiver must necessarily be different from that which is perceived. A good example can be found in USG 2.70, where the student, when asked whether he is identical with his experiences of pain and pleasure, reports, "Well, I can say at once I am not non-different. Why not? Because I am aware of both of them as objects of my knowledge, like a pot. If I were non-different from them I could not know them. But I do know them, so I must be different from them" (Trans. ALSTON, *The Thousand Teachings*, p. 60).

The image of the clear jewel is one that recurs across the pages of the *Upadeśasāhasrī*, as well as in Shankara's other writings, to elucidate the relations among the witnessing self, the individual intellect and the empirical world.[32] This transparent crystal stands for the embodied intellect, which takes on the 'color' or 'shade' of various objects it encounters in the world. That is, we know such objects only through the impressions they make in our intellect. Returning to the analogy, a clear crystal may appear to be red when it passes in front of a red flower, but the sun which illumines flower and crystal alike is not affected by this apparent change in the crystal. Similarly, the witness, which illumines both the intellect and the various objects that make impressions upon it, is not thereby affected by these impressions.

The imagery of USP 7.5 may seem more opaque; in essence, however, it simply turns the metaphor of 7.4 on its head. The prior existence of a red flower is what produces redness in the crystal, but this order is actually reversed when we turn to the embodied intellect. In this case, worldly objects exist only insofar as they make impressions in the mind, and not otherwise. Remove the crystal, in other words, and the flower goes with it. The sunlight alone remains.

The classic Advaita demonstration of this highly counterintuitive claim involves an analysis of the three fundamental states of experience: waking, dreaming and dreamless sleep.[33]

In waking and dream sleep, I am aware of my own existence, mediated to me by my experiences – real in the one case, imagined in the other. In deep sleep, I continue to possess what Paul Hacker calls a "principle of existential unity,"[34] in that I later know that "I" was asleep. I intuitively apprehend that I did not somehow cease to exist during that time. But I have no memories, real or illusory, from the period of dreamless sleep. Hence, Shankara infers, in this state the *Ātman* persists, but the intellect has been dissolved. Like a projector with no film, the light continues to shine; it simply casts no images on the screen. Speaking

[32] MAYEDA (*A Thousand Teachings*, p. 169n11) offers the following as examples: USP 7.4, 17.16, 18.122; BSBh 1.3.19, 3.2.11.

[33] This is a major theme of the *Māṇḍūkya-Kārikā* of Gauḍapāda, as well as Shankara's commentary on them. See COMANS, *Method of Early Advaita Vedānta*, pp. 9-22, and the extended analysis in Arvind SHARMA, *The Experiential Dimension of Advaita Vedānta* (Delhi: Motilal Banarsidass, 1993), esp. pp. 3-37.

[34] HACKER, "Śaṅkara's Conception of Man," in HALBFASS, *Philology and Confrontation*, p. 184.

experientially, the intellect comes and goes in the presence of the eternal Witness, free from distinction or duality.

From this, Shankara draws a radical conclusion:

> Just as the intellect, from absence of discriminating knowledge, holds that the highest does not exist, just so when there is discriminating knowledge, nothing but the highest exists, not even [the intellect] itself. (7.6)

To grasp the startling force of this verse, it is vital to keep in mind that "discriminating knowledge," the subject of this and the preceding verse chapters, is a property of the embodied intellect, not the Witness. It is the intellect of the hearer which differentiates between self and non-self, the intellect which overcomes resistance to the teaching that "I am the Lord," the intellect which shifts its attention from the reflection of the self to its reality, and the intellect which identifies this same self as the eternal Witness of all things, different from the embodied intellect and all the changes that take place in it. It is, finally, a very particular intellect, the intellect of the Hindu teacher Ādi Shankaracharya, which formulated the teachings of USP 2-7 and set them to verse in the first place.

Given these facts, it is truly extraordinary to learn that this intellect, as such, cannot truly be said to exist at all.

At this point, the contemporary hearer of any stripe may feel the urge to characterize Shankara's position as "realist" or "illusionist," "monist" or "solipsist," and so on. Such issues will occupy us in due time. For the present, however, it is worth noting that these kinds of labels do not seem to interest Shankara in the least. He focuses instead on the moment of discovery, when the hearer, exercising her embodied intellect, realizes that this very intellect – the moving center of her body, mind and personality – falls away in the light of the *Ātman* which has been thus uncovered. The categories of bondage and liberation also fall away, at least insofar as these pertain to the individual body, mind and personality of the seeker. So what exactly has happened? Nothing has *happened*, if we take Shankara at his word: no sudden achievement of yogic powers, no mystical revelation, no eclipse of the mind or dissolution of the empirical world. Instead, a paradoxical wisdom has simply dislodged the conventional standards of the world, including any claim this implied hearer might make to status, power, personal identity or even, perhaps, liberation itself. The hearer of USP 2-7 has been brought to the doorstep of *jīvan-mukti*, liberation in this very life, without anything having changed at all.

III.
"God's foolishness is wiser than human wisdom": A Christian *Saṃvāda* with USP 2-7

> For the message about the cross is foolishness to those who are perishing, but to us who are being saved it is the power of God. For it is written,
>
> > 'I will destroy the wisdom of the wise,
> > and the discernment of the discerning I will thwart.'
>
> Where is the one who is wise? Where is the scribe? Where is the debater of this age? Has not God made foolish the wisdom of the world? For since, in the wisdom of God, the world did not know God through wisdom, God decided, through the foolishness of our proclamation, to save those who believe. For Jews demand signs and Greeks desire wisdom, but we proclaim Christ crucified, a stumbling block to Jews and foolishness to Gentiles, but to those who are the called, both Jews and Greeks, Christ the power of God and the wisdom of God. For God's foolishness is wiser than human wisdom, and God's weakness is stronger than human strength (1 Corinthians 1:18-25).

In the treatment of Romans 9-11 in chapter 2, we briefly noted Paul's eschatological approach to the question of historic Israel's final reconciliation. In and of itself, such an emphasis on eschatology was not original to Paul or even to the Christian gospel. Various traditions of Jewish apocalyptic thought likewise envisioned an imminent end to this present sinful age and the establishment, by God, of a new one. According to Paul, however, the new age does not belong exclusively to the future: it has also already dawned with the death and resurrection of Jesus. So Paul can speak of salvation as both "already" and "not yet," beginning in the past and present and straining toward its definitive conclusion in the future. Until the second coming of Christ, the old age of death and the new age of salvation coexist in mutual tension. Both the world and the individual believer, including Paul himself, continue to manifest symptoms of the old age, even as they participate in and look forward to the new one.[35]

In the case of his letter to the Romans, as we have already seen, Paul's struggle with the "already-not yet" of God's salvation leads him to a kind

[35] See especially J. Paul Sampley, *Walking between the Times: Paul's Moral Reasoning* (Minneapolis: Fortress Press, 1991), pp. 7-24, and James D.G. Dunn, *The Theology of Paul the Apostle* (Grand Rapids and Cambridge: William B. Eerdmans Publishing Company, 1998), pp. 461-72.

of double vision on Israel, old and new. In 1 Corinthians, on the other hand, it allows Paul to speak in the continuing present tense of two rival groups undergoing simultaneous but opposed kinds of transformation: "those who are perishing" and "us who are being saved" (1 Cor 1:18, quoted above).[36] The members of these two fundamental divisions have not yet arrived at their respective destinies, but these destinies have, it seems, been fixed. What distinguishes one group from the other are their fundamentally opposed attitudes toward human wisdom and the cross of Christ. The eschatological tension between the new age and old here takes social shape as a tension between those Jews and Greeks who, by God's call, are enabled to see true wisdom for what it is, and those others who prefer their own wisdom to what God has revealed in Christ.

In part, Paul's strong words in this passage reflect a paradox inherent in the Christian claim: the proclamation of a person who died a shameful death by crucifixion as the Messiah of Israel and exalted savior of humankind. This claim would have been highly offensive or ridiculous to many of Paul's contemporaries. Indeed, the earliest extant image of Jesus's crucifixion – a graffito from second-century Rome – depicts Jesus as a donkey, hanging on the cross, with a similarly cartoonish human figure alongside. The scrawled, ironic caption reads: "Alexamenos adores his god."[37]

Beyond bearing witness to the general offensiveness of the Christian proclamation in his contemporary environment, Paul's arguments in 1 Corinthians also address the specific circumstances of the church to which he was writing. Of particular concern were social and economic divisions among the Christians of Corinth.[38] It seems that some of these divisions were related to social status; and social status, in turn, was closely related to rhetorical eloquence and displays of wisdom. Hence, in this passage and throughout the initial chapters of his letter, Paul attempts to undermine such status distinctions by subjecting wisdom itself to a blistering critique.[39] The key element of this critique, for our

36 On Paul's use of the Hellenistic and Jewish "'two-way' tradition" here, see J. Paul SAMPLEY, "The First Letter to the Corinthians," in *The New Interpreter's Bible*, vol. 10 (Nashville: Abingdon Press, 2002), pp. 802, 810-11.

37 See David L. Edwards, *Christianity: The First Two Thousand Years* (Maryknoll: Orbis Books, 1997), p. 72.

38 SAMPLEY, "First Corinthians," pp. 780-81, 801.

39 See Ibid, pp. 802, 808-9, 814-15, and Richard B. HAYS, "Wisdom According to Paul," in S.C. BARTON (ed.), *Where Shall Wisdom Be Found? Wisdom in the Bible, the Church, and the Contemporary World* (Edinburgh: T & T Clark, 1999), pp. 111-23.

purposes, is the apostle's sharp contrast of conventional human wisdom against the true wisdom and power of God: namely, Christ crucified and raised from the dead. In and through this death and resurrection, God inaugurates the new order and upsets the values of the present age, including conventional claims to wisdom and status. "If that shocking event," writes Richard Hays, "is the revelation of the deepest truth about the character of God, then our whole way of seeing the world is turned upside down."[40]

Just how profoundly the wisdom of the cross can upset conventional values finds further witness in Paul's own experience as he describes it in a later letter to the same community (2 Cor 11:21-12:10). Speaking "as a fool" in the face of opposition, Paul rehearses a litany of his apostolic qualifications, including Jewish identity (11:21), ministry (11:22), trials and tribulations (11:23-28, 32-33) and even, obliquely, a dramatic mystical or literal transport to God's own "third heaven" fourteen years prior (12:1-4). At the end of the litany, however, Paul presents himself not as a victor, but as a pathetic figure, reduced to nearly nothing, pleading with God to release him from what he describes as a "thorn" in his flesh (12:7-8). God's response to this pleading, which Paul also makes his own, could be read as a précis of the Christian scandal: "My grace is sufficient for you, for power is made perfect in weakness" (12:9).[41] Worldly wisdom, apostolic status, even the most exalted spiritual translation to a heavenly realm – all of these possess value on their own terms. But they are also dramatically transformed and trans-valued by the foolishness of God.

As we know from our hearing of USP 2-7, above, Shankara offers his own, quite different vision of what counts as the true "wisdom and power of God." One difficulty for the Christian hearer of these chapters may stem from this very fact, for Shankara's claims are in some ways especially scandalous from a Christian point of view. He mounts his

[40] HAYS, "Wisdom According to Paul," p. 113.

[41] Of course, Paul's rhetoric also functions – paradoxically or cynically – to parade before his Corinthian hearers precisely those qualifications that he will go on to dismiss: that is, while he claims only to boast in his weakness (v. 30), he also effectively reminds his hearers that he has superior spiritual credentials to those who are opposing him in the community. This does not significantly detract from his conviction, revealed in Christ and in Paul's own experience, that God's salvation does indeed subvert conventional values. See the discussion in J. Paul SAMPLEY, "The Second Letter to the Corinthians," in *The New Interpreter's Bible*, vol. 11 (Nashville: Abingdon Press, 2000), pp. 24-27, 155-56, 166-67.

arguments entirely in terms of wisdom (*jñāna*) or liberating gnosis (*vidyā*), and his cultivation of discriminating knowledge may be read in parallel with the "discernment" (*sunesis*) that comes under such strong censure by Paul in 1 Cor 1:19. Wedded as it is to an intellectualist programme, as well as to convictions about God and embodied existence that certainly seem to contradict Christian doctrine, the Advaita teaching on *jīvan-mukti* and the *jīvan-mukta* would seem a poor candidate for a any kind of dialogue, much less the dialogue of reconciliation proposed in the previous chapter. Christian hearers of this text might find ourselves concurring with Bhāskara's judgement that we would rather be jackals in a forest than entertain such strange ideas about selfhood and salvation, even for a moment.

Yet Shankara, intriguingly, anticipates just such a rejection. The idiom of apocalyptic eschatology is foreign to him, but his teaching on the self nevertheless represents itself as a kind of *skandalon*, a "stumbling block" which offends those invested in worldly status, wisdom, achievement or any distinguishing characteristics of finite, embodied existence. In the light of *Brahma-vidyā*, our whole way of seeing the world is again turned upside down. Rather than dismissing the wisdom of this teaching, then, we may well discern in the sharp challenge it poses an echo of and movement towards the scandal of the cross.

As a first step in such discernment, we can simply note that Shankara's resolutely practical focus in USP 2-7 may help us become better hearers, rather than merely readers and interpreters, of the apostle Paul and his preaching of Christ crucified. If God's true wisdom should be encountered not as clever ideas but as a life-transforming event, then it also seems clear enough that the authentic hearer encounters this event precisely as a *bubhutsu* or spiritual aspirant (USP 3.4) – that is, to play on a shared Sanskrit root (*budh-*), as an embodied intellect (*buddhi*) yearning for her own radical transformation and transvaluation. Paul's rhetoric is directed primarily at social divisions in the Christian community and dynamics of power and privilege in the Greco-Roman culture of ancient Corinth. Shankara, by contrast, takes aim at the most fundamental distinctions of self-identity and the most basic experiences of perception. But we should be cautious about making too much of this difference. We come to know social divisions only through perception and experience, after all, while even our most fundamental apprehensions of selfhood carry the indelible mark of culture. If we hear the teaching aright, we hear it in and through the whole range of experience available to us. If we encounter it as a world-transforming, eschatological event, then no aspect of our embodied experience will remain untouched. With Shankara and with the Paul of 2 Corinthians, we might find ourselves striving against our instinctive clinging to social status, to authority, to personal strength, to ecstatic experience and indeed to *anything* about which we could say "*that* is [my] self" (*idam-ātman*), in favor of the self-revealing, self-sufficient and utterly foolish grace of God.

The scandal of the cross, moreover, is not merely a scandal about the proclamation of the crucified Jesus as the Christ; it is also the scandalous truth that this proclamation reveals about human existence itself, in this present age. When Paul proclaims that those who are being saved recognize the cross as the power of God (1 Cor 1:18), for example, it may seem natural to presume that this recognition follows from their saving participation in Christ's death and resurrection. Yet, with Shankara's paradoxical deployment of the crystal metaphor in USP 7.4-5 in mind, we may recall that it is equally appropriate to turn this formulation on its head, such that salvation follows from such recognition and is, in a certain sense, identical with it. Insofar as the death and resurrection of Christ can be heard to include the death and resurrection of all humankind – or even, perhaps, all conscious beings – then this foolishness of God is always and already reflected in each and every human life. The difference between those who are being saved and those who are perishing may be precisely this: the firm conviction that we truly exist only insofar as we discover Christ's life in our own. And this life has been revealed as a life characterized by its willingness to allow every aspect of embodied existence, everything we might be tempted to call our own, to be radically stripped away.

If our whole embodied reality has indeed been newly re-founded in the utter and unflinching weakness of Christ, then those who hear this gospel really have only two choices. We can shrink away in fear, or we can proclaim, in a sense distinct but not absolutely different from that proclaimed in these scripted dialogues, "I am the Lord" and "Nothing but the Highest exists" in me. All else is perishing, and those who resist this proclamation risk perishing with it.

To develop this line of inquiry further, we again reach beyond the apostle Paul to a later Christian work that also takes up similar questions of scandal, controversy and the transvaluation of embodied existence: the treatise *Against Heresies* (hereafter AH) by the second-century theologian Irenaeus of Lyons.[42] *Against Heresies*, as its name suggests, is a work of

[42] In the paragraphs that follow, I have used the English translation available in Robert M. GRANT, *Irenaeus of Lyons*, The Early Church Fathers (London and New York:

refutation, directed against a variety of cosmological and soteriological doctrines promulgated by various Gnostic Christian groups.[43] According to Irenaeus, one of the common characteristics of these otherwise disparate errors is their shared claim to possess a secret gnosis or esoteric knowledge bestowed by Christ to a small group of elect. So, to counter such claims, he holds out the Catholic successions of bishops, the biblical canon, and the rule of faith as public, defining features of Christian orthodoxy.[44]

In addition to setting such ecclesial boundaries, Irenaeus also confronts his opponents with what he judges to be a fuller, richer and more orthodox understanding of salvation history, with its climax in the life, death and resurrection of Jesus the Christ. In AH 5.18.3, for example, Irenaeus offers the following short summary of the gospel message:

> The Maker of the world is truly the Word of God; he is our Lord, who in the last times was made man, existing in this world (John 1:10), and invisibly contains everything that was made (Wisd. 1:7) and was imprinted in the shape of a Chi in everything, as Word of God governing and disposing everything. Therefore he came in visible form into his own region (John 1:11) and was made flesh (1:14) and was hanged from the wood in order to recapitulate everything in himself.

Even in such a short excerpt, distinctive features of Irenaeus's thought come vividly to the fore, including especially one aspect of his teaching that would emerge as one of the Christian tradition's strongest claims about the universal significance of the crucified Christ: namely, the proclamation of this Christ as the "summary" or "recapitulation" (*anakephalaiōsis*) of the whole of embodied existence.[45] Through the incarnation and crucifixion of the Word of God, on whose model the world was fashioned, the history that began with Adam and Eve's fall is re-enacted and radically reversed; through the resurrection, on the other hand, death is defeated and the creation renewed in the body of the Lord. It is precisely the scandalous assertion of divine corporeality, Ireneaus argues, that most offends the Gnostics and gives rise to their impious speculations (see, e.g., 5.2.2-3; 5.14.1-3).

Routledge, 1997). For convenience, I have confined my attention to a short sequence of ideas from the fifth and final book of this treatise.

[43] For a capable survey of Christian and other Gnostic traditions, see Birger A. PEARSON, *Ancient Gnosticism: Traditions and Literature* (Minneapolis: Fortress Press, 2007).

[44] See Robert B. ENO, *Teaching Authority in the Early Church*, Message of the Fathers of the Church 14 (Wilmington: Michael Glazier, 1984), pp. 42-50.

[45] See the discussion in GRANT, *Irenaeus of Lyons*, pp. 50-53.

All this may seem quite remote from Shankara's teaching of *Brahma-vidyā*; if anything, Shankara appears to resemble Irenaeus's Gnostic opponents far more closely than he resembles the claims of either the apostle Paul or Irenaeus. Of these opponents, Irenaeus writes:

> Then all the heretics are stupid and do not know the 'economies' of God and do not know his 'economy' for man – blind as they are concerning the truth – when they contradict their own salvation, some introducing a Father other than the Demiurge, others saying that the world and its substances were made by angels... Yet others despise the visible coming of the Lord and reject his incarnation. Still others, again, ignorant of the 'economy' of the Virgin, say he was generated by Joseph. Some say neither soul nor body can receive eternal life, but only the 'inner man,' which they identify with their mind, judging it to rise to perfection... (AH 5.19.2).

Irenaeus here moves from the particular to the general, condemning a broad sweep of rival views with a single common thread: all divide spiritual realities from material ones and thus seek liberation apart from any physical embodiment, their own or the Lord's. In their dualism, they fail fully to embrace the wisdom of the crucified Christ.

At first glance, it seems very natural to close the circle, to see in Shankara's teaching precisely this kind of position; for the Hindu teacher does indeed reduce not only the body but all phenomenal reality to the realm of mere appearance. In light of our slower, more patient reading above, however, we may wonder whether the situation is more complex than it initially appears. Though, from one point of view, Shankara might be accused of identifying eternal life with an "inner man," he would clearly reject associating such an inner reality too closely with the "mind" or somehow working to transform *Ātman* by raising it "to perfection." Anything about which one can say, "this is the self," we recall, falls away by that very act of identification, no matter how spiritual "this" might appear to be: the mind and individual soul are, at the end of the day, as deeply implicated in phenomenal existence as the physical body. The troubling claim of "liberation-in-life" (*jīvan-mukti*) is not that *Ātman* can somehow escape bodily life and return to the immaterial God; it is, rather, that liberation is already the core reality of the embodied hearer, as revealed in the statement, "I am *Brahman*, the Lord."

Advaita Vedanta is not a Christian heresy, and it stands, at least in its self-understanding, opposed to any and all forms of dualism (*dvaita*); so perhaps it comes as no great surprise that Shankara's teachings do not quite match those which Irenaeus finds so offensive. Scandal it may well be, but the challenge Advaita offers is not so easily domesticated to familiar

Christian categories. In fact, we might even ask whether the essential vision of this Hindu teacher may actually resonate more richly and more interestingly with Irenaeus's own notion of "recapitulation" than it does with the esoteric cosmological theories of the Gnostics. For Irenaeus, it is the divine Word, imprinted on and invisibly containing all things, who takes human form in Jesus the Christ; all flesh is, at least potentially, re-created, renewed and drawn together in this same Christ's death and resurrection. For Shankara, it is the divine "witness" (*sākṣin*), the foundation and sole reality of all creation, who illumines all intellects and all possible experience. As already suggested above, those who shift their personal identification from their bodies, minds and personalities to this interior witness die to themselves, at least as these selves are conventionally understood, in order to live in a new way. The embodied intellect is the means by which this radical reorientation takes place, but the intellect itself does not thereby transcend the limitations of embodied life. The scandal of the Advaita teaching for objectors like Bhāskara arises at least in part from the fact that "liberation-in-life" (*jīvan-mukti*) is liberation in *this* life, with all the tension and problems this seems to entail.

These observations may gain further clarity if we shift our attention from Irenaeus's refutation to the more enduring visions of truth and liberation any such refutation is intended to serve, this time attempting to hear the two great teachers together:

Therefore the Apostle says, 'Do not think more highly than you ought to think, but think with sober judgement' (Rom. 12:3), so that we might not taste their 'knowledge,' which is more than one ought to think, and be expelled from the paradise of life.... The things in the heavens are spiritual, while those on earth are the dispensation related to man. Therefore [the Lord] recapitulated these in himself by uniting man to the Spirit and placing the Spirit in man, himself the head of the Spirit to be the head of man: for it is by this Spirit that we see and hear and speak (AH 5.20.2).

Just as [I] am the Witness of the movements in My own intellect, so am I [also the Witness of the movements] in others' [intellects]. I can be neither rejected nor accepted. Therefore I am indeed the highest.

There is no change in the *Ātman*, nor impurity, nor materiality, and because it is the Witness of all intellects, there is no limitation of its knowledge, as there is in the case of knowledge of intellect (USP 7.2-3).

Encountering these more positive formulations side-by-side, we are reminded that Irenaeus, for all his criticisms of Gnostic views, does not hesitate to distinguish between earthly and spiritual realities, between the embodied human person and the divine Spirit by which such persons find themselves joined to Christ. It is through this very Spirit, Irenaeus asserts, that "we see and hear and speak," thereby echoing, at least to some degree, Shankara's insistence upon the true self – God – as the eternal witness within each and every conscious being.

For his part, as we have already noted, Shankara does not explicitly denigrate human embodiment or attempt to engineer some escape into another, more spiritual realm of existence. Even if Shankara's tone suggests a strong bias against the body, endemic not only to Advaita but to many Christian traditions throughout history,[46] the Christian hearer can question whether such a bias is essential to either tradition, and whether internal logic of Advaita might indeed press it in another direction altogether. Lance Nelson, with whom we began our treatment of Shankara in this chapter, suggests the following alternative construction:

> The logic of Advaita requires that, with the attainment of liberation, the sage's false identification with the mind-body complex must vanish. Having realized his nature as *Ātman*, the *mukta* should have completely withdrawn from connection with empirical limitations, like – says the *Chāndogya* Upaniṣad – the snake who has shed his skin. What appears to be his own activity ought now to be completely surrendered to, and governed by, Īśvara [the Lord].[47]

Nelson goes on to elaborate a strong parallel between this liberated sage and the presentation of Lord Krishna in the *Bhagavad-Gītā*.[48] For our purposes, however, it is sufficient to dwell on his more basic notion of self-surrender.

The embodied intellect, as we have seen, does not somehow shake off its limitations in the process of self-inquiry; it merely surrenders its false claim to delimit and define human selfhood. The *jīvan-mukta* can recognize herself as "the highest" precisely because this highest is available in and through embodied experience. It is the limited, embodied intellect who engages in self-inquiry, this same intellect who recognizes the self as the eternal witness of all and who, in the wake of this recognition, finally surrenders. To adopt the idiom of Irenaeus, these limited, earthly

[46] See especially NELSON, "Living Liberation," pp. 31-34, 44-47; and Lance E. NELSON, "The Dualism of Nondualism: Advaita Vedānta and the Irrelevance of Nature," in L. NELSON (ed.), *Purifying the Earthly Body of God: Religion and Ecology in Hindu India*, SUNY Studies in Religious Studies (Albany: State University of New York Press, 1998), pp. 61-88.

[47] NELSON, "Living Liberation," p. 40.

[48] Ibid, pp. 39-44.

"dispensations" become the privileged means by which *Ātman*, pure Spirit, the Lord (*Īśvara*) is revealed as the authentic head of the human person, here and now, in this embodied state. That this self-revelation must find its ultimate basis – at least for the Christian hearer – in the recapitulation of all things in Christ need not detract from appreciation for its life-changing and transformative potential. Shankara might even be interpreted to provide a new vocabulary for similarly paradoxical Christian claims about renewed life in this present age.

Both Shankara and Irenaeus recognize profound limits on human knowledge and inquiry. For the Hindu *ācārya*, it is the *Ātman* that is all-knowing, never the individual intellect, and the Christian theologian for his part severely cautions against risking one's salvation by indulging in false, so-called 'knowledge' outside the boundaries of Christian communion. Nevertheless, suspended between the "already" and the "not yet" of God's salvation in Christ, the Christian hearer of the *Upadeśasāhasrī* might fruitfully risk emulating the concrete, phenomenological and ascetic practice of discrimination the Hindu teacher models in these few verse chapters. Accepting, even provisionally, Shankara's pedagogical redescription of the self, such a hearer may come to see this life as a mere reflection of the light of Christ and thereby to resist any temptation to identify too closely with "*my* body," "*my* mind," "*my* personality," "*my* spiritual experiences" and even, perhaps, "*my* salvation" as anything more than provisional realities on the way to an ever-greater surrender to and identification with the Lord. Always trusting in Christ crucified, in other words, Christian hearers may nevertheless be well advised to sip gingerly or even drink deeply of the scandal offered in this sacred text.

Lest, like Udaṅka, we merely shrink away in fear.

Chapter 4

SOWING THE WORD: COMMENTARY ON USG 1

I.

Upadeśasāhasrī Gadyabandha 1.1-3

Now we shall explain how to teach the means to final release for the benefit of seekers thereafter with faith and desire.

The means to final release is knowledge. It should be repeatedly related to the pupil until it is firmly grasped, if he is dispassionate toward all things non-eternal which are attained by means; if he has abandoned the desire for sons, wealth, and worlds and reached the state of a *paramahaṃsa* wandering ascetic; if he is endowed with tranquility, self-control, compassion, and so forth; if he is possessed of the qualities of a pupil which are well-known from the scriptures; if he is a Brahmin who is pure; if he approaches his teacher in the prescribed manner; if his caste, profession, behavior, knowledge, and family have been examined.

The *Śruti* also says: 'Having scrutinized...'; for when knowledge is firmly grasped, it is conducive to one's own beatitude and to continuity. And the continuity of knowledge is helpful to people, as a boat [is helpful] to one wishing to get across a river. The scripture also says: 'Even if one should offer him this [earth] that is encompassed by water and filled with treasure, [he should say,] "This, truly, is more than that,"' since knowledge is not obtained in any other way according to passages from the *Śruti* and the *Smṛti* such as: 'One who has a teacher knows...,' 'The knowledge which has been learned from a teacher...'; 'A teacher is a boatman; his [right] knowledge is called a boat here.'

II.

The Continuity of Knowledge: Hearing USG 1 (Selections)

In our hearing of first few chapters of the verse portion, we have become familiar with the essential teaching of Advaita, including the challenge it poses to conventional assumptions. In this chapter, as we turn forward to the first prose chapter, we also turn back to more concrete questions of pedagogy, to the moment when the prospective student receives the Advaita teaching for the first time. Shankara begins this exposition with a clipped statement of intent:

> Now we shall explain how to teach the means to final release for the benefit of seekers thereafter with faith and desire. (USG 1.1)

The chapter begins with the term *atha*, "now." This suitably connects the prose portion to the verse portion which precedes it. Or, in those manuscript traditions in which the prose portion claims priority, the term places the teaching of the *Upadeśasāhasrī* in a relation of continuity and discontinuity with its Pūrva-Mīmāṃsā forebear, parallel to the "thereafter now" (*atha-idānīm*) of USP 1.2.[1] Either way, Shankara suggests that a new topic of inquiry, called *upadeśa-vidhi*, "how to teach" or a "method of teaching," is being initiated here.

Each major element of this introductory statement receives further development in the chapter that follows. For the purposes of the present volume, we will focus on just three thematic clusters, all of which – from different angles – unfold a distinctively Advaita theology of revelation. Beginning with Shankara's descriptions of teacher and student, moving through a brief treatment of the teacher's use of the Upanishadic sentences to convey self-knowledge, and concluding with this same teacher's defense of the *Veda* itself, we will come to see revelation not merely as a static content of the scriptural word, but also as the dynamic accommodation of this word to the qualified disciple, as well as to countless teachers and disciples to come. Revelation in its fullest sense emerges in and through what Shankara calls the "continuity of knowledge" (*vidyā-santati*), the ongoing communication of liberation from one generation to the next.

> **An Initial Reflection**: In our hearings of the *Upadeśasāhasrī*'s initial verse chapters, we have been drawn directly into *saṃvāda* with the Advaita teaching through engaged debate with *pūrva-pakṣa* or adversarial positions in USP 1, through the direct address of *Ātman* in USP 7, and through the anticipation of questions and concerns of implied hearers across all of these sacred scripts. In USG 1, by contrast, we hear a literal, scripted *saṃvāda*

[1] See above, ch. 2, pp. 58-59. The commentators also indicate that *atha* can be read as a traditional invocation (*maṃgala*). See V. NARASIMHAN, *Upadeśa Sāhasrī: A Thousand Teachings of Adi Śaṅkara* (Bombay: Bharatiya Vidya Bhavan, 1996), p. 281, and RĀMATĪRTHA'S comment in D. GOKHALE (ed.), *Shri Shankarāchārya's Upadeśasāhasrī with the Gloss Padayôjanīkā by Shrī Rāmatīrtha* (Bombay: Gujurati Printing Press, 1917), p. 1.

between teacher and disciple from a third-person point of view. This poses a distinct challenge for the interpreter, for this *saṃvāda* must now be heard on at least two levels: as a model for employing the *Upadeśasāhasrī*'s various teaching scripts in the verse portion, on the one hand, and as yet another such script, on the other. For the purposes of Christian commentary, such double valence invites us to hear the script reflexively, attentive both to the content and embodied practice of its teaching and to the implications this teaching offers for articulating a theology of revelation that adequately comprehends these Advaita scripts – including, of course, USG 1 itself.

Teacher and Student (USG 1.2-6a)

As we have seen in previous chapters of this commentary, Shankara readily invokes the *Upanishads* in his teaching scripts, drawing out short declarations like "Not thus! Not so!" (*na-iti, na-iti*), as well as more extended narratives such as the tale of the person from Gandhāra, to illustrate the truth of Advaita. The precise place and role of such scriptural citations is clarified in USG 1, as Shankara demonstrates how they can be employed to make their revelatory power effective in the understanding of the hearer. In this short chapter, the teacher cites scripture some 130 times, drawing mostly from the *Upanishads* but also from the *Bhagavad-Gītā* and other less authoritative texts. The "hearing" (*śravaṇa*) modeled by Shankara in this prose chapter is bounded by the scriptures, from beginning to end.

Significantly for our present purposes, this observation holds true not merely for the content of the instruction, but also for the teachers, students and tradition who participate in it. Shankara thus begins the prose portion of the *Upadeśasāhasrī* with a scripturally circumscribed account of the key agents in this process of instruction, beginning with the student:

> The means to final release is knowledge. It should be repeatedly related to the pupil until it is firmly grasped, if he is dispassionate toward all things non-eternal which are attained by means;[2] if he has abandoned the desire for sons, wealth, and worlds and reached the state of a *paramahaṃsa* wandering ascetic; if he is endowed with tranquility, self-control, compassion,

[2] Although the Sanskrit term *sādhana* has previously been used to describe knowledge as the "means to final release" (*mokṣa-sādhana*), here *sādhana* refers to those actions, especially ritual actions, intended to procure worldly or heavenly rewards, as clarified by the phrase "sons, wealth and worlds," which follows. See Paul HACKER (trans.), *Upadeśasāhasrī: Unterweisung in der All-Einheits-Lehre der Inder, von Meister Shankara: Gadyabandha oder das Buch in Prosa*, Religionsgeschichtliche Texts Herausgegeben von Gustav Mensching 2 (Bonn: Ludwig Röhrscheid Verlag, 1949), p. 11n2.

> and so forth; if he is possessed of the qualities of a pupil which are well-known from the scriptures; if he is a Brahmin who is pure; if he approaches his teacher in the prescribed manner; if his caste, profession, behavior, knowledge, and family have been examined. (1.2)

Although this section offers thumbnail sketches of both the fundamental Advaita claim and the basic method to be employed in its communication, its emphasis falls squarely on the question of *adhikāra*: "qualification," "competence," or "fitness" to receive the teaching.[3] The list of qualifications includes, first, marks of social location. The disciple is a Brahmin who has adopted a renunciant life, applied for instruction appropriately,[4] and, upon examination, been found to be of good conduct, learning, and parentage. We have good reason to doubt whether Shankara considers either Brahmin ancestry or formal renunciation as absolutely necessary for liberation;[5] it is, nevertheless, very clear that he ascribes normative value to them.[6]

But, significantly, these are not the only such norms. Shankara also enumerates a number of personal qualities conducive to assimilating the teaching: compassion and other virtues, a well-controlled mind, and the more vaguely defined "qualities of a pupil."[7] Most importantly, the

[3] See especially Francis X. CLOONEY, S.J., *Theology after Vedānta: An Experiment in Comparative Theology* (Albany: State University of New York Press, 1993), pp. 134-41.

[4] On the norms for approaching the teacher, see William CENKNER, *A Tradition of Teachers: Śaṅkara and the Jagadgurus Today* (Delhi: Motilal Banarsidass, 1983, 1995 [reprint]), pp. 13-14, 45-46; and Sengaku MAYEDA (trans.), *A Thousand Teachings: The Upadeśasāhasrī of Śaṅkara* (Albany: State University of New York Press, 1992), p. 228n8.

[5] ĀNANDAGIRI, for example, clarifies that, although Brahmins are preferred, members of the Kṣatriya or warrior class and others also possess fitness (*adhikāra*) to receive the teaching. See S. SUBRAHMANYA SASTRI (ed.), *Shri Shankarabhagavatpada's Upadeshasahasri with the Tika of Shri Anandagiri Acharya*, Advaita Grantha Ratna Manjushi Ratna 15 (Varanasi: Mahesh Research Institute, 1978), p. 121, lines 25-26.

[6] In USP 13.27, for example, Shankara states: "It [the Upanishadic teaching] should only be taught to peaceful renunciates," following A.J. ALSTON (trans.), *The Thousand Teachings (Upadeśa Sāhasrī) of Śrī Śaṃkarācārya* (London: Shanti Sadan, 1990), p. 158. See the further discussion and debate in MAYEDA, *A Thousand Teachings*, pp. 90-92; Roger MARCAURELLE, *Freedom through Inner Renunciation: Śaṅkara's Philosophy in a New Light* (Albany: State University of New York Press, 2000), pp. 38-39; Lance E. NELSON, "Theism for the Masses, Non-Dualism for the Monastic Elite: A Fresh Look at Śaṃkara's Trans-Theistic Spirituality," in W. SHEA (ed.), *The Struggle over the Past: Fundamentalism in the Modern World* (Lanham: University Press of America, 1993), esp. pp. 72-74; and Sengaku MAYEDA, "Ādi-Śaṅkarācārya's Teaching on the Means to Mokṣa: Jñāna and Karman," *Journal of Oriental Research* 34-35 (1966): pp. 72-73.

[7] ĀNANDAGIRI (*Upadeshasahasri,* p. 121, line 24) cites *Bhagavad-Gītā* 13:7 to fill out these qualities: "To shun conceit and tricky ways, to wish none harm, to be long-suffering and upright, to reverence one's teacher, purity, steadfastness, self-restraint..."

qualified disciple is detached from means and ends and has renounced all temporal desires.

Shankara supports and amplifies this description by turning to the scriptures themselves:

> The *Śruti* also says: 'Having scrutinized...' [MuU 1.2.12-13]; for when knowledge is firmly grasped, it is conducive to one's own beatitude and to continuity. And the continuity of knowledge is helpful to people, as a boat [is helpful] to one wishing to get across a river. (1.3a)

We have seen that Shankara does not shrink from identifying the Advaita tradition with a very particular set of social markers, delimited by birth and state of life. Nevertheless, it is the sheer desire for liberation, combined with detachment from ritual action and its fruits, which primarily occupies his attention, both here and in other places where he takes up the question of *adhikāra*.[8]

This desire for liberation has already been mentioned in USG 1.1. To draw further emphasis to it, Shankara refers here to a famous episode from the *Muṇḍaka Upanishad*:

> When he perceives the worlds as built with rites, a Brahmin should acquire a sense of disgust: "What's made can't make what is unmade!" To understand it he must go, firewood in hand, to a teacher well-versed in the Vedas and focused on *brahman*.[9]

Through this brief citation of an Upanishadic text, Shankara places his own presentation of teacher and student squarely within a scriptural frame. But he also, in a sense, re-inscribes the scriptural account within the frame of his own teaching. The anonymous "Brahmin" of MuU 1.2.12 becomes the *paramahaṃsa* ascetic already described, the similarly anonymous teacher becomes the carefully authorized *ācārya* of USG 1.6, below, and the episode as a whole becomes a typical moment in what Shankara here calls the "continuity of knowledge" (*vidyā-santati*).

There is no consensus on the precise meaning of the term *santati* as it is used here. Derived from the verb root *saṃ-tan-*, it refers to spreading

Romanized Sanskrit text and English translation in R.C. ZAEHNER (trans.), *The Bhagavad-Gītā, with a Commentary Based on the Original Sources* (London, Oxford and New York: Oxford University Press, 1969), p. 336. Further virtues are enumerated in BG 13:8-11; all may be intended here.

[8] See CLOONEY, *Theology after Vedānta*, pp. 129-34.

[9] Sanskrit text and English translation in Patrick OLIVELLE (trans.), *The Early Upaniṣads: Annotated Text and Translation*, South Asia Research Series (New York and Oxford: Oxford University Press, 1998), pp. 440-41.

out, stretching or covering something over, making a connection or simply having an effect. In its extended usage, it can indicate "continuity," "succession" or "family."[10] Hence, the term could refer here to sustained effort in meditation or another supporting practice,[11] to the continuous flow of knowledge from one generation of disciples to the next through the lineage of teachers,[12] or – stretching the term a bit – to the precise method of teaching modeled in USG 1.[13] It is used in parallel with "one's own beatitude" as well as in an instrumental role as "helpful to living beings," a means of knowledge, "like a boat to cross a river."

The boat analogy, which we already encountered in chapter 1, suggests that we need not choose between these various options. *Santati* can be interpreted as continuity of the tradition from one generation to the next, along with continuity in teaching and supporting practices, here and now – what one scholar refers to as a "culture of liberation," past, present, and future.[14] If "method of teaching" may be interpreted as the immediate objective of the *Upadeśasāhasrī*, then "continuity" (*santati*) nicely captures the broader vision such a practical method aims to serve.

Shankara concludes USG 1.3 with more evidence from the scriptures, drawing several passages from the *Chāndogya Upanishad* to underscore the central importance of the teacher in this method of teaching and the continuity of teaching itself (1.3b). Before offering a full description of this teacher, however, Shankara slightly tempers his account of the disciple:

> When [the teacher] finds from some indications that the pupil has not grasped [this] knowledge, he should remove the causes which hinder his grasping it – demerit, worldly laxity, absence of firm preliminary learning concerning the discrimination between things eternal and non-eternal, care about what other people think, pride of caste and the like – by the means contrary to those causes and enjoined by the *Śruti* and the *Smṛti*, that is to

[10] See M. MONIER-WILLIAMS, E. LEUMANN, C. CAPELLER, and others, *Sanskrit-English Dictionary, Etymologically and Philologically Arranged with Special Reference to Cognate Indo-European Languages*, rev. ed. (New Delhi: Munshiram Manoharlal Publishers, 2004), s.v. "saṃtati," pp. 1141-42.

[11] See Bradley J. MALKOVSKY, *The Role of Divine Grace in the Soteriology of Śaṃkarācārya*, Numen Studies in the History of Religions 91 (Leiden: Brill, 2001), pp. 369-70.

[12] See NARASIMHAN, *Upadeśa Sāhasrī*, pp. 284-85, as well as HACKER, *Upadeśasāhasrī*, p. 12, who renders the term "uninterrupted Tradition" (*ununterbrochene Tradition*).

[13] Thus the term is simply rendered as as "transmission" in Swāmi JAGADĀNANDA (trans.), *A Thousand Teachings in Two Parts – Prose and Poetry – of Srī Sankarāchārya* (Madras: Sri Ramakrishna Math, [1941]), p. 4.

[14] Thomas A. FORSTHOEFEL, *Knowing Beyond Knowledge: Epistemologies of Religious Experience in Classical and Modern Advaita*, Ashgate World Philosophies (Hants and Burlington: Ashgate Publishing, 2002), pp. 56-71.

> say, non-anger, etc., non-injury and other abstentions,[15] and the observances which are not contradictory to knowledge.[16] (1.4)
> He should also let [him] properly achieve the virtues such as modesty, which are the means to attain knowledge. (1.5)

In USG 1.2, the qualified Advaita disciple has been described as someone of good parentage and personal virtue, dispassionate, with a clear mind and a clean lifestyle. Similarly, in his comment on *Muṇḍaka Upanishad* 1.2.12, Shankara presumes that the disciple who comes to the teacher has already "overcome flaws like pride" and "become indifferent to everything."[17] In this section of the *Upadeśasāhasrī*, we discover that this ideal student may not be so ideal after all. Some of the flaws enumerated here seem explicitly at odds with the previous description; others may simply indicate further work to be done. Either way, it seems clear that the ideal state of fitness, presumed to some extent before the teaching begins, may also be said to emerge only gradually in the course of instruction.

Having thus completed his portrait of the disciple, Shankara turns his attention to the qualities of the more reliably ideal *ācārya*:

> And the teacher is able to consider the pros and cons [of an argument], is endowed with understanding, memory, tranquility, self-control, compassion, favor and the like; he is versed in the traditional doctrine; not attached to any enjoyments, visible or invisible; he has abandoned all the rituals and their requisites; a knower of *Brahman*, he is established in *Brahman*; he leads a blameless life, free from faults such as deceit, pride, trickery, wickedness, fraud, jealousy, falsehood, egotism, self-interest, and so forth; with the only purpose of helping others he wishes to make use of knowledge. (1.6a)

In USG 1.3, Shankara drew on *Muṇḍaka Upanishad* 1.2.12 to set up the teaching situation. This verse, as we have seen, includes two

[15] RĀMATĪRTHA (*Upadeśasāhasrī*, p. 9) cites the list of "abstentions" (*yama*) from *Yoga-Sūtra* 2.30 to fill out this list: non-injury (*ahiṃsā*), truthfulness (*satya*), non-stealing (*asteya*), chastity (*brahmacarya*), and non-possession (*aparigraha*). VIDYĀRAṆYA cites *Yoga-sūtra* 2.30 and 2.35-39 both to prescribe the yamas and to describe their benefits for the seeker after liberation, in Swāmī MOKṢADĀNANDA (trans.), *Jīvan-mukti-Viveka of Swāmī Vidyāraṇya* (Kolkata: Advaita Ashrama, 1996), pp. 209-11.

[16] RĀMATĪRTHA (*Upadeśasāhasrī*, p. 9) again draws on the *Yoga-Sūtras* to fill out the list of "observances" (*niyama*), this time at 2.32: purity (*śauca*), contentment (*saṃtoṣa*), asceticism (*tapas*), study (*svādhyāya*), and devotion to the Lord (*īśvara-praṇidhāna*).

[17] MuUBh 1.2.12. Sanskrit text and English translation in V. PANOLI (trans.), *Upanishads in Sankara's Own Words*, vol. 2, rev. ed. (Calicut: Mathrubhumi Printing and Publishing Co. Ltd., 1996), p. 148.

important qualifications for the *ācārya*: such an ideal teacher is both *śrotriya*, "learned in the *Śruti*" and *brahma-niṣṭha*, "steadfast in *Brahman*."[18] The latter term reappears as a description of the teacher in the *Upadeśasāhasrī*'s second prose chapter, along with two others: *brāhmaṇa*, "a knower of *Brahman*," and *sukham āsīna*, "sitting at ease" (USG 2.45). Placing these two passages together with USG 1.6a, above, we can say that one qualification emerges most consistently: the teacher is a knower of *Brahman*, firmly established in *Brahman*, liberated in this very life. It stands to reason, based on this fundamental affirmation, that such a teacher is also well-versed in the scriptures that alone provide this liberating knowledge. But it also follows that, having accomplished the highest possible goal of human life, this teacher need accomplish nothing else for himself. He can sit at ease, without troubles, and acts only out of unselfish motives. Above all, he acts out of a desire to teach *Brahman*. Hence he is characterized here, as elsewhere in Shankara's writings, as a person of overflowing grace and compassion.[19] Finally, Shankara adds that the teacher, no less than the student, possesses great virtue and personal detachment.

Once we have seen the fitness of the student as, at least in part, an ideal to be achieved through persistence in the path of knowledge rather than a rigid set of criteria for admission, it will come as no surprise that the student ideal closely resembles that of the authorized *ācārya*.[20] Save that one is a seeker, who desires only liberation, and the other a knower, who desires only to convey the liberating truth, both operate within the same parameters: they are unattached from worldly pleasures, have renounced all temporal means and ends, live virtuous lives and possess personal qualities such as compassion, a disciplined mind and humility. Indeed, we might interpret this mutual relation as yet another, implied meaning of the "continuity of knowledge," for teachers and students themselves exhibit continuity in a personal, embodied way. They are mirror images of one another, the distinguishing marks of the teacher becoming means of liberation for the student.[21]

[18] See CENKNER, *Tradition of Teachers*, pp. 8-10.

[19] See J.G. SUTHREN HIRST, "The Place of Teaching Techniques in Śaṃkara's Theology," *Journal of Indian Philosophy* 18 (1990): pp. 130-31.

[20] MAYEDA, *A Thousand Teachings*, p. 229n16, and Jonathan BADER, *Meditation in Śaṅkara's Vedanta* (New Delhi: Aditya Prkashan, 1990), pp. 59-60.

[21] In BGBh 2.55, in discussing the characteristics of the "person of steadfast wisdom," Śaṅkara writes: "... in all the texts for studying the self, the very characteristics of the perfected sage have been set forth as means [*sādhana*], too, to be cultivated [by

A Christian Reflection: The Advaita tradition is, at some level, unavoidably elitist. Shankara addresses himself primarily if not exclusively to a small group of religious elites, presumes their high station in the social hierarchy, and insists that their desire for the teaching impel them to formal renunciation. Yet, Christian hearers can also note the way that Shankara shifts our attention from such markers of social location toward intellectual and moral virtues like compassion, humility, personal detachment and intense desire. Just as Shankara re-frames the teacher and student of MuU 1.2.12 in terms of the Advaita scripts, then, so also might contemporary Christian hearers re-frame these social markers precisely in terms of the more recognizable, interior virtues.[22] The idea that disciples must develop *adhikāra* or eligibility to receive the teaching fruitfully is not, in itself, foreign to most Christian sensibilities; and Shankara's acknowledgment that such eligibility both precedes and arises in the course of instruction corresponds closely to Christian practices of continuous preaching, teaching and ritual. Conversion to Christ is, from one point of view, a once-and-for-all event and, from another, a life-long pursuit inseparable from the cultivation of moral virtue, intellectual assent and an increasingly intense desire for salvation.

Origin of the Body (USG 1.9-11, 16-21, 23a)

Thus far in USG 1, we have heard Shankara construct idealized portraits of teacher and student, exhibiting their mutual continuity as a living example of that broader continuity that is the Advaita tradition. These portraits find support in the words of scripture, to be sure, especially the *Muṇḍaka Upanishad,* but they also create a specific interpretative context for these same scriptures, implying that it is only in the presence of a teacher and student such as these that the scriptural word fruitfully conveys final release. For this reason, Shankara will frequently speak interchangeably of "scripture" or "scripture *and the teacher*" to describe that verbal, scriptural means of knowledge (*śabda-pramāṇa*) that alone reveals the truth of *Brahman.*

the aspirant]. Thus, indeed, are these characteristics acquired through directed effort. The blessed lord recounted these [characteristics] that are at once the means [*sādhana*], demanding effort, and also the marks [*lakṣaṇa*]." Sanskrit text and English translation in A.G. Krishna WARRIER (trans.), *Śrīmad Bhagavad Gītā Bhāṣya of Sri Saṃkarācārya, with Text in Devanagiri & English Rendering, and Index of First Lines of Verses* (Madras: Sri Ramakrishna Math, 1983), p. 76.

[22] This is, in fact, the common interpretative strategy of Swami Parmarthananda, his teacher Swami Dayananda and many other modern Vedantins. See, for example, Swami DAYANANDA, *The Value of Values* (Saylorsburg, PA: Arsha Vidya Gurukulam, 1984, 1993), esp. pp. 85-90; and Swami DAYANANDA, *Introduction to Vedānta: Understanding the Fundamental Problem*, B. THORNTON (ed.) (New Delhi, Bombay and Hyderabad: Vision Books, 1989, 1997), pp. 24-27.

The remainder of the first prose chapter provides a series of examples of this *pramāṇa* being unfolded in an efficacious way by the authorized teacher. Before turning to our first such example, however, it might be helpful to see an outline of the whole:

USG 1.1-44

1	Introduction
2-6a	General Method and Qualifications of the Student and Teacher

6b-8 Establishing a Framework from Scripture

6b	Demonstration of the unity of *Ātman* and *Brahman* from scripture
7-8	Definition of *Brahman* from scripture
9	The Fundamental Question: "Who are you, my child?"

10-24 Teaching the Difference between Self and Embodied Individual

10-15	Repudiating false identification with the body, mind and personality
16	Student's question: how am I different from this body?
17-18a	Recalling the definition of *Ātman* from scripture
18b-22	An illustrative example: the progressive manifestation of name-and-form
23-24	Laying the error to rest through further scriptural citations

25-38 Teaching the Unity between Self and *Brahman*

25-26a	Repudiating false identification with the transmigrating soul Student's question: how am I "the God" (*deva*) Himself?
26b-29	Recalling the unity of *Ātman* and *Brahman* with scriptural citations
30-32	Proscribing rites and rituals with scriptural citations
33-35	Reconciling this scriptural teaching with empirical experience
36-38	Laying the error to rest through further scriptural citations

39-43 Re-Establishing the Authority of Scripture

39	Student's question: why do the scriptures prescribe rituals?
40-43	Differentiating levels of scriptural discourse and their intended recipients
44	Summary of the Teaching

Unlike the verse chapters we have been hearing thus far, USG 1 does not explore a single main theme or idea. Instead, its structure is determined, on the one side, by the words of scripture and, on the other, by the questions and misunderstandings of the student.

The fundamental unit of scripture for Shankara is the *vākya*, the "word" or "sentence," and especially those sentences where the scriptures step free of their narratives or ritual accounts and speak in short, unambiguous phrases about the truth of *Brahman* and *Ātman* – a number of which later tradition would designate as *mahā-vākyas*, "great sayings."[23] To establish the oneness of the *Ātman* in USG 1, for example, Shankara's model teacher cites five important *vākyas*, drawn primarily from the *Chāndogya Upanishad* (1.6b). To show how the definition of *Brahman* coincides with this *Ātman,* he turns mainly to the *Bṛhadāraṇyaka Upanishad* and then to the *Bhagavad-Gītā*, quoting no fewer than 25 passages (1.7-8). It is presumed that the student will hear these passages, learn them and be able to recall them later.

We pick up this script in the ninth section of the chapter, where the teacher, having sown such scriptural seeds, poses a question and receives a troubling response:

> If the pupil who has thus grasped the marks indicative of the highest *Ātman* according to the *Śrutis* and the *Smṛtis* wishes to get out of the ocean of transmigratory existence, [the teacher] should ask him: 'Who are you, my dear?' (1.9)
> If he answers: 'I am a Brahmin's son belonging to such and such a family. I was a student – or, I was a householder – [but] now I am a *paramahaṃsa* wandering ascetic. I wish to get out of the ocean of transmigratory existence infested with great sharks of birth and death;' (1.10)
> [then] the teacher should say: 'My dear, when you are dead your body will be eaten by birds or will turn into earth right here. How then do you wish to get out of the ocean of transmigratory existence? Because if you turn into ashes on this bank of the river you cannot get across to the other side of the river.'[24] (1.11)

In this section, the teacher asks the same question that dominated the various treatments of USP 2-7 we heard in the previous chapter: who are you? Though the student's answer is from one point of view, unsurprising – the particular identifying marks cited by the student are, after all, precisely those that qualified him for instruction – it is also

[23] See K. Satchidananda MURTY, *Revelation and Reason in Advaita Vedanta* (Waltair: Andhra University; New York: Columbia University Press, 1959, 1961), pp. 68-98; MAYEDA, *A Thousand Teachings*, p. 50; and VETTER, *Studien*, pp. 139-40.

[24] This presumably refers to a funeral rite like that described in Gavin FLOOD, *An Introduction to Hinduism* (Cambridge, New York and Melbourne: Cambridge University Press, 1996), p. 207: "A person is cremated on the day of death is possible. The corpse is bathed, anointed with sandalwood paste, shaved if male, wrapped in a cloth and carried to the cremation ground... The funeral pyre is lit, theoretically with the domestic fire of the deceased if he is twice-born, and the remains are gathered up between three and ten days after the funeral and buried, placed in a special area of ground or immersed in a river, preferably the holy Ganges."

disappointing, as the teacher's sharp rebuke makes abundantly clear. In the formula that dominates the subsequent narrative, the student has wrongly identified himself with a body possessed of birth (*jāti*), lineage (*anvaya*) and ritual purification (*saṃskāra*).

The hearing of the scriptures alone has not yet removed this error, so the student presses the teacher for further explanation:

> If he asks: 'How does the body have different caste, family, and purifying ceremonies?' or, 'How am I free from caste, family, and purifying ceremonies?' (1.16)
> [then] the teacher should reply: 'Listen, my dear, [this is] how this body, different from you, has different caste, family and purifying ceremonies and how you are free from caste, family, and purifying ceremonies.'
> Thereupon [the teacher] should remind him: 'You should remember, my dear, that you have been taught that the highest *Ātman*, the *Ātman* of all, is endowed with the marks described above according to such *Śruti* and *Smṛti* passages as: "my dear, this universe was the Existent only" [CU 6.2.1] and [that you have also been taught] the marks indicative of the highest *Ātman* according to *Śruti* and *Smṛti* passages.' (1.17)
> When [the pupil] has recalled to mind the marks indicative of the highest *Ātman*, [the teacher] should tell him: 'This [highest *Ātman*] which is called "Space" is something different from name-and-form, bodiless, characterized as "not coarse," etc., and as "free from evil," etc. It is not afflicted with any attributes of transmigratory existence; "the manifest, unconcealed *Brahman is*... your *Ātman* which is within everything" [BU 3.4.1].[25] It is "the unseen Seer, the unheard Hearer, the unthought Thinker, the unknown Knower" [BU 3.7.23]. It is of the nature of eternal knowledge, "without an inside and without an outside" [BU 2.5.19], "just a mass of knowledge" [BU 2.4.12].' (1.18a)

When prompted to explain how the student is different from his body, the *ācārya* first points out that such self-identification has been ruled out by the scriptures, directing attention back to those definitions already established from the *Upanishads*... and adding a few more *vākyas* for good measure (1.18a). Later, he will further substantiate this claim with a number of passages that specifically demonstrate *Ātman*'s freedom from birth, lineage and ritual purification (1.23b-24).

The *vākyas* are not employed as mere assertions, for Shankara also goes on to show how they can be made intelligible within the proper cosmological framework. Specifically, his model teacher attempts to reveal to the student how *Ātman* is both the material basis of the created world

[25] I have modified MAYEDA's translation of this quotation.

and also, ultimately, unrelated to it.[26] This he accomplishes by recourse to the notions of "name-and-form" and "inconceivable power" in the sections that follow:

> 'It is all-pervading like ether, possessed of infinite power, the *Ātman* of all, free from hunger, etc., and free from appearance and disappearance. This is the Evolver of the unevolved name-and-form merely by being existent since It is possessed of inconceivable power. The unevolved name-and-form is different in essence from this [*Ātman*] and it is the seed of the world, abiding in It, indescribable as this or something else, and known to It.' (1.18b)

In the previous chapter of this commentary, we encountered Shankara's declaration that, from the highest point of view, "nothing but the Highest exists" (USP 7.6). This has led some interpreters to assume that Shankara espouses a form of subjective idealism.[27] In other words, following the analysis of a text like USP 7 to its logical conclusion, one might surmise that worldly experience is a massive imaginary construct of a single deluded mind.

Other interpreters, both critics and admirers, have raised questions about such "illusionism" as a feature of the Advaita teaching. Jacqueline G. Suthren Hirst, for example, notes that Shankara actually uses a variety of images to speak about the created world, each of which removes a particular kind of error.[28] In some places, especially in his commentary on the *Brahma-Sūtras*, Shankara will employ the well-trodden Upanishadic analogy of the clay pot: just as the pot is nothing but a modification of clay, so also the world can be seen as a modification of *Brahman* as its material cause.[29] At the same time, to clarify this idea, he will qualify the clay-pot analogy with the rather different image of a piece of

[26] See Francis X.CLOONEY, S.J., "Evil, Divine Omnipotence, and Human Freedom: Vedanta's Theology of Karma," *The Journal of Religion* 4 (1989): pp. 536-40.

[27] See, for example, Paul HACKER, "Being and Spirit in Vedānta," in W. HALBFASS (ed.), *Philology and Confrontation: Paul Hacker on Traditional and Modern Vedānta* (Albany: State University of New York Press, 1995), esp. pp. 192-97.

[28] The argument in the next two paragraphs closely follows J.G. SUTHREN HIRST, *Śaṃkara's Advaita Vedānta: A Way of Teaching*, RoutledgeCurzon Hindu Studies Series (London and New York: RoutledgeCurzon, 2005), pp. 103-15, which is paralleled in SUTHREN HIRST, "Teaching Techniques," pp. 124-25.

[29] This theory of creation is called *sat-kārya-vāda*, and the Advaita tradition shares it, to a limited extent, with the Sāṃkhya tradition. See John GRIMES, *A Concise Dictionary of Indian Philosophy: Sanskrit Terms Defined in English*, rev. ed. (Albany: State University of New York Press, 1996), p. 289, and Eliot DEUTSCH, *Advaita Vedānta: A Philosophical Reconstruction* (Honolulu: University of Hawaii Press, 1968), pp. 35-45.

rope mistaken for a snake. This very common trope, which Advaita shares with Buddhism and other traditions, implies that the transformation of *Brahman* into the world is not real, but only apparent. In other contexts, Shankara will again change idiom, speaking of the *Ātman* as a grand magician who uses his "miraculous power" (*māyā-śakti*) to create illusions for the pleasure of his audience.

Read in isolation, each of these analogies can lead to serious misunderstandings. For example, the rope mistaken for a snake suggests that the world is indeed a mere delusion of a single mind, but this is qualified in one way by the clay pot, which removes the notion of illusion, and in another by the magician, which adds the notion of divine intention and agency. Together, the three images hold apparently contradictory truths in creative tension, refusing to compromise either the absolute, sole true reality of *Ātman* or the relative, dependent and purely provisional reality of the created world.[30]

We witness a similar kind of balancing act in Shankara's account of "name-and-form" (*nāma-rūpa*) in USG 1.18-22. This term is, as we might expect, drawn from the scriptures. One of the last lines of the *Chāndogya Upanishad*, for example, reads:

> Now, what is called space is that which brings forth name and visible appearance [*nāma-rūpa*]. That within which they are located – that is *brahman*; that is the immortal; that is the self (*ātman*).[31]

Shankara's model teacher has already identified *Ātman* as "space" and has insisted that it is "different from name-and-form" (USG 1.18a), which difference he re-emphasizes in 1.18b. In order to explain the *Chāndogya Upanishad*'s assertion that *Ātman* "brings forth" this same name-and-form, however, the teacher introduces a new theme: *Ātman* as the "evolver" of "unevolved" or "unmanifest" name-and-form. By virtue of its infinite and inscrutable power (*acintya-śakti*), the divine *Ātman* can be spoken of as a conscious, efficient cause of the evolution of the created world, beginning with unmanifest name-and-form as its seed.

[30] The position developed in this chapter has affinities with what Chakravarthi RAM-PRASAD calls Advaita "non-realism," developed in distinction from both 1) a naïve realism which affirms the "irreducible" reality of the phenomenal reality and 2) an idealist or "anti-realist" view which reduces the world entirely to cognition. See his *Advaita Epistemology and Metaphysics: An Outline of Indian Non-Realism* (London and New York: RoutledgeCurzon, 2002), esp. pp. 9-12, 80-92, as well as the discussion in DEUTSCH, *Advaita Vedanta*, pp. 15-26.

[31] Sanskrit text and English translation in OLIVELLE, *Early Upaniṣads*, pp. 286-87.

Yet, this seed does not constitute an independent material cause. Its status is instead defined as indefinable, neither identical with nor absolutely different from the divine self, preserving *Ātman* from either real transformation or real relation with another existent.[32] *Ātman* remains changeless, one only without a second, in whose witnessing presence the whole creation simply unfolds according to its own exceedingly subtle potentiality.

To illustrate this point further, the teacher offers yet another analogy:

> '[Originally] unevolved, this name-and-form took the name-and-form of "ether" in the course of its evolution from this very *Ātman*. And in this manner this element named "ether" arose from the highest *Ātman* as dirty foam from clear water. Foam is neither [identical with] water nor absolutely different from water since it is not seen without water. But water is clear and different from foam which is of the nature of dirt. Likewise, the highest *Ātman* is different from name-and-form which corresponds to foam; *Ātman* is pure, clear, and different in essence from it. This name-and-form, [originally] unevolved, took the name-and-form of "ether," which corresponds to foam, in the course of its evolution. (1.19)

To understand the force of this argument, we should keep in mind that the term translated as "ether" (*ākāśa*) is, in Sanskrit, identical to the "space" (*ākāśa*) identified as *Ātman* in USG 1.18a. Because *Ātman* is subtle and all-pervasive, the invisible "element called *ākāśa*" represents an appropriate metaphor. But *ākāśa* is also the first element to evolve out of name-and-form or, as the text reads here, to arise "from the highest *Ātman,*" at the first moment of creation. "*Ākāśa*" emerges from "*Ākāśa*," what is not-self from that very self.

Does this mean that, following the example of the clay pot, the material world can be viewed as a modification of *Ātman*? The answer is both yes and no, illustrated here by the contrast between pure, transparent water and the "dirty foam" that forms on its surface.[33] There is no foam without water, but there *is* water without foam. By analogy, we can

[32] See MAYEDA, *A Thousand Teachings*, pp. 20-21; Michael COMANS, *The Method of Early Advaita Vedānta: A Study of Gauḍapāda, Śaṅkara, Sureśvara and Padmapāda* (Delhi: Motilal Banarsidass, 2000), pp. 241-46; and L. Thomas O'NEIL, *Māyā in Śaṅkara: Measuring the Immeasurable* (Delhi: Motilal Banarsidass, 1980), pp. 148-53.

[33] On the characterization of foam as dirt, see MAYEDA, *A Thousand Teachigs*, pp. 23-25; and Donald R. TUCK, "Lacuna in Śaṅkara Studies: *A Thousand Teachings (Upadeśasāhasrī)*," *Asian Philosophy* 6/3 (1996): pp. 225-26. MAYEDA's specification of "dirt" as a stand-in for the ignorance (*avidyā*) of USG 2 presses the point further than required; it is sufficient to see this as a rhetorical device to distinguish the nature of *Ātman* from that of the world.

conclude that the indefinable relation between name-and-form and *Ātman* is real from the perspective of empirical reality, but unreal from the perspective of highest truth. It is what one interpreter has called a "non-reciprocal dependence relation."[34]

In this pedagogical context, however, Shankara's purpose is not primarily to unfold an intellectually satisfying view of God and the world. Instead, his model teacher is attempting to answer an urgent question of personal identity. He must situate the student intelligibly, here and now, by showing how the "seed of the world" is also the seed of the hearer's very own empirical self. With this purpose in view, the teacher continues:

> 'Becoming grosser in the course of evolution, the name-and-form becomes air from ether, fire from air, water from fire, earth from water.[35] In this order each preceding [element] entered each succeeding one and the five gross elements, [ether, air, fire, water, and] earth, came into existence. Consequently earth is characterized by the qualities of the five gross elements. And from earth, rice, barley, and other plants consisting of the five elements are produced; from them, when they are eaten, blood and sperm are produced, related respectively to the bodies of women and men. Both blood and sperm, produced by churning with the churning stick of sexual passion driven by nescience and sanctified with sacred formulas,[36] are poured into the womb at the proper time. Through the penetration of fluid from the womb, they become an embryo and it is delivered in the ninth or tenth month. (1.20)

The contemporary hearer of this script might find herself questioning Shankara's understanding of physics and biology. His model teacher offers a vision of the universe as a composite of ether, air, fire, water and earth and portrays conception as a churning of blood and semen in the

[34] Sara GRANT, R.S.C.J., *Toward an Alternative Theology: Confessions of a Non-Dualist Christian: The Teape Lectures, 1989* (Notre Dame: University of Notre Dame Press, 2002), pp. 40-43. Also see the more extensive treatments in Sara GRANT, *Śaṅkarācārya's Concept of Relation* (Delhi: Motilal Banarsidass Publishers, 1998); K.P. ALEAZ, *The Relevance of Relation in Śaṅkara's Advaita Vedānta* (Delhi: Kant Publications, 1996), esp. pp. 80-87; and R.V. DE SMET, "Śaṅkara and Aquinas on Creation," *Indian Philosophical Annual* 6 (1970): pp. 112-18.

[35] The theory enumerated here closely resembles the so-called *pañcīkaraṇa*, the "theory of five elements," which can be derived from the *Taittirīya Upanishad*. Elsewhere, following the *Chāndogya Upanishad*, Shankara will speak of only three elements: fire, water, and food. See MAYEDA, *A Thousand Teachings*, pp. 26-27.

[36] Likely a reference to the "prenatal *saṃskāras*" which are intended to facilitate conception, to ensure a male child and to bring the child to term. See Patrick OLIVELLE, "Rites of Passage: Hindu Rites," in L. JONES (ed.), *Encyclopedia of Religion*, rev. ed., vol. 11 (Detroit: McMillan Reference USA, 2005), p. 7814.

womb. Most natural scientists in the twenty-first century would presumably disagree.

If they did so, however, they would be tacitly acknowledging the realism of the account. Having established the indeterminate status of "unevolved name-and-form" relative to *Ātman*, the teacher now feels free to trace its evolution in highly realistic language. From immaterial ether to the five elements; from these elements to rice, barley and other plants, and, when they are taken as food, to blood and semen; and, finally, from blood and semen to a human embryo, the account betrays no sense that the transformations and differentiations of the physical world are mere illusions. Taken on their own terms, they are palpably and unmistakably real.[37]

The mention of "sacred formulas," moreover, reveals that we are not speaking of a merely physical world, but also a social and ritual one. This is developed further, as follows:

> 'When it is born it obtains its name-and-form, sanctified with sacred formulas by means of a birth ceremony and other [purifying ceremonies]. Again it obtains the name of a student through the performance of the purifying ceremony for initiation. This same body obtains the name of a householder through the performance of the purifying ceremony for union with a wife. This same body obtains the name of an ascetic through the purifying ceremony of becoming a forest-dweller. This same body obtains the name of a wandering ascetic through the purifying ceremony which ends the ritual actions.[38] Thus the body is different from you and is possessed of different caste, family, and purifying ceremonies. (1.21)

[37] For realist approaches to Shankara's thought, see HIRST, *Śaṃkara's Advaita Vedanta*, pp. 94-115; ALEAZ, *Relevance of Relation*, pp. 37-73; Francis X. CLOONEY, S.J., "Śaṃkara's Theological Realism: the Meaning and Usefulness of Gods (*devata*) in the *Uttara Mīmāṃsā Sutra Bhāṣya*," in B. MALKOVSKY (ed.), *New Perspectives on Advaita Vedanta: Essays in Commemoration of Professor Richard De Smet, S.J.* (Leiden, Boston and Köln: Brill, 2000), pp. 30-50; S.L. MALHOTRA, *Social and Political Orientations of Neo-Vedantism: Study of the Social Philosophy of Vivekananda, Aurobindo, Bipin Chandra Pal, Tagore, Gandhi, Vinoba, and Radhakrishnan* (New Delhi: S. Chand and Company, 1970), pp. 31-50; Anantanand RAMBACHAN, *The Advaita Worldview: God, World, Humanity* (Albany: State University of New York Press, 2006), esp. pp. 67-81; and Srinivasa RAO, "Two 'Myths' in Advaita," *Journal of Indian Philosophy* 24 (1996): pp. 265-79. Bradley MALKOVSKY also offers a helpful survey of illusionist and realist strands of Advaita interpretation in his articles "The Personhood of Śaṃkara's *Para Brahman*," *Journal of Religion* 77 (1997): pp. 541-62, and "Advaita Vedānta and Christian Faith," *Journal of Ecumenical Studies* 36 (1999): pp. 397-422.

[38] Each stage of life is marked by a purifying rite (*saṃskāra*). For a fuller description of these rites, see OLIVELLE, "Rites of Passage," pp. 7813-18; FLOOD, *Introduction to Hinduism*, pp. 200-208; and Klaus K. KLOSTERMAIER, *A Survey of Hinduism*, 2d ed. (Albany: State University of New York Press, 1994), pp. 183-92.

Here the teacher continues to trace the cosmic evolution from "name-and-form" in general to *this* "name-and-form": the actual disciple with whom he is talking and whose parentage, ritual life and renunciant status have qualified him for instruction. He tells a life-story that begins with the student's birth and proceeds to the present moment, from one stage of life to another, each marked by a rite of purification. All of these differentiations belong squarely to the world of name-and-form, to the realm of empirical existence and hence, the teacher insists, not to "you" (*tvam*). That is, they do not pertain to the highest *Ātman*, from whose inconceivable power and in whose witnessing presence they have emerged, evolved and coalesced into this embodied individual, standing before the teacher. In a subsequent section, we can also note, the teacher will also clarify that "body" here should not be understood in a reductively physical sense, since it also includes the mind and senses (USG 1.22).

The *ācārya* closes by making one additional point:

> '[The second question you asked me earlier was,] "How am I free from caste, family, and purifying ceremonies?" Listen to what [I am going to say]. The Evolver of name-and-form, by nature different in essence from name-and-form, created this body in the course of evolving name-and-form. And [the Evolver] entered the name-and-form [of the body], Itself being free from the duties of purifying ceremonies. Itself unseen by others, [the Evolver] is seeing; unheard, It is hearing; unthought, It is thinking; unknown, It is knowing.' (1.23a)

In USG 1.16, we recall, the student asked two questions, one about the body itself and another about his own relation to it. In this section, the conversation turns from the first of these questions to the second, making it clear that *Ātman*, available in and through embodied experience, is nevertheless free from association with the body and its ritual duties.

Perhaps most importantly, the teacher concludes his argument by returning to the words of scripture, recalling for the student the citations already given in USG 1.18a. But the import of these isolated statements been dramatically transformed. When the teacher alludes to a *vākya* like *Bṛhadāraṇyaka Upanishad* 3.7.23 – "[The self] sees, but he can't be seen; he hears, but he can't be heard," and so on[39] – he does not merely pronounce an abstract proposition, to be memorized and held by a sheer act of will. Rather, he sums up that disciple's own existential situation, here and now, as the divine cause of the body's emergence and, at one and the same time, irreducibly different from this same body.

[39] Sanskrit text and English translation in OLIVELLE, *Early Upaniṣads*, p. 89.

A Christian Reflection: Christian hearers may most fruitfully approach this script by beginning with what it denies about the divine self, rather than what it affirms. For Shankara systematically excludes any change or evolution in *Ātman*, any material cause apart from that same *Ātman*, and also, finally, any ontological identification of creator with creation, evolver with evolved, the deep sea with the crusty, ephemeral foam at its edge. These same exclusions can be inferred as – alongside the scriptural creation narratives themselves – prime motivating concerns behind the classic Christian doctrine of *creatio ex nihilo*, "creation out of nothing." The unquantifiable *nihil* of the Christian teaching cannot be simply equated with the indefinable seed of unmanifest name-and-form, of course, but both may nevertheless be heard to refute false alternatives of dualism and pantheism without thereby falling silent. In neither case, moreover, should the explanatory force of the teaching be severed from its soteriological intent. That is, both teachings function to disclose hearers' complete dependence and dynamic orientation to our transcendent source, ground and end – essentially and categorically *other*, yet also more intimate to us than the space we inhabit, the air we breathe, the sounds we perceive, and the most sublime thoughts of our embodied intellect. But herein lies the crucial difference: whereas the Christian disciple addresses this source, ground and end as "Thou," the Advaita script insists that we speak primarily, and more radically, of the "I."

The Primacy and Coherence of the Word (USG 1.39-43)

For Shankara, the *Vedas* and the scriptural traditions flowing from it represent the sole, fundamental source of the Advaita teaching. The teacher of USG 1 quotes often from the *Upanishads* and the *Bhagavad-Gītā*, employs images and arguments drawn from them, and negotiates within a teacher-student relation that is also, in significant ways, circumscribed by these scriptural texts. From the treatment above, however, it is also apparent that Shankara's ideal teacher uses the scriptures selectively and creatively. Not every passage qualifies as a relevant *vākya*, and those that challenge the strict unity of *Brahman* and *Ātman* do not appear at all.[40] The passages that do appear in this teaching script, moreover, acquire new meaning and relevance through explanatory devices like the progressive evolution of name-and-form, which connect the declarations of the *vākyas* to the student's self-understanding, here and now.

[40] For a discussion of the hermeneutical rules for selecting those *vākyas* which most clearly establish the true intent of the *Vedas*, see Anantanand RAMBACHAN, "Where Words Can Set Free: The Liberating Potency of Vedic Words in the Hermeneutics of Śaṅkara," in J. TIMM (ed.), *Texts in Context: Traditional Hermeneutics in South Asia* (Albany: State University of New York Press, 1992), pp. 40-42.

This issue of scripture and scriptural interpretation is taken up more explicitly in the final sequence of USG 1. The exchange begins, as we might by now expect, with a question:

> If [the pupil] says: 'If, your Holiness, *Ātman* is "without an inside and without an outside" [BU 4.5.13], "without and within, unborn" [MuU 2.1.2], "entirely a mass of knowledge" [BU 4.5.13], like a mass of salt, devoid of all the varieties of forms, and homogeneous like ether, then how is it that the object, means, and agent of actions are [either actually] experienced or stated in the *Śrutis*? This is well-known in the *Śrutis* and *Smṛtis* and among common people, and is a matter which causes differences of opinion among hundreds of disputants'; (1.39)
> [then] the teacher should reply, 'It is the effect of nescience that the object, means, and agents of actions are [either actually] experienced or stated in the *Śrutis*; but from the standpoint of highest truth *Ātman* is one alone and [only] appears as many through the vision [affected] by nescience just as the moon [appears] as many to sight [affected] by *timira* eye-disease. Duality is the effect of nescience, since it is reasonable [for the *Śrutis*] to condemn the view that [*Ātman*] is different [from *Brahman*] by saying, "Verily, where there seems to be another..." [BU 4.3.31];[41] "For where there is a duality, as it were, there one sees another" [BU 2.4.14]; "Death after death attains he..." [BU 4.4.19];[42] "But where one sees something else, hears something else, understands something else – that is the small... but the small is the same as the mortal" [CU 7.24.1]; "... the modification is a verbal distinction, a name" [CU 6.1.4]; "... He is one and I another..." [BU 1.4.10]. And [the same conclusion is reached] from *Śruti* passages which establish oneness, for example: "one alone, without a second" [CU 6.2.1]; 'Where, verily... one's own...?' [BU 2.4.14]; '... what delusion, what sorrow is there?' [IU 7].'[43] (1.40)

The student has made progress. Thus far in the prose script, he has been asking how the scriptural *vākyas* establishing the unity and sole reality of *Ātman* can be reconciled with phenomenal experience. Here, he reverses this order, asking how phenomenal experience can be reconciled with the firm conviction that arises from these same *vākyas*. That is, presuming

[41] This and the following verse underscore the connection between perception and duality – that is, that the very perception of an apparent "other" presumes ignorance and duality.

[42] The half-verse reads (OLIVELLE, *Early Upaniṣads*, pp. 124-25): "From death to death he goes, who sees here any kind of diversity." Here the perception of duality is connected to continued rebirth.

[43] The allusive quotation from BU 2.4.14 is a continuation of the passage quoted above, also cited as BU 2.4.14. IU 7 reads (OLIVELLE, *Early Upaniṣads*, pp. 406-407): "When in the self of a discerning man, his very self has become all beings,// What bewilderment, what sorrow can there be, regarding that self of him who sees this oneness?"

that what the *Upanishads* teach is true, why then do we encounter duality in the world and, even more importantly, in the scriptural *pramāṇa* itself?

To address this issue, the teacher has recourse to a well-traveled Advaitin and Buddhist distinction between two levels of reality: phenomenal experience (*vyāvaharika*) and highest truth (*pāramārthika*). From the *vyāvaharika* point of view, he explains, there are indeed "objects" or "goals" to be achieved in this world and in heavenly worlds, "means" such as ritual performance and ethical striving to achieve them, and "agents" to undertake such means. But this, as we have heard before, is the product of fundamental ignorance. From the highest point of view, such distinctions no longer apply, as demonstrated by additional *vākyas* from the *Upanishads*.

The analogy the teacher uses to illustrate this idea is highly illusionistic: the apprehension of multiple moons by a person with diseased vision. This image should be held in creative tension with more realist approaches, such as the account of "name-and-form" given earlier. The world is not unreal. It is provisional, susceptible to sublation or, following Eliot Deutsch, "subration." It has not been dissolved, but "disvalued" in the light of highest truth.[44]

In the final sections, Shankara extends such provisional status to the *Vedas* themselves:

> [The pupil may ask:] 'If this be so, Your Holiness, for what purpose is the difference in object, means, etc., of actions as well as origination and dissolution [of the world] stated in the *Śrutis*?' (1.41)
> Then [the teacher] replies: 'A person possessed of nescience, being differentiated by the body, etc., thinks that his *Ātman* is connected with things desirable and undesirable; [and] he does not know how to distinguish the means of attaining things desirable from that of abandoning things undesirable, although he desires to attain things desirable and to abandon things undesirable by some means. The scripture gradually removes his ignorance concerning this matter, but it does not establish the difference in object, means, etc., of actions, since the difference [constitutes] transmigratory existence which is undesirable by nature. Thus [the scripture] uproots nescience which is the view that [*Ātman*] is different [from *Brahman*], the root of transmigratory existence, by showing the reasonableness of the oneness of the origination, dissolution, etc. [of the world].' (1.42)

The student presses his earlier question, pointing out that the scriptures not only prescribe rituals; they also describe the creation of an apparently

[44] See DEUTSCH, *Advaita Vedānta*, pp. 15-16.

real world – as, it should be noted, the teacher himself has also done, a few sections earlier in this chapter. Why?

In reply, the model teacher articulates a theory of accommodation. In order to reach those who are still ignorant, scripture accommodates their desire for means and ends, prescribing rituals and teaching the creation and dissolution of the universe. Yet, in the midst of all of these teachings that presume difference, the scriptures also gradually purify their recipients' minds, wean them of ignorance, and direct them toward the true knowledge fully revealed in the *Upanishads*. The *Vedas* do not "establish" or "sanction" the duality born of ignorance. They are adapted to this ignorance, in order to create those conditions conducive to its removal.

This means that there is a direct parallel between the pedagogical structure of the *Vedas* and the pedagogical method exhibited in the *Upadeśasāhasrī*'s sacred scripts. For the first prose chapter begins solidly in the realm of duality, with a certain kind of student, a certain kind of teacher, and a specific goal to be achieved. By the end of the narrative, all such *vyāvaharika* distinctions have been sublated in the light of highest truth. This local example, we now discover, mirrors the broader pedagogical movement of the *Vedas* and even, we might speculate, of the whole created order. In each case, worldly experience gives way to highest truth. Yet, there is no way to arrive at that truth except through these very same provisional, worldly realities. To pick up the metaphor of USG 1.3, such phenomenal realities may well represent the dark and perilous sea of bondage; but they are also, if employed properly, the boat by which seekers can be carried to the farther shore.

Shankara concludes, as we might by now expect, with the word of scripture, quoting back to the student precisely those *vākyas* with which this line of questioning began:

> 'When nescience has been uprooted by means of the *Śrutis*, *Smṛtis*, and reasoning, the only knowledge of one who sees the highest truth is established right in this [*Ātman*] that is described as follows: "Without an inside and without an outside" [BU 2.5.19]; "Without and within, unborn" [MuU 2.1.2]; like a mass of salt, "Entirely a mass of knowledge" [BU 4.5.13]; and the homogeneous *Ātman* which is all-pervading like ether. It is not reasonable that [in *Ātman*] even a trace of impurity should arise from the difference in object and means of actions, origination and dissolution [of the world], and so forth.' (1.43)

This is not the finale of the *Upadeśasāhasrī*'s first prose chapter: in USG 1.44, Shankara's model *ācārya* will again offer a brief summary of his teaching. Nevertheless, the essential questions have already been posed and answered: Who am I? Why does my body possess distinguishing characteristics like lineage and state of life? How am I different from this body, mind and personality? Why do the scriptures address me as though I am not?

At each step of the inquiry, the teacher makes reference to the words of scripture. Even the question of scripture's internal coherence has been resolved with a hermeneutical key provided by certain of its own statements. The circularity of the argument seems deliberate. As an independent means of knowledge (*pramāṇa*), scripture rests on no authority outside itself. In the hands of the competent teacher, it is completely self-sufficient. But it also points beyond and within itself to something higher. The worldly continuity of teacher, student, Vedic revelation and the tradition as a whole inexorably, question by question, citation by citation, give way to the absolute continuity of *Ātman* the divine self.

III.
"Not a human word, but God's word": A Christian *Saṃvāda* with USG 1

> You remember our labor and toil, brothers and sisters; we worked night and day, so that we might not burden any of you while we proclaimed the gospel of God. You are witnesses, and God also, how pure, upright, and blameless our conduct was toward you believers. As you know, we dealt with each one of you like a father with his children, urging and encouraging you and pleading that you lead a life worthy of God, who calls you into his own kingdom and glory. We also constantly give thanks to God for this, that when you received the word of God that you heard from us, you accepted it not as a human word but as what it really is, God's word, which is also at work in you believers (1 Thessalonians 2:9-13).

In our brief forays into Paul's thought thus far we have been moving backwards chronologically, from the letter to the Romans, written towards the end of his ministry, to the earlier Corinthian correspondence. We continue this movement here, to what is likely Paul's earliest extant letter and also, thereby, the earliest book in the NT.[45] In fact, we are pressing still further back, for in this passage Paul refers the Thessalonian

[45] Raymond F. Collins, "The First Letter to the Thessalonians," in R. Brown, J. Fitzmyer, and R. Murphy (eds.), *The New Jerome Biblical Commentary* (Englewood Cliffs: Prentice Hall, 1990), p. 773 [46:9-11].

believers to that moment when he first proclaimed the gospel to them and they accepted it as God's own word.

In the context of this and Paul's other letters, the term "gospel" (*evangelion*) clearly involves more than just the communication of interesting bits of information about Jesus the Christ. James Dunn speculates that the word itself is a "neologism" developed by Paul, a "new usage" of "old vocabulary" drawn from the Hebrew Scriptures and especially from Isaiah.[46] In Isaiah, the prophet offers encouragement and brings good news of God's intervention and care. Paul transforms these verbal forms into the singular noun, "the gospel," representing not merely the proclamation of good news but also a living force in the ongoing transformation of believers. It is precisely this extraordinary power of the gospel, a power beyond mere words, which becomes one of the major themes of Paul's correspondence with the Thessalonians (see, e.g., 1 Thess 1:5). Addressing a community that seems to have become discouraged by the deaths of some of its members and a painful separation from Paul himself, the apostle offers encouragement by drawing attention to the dynamic word which community members first received from him and which, then as now, works powerfully in their midst.[47]

For Shankara, the authority of the Advaita word of liberation is deeply implicated in key assumptions about *Śruti* as an authorless revelation and, at least in the hands of the right teacher, as the sole *pramāṇa* or means for knowing *Ātman*. For the apostle Paul, according to Dunn, the preaching of the gospel rested on a tripartite foundation.[48] First and foremost, Paul presumes the authority of the Jewish scriptures. In practice the Christian apostle, no less than the Hindu *ācārya*, draws on this revealed source in a highly selective way, placing his strongest emphases

[46] James D.G. DUNN, *The Theology of Paul the Apostle* (Grand Rapids and Cambridge: William B. Eerdmans Publishing Company, 1998), pp. 166-69.

[47] On First Thessalonians as a letter of consolation, see Abraham SMITH, *Comfort One Another: Reconstructing the Rhetoric and Audience of 1 Thessalonians*, Literary Currents in Biblical Interpretation (Louisville: Westminster John Knox Press, 1995), esp. pp. 42-60, as well as the more general discussion in Abraham SMITH, "The First Letter to the Thessalonians," in *The New Interpreter's Bible*, vol. 11 (Nashville: Abingdon Press, 2000), pp. 673-85.

[48] For the rest of this paragraph, I am closely following the account in DUNN, *Theology of Paul*, pp. 169-79. See also the helpful treatments in E.P. SANDERS, *Paul*, Past Masters (Oxford and New York: Oxford University Press, 1991), pp. 21-25 and Morna D. HOOKER, "Beyond the Things That Are Written? Paul's Use of Scripture," in *From Adam to Christ: Essays on Paul* (Cambridge: Cambridge University Press, 1990), pp. 139-54.

upon those key passages – including such *mahā-vākyas* as Genesis 15:6, "[Abram] believed the Lord; and the Lord reckoned it to him as righteousness" – which most clearly acquire new meaning and resonance in the light of Christ. Hence, the various formulae of the early *kerygma* about this same Christ represent a second major source of Paul's teaching, both as they stand on their own and as they shape the interpretation of Torah.

Finally, Paul appeals to his own personal revelation of Jesus, a dramatic disclosure which sparked his mission to the Gentiles and shaped his understanding of Jewish scripture and Christian *kerygma* in distinctive ways. In USG 1, as we have seen, the ideal teacher is characterised as *śrotriya* and *Brahma-niṣṭha*, skilled in scriptural interpretation and steadfast in *Brahman*. For Paul, the ideal teacher might instead be described as *śrotriya* and *Christo-niṣṭha*, skilled in scriptural interpretation and steadfast in the Christ made known through oral tradition and personal encounter. The living word of God depends for its fruitfulness upon the particular persons who communicate it, as well as those who receive it in faith. For this reason, in the passage quoted above, Paul presents himself and his fellow workers as models for imitation.[49] Like a father caring for children, the apostle claims, the first evangelists worked without concern for their own needs, providing an example of selflessness, purity and justice.[50] The believers are, by extension, invited to live according to this same pattern. Elsewhere in the letter, Paul will also commend the Thessalonian community itself for its steadfastness in the face of persecution (see 1 Thess 1:6-10; 2:14-16). The Thessalonians provide, in a sense, models for their own walk, mirroring the pace earlier set for them by the first witnesses.[51]

For Shankara, the personal virtue, disposition and mutual relation of teacher and student also play a constitutive role in the communication and reception of the Vedic *pramāṇa*. The Advaitin teacher delimits these social relations in ways that would be inconceivable and probably quite

[49] This is a common rhetorical strategy throughout Paul's letters. See J. Paul SAMPLEY, *Walking between the Times: Paul's Moral Reasoning* (Minneapolis: Fortress Press, 1991), pp. 88-91.

[50] Some interpreters interpret these passages as Paul's self-defence in the face of opposition, but others note that such autobiographical confessions were often employed in Cynic and Stoic literature to introduce a philosopher's teaching. See the discussion in COLLINS, "First Thessalonians," p. 775, and SMITH, "First Thessalonians," p. 698.

[51] SMITH, *Comfort One Another*, pp. 76-80 and SAMPLEY, *Walking between the Times*, pp. 15-17, 87-88.

offensive to Paul: the qualified disciple, the *adhikārin*, is a male Brahmin renunciant of the *paramahaṃsa* order, not a woman, nor a householder, nor a member of the Śūdra class. Nevertheless, the primary such qualifications are the disciple's intense longing for liberation and a correlative, cultivated detachment from ritual means and ends, temporal achievement and indeed all those names and forms that heretofore defined his individual existence. The *Vedas* actively accommodate hearers' desire for such means and ends, while also weaning them of their attachments and re-orienting them to the self-revealing presence of the divine *Ātman*. If, in the apostle Paul's formula, disciples recognize the word of the teaching as God's own word, this follows in a strictly secondary sense from their social station, humility and selflessness, the purity of their teachers or even the disclosive power of the scriptural word itself; it follows, first and foremost, from the fact that the divine self, who lies at the source of the created order and the scriptures, is also at work in the disciples' own phenomenal existence.

Following the lead of Jacqueline G. Suthren Hirst and L. Thomas O'Neil, we can take this insight a further step. For the evidence of USG 1 suggests that a full Advaita theology of revelation may only be conceptually distinct from an Advaita theology of creation, unfolded by the teacher as the manifestation of name-and-form.[52] At one level, it is true, the created world is a product of ignorance and destined to be sublated. It is mere dirty foam on the surface of the pure, clean ocean of *Ātman*. At another level, however, the images employed by the teacher and the *Veda* are drawn from this same created world. *Ātman* has, by inconceivable power, manifested name-and-form in such a way that it can disclose its ultimate source and end. Shankara does not therefore merely introduce cosmology for a pedagogical purpose. He introduces a *pedagogical cosmology*, in which the created universe strains toward transcendence and becomes the privileged means of its own sublation. By inscribing the disciple – corporeally, socially and ritually – within the progressive unfolding of name-and-form, the model *ācārya* also alerts him to a process of self-disclosure already at work therein. The disclosure of the *Upanishads*, though indispensable for authentic self-knowledge, in fact accommodates, presumes and makes apparent the prior self-disclosure and liberating pedagogy of the created order itself.

[52] See SUTHREN HIRST, *Śaṃkara's Advaita Vedanta*, pp. 97-99, and O'NEIL, *Māyā in Śaṅkara*, esp. pp. 154-86.

If this interpretation of the Advaita scripts rings true, then we may need to reach beyond the apostle Paul to engage it more fully. This we do by once again turning our attention to a later work that both builds upon and significantly re-interprets Paul's vision of teaching and revelation: the educational treatise *Teaching Christianity* (*De doctrina Christiana;* hereafter DDC) by the fourth- and fifth-century North African bishop Augustine of Hippo.[53] In a number of his early works, Augustine reflected on Christian pedagogy by means of teaching scripts not unlike USG 1 in form; notably, these include a scripted dialogue with his son Adeodatus in *The Teacher* (*De magistro*) and two scripted catechetical addresses in *Instructing Beginners in the Faith* (*De catechizandus rudibus*).[54] But it is in *Teaching Christianity* where we find his most systematic exposition of what we might now term an *upadeśa-vidhi* or "method of instruction" (USG 1.1) for teaching the Christian scriptures, including basic principles and the rule of faith (book I), tools for biblical interpretation (books II-III) and rhetorical strategies for its effective communication (book IV). As in the previous chapter, we confine our attention to a relatively short sequence of ideas, this time taken from the beginning of Augustine's treatise.

We have already noted that, for both Paul and Shankara, the fruitfulness of the teaching depends upon its source in the revealed scriptures; yet, again for both, this revelation emerges in its fullness only through the proper social medium. Arguing along similar lines, Augustine begins *Teaching Christianity* with an apology and defense of the need for human beings to communicate the word of God, pointing out that Christians who believe they can understand the scriptures without instruction would do well to remember that they learned even their native language from others (Prol.4-5). Such persons can also call to mind the biblical

[53] In what follows, I have used the English translation in Saint AUGUSTINE, *Teaching Christianity: De Doctrina Christiana*, E. HILL, O.P (trans.), J. ROTELLE, O.S.A. (ed.), The Works of Saint Augustine: A Translation for the 21st Century I/11 (Hyde Park: New City Press, 1996).

[54] On the former, which is also important as Augustine's earliest articulation of the theory of signs, see AUGUSTINE OF HIPPO, "The Teacher," in J. BURLEIGH (ed.), *Augustine: Earlier Writings*, Library of Christian Classics (Philadelphia: Westminster Press, 1953), pp. 64-101; and the excellent analysis in R.A. Markus, "St. Augustine on Signs," in R. MARKUS (ed.), *Augustine: A Collection of Critical Essays* (Garden City: Doubleday and Co., 1972), pp. 61-91. On the latter, see AUGUSTINE OF HIPPO, *Instructing Beginners in the Faith*, R. CANNING (trans.), B. RAMSEY (ed.), The Augustine Series 5 (Hyde Park: New City Press, 2006), as well as the discussion in William HARMLESS, *Augustine and the Catechumenate* (Collegeville: Liturgical Press, 1995), pp. 107-55.

examples of the centurion Cornelius and the apostle Paul himself, both of whom, even after they received direct revelations from God, sought out human instruction: "And it could all, of course, have been done by the angel; but then no respect would have been shown to our human status, if God appeared to be unwilling to have his word administered to us by other human beings" (Prol.6). At the outset of this work, then, Augustine places the word of God into the hands of human teachers, while also inscribing these teachers and their students into a biblical frame. And, in so doing, he also mirrors an important dynamic we have seen at work in the early sections of USG 1.

This point of resonance gains depth and difficulty as we read further in *Teaching Christianity*, where Augustine goes beyond the mere fact of human mediation to the inner purification required by teachers and students to render it fully effective. He writes:

> ... since we are meant to enjoy that truth which is unchangeably alive, and since it is in its light that God the Trinity, author and maker of the universe, provides for all the things he has made, our minds have to be purified, to enable them to perceive that light, and to cling to it once perceived. We should think of this purification process as a kind of walk, a kind of voyage toward our home country. We do not draw near, after all, by movement in place to the one who is present everywhere, but by honest commitment and good behaviour (DCR 1.10.10).

Augustine's argument in this passage depends upon a distinction made elsewhere in the work, between God who alone is to be "enjoyed" (*frui*) and everything else, which should instead be "used" (*uti*) with reference to God (e.g. DDC 1.3.3 – 7.7; 1.22.20-21; 1.31.34 – 34.38). Since God is the sole proper object of human enjoyment, all our strivings and relations with others gain relevance only in our shared journey, a "kind of voyage" toward this God's infinite and unchangeable light. Turning the distinction around, we might also add that such created realities *should* be used on the journey to God precisely because they *can* be so used; for creation has been providentially arranged to bear those who qualify themselves, by "honest commitment and good behaviour," to a home country from which, at the most fundamental level, they have not and cannot ever be separated.

Shankara, of course, also evokes the imagery of travel to illustrate the Advaita teaching. Both he, in such texts as USP 17.52,[55] and his model

[55] See above, ch. 1, pp. 19-20.

ācārya, in the present prose chapter, introduce the trope of the boat of knowledge, by which one crosses the river of ignorance to the farther shore of liberation. In the immediate context of USG 1.3, this boat serves as a symbol of *vidyā-santati*, the "continuity" or "spreading out" of self-knowledge in this teaching moment and in the broader tradition constituted by such moments, from one generation to the next. Reading more broadly across the script of USG 1, we might now trace this *vidyā-santati* still further back, behind the teaching tradition to the *Vedas* and behind the *Vedas* to the *acintya-śakti* or inscrutable power of *Ātman*. If the seed of the world is, as I have suggested, also the seed of its own sublation, then the *Ātman* who is the evolver of embodied existence (1.18) is also by implication the evolver of the Upanishadic *vākyas* and of the teacher and tradition that render them effective as a means of liberating knowledge. Following this line of interpretation, the *vidyā-santati* of USG 1 emerges as a privileged social mediation of this broader providential design, of liberating knowledge and indeed of *Ātman* the divine self.

We can read further in Augustine's *Teaching Christianity* to uncover another significant parallel to Shankara's boat of knowledge. For Augustine does not merely speak of travel in a general sense; he also describes Jesus the Christ as *Christus via*, the Wisdom of God who becomes both an example of purity for humankind and, through the incarnation, the road or way on which we can make our arduous journey to our home country in God (DCR 1.11.11; 1.17.16).[56] "So since [Wisdom] herself is our home, she also made herself for us into the way home" (1.11.11). By extension, Augustine goes on to explain, this *Christus via* also includes Christ's body, the church, and indeed the whole of God's saving action in history (1.15.14 – 18.17). The church does not stand apart from the rest of creation and the providential ordering of this creation toward God; yet, as the privileged medium of God's Wisdom – our home country, who took flesh, entered into empirical life and thereby also became our way to himself and to his Father – it possesses a special status and function, comparable to the *vidyā-santati* of USG 1.3.

Such a correlation, once established, carries the potential to re-affirm, to clarify and to de-familiarize Christian teachings about revelation and

[56] For further accounts of the *Christus via* theme in Augustine's writings, see Leo C. FERRARI, "'Christus Via' in Augustine's *Confessions*," *Augustinian Studies* 7 (1976): pp. 47-58, and especially Robert J. O'CONNELL, *Soundings in Augustine's Imagination* (New York: Fordham University Press, 1994), pp. 69-94.

its social mediation in the church. At a first level, in and out of our hearing of this Advaita text, we may be reminded that such mediation refers not primarily to grand metaphors or ecclesiastical structures, but to local situations – such as those modeled in USG 1, alluded to in Paul's first letter to the Thessalonians, and commended in the prologue to Augustine's *Teaching Christianity* – when the word is communicated, received and recognized as what it truly is: the word of God. From one point of view, the church as the bearer and embodiment of divine revelation represents a cumulative, social and soteriological reality constituted entirely by such moments of disclosure and reception, across the generations.[57] "Every day," taught the Venerable Bede, "the Church gives birth to the Church."[58] So also, *ipso facto*, for the *vidyā-santati* of teacher, student and ongoing tradition which mediates and concretely embodies the word of the *Upanishads* wherever and whenever it is properly enacted.

At a second level, the correlation between church and *vidyā-santati* as social mediations of divine revelation also serves to remind the Christian hearer of the radically provisional character of both institutions and indeed of creation itself. According to Shankara, for all his realism at one level of instruction, the revelation of the *Śruti* and the cosmic pedagogy aim for nothing other than their own complete sublation in light of highest truth. The spreading out or diffusion of the tradition does not culminate in any final vindication or glorious transfiguration at the end of time; it culminates only in the end of all such distinctions of name-and-form, beginning with the word of the teacher, extending to the *Vedas* and reaching back to their unmanifest and indefinable seed. The world has no positive value in itself; it gains such value only as a means to self-knowledge and the absolute, divine freedom of *Ātman*.[59]

But this radical vision, too, is not entirely without parallel in Augustine and the broader Christian tradition. We can gain at least some insight on this matter by again juxtaposing core texts, so as to read – or, better, to hear – them together:

[57] See Joseph KOMONCHAK, "The Epistemology of Reception," *The Jurist* 57 (1997): pp. 180-203; and Joseph A. KOMONCHAK, *Foundations in Ecclesiology*, Supplementary Issue of the *Lonergan Workshop* Journal 11 (Chestnut Hill, MA: Boston College, 1995).

[58] Cited in KOMONCHAK, "Epistemology of Reception," p. 193.

[59] Lance E. NELSON argues this point forcefully in "The Dualism of Nondualism: Advaita Vedānta and the Irrelevance of Nature," in L. NELSON (ed.), *Purifying the Earthly Body of God: Religion and Ecology in Hindu India*, SUNY Studies in Religious Studies (Albany: State University of New York Press, 1998), pp. 72-73, 75-78.

'When nescience has been uprooted by means of the *Śrutis*, *Smṛtis*, and reasoning, the only knowledge of one who sees the highest truth is established right in this [*Ātman*] that is described as follows: "Without an inside and without an outside" [BU 2.5.19]; "Without and within, unborn" [MuU 2.1.2]; like a mass of salt, "entirely a mass of knowledge" [BU 4.5.13]; and the homogeneous *Ātman* which is all-pervading like ether. It is not reasonable that [in *Ātman*] even a trace of impurity should arise from the difference in object and means of actions, origination and dissolution [of the world], and so forth' (USG 1.43)

That is, after all, what the Lord meant by saying, *I am the way, and the truth and the life* (Jn 14:6)... From this it can be readily understood how nothing must be allowed to hold us back on the way, when even the Lord himself, insofar as he was prepared to be the way for us, did not wish us to hold onto him, but to pass along him. He did not wish us to cling feebly to any temporal things, even those he took to himself and carried for our salvation, but rather to run eagerly along and through them, and so deserve to be swiftly and finally conveyed to him himself, where he has deposited our nature, freed from all temporal conditions, at the right hand of the Father (DCR 1.34.38).

Both of these passages address the desired ends of their respective pedagogies and, indeed, of life itself. Both cite scripture, but both also go beyond scripture and beyond all conditions of phenomenal existence itself. For Augustine no less than for Shankara, all such temporal realities – including the church and even, at some level, the incarnation of Christ himself – have a strictly provisional character, falling away when the traveler has reached her final destination.

Whither this destination? The Father, one in being with Son and Spirit? *Ātman*, one only without a second? Differences certainly remain. Most pressingly, just as from the Christian point of view it is difficult to conceive of a revelation without a personal Revealer,[60] so also it is difficult if not impossible for the Christian hearer of USG 1 to accept a providential order of self-disclosure without a personal Author to set it in motion and bring it to its final end. But, to adopt Shankara's language, such differences operate within and pertain only to the world of name-and-form. They are not identical with the saving truth they disclose, even if the only way to this truth is through them. Through their mutual relation, Shankara's teacher and student enact a profound tension that cuts across the tradition, the Vedic revelation and the whole created order. The teacher of USG 1 does not so much explain this

[60] See MURTY, *Revelation and Reason*, pp. 241-46.

tension away as intensify it, pushing the student toward that higher plane inculcated by tradition, revelation and creation alike. The point is not to hold on to such realities, but to put them to their proper use. On this point, Augustine – for his own distinctively Christian (and Neo-Platonic) reasons – concurs.

There is much that has escaped our attention in this brief experiment in dialogue, not least what might be considered Augustine's own version of a *mahā-vākya*: the twofold love of God and neighbor (DCR 1.35.39 – 40.42). Such love will claim our primary attention in the next chapter. For the time being, Christian hearers of this Advaita sacred script can be reminded of the indispensable place of both scripture and the church in the mediation of divine revelation, while also finding ourselves sharply challenged to relativize our attachments to these dispensations on the way toward God's own, immediate self-disclosure. Revelation functions within and depends upon the created order, but – at least, when viewed though the lens of the scriptures – this created order also exists for no purpose other than revelation. It possesses value only outside itself, in the disclosure of its transcendent source, ground and end.[61]

For the Christian hearer, revelation and creation come together uniquely in the *Christus via*, the incarnate Christ, who carries hearers by means of his own flesh and his own body, the church, to the one revealer and creator of all. If such a Christian hearer comes to perceive this more clearly in and out of a hearing of USG 1, however, then this teaching script may itself come to be appreciated as yet another providential expression of that same *Christus via*, albeit under a quite different name-and-form. Neither name-and-form is completely resolvable in terms of the other; yet both, when read together, press us beyond any and all such resolutions to the higher kingdom and glory of God the divine self, to whom alone we have been called and to whom alone we look for our final liberation. We respond to this call, as Paul insists, not directly through these names and forms, but through our firm recognition of God's word in them, and even in ourselves.

[61] On this issue, see especially Rowan D. WILLIAMS, "'Good For Nothing'? Augustine on Creation," *Augustinian Studies* 25 (1994): pp. 9-24.

Chapter 5

HEARERS OF THE WORD: COMMENTARY ON USP 18

I.

Upadeśasāhasrī Padyabandha 18.29-30, 110

In the [bearer of the 'I'-notion] there is the reflection, and words referring to the former could indicate the internal Seeing indirectly, [but] never designate It directly.

[This is] because that which is not a member of any genus and so on cannot be indicated by words. As the bearer of the 'I'-notion has the reflection of *Ātman*, it is the intellect that is referred to by the words for *Ātman*.

This is the way of realization that '[I] am the Existent.' And [if] it were not so, it would not be [realized]. If there were no medium, the teaching 'Thou art That' (CU 6.8.7ff) would moreover be meaningless.

II.

"*Tat-tvam-asi*": Hearing USP 18 (Selections)

Like USP 1, the *Upadeśasāhasrī*'s eighteenth verse chapter begins and ends with reverent salutations. Such opening and closing salutations provide indirect evidence that this chapter, along with other parts of the treatise, may once have existed as an independent work. They also, as we might expect, foreshadow major themes to be developed in the chapter's teaching scripts:

> Salutation to that *Ātman*, the Constant Awareness, *Ātman* of the notions of the intellect, through which the modifications [of the intellect] disappear and arise (USP 18.1).
> Salutation to an Indra among ascetics,[1] teacher of the teacher, a person of great intellect, who defeated hundreds of enemies of the *Śrutis* by means

[1] Here the asceticism of the teacher is exalted by comparison to Indra, one of the most important of the Vedic gods. Just as Indra stands out among the gods, so also this teacher stood out among renunciants (*yati*).

> of sword-like words supported by thunderbolt-like reasoning[2] and protected the treasure of the meaning of the *Vedas* (18.2).

Reading backwards, we can see in these verses, first, a strong affirmation of the importance of the Vedic revelation, whose invaluable teachings merit protection from their many enemies (v. 2). In accord with our treatment in the previous chapter, this word of scripture is joined very closely to the teaching tradition, glorifying both the teaching itself and the teaching lineage by means of the somewhat ambiguous phrase "teacher of my teacher."[3] Shankara also, more centrally, offers reverent salutations to *Ātman* the divine self (v. 1). He qualifies this *Ātman* in a distinctive way, as that "Constant Awareness" within which various "modifications" and "notions of the intellect" reside, disappear and arise again.

The precise relation between this pure "awareness" (*avagati*), which is eternal, and those passing notions or convictions (*pratyaya*) which constitute ordinary experience is not entirely obvious. Since we become aware of our consciousness only through our consciousness of particular internal and external objects, is it really possible to distinguish so clearly between the two? And, perhaps more importantly, how can "scripture and the teacher" reveal the eternal awareness of *Ātman* by means of words – which, after all, invariably presume and refer to determinate notions or convictions of the intellect? The seriousness with which Shankara takes these kinds of questions is amply revealed by the length of the chapter he devotes to them. The renowned eighteenth verse chapter of the *Upadeśasāhasrī*, traditionally entitled "*tat-tvam-asi*," runs some

[2] Thunderbolts were among the preferred weapons of Indra, thus extending the metaphor.

[3] See ĀNANDAGIRI's comment in S. SUBRAHMANYA SASTRI (ed.), *Shri Shankarabhagavatpada's Upadeshasahasri with the Tika of Shri Anandagiri Acharya*, Advaita Grantha Ratna Manjushi Ratna 15 (Varanasi: Mahesh Research Institute, 1978), p. 76 (line 13), as well as Swami PARAMARTHANANDA Saraswati, *UPADEŚA SĀHASRĪ*, audio cassettes, Vedānta Vidyārthi Sangha, n.d., cassette #18-1. This verse is sometimes interpreted as a reference to Gauḍapāda, whom Advaita tradition identifies as the teacher of Shankara's own teacher Govinda. The commentators do not identify Gauḍapāda by name, although RĀMATĪRTHA does treat the phrase *guroḥ garīyasa*, literally "greater than the teacher," as a synonym for *parama-guru*, "the highest teacher," a traditional epithet of Gauḍapāda. See the full comment in D. GOKHALE (ed.), *Shri Shankarāchārya's Upadeśasāhasrī with the Gloss Padayôjanīkā by Shrī Rāmatīrtha* (Bombay: Gujurati Printing Press, 1917), p. 323. One need not choose between these options: the identification of Shankara with the teaching tradition is strengthened rather than weakened by naming those teachers from whom he received the liberating truth.

230 verses long in Mayeda's critical edition,[4] nearly three times the size of the next longest verse chapter (USP 17) and comprising over a third of the verse portion as a whole.

As the traditional title indicates, this teaching script defends the revelatory power of the great saying, "Thou art that," of the *Chāndogya Upanishad.* In the course of this argument, Shankara also develops a series of propositions about the nature of divine presence in and as the hearer of these same words. By virtue of the reflection of *Ātman* in each conscious being and across every human experience, he argues, the Upanishadic *vākya* can reveal this *Ātman* in an efficacious way. Without it, even the revealed word will necessarily fall far short of its liberating aim. It will thus become possible, in and out of our hearing of USP 18, to speak of the intimate co-presence and likeness of the divine self in the finite intellect, a likeness that Shankara will call the door or medium (*dvāra*) for the great saying and the liberation it confers.

> **An Initial Reflection:** When we speak of the "likeness" and "reflection" of *Ātman* in the embodied intellect, even briefly, we open the possibility of hearing an echo of Jewish and Christian doctrines about the image and likeness of God in humankind – and rightly so. In hearing such an echo, it is important to remember that the precise character of this divine image has been specified variously throughout Christian history: as pure rationality, natural incorruptibility, conscience, our capacity for relationship, and so on.[5] Most importantly for Christian hearers, teachings about the image of God cannot be treated entirely apart from teachings about Jesus the Christ, in whom this image is renewed and brought to its perfection. So, as we hear the scripts of USP 18, we will listen not merely for their teachings about divine likeness in the abstract, but also for the ways that these teachings may be heard to reflect, to contrast and to clarify that particular divine likeness disclosed in Christ.

A Question of Experience (USP 18.3-4, 9-10)

In verse 2, Shankara has already alluded to the existence of some persons or traditions that can be considered enemies of the sacred scriptures. In many places throughout the *Upadeśasāhasrī* and Shankara's commentaries, the

[4] Traditional recensions of the text – such as those that form the basis of the commentaries of ĀNANDAGIRI, RĀMATĪRTHA and PARAMARTHANANDA and those adopted by the translators ALSTON and JAGADĀNANDA – include 233 verses. In this commentary, I follow MAYEDA's numbering, but I have also given, in brackets, variant verse numbers from Swāmi JAGADĀNANDA (trans.), *A Thousand Teachings in Two Parts – Prose and Poetry – of Srī Sankarāchārya* (Madras: Sri Ramakrishna Math, [1941]).

[5] See, for example, Jack MAHONEY, S.J., "Evolution, Altruism, and the Image of God," *Theological Studies* 71 (2010): esp. 678-83.

voices of such purported enemies appear in the text as one or another *pūrva-pakṣin* – literally, the "prior" (*pūrva*) advocate of a particular "wing" or viewpoint (*pakṣa*) to be clarified or refuted in the course of the discussion. We have already encountered one major *pūrva-pakṣin* in our commentary on USP 1, above, and we will meet several others in USP 16, below. The principal adversary depicted in the present chapter stands out for special notice, however, due in no small part to its very close proximity to Shankara's own teaching. As we shall see, there are some grounds to hypothesize that the primary *pūrva-pakṣa* view of USP 18 may find its source in the Advaita of Shankara's approximate contemporary and rival, Maṇḍana Miśra.[6] More cautiously, the position can be referred to as the "*prasaṃkhyāna-vāda*," because it advocates a form of meditative practice called *prasaṃcakṣā* in USP 18.9 and *prasaṃkhyāna* in USP 18.12 and 18.17.

Why is this so challenging? How could advocating one or another form of meditation pose a threat to the teaching? Anticipating such questions, Shankara advances a fundamental thesis:

> If the understanding, 'I am ever-free, the existent,' could not arise, for what purpose does the *Śruti* teach thus zealously like a [devoted] mother? (USP 18.3). From this [self-]established [*Ātman* which is indicated by the word] 'I' the attribute 'you' is excluded – just as the notion of a serpent [is excluded] in application to a rope – by means of reasoning and such teachings as 'Thou art That' [CU 6.13.3] and so forth (18.4).

From the start, Shankara identifies the core issue of contention in this chapter as the sufficiency of the Upanishadic word to reveal and directly to communicate self-knowledge.

Vedanta, like most classical Indian traditions, inherited from the Nyāya tradition of logical analysis a strong interest in differentiating the various means of acquiring valid knowledge (*pramāṇas*), such as perception, inference, and verbal testimony.[7] The *Pūrva-Mīmāṃsā* tradition of ritual exegesis gave special emphasis and precision to the understanding

[6] See Michael COMANS, "Śaṅkara and the Prasaṅkhyānavāda," *Journal of Indian Philosophy* 24 (1996), pp. 50-55; Jacqueline SUTHREN HIRST, "Weaving the Strands: Cognition, Authority and Language in Śaṅkara's *Upadeśasāhasrī*," in S. RAO and G. MISHRA (eds), *Paramparā: Essays in Honour of R. Balasubramanian* (New Delhi: Indian Council of Philosophical Research, 2003), pp. 143-44; and Sengaku MAYEDA, trans., *A Thousand Teachings: The Upadeśasāhasrī of Śaṅkara* (Albany: State University of New York Press, 1992), p. 196n13.

[7] See Richard KING, *Indian Philosophy: An Introduction to Hindu and Buddhist Thought* (Edinburgh: Edinburgh University Press, 1999), pp. 128-37; Surendranath DASGUPTA, *A History of Indian Philosophy*, vol. 1 (Cambridge: Cambridge University Press, 1957), pp. 332-55; and the extended treatment in D.M. DATTA, *The Six Ways of Knowing: A Critical Study of the Vedānta Theory of Knowledge* (Calcutta: University of Calcutta, 1960).

of the scriptural revelation as the last of these: a *śabda-pramāṇa*, a verbal means of knowledge, in which truth is disclosed immediately, by the correct understanding of words.[8] Viewed against this background, it is not surprising that these initial verses of USP 18 focus our attention on the scriptures by personifying them as a caring mother, who would never proclaim the identity of self and *Brahman* so persistently if such words were incapable of bearing its intended fruit (v. 3). In addition, they clarify the fact that, in proclaiming this message, scripture and teacher alike add nothing new to the hearer, the "I." They merely negate all false associations of this self-established and self-evident "I" with those myriad characteristics objectifiable as "you."

Shankara introduces one of his favorite metaphors to illustrate the point: the rope and the snake.[9] When a piece of rope has been mistakenly identified as a snake, one need not – and, in fact, cannot – address the situation by killing the offending reptile. Since there never really was a snake there in the first place, only the erroneous identification needs to be removed, and this requires merely the proper words of correction: "It is a rope, not a snake." Similarly, since *Ātman* is not now nor ever was truly subject to bondage, the proper hearing of the scriptural word, the *śabda-pramāṇa*, also has the power to effect final liberation, here and now.

A bit further along, the *prasaṃkhyāna-vādin* speaks up to contest this claim:

> [Objection:] 'Even when one is told, "You are indeed the Existent," one does not attain immovable final release of *Ātman*. Therefore, one should take up *prasaṃcakṣā* meditation as well as reasoning (18.9).
> 'Even one who understands the meaning of the sentence does not grasp it from a single utterance. Therefore he needs further things; they are two, [*prasaṃcakṣā* meditation and reasoning], as we have said [above]' (18.10).

To illustrate the *pūrva-pakṣin*'s position, I have selected just two verses from a longer exposition (vv. 9-18). Even stated so briefly, the substance of this objection is fairly straightforward: the opponent asserts that mere hearing of the scriptural words does not, as a rule, immediately produce liberation for most hearers. Something more must be required.

[8] See DASGUPTA, *History*, vol. 1, pp. 394-97.

[9] For further accounts of this trope, see J.G. SUTHREN HIRST, *Śaṃkara's Advaita Vedānta: A Way of Teaching*, RoutledgeCurzon Hindu Studies Series (London and New York: RoutledgeCurzon, 2005), pp. 105-9; and Arvind SHARMA, *The Rope and the Snake: A Metaphorical Exploration of Advaita Vedānta* (New Delhi: Manohar, 1997).

In v. 9, the additional disciplines are specified as "reasoning" and a form of repetition alternately called *prasaṃcakṣā* here and *prasaṃkhyāna* elsewhere. Though Shankara does not clearly define these practices, we can gain some insight from a comparable *pūrva-pakṣin* refuted by his disciple Sureśvara. For, in Sureśvara's *Naiṣkarmya-siddhi*, one of the primary opposing views is characterized as follows:

> Meditation (prasaṅkhyāna) consists in the repeated application of the mind to the ideas evolved by reasoning through agreement and difference on the meaning of 'that thou art' and other holy sentences. When properly performed it generates perfect knowledge... and does so by improving such knowledge as already exists, and not through merely improving the mind's powers of concentration.[10]

If we import these definitions of reasoning and *prasaṃkhyāna* meditation from Sureśvara's work into our reading of USP 18, we find ourselves in a bit of a quandary: for the recommended practices appear to be nearly identical to those promoted in the *Upadeśasāhasrī* itself. As we shall see, Shankara devotes a number of verses of USP 18 to a specific method of reasoning by "agreement and difference," and in USG 2-3 he will prescribe an extended process of reflection and repetition to facilitate its thorough assimilation on the part of the disciple. How, then, does the *prasaṃkhyāna-vāda* represent an "opposing view"?

Unless we have recourse to one or another developmental schema,[11] we may be forced to locate the key difference in the conflicting understandings that lie behind these practices of reasoning and meditation, rather than in the practices themselves. Sureśvara says as much when he specifies that, according to the opponent, the disciplines of reasoning and *prasaṃkhyāna* perfect liberating knowledge "by *improving such knowledge as already exists*, and not through merely improving the mind's powers of concentration."[12] How can self-knowledge be "improved"? Earlier in the *Naiṣkarmya-siddhi*, when he first introduces several adversarial views, Sureśvara offers one possible explanation:

[10] NS 3.89, in A.J. ALSTON (trans.), *The Realization of the Absolute: The 'Naiṣkarmya Siddhi' of Śrī Sureśvara* (London: Shanti Sadan, 1959, 1971), p. 211.

[11] See Tilmann VETTER, *Studien zur Lehre und Entwicklung Śaṅkaras* (Wien: Institut für Indologie der Universität Wien, 1979), pp. 17-19, 89-91, 93-94. We will return to this issue in the next chapter.

[12] In Sanskrit: *pramiti-vardhanayā paripūrṇāṃ pramitiṃ janayati na punar aikāgrya-vardhanayeti*, following the text and translation in ALSTON, *Realization of the Absolute*, p. 211 (emphasis added).

> And another school maintains that the knowledge, 'I am the Absolute' generated by the Upanishadic texts is relational and hence does not penetrate to the real nature of the Self. But they say that in the case of one who meditates on the meaning conveyed by the sentences as continuously as the Ganges flows, another cognition arises which is (not relational because it is) not the meaning of any sentence. It is the latter knowledge alone which eradicates all the darkness of nescience.[13]

Tracing the thread of argument one step further back, we can observe that, in raising these objections, Sureśvara may have the teachings of Maṇḍana Miśra in mind.[14] For Maṇḍana Miśra develops a number of similar arguments about qualitatively distinct forms of self-knowledge in his Advaita treatise *Brahma-siddhi*. In one place, for example, he contrasts the "indirect" nature of verbal knowledge against direct perception of the world; hence, to achieve actual liberation, the verbal knowledge of the self must be verified directly, by means of a continuous meditative practice called *prasaṃkhyāna* or *prasaṃcaksā*.[15]

It matters little whether Shankara specifically intends Maṇḍana Miśra when he articulates the *pūrva-pakṣa* view of USP 18.9-18. What does matter is that this *pūrva-pakṣin* appears to be suggesting that the "indirect" or "relational" knowledge provided by the scriptures must give way to a direct, experiential knowledge acquired through continuous meditation. This is, in any case, the view that Shankara sets out to demolish across the pages of the *Upadeśasāhasrī*'s massive eighteenth verse chapter.

Negatively, his argument in this chapter largely replicates his refutation of the "combination of knowledge and action" position introduced in USP 1.8-11a, also associated with Maṇḍana Miśra and treated in chapter 2 of this commentary: since meditation no less than Vedic ritualism represents yet another finite action that presumes agency, ego and the pursuit of means and ends, it remains solidly in the realm of *karma*, incompatible with liberating *jñāna*.[16] The harder task for Shankara is to

[13] *NS* 1.66, in ALSTON, *Realization of the Absolute,* pp. 45-46.

[14] See Ibid, p. 47n4, and the discussion in Allen Wright THRASHER, "The Dates of Maṇḍana Miśra and Śaṃkara," *Wiener Zeitschrift für die Kunde Südasiens und Archiv für indische Philosophie* 23 (1979): pp. 131-37.

[15] *Brahma-siddhi* III.34, as translated in COMANS, "Śaṅkara and the Prasaṅkhyānavāda," p. 52. An alternate summary/translation of this text by Allen W. THRASHER is available in K. POTTER (ed.), *Encyclopedia of Indian Philosophies: Advaita Vedānta up to Śaṅkara and His Pupils* (Princeton: Princeton University Press, 1981), p. 409.

[16] E.g., USP 18.19-25, 196-97 [199-200], 208-11 [211-14], as well as the discussion in Jonathan BADER, *Meditation in Śaṅkara's Vedānta* (New Delhi: Aditya Prkashan, 1990), esp. pp. 52-64, 75-78.

argue the positive side of this negative judgment on action. How *can* the scriptural words effect liberation, directly, without the need of subsequent disciplines or experiential verification? Shankara builds this more positive case at great length and in no readily apparent order.[17] For convenience, we confine our attention to two recurrent themes, each developed in pieces across the whole chapter.

> **A Christian Reflection:** Christian hearers, encountering the views of the *prasaṃkhyāna-vādin* for the first time, may recall that Christians have also often been tempted to identify faith in Christ with particular kinds of experiential states. Amongst the earliest generations and even today, charismatic inspiration and *glossolalia* often been highly valued – sometimes, we shall hear Paul insist below, too highly valued. During the Great Awakening, prominent evangelists placed great importance on the authentication of conversion experiences, and not a few modern and contemporary theologians have drawn special attention to mystical experience or ecstatic states. Christian hearers who take the scripts of USP 18 fully to heart may find themselves asking whether Shankara's critique of the *prasaṃkhyāna-vādin* might also function as a critique of precisely these views, at least insofar as they seek to verify divine presence, grace and salvation in one or another specific kind of experience. Such hearers are called by Shankara and by his teaching scripts to place their hope not in any particular experiential state – which by nature come and go – but solely in the God revealed by the scriptures, who perdures and transcends all experiences whatsoever.

Agreement and Difference (USP 18.96, 169-71, 188-90)

As we have already noted, and as the traditional title reveals, the major topic of USP 18 is the great saying "*tat-tvam-asi*," "That thou art." Like the negation "Not thus! Not so!", the importance of this great saying follows only in part from the profundity of its message. It is also uttered repeatedly in its original scriptural context, and such repetition, for Shankara and other traditional Vedanta interpreters, lends special gravity to its correct interpretation.[18]

[17] SUTHREN HIRST ("Weaving the Strands," pp. 148-55) argues that the apparent disorder of the text actually reflects the repetitive, cumulative and recursive method by which knowledge arises in the mind of the pupil. Though I find this suggestion persuasive, for convenience I have adopted the more common interpretative strategy of isolating selected themes for special attention.

[18] Repetition (*Abhyāsa*) is one of six criteria for determining the true meaning of the *Veda* in Vedanta exegesis. See PARAMARTHANANDA, *UPADEŚA SĀHASRĪ*, cassette #18-49, and Anantanand RAMBACHAN, "Where Words Can Set Free: The Liberating Potency of Vedic Words in the Hermeneutics of Śaṅkara," in J. TIMM (ed.), *Texts in Context: Traditional Hermeneutics in South Asia* (Albany: State University of New York Press, 1992), p. 41.

The scriptural context is, specifically, a dialogue between the sage Uddālaka Āruṇi and his son Śvetaketu in the sixth chapter of the *Chāndogya Upanishad.*[19] According to the Upanishadic narrative, Uddālaka Āruṇi offers his son instruction in a "rule of substitution" whereby all reality comes to be known by its most fundamental essence rather than by incidental transformations, just as anything made of clay can be identified by the simple designation, "It's clay" (6.1.4). In the course of his instruction, he describes the "existent" (*sat*) as the fundamental root of the individual (6.8) by drawing a series of analogies: bees' honey (9); merging rivers (10); sap in a tree (11); the seeds of a banyan fruit (12); salt dissolved in water (13); the man from Gandhāra (14);[20] the passage of a gravely ill person into death (15); and testing for truth or falsehood by means of a red-hot axe (16). Each illustration of CU 6.8-16 ends with the refrain "*tat-tvam-asi*": "That's how you are," or, more traditionally, "Thou art that." You, Śvetaketu, are none other than that ultimate existent, one without a second, the divine source of all.[21]

Perhaps most importantly for our present purpose, the Upanishad also adds a telling, final gloss: "And he did, indeed, learn it from him" (CU 6.16.3). Śvetaketu did not merely hear the sentence "*tat-tvam-asi*"; on hearing, he understood and, at least in Shankara's interpretation, attained final liberation, there and then.[22] And so, in USP 18, to explain how these words could effect such a dramatic result, Shankara introduces a technical idiom:

> The logical means by which to ascertain [the meanings of] 'this' [and] 'I' should indeed be the method of agreement and difference of the words and of the meanings of the words (USP 18.96).

[19] Sanskrit text and English translation in Patrick OLIVELLE (trans.), *The Early Upaniṣads: Annotated Text and Translation*, South Asia Research Series (New York and Oxford: Oxford University Press, 1998), pp. 245-57.

[20] See above, ch. 3, p. 89.

[21] Joel BRERETON hypothesizes that the phrase was originally the conclusion of CU 6.12 and only subsequently spread to the other verses; it need not, therefore, have a direct reference to the "existent" (*sat*) of 6.2.1. See the full argument in his "'*Tat Tvam Asi*' in Context," *Zeitschrift der Deutschen Morgenländischen Gesellschaft* 136 (1986): pp. 98-109. In rendering the sentence according to the traditional Advaita interpretation, I follow the suggestion of Julius LIPNER that the rendering communicates "the correct *philosophical/theological* import of the text," even if it is not the original or most literal rendering. See his essay "The Self of Being and the Being of Self: Śaṃkara on 'That You Are' (*Tat Tvam Asi*)," in B. MALKOVSKY (ed.), *New Perspectives on Advaita Vedanta: Essays in Commemoration of Professor Richard De Smet, S.J.* (Leiden, Boston and Köln: Brill, 2000), pp. 55-56, 55n9.

[22] See CUBh 6.16.3, in PANOLI, *Upanishads*, vol. 3, pp. 680-82.

In classical Indian grammar, various methods of "agreement and difference" (*anvaya-vyatireka*) were employed to distinguish invariable and variable meanings of words, as well as to establish legitimate grounds of inference.[23] Such applications of *anvaya-vyatireka* always dealt with some form of "positive and negative concomitance," whereby one discerns positive relations (*anvaya*) among concepts, terms or events, as well as salient absences or disjunctions (*vyatireka*).[24]

The precise application of such an analytic procedure in the context of Advaita tradition generally and USP 18 in particular has generated lively debate. Drawing Shankara's scattered statements together with the more specific descriptions in Sureśvara's work, Sengaku Mayeda argues that the compound *anvaya-vyatireka* refers to a distinctive "meditational" method virtually unique to these two teachers.[25] At the other end of the spectrum, Wilhelm Halbfass argues for a much wider semantic valence, suggesting that the term is used by Shankara to indicate, "not just one specific 'mode of reasoning,' but the basic structure of 'reasoning' as such."[26] Swami Paramarthananda broadly concurs. He does not settle on a single definition of *anvaya-vyatireka,* but distinguishes three distinct levels of meaning in Advaita tradition: 1) grammatical analysis, 2) discrimination between what is continuous and variable in human experience, and 3) a method of interpreting scriptural sayings like *tat-tvam-asi* to good effect.[27]

If we accept Paramarthananda's classification, it seems evident that the use of *anvaya-vyatireka* in the present verse works primarily on the second of these three levels. A few verses earlier (USP 18.90), Shankara has highlighted the central importance of "discrimination between 'you' and 'I'" for a proper understanding of the scriptures, and in the verse following he adverts to the persistence of one's "own Seeing" even in the state of dreamless sleep (18.97). When Shankara speaks of applying the method of *anvaya-vyatireka* to the words and meanings of "I" and "this"

[23] See the discussion in G. CARDONA, "*Anvaya and Vyatireka* in Indian Grammar," *Adyar Library Bulletin* 31-32 (1967-68), pp. 313-52.

[24] Wilhelm HALBFASS, "Human Reason and Vedic Revelation in Advaita Vedanta," in *Tradition and Reflection: Explorations in Indian Thought* (Albany: State University of New York Press, 1991), p. 174.

[25] See MAYEDA, *A Thousand Teachings*, pp. 50-57; Sengaku MAYEDA, "Śaṃkara and Sureśvara: Their Exegetical Method to Interpret the Great Sentence '*Tat Tvam Asi*,'" *Adyar Library Bulletin* 44-45 (1980-81), pp. 147-60.

[26] HALBFASS, "Human Reason," pp. 170-71.

[27] PARAMARTHANANDA, *UPADEŚA SĀHASRĪ*, #18-28.

in v. 96, then, it stands to reason that he refers to a process of differentiating between the conscious subject and the states of waking, dreaming and deep sleep. This consciousness is present along with the experiences of waking and dream, but it also persists in their absence, in dreamless sleep. Hence, it alone qualifies as the true self, the constant witness at the base of all changing phenomena.[28]

Such reasoned inquiry represents the necessary precondition for an efficacious hearing of the scriptures, but it does not go nearly far enough. For even the most discriminating intellect, working by its own power to differentiate self from non-self, could not guess the true identity of this enduring self. To come to such an understanding, a similar method must also be applied to such scriptural statements as "*tat-tvam-asi.*" Shankara later explains:

> Since [in the sentence 'Thou art That' the words] 'Thou' and 'The Existent' have the same referent, this [sentence] is comparable to [the sentence] 'The horse is black.' Since the word 'Thou' is [used] in apposition to [a word – 'Existent' – which] refers to the Painless One, it [too] refers to that [Painless One] (18.169 [170-71a]).
> Likewise, since the word 'That' is [used] in connection with [the word which] denotes the inner *Ātman*, [it refers to the inner *Ātman*]. [Just like the sentence] 'You are the tenth,' the sentence ['Thou art That'] means the inner *Ātman* (18.170 [171b-72]).

Later in the same section, Shankara will refer to these verses as yet another example of *anvaya-vyatireka*, similar to that proposed in v. 96 (see USP 18.178-79). But here the object of inquiry has shifted from human experience in general to the specific words of the Vedic revelation.

Shankara's analysis proceeds in several steps. First, from the context of the *Upanishad*, Shankara takes it as given that *tat* refers to none other than *sat*, "the existent," the original topic of Uddālaka Āruṇi's teaching.[29] Second, he asserts that the verb *asi* or "is" in the sentence functions, not as a metaphor or injunction, but in a relationship he calls "shared referentiality" or simply "connection" (v. 169), which the commentators gloss as apposition.[30] Shankara offers a somewhat misleading

[28] See HALBFASS, "Human Reason," pp. 162-68, and COMANS, "Śaṅkara and the *Prasaṅkhyānavāda*," pp. 59-61.

[29] See LIPNER, "Self of Being," p. 57, and HIRST, *Śaṃkara's Advaita Vedānta*, pp. 157-58. Following Brereton (esp. pp. 102-3), it should be noted that this identification is not self-evident in the original context.

[30] See the comment by ĀNANDAGIRI, in*Upadeśasāhasrī*, p. 104, lines 14-15; RĀMATĪRTHA, *Upadeśasāhasrī*, p. 397; and Shankara's more extended defence of the strictly

parallel to illustrate the point: "the horse is black." His point here is not that *tvam* functions as a qualification or attribute of *sat*, as "black" is an attribute of "horse." It is, instead, that when the terms are placed in apposition, they spontaneously restrict each other's meanings. When I say, "the horse is black," I negate all non-horse objects from the idea of "blackness" and negate from the idea "horse" all brown, white and other colorations.[31]

The result of such apposition, in the case of *tat-tvam-asi*, is quite startling, because the conventional meanings of the two terms appear, at first glance, to be mutually exclusive. "The existent," *Brahman* the divine self, normally indicates a reality other than the "inner self," mine or anyone else's. Similarly, the pronoun "you" normally indicates an individual person, who can be presumed to undergo experiences of pain or limitation throughout her life. If the hearer has engaged in the kind of careful discrimination between self and non-self alluded to in USP 18.96, however, and if this hearer accepts the teaching of Uddālaka Āruṇi in the *Chāndogya Upanishad* as revealed truth, then the awkward juxtaposition of these terms can yield a surprising result. As in "the horse is black," these apparent contraries are excluded, each in the other, the very moment the words are pronounced: distance or otherness is removed from the notion of the divine existent, and suffering excluded from the individual self. The innermost *Ātman* is thus revealed as none other than that divine being who is "free from pain," here and now.[32]

Shankara illustrates this teaching with an image that recurs across a number of his writings: the analogy of the "tenth person." Jacqueline G. Suthren Hirst explains:

copulative, rather than merely injunctive or eulogistic, force of *asi* in CUBh 6.16.3 (Panoli, *Upanishads*, vol. 3, pp. 683-87).

[31] See A.J. ALSTON (trans.), *The Thousand Teachings (Upadeśa Sāhasrī) of Śrī Śaṃkarācārya* (London: Shanti Sadan, 1990), pp. 360-61n1 and pp. 364-65n1.

[32] With few exceptions, I am following the interpretation given to these verses in MAYEDA, *A Thousand Teachings*, pp. 52-53; COMANS, "Śaṅkara and the *Prasaṅkhyānavāda*," pp. 62-63; and Eliot DEUTSCH, *Advaita Vedānta: A Philosophical Reconstruction* (Honolulu: University of Hawaii Press, 1968), pp. 49-50. LIPNER ("Self of Being," pp. 63-64) insists strenuously that only the meaning of *tvam* is restricted. He thus offers the following translation of the verse: "The word 'that' has the inner Self for its referent/ designates the inner Self; 'you' has the sense of the word 'that'/has the same referent as the word 'that.' Both words (jointly exclude) the condition of the non-inner Self, which is the condition of the suffering Self." According to both interpretations, the application of *anvaya-vyatireka* to the sentence has the primary effect of removing the idea of suffering from *Ātman*. See also the more extensive discussion in HIRST, *Śaṃkara's Advaita Vedānta*, pp. 154-59.

> A party of ten men crosses a river. Once on the other side, one of their number tries to count them up to make sure no-one is missing. But he can only find nine. All bewail their loss, until a passer-by says, "You are the tenth," to the man who had failed to count himself. At which point, the truth dawns.[33]

The *Upanishads* function, in this analogy, as the compassionate passer-by, reminding students to see their innermost selves as, here and now, that divine reality they have been so assiduously seeking to find. The teacher pronounces the scriptural words *tat-tvam-asi* and, presuming a suitably attentive and prepared hearer, the truth dawns.

Foreseeing possible objections, Shankara offers a further clarification:

> Without abandoning their own meanings [the words 'Thou' and 'That'] convey a special meaning and result in the realization of the inner *Ātman*. Therefore there is no other meaning contradictory to this meaning (18.171 [173]).

It is significant that the conventional meanings of the terms *tat* and *tvam* are not entirely abandoned in this process. For it is only by means of the conventional meanings of the two terms as "divine existent" and "innermost self," respectively, that the sentence *tat-tvam-asi* can achieve its intended purpose. Through their juxtaposition, the two terms convey what Shankara describes as a "special meaning" and distinctive "awareness" of the divine *Ātman* within. This special meaning is achieved, moreover, by the mere pronouncement of the words. It cannot be contradicted and, we might add, does not await some further verification.[34]

A bit further along in the chapter, Shankara strongly underscores this point:

> The knowledge that one is ever-free arises from the sentence and not from anything else. The knowledge of the meaning of the sentence is also preceded by recollecting the meaning of the words (18.188 [190]).
> By the method of agreement and contrariety the meaning of words is certainly recollected. Thus one realizes that one is oneself free from pain and actionless (18.189 [191])

[33] SUTHREN HIRST, "Teaching Techniques," pp. 127-28.

[34] PARAMARTHANANDA (*UPADEŚA SĀHASRĪ*, cassette #18-49) offers the example of a person who sees the reflection of the moon in a deep well. Mistaking the reflection for the reality, she lowers a rope to rescue the moon and return it to its proper place in the sky. The rope catches on a rock, and our hero, thinking she has hooked the sunken moon, pulls and pulls until the rope breaks, throwing her backwards on the ground. From where she has fallen, she looks into the sky and says, "There is the moon, back in the sky. I did it!", when nothing has changed.

These two verses, and the one following, are cited by Sureśvara as a "summary of the whole argument" against the *prasaṃkhyāna-vādin.*[35] In them, Shankara brings the preceding reflections to bear on the specific objection raised in USP 18.9-10.

There, we encountered a position that placed liberation at the end of a process of hearing, reasoning and *prasaṃkhyāna* meditation. Here, Shankara inverts this scheme, positing the efficacious hearing of the scriptural word as the desired end of the process, rather than its beginning.[36] First, he appears to suggest, one undertakes the kind of discernment on self and non-self alluded to by the phrase "agreement and difference" in v. 96. Next, recalling both the results of such discernment and the conventional meanings of words such as *tat* and *tvam* individually, one hears them paradoxically juxtaposed in a scriptural sentence such as *tat-tvam-asi.* Thus prepared and exposed to the scriptural revelation, the hearer comes naturally and spontaneously to see herself as "ever-liberated" (v. 188 [190]), "free from pain" and "free from action" (v. 189 [191]).[37] And this follows from the sentence itself, "not from anything else" – presumably including, above all, the *prasaṃkhyāna* meditation commended by the *pūrva-pakṣin.*

Shankara succinctly summarizes this teaching script:

> Through such sentences as '[Thou art] the Existent,'[38] like the [sentence] 'You are the tenth,' right knowledge concerning the inner *Ātman* will become clearer (18.190 [192]).

Again calling to mind the example of the tenth person, who forgot to count himself, Shankara reminds us that the object of inquiry here is none other than the "innermost self" of the hearer. Because of this, the student of the teaching need not seek fulfillment outside of herself, in one or another meditative practice. She needs only a word she can trust, a word that re-directs her attention to the divine reality behind all appearances. And this is precisely what the scriptures provide in short, startling pronouncements like "*tat-tvam-asi.*"

35 NS 4.31-33, in Alston, *Realization of the Absolute*, pp. 248-49.

36 See especially SUTHREN HIRST, "Weaving the Strands," p. 155.

37 PARAMARTHANANDA, *UPADEŚA SĀHASRĪ*, cassette #18-55.

38 Here, as we have already noted, Shankara takes it for granted that *tat* can be read as a synonym of "the existent" (*sat*); hence *sat-eva*, "The existent only" from CU 6.2.1 can simply be substituted for the sentence *tat-tvam-asi.* For the argument, see ALSTON, *The Thousand Teachings*, p. 373n1.

A Christian Reflection: It may seem rather remote from most Christian understandings to locate the attainment of final liberation in highly technical analyses of embodied experience and the grammar of the scriptures. Christian hearers would do well, however, to remember that the apostle Paul's decisive positions on righteousness by faith depended on his grammatical analysis of the Greek Septuagint,[39] and subsequent generations of Christian theologians have continued to adopt a highly technical idiom to argue about such issues as grace, free-will and the Eucharist – in the latter case, at least in English, many controversies can be reduced to arguments about the use of prepositions. At one level, this reflects a deep conviction, shared with Shankara and Advaita tradition generally, that if the scriptures do truly communicate God's liberation in language, then language and grammar have themselves been invested with extraordinary significance. What Shankara may add is a heightened awareness of the soteriological significance of that very fact, a sustained reflection on what liberation must (and must not) entail if it can indeed be effected by means of language. Specifically, such liberation should not be understood in terms of one or another change of state or substantive achievement on the part of the hearer; it must refer to what is intrinsic, fundamental and prior to the language that makes it known. In Christian terms, if salvation is truly and fully disclosed in the word of the scriptures, then such salvation must be seen first and foremost as already given – as gift, as grace – in the life and consciousness of the hearer.

The Reflection of the Self in the Mind (USP 18.26, 29-30, 109-10, 202-3)

In chapter 3, we noted that the process of negation described in USP 2-3 can be regarded as a kind of guided apprenticeship, a progressive discovery of the true self by means of the disciplined removal of all that is foreign to it. Reasoning by "agreement and difference," as described in USP 18, functions in a similar way. Indeed, elsewhere in the chapter, Shankara asserts that, by removing the idea of suffering in the hearer, the conjunction of *tat* and *tvam* in the sentence *tat-tvam-asi* conveys precisely the same message as the negative formula, "Not thus! Not so!"[40] Like such negations, the words "Thou art that" offer no new information about *Ātman,* as such; they merely remove the hearers' false identification with suffering and all the limiting conditions of empirical life, until only *Ātman* remains.

[39] This is brought out very nicely in E.P. SANDERS, *Paul: A Very Short Introduction* (Oxford: Oxford University Press, 1991), pp. 44-64.

[40] See USP 18.194-95, and the discussion in SUTHREN HIRST, *Śaṃkara's Advaita Vedanta*, pp. 159-60.

But what, precisely, is this divine *Ātman*? How can we describe what is left after all these limiting characteristics have been removed? Shankara does not say, nor can he. Thus, reflecting on such strategies of negation throughout Shankara's works, comparative theologian John Thatamanil has recently suggested that the Hindu sage can be intelligibly situated within the frame of "apophatic theology," characteristic of Pseudo-Dionysius and other Christian mystical writers; that is, he articulates a "theology that knows ultimate reality as language-transcending mystery beyond either positive or negative description."[41] Language serves a vital role in this theology, as we have already heard, but this role is functional and performative rather than strictly descriptive: it dynamically re-directs its hearers' attention to that sole, divine reality that pervades all finite words and experiences even as it ultimately eludes their grasp.

At this point, however, a further question might arise about the specific character of this divine presence in Shankara's apophatism. Arguably, the successive applications of *anvaya-vyatireka* to experience and to the phrase *tat-tvam-asi* described in this chapter seem to introduce an element of absolute transcendence to his account – what Lance Nelson calls the "dualism of nondualism."[42] For, in affirming the radical immanent presence of *Brahman* as the very self of the hearer, Shankara also proclaims a radical disjunction between that divine self and all those particular, embodied experiences of phenomenal existence. On this reading, Shankara offers a robust sense of divine presence with one hand, only to sweep it away with the other.

We have already addressed this issue, at least in part, in our treatment of the evolution of "name-and-form" and the ambivalent, "indescribable" status of the created order – as both source of bondage and means of liberation – in the previous chapter. To develop this idea further, however, we can turn to a second major theme developed in USP 18. Divine presence turns out to be a complex issue in Shankara's teaching, precisely because a word like *tvam*, as we saw in USP 18.171 [173], never entirely divests itself of its conventional meanings when placed in apposition to *tat* or *sat*. It continues to refer to the finite

[41] John J. THATAMANIL, *The Immanent Divine: God, Creation, and the Human Predicament* (Minneapolis: Fortress Press, 2006), p. 61.

[42] THATAMANIL, *Immanent Divine*, p. 91; and Lance E. NELSON, "The Dualism of Nondualism: Advaita Vedānta and the Irrelevance of Nature," in L. NELSON (ed.), *Purifying the Earthly Body of God: Religion and Ecology in Hindu India*, SUNY Studies in Religious Studies (Albany: State University of New York Press, 1998), pp. 61-88.

hearer, even as it points within and beyond that hearer to the ever-liberated *Ātman*.

How can this one term, when spoken by the teacher, accomplish such a subtle task? To answer, Shankara first reiterates the fundamental Advaita teaching on *Ātman*:

> [*Ātman*] is the self-effulgent Perception, the Seeing, internally existing and actionless. [It] is the Witness which is directly cognized and in the interior of all, and the Observer which is constant, attributeless, and non-dual (USP 18.26).

In this verse, and the two following, we encounter a good example of what Thatamanil characterizes as Shankara's apophatic theology. On the one hand, *Ātman* is characterised as being without action, change, attributes or distinctions of any kind. On the other, even the positive descriptors of *Ātman* imply its inaccessibility to ordinary means of knowledge, at least as a determinate object. It is the interior "Seeing" and "Witness," unavailable to sight. It is the constant "Observer," incapable of being itself observed. It is the "self-luminous" and "directly evident" awareness which cannot be illumined by any other source. As the ground of all perception and inference, in other words, *Ātman* cannot by definition become their object.

Surely the great exception to such limitations would be the words of scripture, the *śabda-pramāṇa*. What does the sentence *tat-tvam-asi* do, if not reveal *Ātman*? Shankara explains:

> In the [bearer of the 'I'-notion] there is the reflection, and words referring to the former could indicate the internal Seeing indirectly, [but] never designate It directly (18.29).
> [This is] because that which is not a member of any genus and so on cannot be indicated by words [18.30]. As the bearer of the 'I'-notion has the reflection of *Ātman* [in it and appears to be *Ātman*], it is the intellect that is referred to by the words for *Ātman* (18.30 [18.31a]).

Shankara has already indicated that *Ātman* stands outside the realm of attribution (v. 26); even, Swami Paramarthananda will add in one of his discourses, the attribute "without attributes" fails truly to describe the divine self.[43] Why? This is specified here. All words presume connection with some "genus" or category (v. 30). In contemporary English, for example, a "horse" is defined as a mammal of a particular type, and even such specialized terms as "*Ātman*" or "divine self" in this commentary

43 Paramarthananda, *Upadeśa Sāhasrī*, cassette #18-9.

have presumably become familiar to most readers by modifying their understandings of broader categories – such as "self" – already present in memory.[44] But *Ātman* the divine self is singular in an absolute sense. It does not belong to a genus and is therefore out of the reach of categorical language, including words such as "*Ātman*," "*tat*," or "*tvam*."

Nevertheless, Shankara insists, the sentences of the *Upanishads* do reveal *Ātman*. How? That's simple enough: they operate indirectly, rather than by direct signification (v. 29).

Much has been written on "implication" or "oblique predication" (*lakṣaṇā; lakṣārthya*) as a feature of Shankara's teaching, and surveying these discussions here would take us rather far afield.[45] Most importantly for our present purpose, Shankara indicates that the descriptive words we use for *Ātman* do have a literal referent; it's just that this referent is not, strictly speaking, the divine self. It is, instead, the "reflection" (*ābhāsa*) of this self in the hearer, the finite "bearer of the 'I'-notion," which Paramarthananda and Jagadānanda gloss as "ego," Alston as "ego-sense," and Mayeda as "intellect."[46]

We have already encountered the notion that the finite intellect is pervaded by the "reflection of Pure Consciousness" in our treatment of USP 5.3-5.[47] In the context of that discussion, this fact became an occasion for error, whereby the ignorant person mistakes reflection for reality and thus remains in bondage. In the present context, the same idea appears under a different Sanskrit idiom and with a more positive connotation. For it is only by means of this reflection that scriptural

44 See ALSTON, *The Thousand Teachings*, p. 283-84n1.

45 For more extensive and detailed treatments, see Richard V. DE SMET, S.J. "Langage et Connaissance de L'Absolu chez Çaṃkara," *Revue Philosophique de Louvain* 3e série 52 (1954): pp. 31-74; Guy MAXIMILIEN, "Le Langage et L'*Ātman* d'après USP 18 (I)," *Wiener Zeischrift für die Kunde Süd-Asiens* 19 (1975): pp. 117-33: Guy MAXIMILIEN, "Le Langage et L'*Ātman* d'après USP 18 (II)," *Wiener Zeischrift für die Kunde Süd-Asiens* 20 (1976): pp. 125-39; Julius LIPNER, "Śaṃkara on Metaphor with reference to Gītā 13.12-18," in R.W. PERRETT (ed.), *Indian Philosophy of Religion* (Dordrecht: Kluwer Academic Publishers, 1989), pp. 167-81; and Julius LIPNER, "Śaṃkara on satyaṃ jñānam anantaṃ brahma (TaiUp. 2.1.1)," in P. BILIMORIA and J.N. MOHANTY (eds.), *Relativism, Suffering and Beyond: Essays in Memory of Bimal K. Matilal* (Delhi: Oxford University Press, 1997), pp. 301-18.

46 See JAGADĀNANDA, *A Thousand Teachings*, p. 31; PARAMARTHANADA, *UPADEŚA SĀHASRĪ*, cassette #18-10; ALSTON, *Thousand Teachings*, p. 284; and MAYEDA's translation, included above. JAGADĀNANDA and PARAMARTHANANDA seem to be following the commentators, who also gloss *ahaṃ-kṛt* as *aham-kāra*. See ĀNANDAGIRI, *Upadeśasāhasrī*, p. 80, lines 24-25, and RĀMATĪRTHA, *Upadeśasāhasrī*, p. 664.

47 See above, ch. 3, pp. 94-97.

sentences such as *tat-tvam-asi* can properly be said to reveal the self in the mind of the hearer. That is, by referring directly to the reflection, a word like *tvam* refers indirectly to the primary reality beyond such words. What is, at one level, the cause of continuing error again becomes, at a deeper level, a privileged means for its correction.[48]

Further along in the chapter, Shankara makes this positive function more explicit:

> Only in the sense that the mirror which has the reflection of a face and appears to be the face is the face, can the mirror of the intellect's notion which has the reflection of *Ātman* [and appears to be *Ātman* be what is called *ātman*]. In that sense the 'I' is indeed [*ātman* but not in the true sense] (18.109).
> This is the way of realization that '[I] am the Existent.'[49] And [if] it were not so, it would not be [realized]. If there were no medium, the teaching 'Thou art That' (CU 6.8.7ff) would moreover be meaningless (18.110).

In USP 18.31-32 [18.31b-33a], Shankara has previously introduced two analogies to illustrate the relation between the infinite *Ātman* and its reflection in the mind: a burning torch and the image of a face reflected in a mirror. In both cases, words such as "fire" and "face" are applied both to the primary reality and to the secondary bearer of that primary reality: both the actual fire and the wooden torch are called "fire," both the face and its reflection are called "my face."

The present verses extend the second of these analogies and apply it to the controverted phrase *tat-tvam-asi*. Just as we comfortably say, "there is my face" of a reflected image without necessarily falling into confusion, so also we can truthfully refer to the divine *Ātman* by referring to its reflection in the embodied intellect of the hearer and, by extension, in any other conscious being. Michael Comans summarizes the argument as follows:

> Words... directly refer to the ego, the "I" of everyday discourse which is the mind with the reflection of Awareness. If this is so, the words of the *Śruti* such as "*tat tvam asi*" now have a medium through which to function. The word "you" (*tvam*) directly refers to the ego, the reflection of Awareness in the mind; and since the reflection is not something other than – nor is it separate from – the original Awareness, the word "you" can

[48] See SUTHREN HIRST, "Weaving the Strands," pp. 145-46, and further discussion in VETTER, *Studien*, pp. 96-102.

[49] The quoted phrase is, "*Sad-asmi.*" This is probably intended as a shorthand for the *Aham-brahma-asmi*, "I am *Brahman*," of BU 1.4.10. See ALSTON, *The Thousand Teachings*, p. 327n1.

> directly imply the subject, pure Awareness, if the hearer is ready to negate the ego as the Self.[50]

The word translated by Mayeda and Comans as "medium" (*dvāra*) could also be rendered as "door" or, following Alston, as "bridge."[51] The reflection thus functions as an essential link between the hearer's experience of embodied selfhood and her true identity as the self of all. She images the infinite, divine consciousness through her finite activity of conscious intending. Were it otherwise, the scriptural sentences would be rendered ineffective, and *Ātman* would be truly unknowable, rather than merely unreachable by words.

We should keep in mind that Shankara employs this theory of reflection primarily to defend the authority and sufficiency of the scriptures. Yet, once articulated, the theory has profound implications for our understanding of divine presence. To extend the metaphor: one should not confuse the original face with the reflected image, but both genuinely manifest the reality of that same face. So also our various experiences as conscious beings really do manifest the divine *Ātman*. Hence, Swami Paramarthanananda explains that it is only by means of the *ābhāsa,* the reflection of *Ātman* in the finite mind, that the empirical self can be said to become liberated – which belongs properly to the changeless *Ātman* – or that the divine self can be said to acquire self-knowledge – which presumes intellect, ego and a process of transformation antithetical to *Ātman.*[52] It is the scriptural word which facilitates such a 'miraculous exchange' of empirical knowledge and eternal liberation, but efficacious hearing of this word depends critically upon the fact that the hearer already bears the inextricable mark of the divine.

Towards the end of USP 18, Shankara draws out some further implications and consolidates his argument against the *pūrva-pakṣin*:

> It is only Itself that is aware of the Seeing, for Its nature is Awareness. The Awareness of this [inner *Ātman*] is described as the intellect's coming into being as a possessor of Its reflection (18.202 [205]).
> You here and now are final release, [self-]established and free from hunger, etc. How can such a contradictory statement be made [in the *Śruti*] that [*Ātman*] is to be heard, etc., by you? (18.203 [206]).

[50] COMANS, "Śaṅkara and the *Prasaṅkhyānavāda,*" p. 58.

[51] ALSTON, *The Thousand Teachings*, p. 327.

[52] PARAMARTHANANDA, *UPADEŚA SĀHASRĪ,* cassette #18-34. Cf. RĀMATĪRTHA, *Upadeśasāhasrī*, pp. 370-71, and ALSTON, *The Thousand Teachings*, pp. 326-27n2.

At the end of v. 203 [206], Shankara appears to refer to the great sage Yājñavalkya's words to his wife Maitreyī in *Bṛhadāraṇyaka Upanishad* 2.4.5: "You see, Maitreyī – it is one's self (*ātman*), which one should see and hear, and on which one should reflect and concentrate."[53] This passage is of central importance, not only because it supplies the scriptural warrant for the traditional threefold method of "hearing," "reflection" and "contemplation" mentioned in the introduction to this commentary, but also because it seems very strongly to support the position of the *prasaṃkhyāna-vādin*, as articulated in USP 18.9-10. That is, it implies that one first hears the scriptures and then subsequently engages in reasoning and meditation to verify this knowledge and to bring it to perfection.

Interestingly, Shankara has quoted and apparently criticized only that portion of the passage that we would expect him most vociferously to affirm – namely, that *Ātman* "should be heard." He does not, however, intend to discredit one or another element of the threefold process.[54] He aims, instead, to draw our attention to these Sanskrit verbal forms as future passive participles. The *Ātman*, Yājñavalkya says, "is to be heard" (*śrotavya*), "is to be reflected upon" (*mantavya*), and "is to be concentrated upon" (*nididhyāsitavya*). Such grammatical constructions by definition imply an action to be completed at some point in the future, a result which has yet to be achieved and, therefore, an injunction to act accordingly. But no such injunctions are possible in the case of self-knowledge, as we have heard again and again and which is strongly underscored here. The hearer – "you" – is already free from hunger and other limitations, and she need not and cannot be established by any means outside herself. She is, here and now, identical with liberation, with *Brahman* the divine self (v. 203 [206]).

This brings us very close to the heart of Shankara's refutation across the pages of USP 18. For Yājñavalkya's first instruction to Maitreyī in BU 2.4.5 is not that she should hear, reflect or concentrate, but that she "should see" *Ātman* directly.[55] Such a command again implicates the hearer in a paradox, as specified in v. 202 [205], for the divine self is not

[53] Sanskrit text and English translation in OLIVELLE, *Early Upaniṣads*, pp. 68-69.

[54] On this point, see especially Jacqueline SUTHREN HIRST, "Strategies of Interpretation: Śaṃkara's Commentary on Bṛhadāraṇyakopaniṣad," *Journal of the American Oriental Society* 116 (1996): pp. 59-66.

[55] In BUBh 2.4.5, Shankara separates *draṣṭavya* from the other three injunctions, pointing that a "right vision" (*samyag-darśana*) is the intended result of the entire process, including hearing, reflection and meditation. Sanskrit text and English translation in

an object of sight but Seeing itself, not accessible to experience but Experience itself. Why then the injunction? Why do the scriptures speak this way? The *pūrva-pakṣin*, as we have seen, attempts to resolve this apparent contradiction by moving back into the idiom of means and ends, postulating a sequence of actions that will, if performed correctly, generate direct perception of *Ātman* as a future result.

But final liberation, Shankara insists, does not depend upon any finite human effort whatsoever. It is a permanent feature of human existence, given in and through every possible experience, from the most acute suffering to the most concentrated moment of meditative practice. Or, perhaps more accurately, the divine *Ātman* is present *with* all such finite experiences, in what is called "the possessor of its reflection" – that is, in the finite intellect of the conscious subject (v. 202 [205]). Due to this reflection, this divine image in the human person, simple words like "I" and "you" bear a double-referent. They refer directly to the empirical self, who can hear, reflect and meditate, and who is subject to injunctions like "it is to be seen." Insofar as this empirical self reflects the divine self, it also becomes a privileged bridge or door to the *Ātman* beyond the reach of such injunctions. The point, then, is not to resolve the apparent contraries of the scriptures by dragging this pure "Seeing" back into the realm of achievements and results, as the *prasaṃkhyāna-vādin* appears to do. It is, rather, to enter completely into the mystery of such words, to come to perceive all finite achievements, results and myriad experiences of ordinary life in the light of a divine self that is always and everywhere co-present with them.

Shankara concludes USP 18 exactly as he began, with reverent salutations:

> Salutation to this good teacher who, like a bee, has collected for us from the flowers of the Upaniṣadic sentences the best honey of the nectar of knowledge (18.230 [233]).

This concluding verse draws our attention resolutely back to the sentences of the scriptures and to the mediation of the teacher, who draws the essential meaning from these sentences and communicates them to the student. We are thus reminded that the teaching scripts of USP 18, such as reasoning by "agreement and difference" or adverting to the reflection of *Ātman* in the finite consciousness of the hearer, are not intended to stand on their own. They, like Ādi Shankaracharya himself,

V. Panoli (trans.), *Upanishads in Sankara's Own Words*, vol. 4 (Calicut: Mathrubhumi Printing and Publishing Co. Ltd., 1994), pp. 523-24.

need to be understood within parameters of the teaching tradition. The "nectar of knowledge" has not been drawn out of the scriptures for its own sake. It is, rather, intended "for us" (*naḥ*), for the collective good of all those Advaitin disciples – past, present and future – who desire to seek, to hear and to be set free.

III.
"It is God who is at work in you": A Christian *Saṃvāda* with USP 18

> Let the same mind be in you that was in Christ Jesus,
>
> who, though he was in the form of God, did not regard equality with God as something to be exploited, but emptied himself, taking the form of a slave, being born in human likeness. And being found in human form, he humbled himself and became obedient to the point of death – even death on a cross.
>
> Therefore God also highly exalted him and gave him the name that is above every name, so that at the name of Jesus every knee should bend, in heaven and on earth and under the earth, and every tongue should confess that Jesus Christ is Lord, to the glory of God the Father.
>
> Therefore, my beloved, just as you have always obeyed me, not only in my presence, but much more now in my absence, work out your own salvation with fear and trembling; for it is God who is at work in you, enabling you both to will and to work for his good pleasure (Philippians 2:5-13).

The previous chapter was occupied with issues of revelation, teaching authority and pedagogy. For Shankara's model teacher and student, no less than for the apostle Paul's small communities of believers, much depends upon hearing the revelation of the scriptural word aright. This word possesses an intrinsic dynamism, tending towards its own full realization in the light of highest truth. In fact, the scriptures become revelation in the full sense only in and through a process of communication, reception and purification – a process which is, I have suggested, coextensive with creation itself. For both Paul and Shankara, however, the communication of the revealed word represents only one side of the gospel equation. The transformation effected by this teaching presumes hearers who are disposed to be so transformed. And this, in turn, presumes the prior, empowering presence of the divine self.

We have already encountered this idea briefly, in Paul's assertion that the gospel, which the Thessalonians recognized as God's own word, is "also at work in you believers" (1 Thess 2:13). To explore it further, in conversation with USP 18, we turn now to his letter to the Philippians.[56] The short selection quoted above sums up major themes of Paul's broader exposition in Phil 1:27 – 2:18. As in 1 Thessalonians, the apostle offers a word of encouragement in the face of his extended absence, as well as their experiences of opposition and social exclusion (see Phil 1:27-29).[57] Here, as there, Paul also commends a model of steadfastness, love and service for their imitation. But this time the model is provided, not primarily by Paul, his fellow workers or members of the community, but by Jesus the Christ.

Indeed, at the center of Philippians 2 stands one of the most significant Christological confessions of the NT (2:6-11). In these verses, Christ is praised as the one who, though "in the form of God" (v. 6), willingly submitted himself to "human likeness" and to "death on a cross" (vv. 7-8), only to be thereafter exalted by God and acclaimed as "Lord" (vv. 9-11). This passage, which may or may not pre-date Paul and his communities as a doxological hymn, nevertheless offers a strong expression of Christian devotion to the person of Jesus and an early witness to developing convictions about his "special significance" relative to God the Father.[58] More importantly for our purposes, the doxology is not employed by Paul primarily to make one or another claim about the identity of Christ, in the abstract. It is intended for a pedagogical purpose: to inculcate a distinctive attitude on the part of those who hear it. Through these verses of praise, the Philippians are called radically to conform themselves to Christ, taking consolation from his self-emptying love, sharing the gift of his Spirit and thereby sharing also in the "same mind" of humble service.[59] Paul's

[56] The date of this letter is by no means certain. It is written from prison and thus possibly from Rome in the early 60s CE (see Phil 1:7, 12-18). Many interpreters would, however, place it earlier in Paul's career and trace it to his imprisonment in Caesarea, Corinth or Ephesus. Brendan BYRNE, S.J., summarizes the various criticisms of the Roman hypothesis, as well as of the literary integrity of the letter in his "The Letter to the Philippians," in R. BROWN, J. FITZMYER, and R. MURPHY (eds.), *The New Jerome Biblical Commentary* (Englewood Cliffs: Prentice Hall, 1990), pp. 791-92 [48:4-6]. Morna D. HOOKER offers a judicious response to these objections in "The Letter to the Philippians," in *The New Interpreter's Bible*, vol. 11 (Nashville: Abingdon Press, 2000), pp. 471-75, without settling on Rome as the definitive place of origin.

[57] See HOOKER, "Philippians," pp. 496-98, and Larry W. HURTADO, *How on Earth Did Jesus Become God? Historical Questions about Earliest Devotion to Jesus* (Grand Rapids and Cambridge: William B. Eerdmans Publishing Company, 2005), pp. 72-73.

[58] HURTADO, *How on Earth?*, pp. 83-107, quoting p. 83.

[59] See HOOKER, "Philippians," 498-99, and Morna D. HOOKER, "Philippians 2.6-11," in *From Adam to Christ: Essays on Paul* (Cambridge: Cambridge University press, 1990), pp. 88-100.

hearers are reminded of their past obedience and summoned to work out their salvation in "fear and trembling" (Phil v. 12) – that is, in the intimate and awesome presence of God. So intimate is this presence that Paul ultimately refers all such "working" and "willing," not to the Philippians' own efforts, but to God (v. 13).[60] In 1 Thess 2, God's word worked in believers; here, the work is unambiguously that of God the divine self.

What is the basis of such claims? In the views of James Dunn, Morna D. Hooker and other scholars, the intimate connection between God and humanity follows fundamentally from Paul's understanding of Christ as the "new Adam," alluded to in the Philippians hymn as well as in such parallels as 1 Corinthians 15 and Romans 5.[61] Christ emerges in this interpretation as the universal human being, "the pattern of what humanity was meant to be: the perfect image of God and the reflection of God's glory."[62] This promised perfection, as we have seen before, both bears fruit in the lives of Christians here and now and looks to its decisive fulfillment at the end of time – but the fundamental reality remains constant and eternal. "In Christ," writes Dunn, "the infinite gap between the 'image' which is God's creative wisdom and the 'image' which is created humanity is bridged, both image which stamps and image which is stamped."[63] What applies to Christ, we might add, also applies to every believer, at least potentially.

Applying this "revelatory insight" to the concrete exigencies of human living is no easy matter.[64] What precisely does it mean to say that that the infinite gap between God and humankind has been bridged or that the unlimited and eternal God works in the striving of limited human beings? If the record of his letters is any indication, Paul himself struggled with his communities to discipline extravagant claims to divine presence and inspiration.[65] To ensure the veracity of elevated spiritual

[60] HOOKER, "Philippians," p. 512.

[61] See the discussion in Ibid, pp. 503-10; James D.G. DUNN, *The Theology of Paul the Apostle* (Grand Rapids and Cambridge: William B. Eerdmans Publishing Company, 1998), pp. 281-93; and especially Morna D. HOOKER, "Adam *Redivivus*: Philippians 2 Once More," in S. MOYISE, ed., *The Old Testament in the New Testament: Essays in Honour of J.L. North*, Journal for the Study of the New Testament Supplement Series 189 (Sheffield: Sheffield Academic Press, 200), pp. 220-34.

[62] HOOKER, "Philippians," p. 505.

[63] DUNN, *Theology of Paul*, p. 293.

[64] Ibid.

[65] See Ibid., pp. 426-34 and the discussion in James D.G. DUNN, *Unity and Diversity in the New Testament: An Inquiry into the Character of Earliest Christianity*, 3d Ed. (London: SCM Press, 2006), pp. 189-217.

experiences, Paul insisted that they be tested against the Christian *kerygma*, against the concrete ways they benefit the community and against the criterion of love.[66] Again we can follow Dunn, who explains:

> Now the point is that experience of union with Christ is experience of life being moulded by Christ, taking its characteristic features from Christ, manifesting the same character as was manifested in the ministry of Christ. That is to say, union with Christ for Paul is *characterized* not by lofty peaks of spiritual excitement or high inspiration, but more typically by self-giving love, by the cross....[67]

This observation brings us squarely back to the vision of Philippians 2, where the promise of divine presence is nearly identified with disciples' conformity to Christ. The Philippians manifest the image of God, not through one or another particular kind of experience, but in their working and willing for God's good pleasure: that is, we might venture to say, God works in them in the various ways they actually embody God's self-giving love.

Paul's vision of divine presence, as expressed in Philippians 2 and its parallels, offers what may be the strongest provocation and parallel to Shankara's *Upadeśasāhasrī* that we have yet seen in this commentary project. First and foremost, this vision is thoroughly Christocentric, and thus significantly complicates any attempt to locate God's "working and willing" in something innate to the human constitution, apart from Christ. It is no mistake that the verses of praise in Phil 2:6-11 eventually became key texts in the formation of classical Christology.[68] Yet, insofar as Paul invokes Christ as the new Adam, who bridges the gap between divine wisdom and the vitiated reflection of this same wisdom in each and every human person, his vision also resembles Shankara's theory of *ābhāsa* in USP 18. In the one case, the movement is from the innermost, highly subtle *Ātman*, unreachable by human language and unrelated to phenomenal existence, to the reflection of this *Ātman* in the empirical human consciousness. In the other, the movement is from the self-emptying and exaltation of Jesus the Christ, enacted in history, to their

[66] See DUNN, *Unity and Diversity*, esp. pp. 207-9, as well as DUNN, *Theology of Paul*, pp. 594-98.

[67] DUNN, *Unity and Diversity*, p. 210.

[68] See, for example, SANDERS, *Paul*, pp. 91-97; Richard A. NORRIS, Jr., *The Christological Controversy*, Sources of Early Christian Thought (Philadelphia: Fortress Press, 1980), esp. pp. 1-5; and Gerald O'Collins, S.J., *Christology: A Biblical, Historical, and Systematic Study of Jesus* (Oxford and New York: Oxford University Press, 1995), esp. pp. 33-36, 136-43, 237-44.

subsequent manifestation in the life of the Christian believer. In both cases, however, God can be identified as co-present in human experience precisely because human experience bears, or has been made to bear, the indelible stamp or likeness of God. This divine reflection is purely *given* in the most important sense: it is not the result of any human striving. Disciples can nevertheless manifest it to a greater or lesser degree, by putting on the "mind of Christ" through self-giving love in the one case, by applying the method of "agreement and difference" in the other, so that the reflection of *Ātman* in the embodied intellect emerges as a medium or bridge between human and divine – not unlike the constitution of Christ himself.

This correlation between image of God and reflection of *Ātman* carries rich potential for dialogue. As stated, however, it risks stripping the *ābhāsa* theory from its pedagogical context in the USP 18 teaching script. When we encountered the idea of the reflection of *Ātman* in the mind in chapter 3 of this commentary, we recall, it was part of the problem, not part of the solution. If we had constructed a correlation with anything in Christian tradition in that context, it would have been with the divine image corrupted by sin. The *ābhāsa* gains positive valence as a privileged medium for liberation only in the context of a highly technical defense of the Upanishadic phrase *tat-tvam-asi* as an efficacious *śabda-pramāṇa* or verbal means of liberating self-knowledge. In seeking out a Christian dialogue with this script, therefore, core convictions about divine presence and conformity to Christ may not, in and of themselves, possess sufficient interpretive heft; ideally, we would want to establish a correlation that brings these core convictions forward in an idiom that is similarly technical, hermeneutical and attentive to the ambivalent character of the divine image in the human constitution.

This is, as it happens, what we find in the twelfth-century *Sentences* of Peter Lombard (*Sententiae in IV libris distinctae*; hereafter *Sent.*).[69] This work, though rarely read in the modern era, served as the primary textbook for the theology of the great universities, beginning shortly after the Lombard's death in 1160 and continuing well into the sixteenth century.[70]

[69] English translations follow those in Peter LOMBARD, *The Sentences*, G. SILANO (trans.), 4 vols., Saint Michael's College Mediaeval Translations (Toronto: Pontifical Institute of Mediaeval Studies, 2007-2010). The Latin text is available in Magistri Petri LOMBARDI, *Sententiae in IV libris distinctae*, I. BRADY (ed.), 2 vols., Spicilegium Bonaventurianum 4-5 (Grottaferrata: Editiones Collegii S. Bonaventurae Ad Claras Aquas, 1971-81).

[70] See Marcia COLISH, "The Development of Lombardian Theology, 1160-1215," in J. DRIJVERS and A. MACDONALD (eds.), *Centres of Learning: Learning and Location in*

In form, the *Sentences* is true to its name: drawing on the prior compilations available in various Bible glosses and in the works of such great lights as Peter Abelard and Hugh of St. Victor, the Lombard drew together a variety of "sentences" or authoritative statements from prior tradition, set them in order and juxtaposed them in deliberately problematic ways, so that both teacher and student would have to exercise considerable dexterity to reconcile their disparate and discordant claims.[71] As is well known, the *Sentences* thus offered a very suitable basis for such later masters as Thomas Aquinas and Bonaventure to construct their grand syntheses.

Less well known, perhaps, is the Lombard's own creativity in drawing these sentences together and offering his own attempts at hermeneutic reconciliation. The work's four books follow a definite and original order, based upon Augustine's twofold distinction in *Teaching Christianity* between signs and things, on the one hand, and between "things to be used" (*uti*) and those "to be enjoyed" (*frui*), on the other – the latter of which distinction we touched on briefly in the previous chapter.[72] The first two books of the *Sentences* treat "things," including both the Trinitarian God who alone should be enjoyed (Book I) and those lesser, created realities which must instead be used in reference to God (Book II). Book IV, in contrast, focuses on "signs," understood broadly to include not only the sacraments of the church – here numbered seven for the first time in Christian history – but also the "last things" of Christian eschatology.

Book III, in which the Lombard turns to Christology and soteriology, fits less easily into this schema, and his inclusion of charity and the other virtues in this book has provoked bewilderment on the part of some interpreters.[73] The decision to integrate the moral virtues into a treatment of Christology makes good sense, however, if we situate Book III of the *Sentences* within the framework of Philippians 2, wherein Christ

Pre-Modern Europe and the Near East, (Leiden: E.J. Brill, 1995), pp. 207-16, as well as the more extensive treatments in her magisterial *Peter Lombard,* 2 vols., Brill's Studies in Intellectual History 41 (Leiden: E.J. Brill, 1994) and in Philipp W. ROSEMANN, *Peter Lombard,* Great Medieval Thinkers (New York: Oxford University Press, 2004).

71 See the discussion in Reid B. LOCKLIN, "Interreligious *Prudentia*: Wisdom from Peter Lombard for the Post-Conciliar Church," in W. MADGES (ed.), *Vatican II: Forty Years Later* (Maryknoll: Orbis, 2006), pp. 285-91.

72 See above, ch. 4, p. 140, as well as the discussion in ROSEMANN, *Peter Lombard,* pp. 57-61.

73 COLISH (*Peter Lombard,* vol. 2, p. 471) remarks that, "From a schematic point of view, ethics is the major subject on which [Peter Lombard's] gift for lucid organization deserts him."

emerges as the "new Adam," true image of God and perfect model for humankind. Philip W. Rosemann suggests that, for the Lombard,

> ... [t]he foundation of the moral life of the Christian is not virtue, really, but the person of Christ Himself – Christ who literally embodies God's love, which human beings are invited to return... In the Incarnation, God implanted His love in humanity, in order to allow us to participate in the return to Him of His Son, if only we recognize Christ for what He is and cling to Him with all our hearts. This recognition, this faith, is facilitated by Christ's works, which reveal His love to us; our love, in turn, will give rise to similar works of virtue in order to make itself known and to disseminate God's love. Naturally, then, 'charity is the mother of all the virtues.'[74]

Every virtue, the Lombard affirms with the broader tradition, emanates from self-giving love; and authentic human love, in turn, flows from and participates in the more perfect love of Christ. Hence, the human Christ becomes the sole true model of the moral life, and the topic of ethics fits quite suitably in the midst of a treatment of the Incarnation.[75] Peter Lombard offers, we might say, a technical expression of Paul's central insight in his letter to the Philippians.

But what, even the patient reader may wish by this point to ask, has the Lombard's account of charity and the other virtues to do with the detailed analyses of USP 18? In our hearing of such verses as USP 18.30, 18.109, and 18.202, above, we noted how Shankara's doctrine of *ābhāsa*, of the reflection of the divine self in the finite intellect, meant that a word like *tvam* in *"tat-tvam-asi"* possesses a paradoxical double-referent, referring primarily to the intellect and secondarily to the divine self reflected therein. So also in Peter Lombard's *Sentences*, we observe that the term *caritas* or self-giving love carries a similarly paradoxical double valence, albeit in reverse order: primarily, the term refers to the pure *caritas* of God's incarnation in Christ; secondarily, it also refers to the finite and fragile *caritas* that Christ kindles in the human heart. The Lombard will often refer to this love as "the affection of charity," but his technical exposition makes it clear that he is speaking less of a particular experiential state than of a more fundamental mode of intentionality, a basic orientation or pattern of "movements in the mind" toward God and the good of the neighbour.[76] As such a mode of conscious intending,

[74] ROSEMANN, *Peter Lombard*, pp. 139-40, quoting *Sent.* III.23.9.2.

[75] See Ibid, pp. 60-61, 139-42.

[76] See, e.g., *Sent.* III.27.2-4 and III.29.2.7-9, as well as the discussion of the Lombard's "intentionalism" in COLISH, *Peter Lombard*, vol. 2, esp. pp. 480-84 and pp. 501-503.

caritas might, no less than the *ābhāsa* of Shankara's teaching, be meaningfully interpreted as the immediate, intimate and all-pervasive medium (*dvāra*) by which Christ becomes co-present with the myriad experiences of the Christian disciple, from the highest point of spiritual elevation to the darkest moments of abandonment and desolation.

Once this correlation has been established, it becomes possible once again to hear Shankara together and in tandem with his Christian interlocutor. For this purpose, I have selected an excerpt from Book III of the *Sentences*, in which the Lombard considers the relationship between the perfect love of Christ and of the saints, which the apostle Paul proclaims will never end (1 Cor 13:8), and the less than perfect love of the ordinary disciple, striving and sometimes failing, in the here and now:

But this and the other things which have been said of charity can be understood about the perfect charity, which only the perfect have. Once that one is had, it is not lost; but the beginnings of charity at times grow, at times fail. For there are beginnings, progress and perfection of this virtue… Charity too [like faith, hope and knowledge] is in part, as the saints frequently teach, because we now love in part; and so it too will be made void insofar as it is in part, because imperfection will be taken away and perfection will be added, but charity itself will remain, but increased, both its acts, and the manner of loving, so that you may love God for his own sake and with your whole heart and your neighbour as yourself, but the mode of imperfection shall be eliminated. But faith and hope shall be made entirely void (*Sent.* III.31.1.9, 2.2).

In the [bearer of the 'I'-notion] there is the reflection, and words referring to the former could indicate the internal Seeing indirectly, [but] never designate It directly… As the bearer of the 'I'-notion has the reflection of *Ātman* [in it and appears to be *Ātman*], it is the intellect that is referred to by the words for *Ātman* (18.29-30 [18.29-31a]).

Since the word 'Thou' is [used] in apposition to [a word – 'Existent' – which] refers to the Painless One, it [too] refers to that [Painless One]. Likewise, since the word 'That' is used in connection with [the word which] denotes the inner *Ātman*, [it refers to the inner *Ātman*]. [Just like the sentence] 'You are the tenth,' the sentence ['Thou art That'] means the inner *Ātman* (18.169b-70 [172]).

The Lombard speaks in the Pauline language of "already-not yet," of a beginning of love in the present which will, should the Christian persevere, come to its fulfillment at the end of time. Shankara, on the other hand, speaks in the idiom of truth and appearance, of the infinite, indescribable self of each human person and its many finite reflections in individual human minds. But at the end of the day, whether in part or in perfection, in reflection or in reality, it is just one love and just one innermost self, free from suffering and all the vagaries of phenomenal existence. Though the *modus* of present love may change, the Lombard thus adds, the core reality will continue to all eternity, when so many other things – even faith and hope – have long since passed away. We might therefore hear in his teaching a kind of *anvaya-vyatireka* reasoning, distinguishing the enduring reality of perfect *caritas* from its partial and inchoate manifestations in the present experience of the disciple.

This last point acquires even greater significance if we turn to another related issue, on which the Lombard's teaching eventually provoked controversy and dissent: namely, his claim that this perfect *caritas* is ultimately non-different from the Holy Spirit and Spirit of Christ, God the divine self. The preeminent Peter Lombard scholar Marcia Colish denies that he ever held such a "participationist" and incipiently "pantheist" view,[77] but others such as Rosemann and Aege Rydstrøm-Poulsen maintain the integrity of the idea, which may well have been the more traditional Christian teaching in the Lombard's own time.[78] We have already encountered Irenaeus's proclamation that it is through God's Spirit, placed in us by Christ, that "we see and hear and speak."[79] The Lombard merely adds technical clarity to such claims, insisting that, if it is *by* the Spirit that we see, hear, speak and especially love, then charity itself can and should be identified with God who is Love, co-present and reflected – albeit imperfectly – in ordinary human consciousness. Only later would the Lombard's view come under the stern criticism of Thomas Aquinas, among others, who preferred to speak of charity as a "special virtue" created in the soul: a gift of God, to be sure, but not God's own divine self.[80]

For Peter Lombard, however, the pre-eminent gift of God *is* the Spirit of Christ, co-equal with God, and to speak rightly of this gift one must

77 COLISH, *Peter Lombard*, vol. 1, pp. 261-62.

78 See ROSEMANN, *Peter Lombard*, pp. 87-90, quotation at p. 89; Philipp W. ROSEMANN, "*Fraterno dilectio est Deus*: Peter Lombard's Thesis on Charity as the Holy Spirit," in T. KELLY and P. ROSEMANN (eds.), *Amor amicitiae: On the Love that is Friendship: Essays in Medieval Thought and Beyond in Honor of the Rev. Professor James McEvoy* (Leuven, Paris, and Dudley: Peeters, 2004), pp. 409-36; and Aege RYDSTRØM-POULSEN, *The Gracious God: Gratia in Augustine and the Twelfth Century* (Copenhagen: Akademisk, 2002), pp. 384-89, esp. pp. 388-89n283.

79 See above, ch. 3, pp. 109-12.

80 ROSEMANN, *Peter Lombard*, pp. 141-42. RYDSTRØM-POULSEN also surveys a range of twelfth-century critics of this teaching in *The Gracious God*, pp. 435-66.

speak of this divine self's immediate presence in the human self. As he comments in Book I of the *Sentences*:

> It has been said above, and it has been shown by sacred authorities, that the Holy Spirit is the love of the Father and the Son by which they love each other and us. It must be added to this that the very same Holy Spirit is the love or charity by which we love God and neighbour... and whoever loves the very love by which he loves his neighbour, in that very thing loves God, because that very love is God, that is, the Holy Spirit (*Sent.* I.17.1.2)

Thomas objected to such an assertion, insofar as it seems to make of each Christian yet another incarnation of God.[81] But this is, of course, precisely what makes the Lombard's teaching so attractive for our Christian *saṃvāda* with USP 18. When the *Sentences* are head in tandem with the verses of Shankara's chapter, for example, the scriptural injunction to "love the Lord your God with all your heart, and with all your soul, and with all your strength, and with all your mind; and your neighbor as yourself" (Luke 10:27) can be interpreted to function in a dynamic, revealing way not unlike the great saying *tat-tvam-asi*. It no longer merely enjoins the Christian to certain, specific kinds of intentions and behaviors; it discloses the divine self already present in that Christian person – or any person at all – now and in eternity. And it does so through a process of mutual exclusion, removing from the hearer any imperfection or limitation in her single-hearted love of God and neighbor and removing from God any essential difference from that unlimited, self-giving love. The twofold love of God and neighbor is, at its most profound level, just one love: God the divine self, as revealed in the person of Christ and eternally joined, by grace, to this particular hearer, here and now.

Of course, our analogy may appear to break down at precisely this point: the juncture between limited experience and unlimited self. For our two teachers address this issue in strikingly different ways. For Shankara, the tension between reflection and reality, between individual embodied self and the divine self of all, can be resolved only through sublation, as we have heard again and again. The divine self has no positive relation with the empirical self, and cannot properly be said to hear, to reflect or to engage in any other activity at all. The Lombard, by contrast, draws explicitly on the language of relation to resolve this tension, differentiating between the unchangeable essence of divine *caritas* in

[81] See ROSEMANN, *Peter Lombard*, pp. 88-89.

itself and the temporal effect of this same divine *caritas* relative to created beings.[82] Yet, in both cases, the relationship between divine reality and its reflection in the embodied intellect is radically asymmetrical.[83] The divine self – the unknown Knower of all possible objects, the uncaused Cause of the Christian moral life – pervades its hearers' every experience without thereby becoming bound to them.

Notwithstanding significant differences, Christian hearers of USP 18 may come to a new appreciation for the Lombard's distinctive, controversial, yet authentically Christian teaching, in and out of our hearing of these Advaita scripts. Self-giving love may initially appear to be a derived, secondary feature of existence, intrinsically bound up with the exigences of individual, embodied life, and thus a poor candidate for identity with God. Indeed, understood as the *ābhāsa* or reflection of God in the body, mind and personality of the hearer, human charity invariably possesses all of the limitations of that body, mind and personality. It is not reducible to those limitations, any more than pure consciousness – *Ātman* the divine self – is reducible to the individual consciousness of the embodied intellect. It is, nevertheless, the sole foundation of such loving, of the human person and of creation; insofar as we do love truly, we reveal the God who is that love, within and beyond its limited reflection in the embodied individual. Christians put on the mind of Christ and strive to love selflessly, then, not primarily to achieve moral perfection or to attain some particular experience of love, but to acknowledge and disclose their own deepest reality, the image and co-presence of God the Spirit in them. Finally, of course, if this is true of the Christian hearer, it is at least potentially true of each and every being capable of giving and receiving love, no matter how faint, partial or imperfect that love may be.[84]

[82] E.g., *Sent.* III.32.2-4.

[83] Richard DE SMET and several of his students have questioned whether the theory of relation and the provisional reality of the world one finds in Shankara is really all that different from the ideas found in Thomas Aquinas. See, for example, Bradley J. MALKOVSKY, "Introduction: The Life and Work of Richard V. De Smet, S.J.," in MALKOVSKY, *New Perspectives*, pp. 1-17; K.P. ALEAZ, *The Relevance of Relation in Śaṅkara's Advaita Vedānta* (Delhi: Kant Publications, 1996); Sara GRANT, *Śaṅkarācārya's Concept of Relation* (Delhi: Motilal Banarsidass Publishers, 1998); and the discussion in ch. 4, above, pp. 121-31.

[84] Though, it should be noted, this is one place where the dialogue with Shankara pushes this teaching of Peter Lombard beyond what he himself would have recognized or likely approved. ROSEMANN ("*Fraterno dilectio*," 432) puts the matter as follows: "The total dependence of the virtues, including the cardinal virtues, upon charity means that the theology of the *Sentences* has no room for a natural habit of virtue. Peter Lombard

Words inevitably fall short, but that does not render the mystery inaccessible or somehow removed from human existence. On the contrary. For those graced to become authentic hearers, the divine self can indeed be said to be "at work in you," albeit worklessly at work, in the present and in eternity. The words of the teaching may not capture this divine mystery. Due to its intimate presence in the life and mind of the hearer, however, they can nevertheless find a home.

knows that there are people, such as non-Christians, who are capable of performing good acts without having received the spirit of charity. But these acts have no merit in the eyes of God. In the Lombard's ethics, it is all or nothing."

Chapter 6

DISCERNMENT AND COMMUNION: COMMENTARY ON USG 2

I.

Upadeśasāhasrī Gadyabandha 2.62-65

> [The pupil asked,] 'Your Holiness, is the mutual superimposition of the body and *Atman* made by the composite of the body and so on or by *Ātman*?'
>
> The teacher said, 'What would happen to you, if [the mutual superimposition] is made by the composite of the body and so on, or if [it] is made by *Ātman*?'
>
> Then the pupil answered, 'If I am merely the composite of the body and so on, then I am non-conscious, so I exist for another's sake; consequently, the mutual superimposition of body and *Ātman* is not effected by me. If I am the highest *Ātman* different from the composite [of the body and so on], then I am conscious, so I exist for my own sake; consequently, the superimposition [of body] which is the seed of every calamity is effected upon *Ātman* by me who am conscious.'
>
> To this the teacher responded, 'If you know that the false superimposition is the seed of [every] calamity, then do not make it!'

II.

Discerning the Self: Hearing USG 2 (Selections)

The second prose chapter begins much as the first prose chapter did, with a student approaching a teacher to seek self-knowledge. But Shankara also signals that this is a different teaching script, with its own distinctive purpose and themes:[1]

> A certain student, who was tired of transmigratory existence characterized by birth and death and was seeking after final release, approached in the

[1] See Tilmann Vetter, *Studien zur Lehre und Entwicklung Śaṅkaras* (Wien: Institut für Indologie der Universität Wien, 1979), pp. 75-78.

> prescribed manner a knower of *Brahman* who was established in *Brahman* and sitting at his ease,[2] and asked him, 'Your Holiness, how can I be released from transmigratory existence? I am aware of the body, the senses and [their] objects; I experience pain in the waking state, and I experience it in the dreaming state after getting relief again and again by entering into the state of deep sleep again and again. Is it indeed my own nature or [is it] due to some cause, my own nature being different? If [this is] my own nature, there is no hope for me to attain final release, since one cannot avoid one's own nature. If [it is] due to some cause, final release is possible after the cause has been removed.' (USG 2.45)

Whereas the first prose chapter described a "method of instruction" to be employed in the present, the second narrates a past event, when a "certain student" approached a teacher seeking such instruction. In USG 1.2 and 1.10, as we have heard, the disciple was described as a *paramahaṃsa* renunciant, who has left behind life as a student or as a householder. Here, Shankara characterizes the disciple precisely as a celibate student, possibly in an earlier stage of life. Judging from these features, it might seem appropriate to reverse the chapters' present order, positioning USG 2 as remote preparation for the hearing of the scriptures in USG 1.

These differences need not be pressed, and they do not invalidate upholding a close relation between these two chapters in the *Upadeśasāhasrī*'s final form. The commentators, for example, see in the description of the student here, and particularly in the nature of his questions, hints that he must in fact be a renunciant who has already heard the teaching of the *Upanishads*, exactly as depicted in the first prose chapter.[3]

[2] See the discussion above, ch. 4, pp. 119-20. The term translated here as "knower of *Brahman*" (*brāhmaṇa*) could be rendered as "Brahmin." The context supports MAYEDA's reading, however, as do the English translations in A.J. ALSTON (trans.), *The Thousand Teachings (Upadeśa Sāhasrī) of Śrī Śaṃkarācārya* (London: Shanti Sadan, 1990), p. 46; Swāmi JAGADĀNANDA (trans.), *A Thousand Teachings in Two Parts – Prose and Poetry – of Srī Sankarāchārya* (Madras: Sri Ramakrishna Math, [1941]), p. 33; and Deb Kumar DAS (trans.), *Śaṅkarācārya: A Discourse on the Real Nature of the Self* (Calcutta: Writers Workshop, 1970), p. 1. The close relation of the two meanings is not incidental: Brahmin ideals of religious life thoroughly pervade Shankara's teaching, even as he proclaims a higher unity that transcends all distinguishing marks of caste and state of life.

[3] See RĀMATĪRTHA's comment in D. GOKHALE (ed.), *Shri Shankarāchārya's Upadeśasāhasrī with the Gloss Padayôjanīkā by Shrī Rāmatīrtha* (Bombay: Gujurati Printing Press, 1917), pp. 50-51; ĀNANDAGIRI's comment in S. SUBRAHMANYA SASTRI (ed.), *Shri Shankarabhagavatpada's Upadeshasahasri with the Tika of Shri Anandagiri Acharya*, Advaita Grantha Ratna Manjushi Ratna 15 (Varanasi: Mahesh Research Institute, 1978), pp. 138-39; and the summary in V. NARASIMHAN, *Upadeśa Sāhasrī: A Thousand Teachings of Adi Śaṅkara* (Bombay: Bharatiya Vidya Bhavan, 1996), pp. 323-24.

The student initiates the discussion, rather than the teacher, and he seeks to probe the precise cause of worldly experience, the three states of waking, dreaming and deep sleep, and the phenomenon of pain. The very construction of the questions seems to presume the Advaita position on bondage and final release. Either this student is unbelievably astute, then, or he is already quite well-rehearsed.

The student's questions also, of course, introduce and anticipate the structure of USG 2. In a first major unit (2.51-73), student and teacher engage in an examination of the cause of suffering: primordial ignorance, its locus and the existential possibility of its removal. A second unit (2.74-108) delves more deeply into the essential nature of *Ātman* as changeless knowledge, which grounds and becomes manifest in empirical knowing. The underlying unity of both of these inquiries is, moreover, nicely captured by two titles attached to the chapter in different manuscript traditions: "Awareness" and "Knowledge of the Self as Non-Dual and Transcendentally Changeless."[4] One of the major purposes of this teaching script is, we might say, to discern how ordinary human awareness opens into and is indissolubly related to the non-dual and transcendentally changeless self.

An Initial Reflection: Thus far in this commentary, we have encountered the essential message of Advaita, as well as important presuppositions about its teachers, its hearers and the liberating power of the *Upanishads*, rightly understood. Despite the apparent simplicity of such great sayings as "I am *Brahman*" (*ahaṃ brahma-asmi*) and "Thou art that" (*tat-tvam-asi*) neither text nor tradition is susceptible to easy reduction. They embody complex, layered convictions about the nature of reality, final release and the means thereto, and these layers become still more complex as they are brought into conversation with Christian witnesses like the apostle Paul, Irenaeus of Lyons, Augustine of Hippo and Peter Lombard. In this chapter and the two that follow, we delve more deeply into this layered complexity and somewhat shift our primary focus from the component parts of the teaching to the broader movement they presume, model and re-create. In USG 1.3, as we have seen, Shankara refers to this movement with the Sanskrit term *vidyā-santati*, the ongoing "continuity of knowledge" constituted by teacher, disciple and living tradition. Now, in and out of our hearing of this prose chapter, we can begin to bring this *vidyā-santati* into dialogue with the Christian notion of *koinonia*, that privileged "sharing" or "communion" in God's life that follows from shared participation in the life, death and resurrection of Jesus the Christ. For Shankara, one can

[4] In Sanskrit: *avagati* and *kūṭastha-advaya-ātma-bodha*, respectively. See MAYEDA, *Upadeśasāhasrī*, pp. 215, 285n275.

speak of a common sharing or communion of all conscious beings in the divine reality of *Ātman* by the bare fact of their conscious awareness. Yet, such sharing emerges as an explicit and liberating feature of the disciple's own self-understanding only slowly, through an assiduous process of self-inquiry and discernment, as we hear especially clearly in the scripted dialogues of USG 2.

"Mā Kārṣīs-Tarhi!" (USG 2.51, 54a, 62-66, 69-70, 71-73a)

We have already noted some features that set USG 2 apart from USG 1. A deeper dissonance can be heard in the specific, concrete terms of the dialogue itself. Rather than citing scripture, for example, this model teacher responds to the student's initial questions with the simple assertion that pain and suffering do not belong to the student's own nature (2.46). Their cause is fundamental ignorance (*avidyā*); due to this ignorance, the student identifies himself as an agent and experiencer, subject to rebirth, when in fact he is none other than the "highest *Ātman*," ever-free (2.48-50). As we shall see, the disciple attempts to refute this claim, and the conversation continues apace. Not once, however, does the teacher refer directly to the words of the *Upanishads* – not even to the great saying *tat-tvam-asi*. For this and other reasons, Tilmann Vetter characterizes the present prose chapter as one of Shankara's earliest writings and "perhaps [his] most important philosophical endeavor." After this, in such works as USG 1 and his all-important commentary on the *Brahma-Sūtras*, the great sage would lose confidence in reason and place increasingly strong emphasis on scriptural revelation.[5]

Certainly, one cannot overlook the differences between these texts, and the kind of historical development postulated by Vetter cannot be completely excluded. Nevertheless, the work of Wilhelm Halbfass and Jacqueline G. Suthren Hirst in particular opens a door to viewing the relation between USG 1 and USG 2 in a more nuanced manner than his method allows. Halbfass, first and foremost, softens the purported contrast between reason and revelation in Shankara's teaching: although the great teacher uniformly insists that the *Upanishads* alone "lend final

[5] VETTER, *Studien*, pp. 89-91 (quotation at p. 89). Paul HACKER offers the more commonsense suggestion that scriptural citations are for beginners and pure reasoning for more advanced pupils, but this too presumes a significant discontinuity between reliance on the scriptural revelation and reliance on reason. See Paul HACKER (trans.), *Upadeśasāhasrī: Unterweisung in der All-Einheits-Lehre der Inder, von Meister Shankara: Gadyabandha oder das Buch in Prosa*, Religionsgeschichtliche Texts Herausgegeben von Gustav Mensching 2 (Bonn: Ludwig Röhrscheid Verlag, 1949), pp. 7-9, and the discussion in VETTER, *Studien*, pp. 77-78.

validity to statements about the self or the absolute," these same *Upanishads* respond to and model patterns of human reasoning and thus legitimize the robust use of reason itself.[6] And Suthren Hirst, for her part, has shown that Shankara's rhetorical structures are generally rooted firmly in the *Upanishads*, even when the particular arguments he employs may differ in significant ways.[7] One can reason within the limits of scripture, in other words, even if scripture is never cited.[8] With or without such citations, the *Upanishads* ideally direct, support and nourish the use of reason, from beginning to end.

Following Halbfass and Suthren Hirst, then, we need not hear in USG 2 any contradiction of those other scripts focused more explicitly on the word of the *Upanishads*, such as USG 1 and USP 18; indeed, this dialogue can be credibly interpreted as an extended application of precisely that method of "agreement and difference" described in USP 18, whereby one differentiates self from non-self for the specific purpose of understanding the scriptural teaching aright. By means of disciplined inquiry, inferior modes of reasoning are progressively corrected, purified and transformed into what reason could and should be, in light of Upanishadic truth.

But this, of course, presumes that there are conventional patterns of reasoning in need of purification. The model disciple, as it turns out, obligingly provides just that:

> The pupil said, 'Even though I exist [eternally], still I am not the highest *Ātman*. My nature is transmigratory existence which is characterized by agency and experiencership, since it is known by sense-perception and other means of knowledge. (USG 2.51a)

Having first posed a series of questions about the source of suffering and pain, and having then been told that he is the eternal self of all

[6] W. HALBFASS, "Human Reason and Vedic Revelation in Advaita Vedanta," in *Tradition and Reflection: Explorations in Indian Thought* (Albany: State University of New York Press, 1991), pp. 179-80.

[7] See Jacqueline SUTHREN HIRST, "Strategies of Interpretation: Śaṃkara's Commentary on Bṛhadāraṇyakopaniṣad," *Journal of the American Oriental Society* 116 (1996): pp. 66-69; J.G. SUTHREN HIRST, "The Place of Teaching Techniques in Śaṃkara's Theology," *Journal of Indian Philosophy* 18 (1990): esp. pp. 122-27; and J.G. SUTHREN HIRST, *Śaṃkara's Advaita Vedānta: A Way of Teaching*, RoutledgeCurzon Hindu Studies Series (London and New York: RoutledgeCurzon, 2005), esp. pp. 69-74.

[8] SUTHREN HIRST provides a good example of this in Shankara's refutation of Buddhist positions in the *Bṛhadāraṇyaka Upanishad*, in which Shankara's arguments are clearly "scripturally based" without ever citing scripture. See SUTHREN HIRST, "Śaṃkara's Commentary," pp. 69-74.

(USG 2.50), the student responds by refusing to grant the validity of the claim. He does not deny everything: in line with all the so-called orthodox schools of Hinduism and against such heterodox adversaries as the Buddhists, the disciple grants his own substantial and perduring existence as a presupposition for further enquiry. Such an assumption, by itself, situates the entire discussion within a broadly Vedic frame.

Nevertheless, the key Advaita teaching on *Ātman* has been flatly denied, on the evidence of perception, inference and possibly the scriptures themselves. Nor can some doctrine of *avidyā* or primordial ignorance invalidate such evidence, as the disciple goes on to explain:

> [Transmigratory existence] has not nescience as its cause, since nescience cannot have one's own *Ātman* as its object. Nescience is [defined as] the superimposition of the qualities of one [thing] upon another. For example, fully known silver is superimposed upon fully known mother-of-pearl, a fully-known person upon a [fully known] tree trunk, or a fully known trunk upon a [fully known] person; but not an unknown [thing] upon [one that is] fully known nor a fully known [thing] upon one that is unknown. Nor is non-*Ātman* superimposed upon *Ātman* because *Ātman* is not fully known, nor *Ātman* [superimposed] upon non-*Ātman*, [again] because *Ātman* is not fully known.' (2.51b)

In this passage, the disciple defines fundamental ignorance or "nescience" (*avidyā*) as a form of "superimposition" (*adhyāropaṇā*), the erroneous attribution of the qualities of one object to another such object. In his commentary on the *Brahma-Sūtras*, Shankara similarly treats *avidyā* in terms of superimposition (*adhyāsa*), which he defines as "an awareness, similar in nature to memory, that arises on a different (foreign) basis as a result of some past experience."[9] Remembering the characteristics of silver perceived in the past, one imposes these characteristics on something else, perceived in the present, such as mother-of-pearl. So also in the case of the person mistaken for a tree or, reaching beyond the present chapter to other scripts, the rope mistaken for a snake. There is no problem with the characteristics themselves; the problem is that they have been falsely associated with the wrong object.

The very close association of "nescience" (*avidyā*) and "superimposition" (*adhyāsa; adhyāropaṇā*) in the *Upadeśasāhasrī*, in the *Brahma-Sūtra* commentary and in other works have led some scholars to suggest that

[9] BSBh Introduction, in Swami GAMBHIRANANDA (trans.), *Brahma-Sūtra-Bhāṣya of Śrī Śaṅkarācārya* (Calcutta: Advaita Ashrama, 1965, 1972), p. 2. See also MAYEDA, *A Thousand Teachings*, p. 77, and HACKER, *Upadeśasāhasrī*, p. 34n5.

Shankara regarded the two ideas as virtual synonyms, distinguishing his view from those later traditions that would treat *avidyā* as a kind of material cause prior to the act of superimposition.[10] Others argue for greater continuity between Shankara and his followers on this point.[11] In the present context, neither teacher nor student appears to be unduly preoccupied with such subtleties. The teacher has described *avidyā* as the cause of transmigratory existence, and this *avidyā* takes existential shape in the conscious act of superimposing such characteristics as "agency" and "experiencership" on the supreme *Ātman*. Further clarity of definition is not required at this point.

This does not mean, of course, that either subtlety or a desire for clarity have themselves been set aside. To the contrary: the student goes on to contend that *avidyā*, thus defined, does not and cannot apply to *Ātman*. Why? The argument rests upon a distinction between things "fully known," or determinable as objects of knowledge, and their opposite. Silver, mother-of-pearl, a tree trunk, a person, a rope, a snake – all of these involve determinable objects, whose characteristics can be thoroughly established through perception, inference and other means of knowledge. But *Ātman* is inaccessible to any such means. Hence the highest self is "not fully known." To superimpose one thing on another, one must have at least a vague prior notion of both objects, which seems not to be possible in the case of *Ātman*.

The teacher responds by changing the terms of the conversation, attempting to expand the student's understanding of what it means for something to be "fully known" in the first place:[12]

> The teacher[13] replied, 'Listen. It is true that the body and *Ātman* are fully known; but they are not fully known to all people as the objects of distinct

[10] E.g. Paul HACKER, "Distinctive Features of the Doctrine and Terminology of Śaṅkara: *Avidyā, Namarupa, Maya, Īśvara*," in W. HALBFASS (ed.), *Philology and Confrontation: Paul Hacker on Traditional and Modern Vedānta*, (Albany: State University of New York Press, 1995), pp. 58-67, and MAYEDA, *A Thousand Teachings*, pp. 76-79.

[11] See Michael COMANS, *The Method of Advaita Vedānta: A Study of Gauḍapāda, Śaṅkara, Sureśvara and Padmapāda* (Delhi: Motilal Banarsidass, 2000), pp. 246-67, and especially Martha J. DOHERTY, "A Contemporary Debate in Advaita Vedanta: Avidyā and the Views of Swami Satchidanandendra Saraswati," Ph.D. thesis, Harvard University, 1999.

[12] See ĀNANDAGIRI, *Upadeśasāhasrī*, p. 140, lines 28-29; RĀMATĪRTHA, *Upadeśasāhasrī*, p. 55, and the summary in NARASIMHAN, *Upadeśa Sāhasrī*, p. 327.

[13] One of the stylistic differences between USG 1 and USG 2 is the way the teacher is described: in USG 1, he is characterised by the slightly more formal and institutional term *ācārya*, whereas here Shankara employs the more personal term *guru*. See Minoru

> notions like a tree-trunk and a person.' 'How [are they known] then?' '[They are] always [known] as the objects of constantly non-distinct notions. Since nobody grasps the body and *Ātman* as two distinct notions, saying, "This is the body, that is *Ātman*," people are deluded with regard to *Ātman* and non-*Ātman*, thinking, "*Ātman* is thus" or "*Ātman* is not thus."' (2.54a)

Shankara's model teacher aims to illustrate that the student's objection falls short precisely because of *Ātman*'s unique status. This *Ātman*, he readily grants, is not known as an "object of a distinct notion," as silver, tree trunks and other persons are known, but neither is it unknown. *Ātman* is presented in our awareness together with finite body, mind and personality, in what the teacher calls "constantly non-distinct notions." Since we are conscious precisely as embodied beings, we invariably confuse the characteristics of embodied life with the self-evident *Ātman*. But neither the body nor *Ātman* can, on that basis, be dismissed as unknowable.[14]

Further along in the dialogue, the teacher will extend this argument along familiar lines, demonstrating that *Ātman*, though given in constant combination with whatever is known through bodily senses, actually rests on a firmer epistemological foundation (see USG 2.59-61). Unlike perceptions, which come and go as objects of knowledge, the self is always known as that in and through which all such finite experiences occur. It is the overarching reality that must be presupposed before we can conceive of any such experiences at all, like the air we breathe or the open sky. Not only is it possible to know *Ātman*, then, but unlike ordinary objects of knowledge, it actually belongs to the very nature of *Ātman* to be fully known (2.61). Conventional reasoning has not been denied; it has been refined and re-oriented in light of a higher truth.

By the end of this initial sequence (2.51-61), the student is ready to grant the origin of pain and suffering in what he specifies as a "mutual superimposition" (*itara-itara-adhyāropaṇā*) of *Ātman* and the body, mind and personality, by which the qualities of each are falsely and mutually attributed to the other. But this, in turn, gives rise to a further problem:

HARA, "Hindu Concepts of Teacher, Sanskrit *Guru* and *Ācārya*," in M. NAGATOMI, B. MATILAL, J. MASSON, and E. DIMOCK (eds.), *Sanskrit and Indian Studies: Essays in Honor of Daniel H.H. Ingalls*, (Dordrecht, Holland: D. Reidel Publishing Company, 1980), pp. 93-118.

[14] See also the similar discussion in BSBh Introduction, in GAMBHIRANANDA, *Brahma-Sūtra-Bhāṣya*, pp. 3-4.

> [The pupil asked,] 'Your Holiness, is the mutual superimposition of the body and *Ātman* made by the composite of the body and so on or by *Ātman*?' (2.62)

The student here asks a classic question about the agent or locus of *avidyā*.[15] That is, granting that suffering originates in ignorance, is it *Ātman* the divine self who has made this error? Or is it the finite ego, in combination with a body, mind and personality? Or perhaps both?

Like any competent instructor, Shankara's model teacher does not deign to answer such a difficult question on such an all-important issue. He turns it back on the student:

> The teacher said, 'What would happen to you, if [the mutual superimposition] is made by the composite of the body and so on, or if [it] is made by *Ātman*?' (2.63)
> Then the pupil answered, 'If I am merely the composite of the body and so on, then I am non-conscious, so I exist for another's sake; consequently, the mutual superimposition of body and *Ātman* is not effected by me. If I am the highest *Ātman* different from the composite [of the body and so on], then I am conscious, so I exist for my own sake; consequently, the superimposition [of body] which is the seed of every calamity is effected upon *Ātman* by me who am conscious.' (2.64)

The assumption governing this section and those that follow may have been borrowed from the rival tradition of Sāṃkhya, which maintained that any composite entity must, by virtue of that very fact, exist "for the sake of another" or in a way that is "other-valued" (*para-artha*).[16] Earlier in this chapter and elsewhere, Shankara offers the image of a house to illustrate the idea.[17] Such a house is composite, constructed of bamboo

15 See MAYEDA, *A Thousand Teachings*, p. 249n15.

16 See DAS, *Discourse*, pp. 17, 23; *Sāṃkhya-kārikā* 17, summarised in G. LARSON and R. BHATTACHARYA (eds.), *Encyclopedia of Indian Philosophies, Volume IV: Sāṃkhya, A Dualist Tradition in Indian Philosophy* (Delhi: Motilal Banarsidass, 1987), pp. 155-56; and the discussion in Mikel BURLEY, *Classical Sāṃkhya and Yoga: An Indian Metaphysics of Experience*, Routledge Hindu Studies Series (London and New York: Routledge, 2007), pp. 74-77, 141-47.

17 See USG 2.56, and especially BUBh 2.1.15, in V. PANOLI (trans.), *Upanishads in Śaṅkara's Own Words*, vol. 4 (Calicut: Mathrubhumi Printing and Publishing Co. Ltd., 1994), p. 407 (modified): "Seeing that the parts of a house such as pillars, walls, straw and timber, as well as the aggregate of all these, are meant for the benefit of someone who sees, hears, thinks, and knows these objects and whose existence etc. does not depend upon the origination, rise and fall, destruction, name, form, and attributes in the form of effects of these objects, we infer that the parts of the vital air etc., as well as the aggregate must be for the benefit of some entity that sees, hears, thinks and knows

pillars, walls and a thatch roof, and without inherent meaning and value; its parts have been brought together for the purpose of some conscious being different from it, presumably the occupant. Unlike the house but like the occupant, *Ātman* as pure consciousness exists for its own sake. Unlike the occupant but like the house, the composite of body, mind and personality – indeed, the whole created order – exists only in dependence upon and, hence, "for the sake of" this same pure consciousness.[18]

Continuing this line of reasoning, the student asks: who actually has the capacity to superimpose foreign notions on this *Ātman*? Only a conscious being. Since on this reading the composite of body, mind and personality is not conscious in and of itself, but only in dependence upon and "for the sake of" *Ātman*, *avidyā* cannot be assigned to it. But it cannot exactly be assigned to *Ātman* either. For this *Ātman* has been made the object, rather than the subject, of false superimposition. So who is left? Only "me," the conscious hearer, the one who has raised the question in the first place. So the student concludes: this false superimposition, the seed of all pain and suffering, must have been made, in a paradoxically unclassifiable way, "by me."

Such a cryptic, asymptotic conclusion naturally merits a still more cryptic reply:

> To this the teacher responded, 'If you know that the false superimposition is the seed of [every] calamity, then do not make it!' (2.65)
> 'Your Holiness, I cannot help [it]. I am driven to do it by another; I am not independent.' (2.66)

Shankara's model teacher, we note, does not even slightly clarify the question, "Whose is *avidyā*?" or help us assign the student's "by me" to the realm of *Ātman* or to the composite of body, mind and personality. Instead, simply taking the student at his word, he issues a command: "*Mā kārṣīs-tarhi*," "Then do not make it!" or, more colloquially, "So cut it out already!" The student professes himself unable to comply, and the dialogue continues.

these objects and whose existence, etc. do not depend upon the origination, rise and fall etc. of those things."

[18] The parallel to Sāṃkhya is limited by the fact that, in Sāṃkhya, pure spirit can be characterized as an "enjoyer" (*bhoktṛ*) of material reality, while Shankara specifically negates such enjoyership (*bhoktṛ-tva*) in *Ātman*. See BURLEY, *Classical Sāṃkhya*, pp. 78-79; Gerald James LARSON, "Introduction to the Philosophy of Sāṃkhya," in LARSON and BHATTACHARYA, *Sāṃkhya*, esp. pp. 73-83; and the further discussion of Sāṃkhya in ch. 7, below, pp. 223-26.

Studies by Paul Hacker and Daniel Ingalls have convincingly demonstrated that the model teacher's strategy here exactly mirrors Shankara's own approach in the three places where questions about the source or locus of *avidyā* arises in his commentaries (BSBh 4.1.3; BUBh 4.1.6; BGBh 13.2).[19] "In all these passages," Ingalls affirms, "one sees that Śaṃkara never admits either horn of the dilemma. *Avidyā* is never said to be real. It is never said to be unreal. But no new modality is set up to solve the difficulty."[20] Ingalls and Hacker both ascribe Shankara's distinctive position on this issue – or, perhaps, his non-position – to his thoroughly practical orientation. As Hacker puts the matter, the great teacher's "answers are not philosophically exact; rather, they are pedagogically compelling."[21]

While in general agreement on this score, John Thatamanil also suggests that Shankara may deliberately assign *avidyā* to the category of mystery, as the "impossible possibility" that accounts for empirical suffering without rendering it ontologically necessary or rationally explicable.[22] Shankara is not, of course, mute about the origins of empirical life itself: in USG 1, as we have seen, he draws on the Upanishadic idiom of "name-and-form" to unfold the emergence of the world and the embodied individual from *Ātman*. But how and why does such emergence become the cause of so much suffering? There is no satisfactory answer to this question. The point, Shankara appears to have maintained, is never to offer a rational defense of *avidyā* as the root of all evil. The point is to remove it.

With this goal in mind, the teacher poses a further question:

> The teacher said, 'Are you different from feelings of pleasure and pain and from [the words] I have spoken, or are you identical [with them]?' (2.69) The pupil answered, 'I am indeed not identical.' 'Why?' 'Because I perceive both of them as objects just as [I perceive] a jar and other things [as objects]. If I were identical [with them] I could not perceive either of them; but I do perceive them, so I am different [from both of them]. If [I were] identical [with them] it would follow that the modifications of the feelings of pleasure and pain exist for their own sake and so do [the words] you have spoken; but it is not reasonable that any of them exists

19 HACKER, "Distinctive Features," pp. 65-66, and Daniel H.H. INGALLS, "Śaṃkara on the Question: 'Whose is Avidyā?'" *Philosophy East and West* 3/1 (1953): pp. 69-72.

20 INGALLS, "Śaṃkara on the Question," p. 71.

21 HACKER, "Distinctive Features," p. 66.

22 John J. THATAMANIL, *The Immanent Divine: God, Creation, and the Human Predicament* (Minneapolis: Fortress Press, 2006), pp. 54-57.

> for their own sake, for the pleasure and pain produced by a sandal and a thorn are not for the sake of the sandal and the thorn,[23] nor is use made of a jar for the sake of the jar. So, the sandal and other things serve my purpose, *i.e.*, the purpose of their perceiver, since I who am different from them perceive all the objects seated in the intellect. (2.70)

In section 2.66, the student explained his inability to eradicate ignorance by placing the blame elsewhere: that is, he claimed that he is not independent, wholly determined by some outside power. But this would, based on the position developed in USG 2.64, render him non-conscious and "for the sake of another" (*para-artha*; see USG 2.67).

To address this claim, teacher and student together make a critical examination of pain and pleasure as they concretely arise in the individual consciousness. Such experiences, the student concedes, do not possess positive or negative value in and of themselves, but only in relation to another: namely, the one who becomes conscious of them. As in the earlier example of a house and its occupant, the one whose purpose is served by such experiences must also be different from the experiences. How then are they related? The student's answer echoes a key theme of USP 7.1: I, the conscious subject, perceive all such objects of experience as "seated in the intellect," much like – to draw on Swami Paramarthananda's illustration from chapter 3 – frames passing through a film projector.[24]

The model teacher draws what must be, given the assumptions that govern the entire debate, the only possible conclusion:

> The teacher said to him, 'So, then, you exist for your own sake since you are conscious. You are not driven [to act] by another. A conscious being is neither dependent on another nor driven [to act] by another, for it is not reasonable that a conscious being should exist for the sake of another conscious being since they are equal like two lights. Nor does a conscious being exist for the sake of a non-conscious being since it is not reasonable that a non-conscious being should have any connection with its own object precisely because it is non-conscious. Nor does experience show that two non-conscious beings exist for each other, as for example a stick of wood and a wall do not fulfill each other's purposes.' (2.71)

[23] The example of the thorn may seem an odd addition to this list. The English translation "for the sake of" seems to imply "for the good of," but it need not carry such a connotation. The point here is that the thorn, like the sandal and the jar, generates a sensible reaction – in this case, pain – and thus "serves the purpose," not of itself, but of the one who becomes conscious of it.

[24] See above, ch. 3, pp. 99-100; MAYEDA, *A Thousand Teachings*, pp. 36-37; and the further discussion in VETTER, *Studien*, pp. 80-81.

The teacher attempts to demolish all possible avenues by which the student could sustain his earlier assertion, "I am not independent." In the main, the second half of the section re-articulates the view that non-conscious things acquire purpose and value only in relation to conscious beings, just as a house possesses value in relation to its occupant and a jar possesses value in relation to the one who uses it to carry water.

In the first half, however, the teacher also anticipates a further objection. For, even if one grants that a conscious subject cannot exist "for the sake of" non-conscious things, it might still be possible for one conscious being to exist in intrinsic relation to and thus "for the sake of" another conscious being.[25] To resolve this doubt, the teacher asserts that all conscious beings possess a fundamental "equality," just as two lights can be regarded as fundamentally the same.[26]

The student does not initially grant this new element in the teacher's argument:

> [The pupil objected,] 'Is it not experienced that a servant and his master, though they are equal in the sense of being conscious, exist for each other?' (2.72)
>
> [The teacher said,] 'It is not so, for what [I] meant was that you have consciousness just as fire has heat and light. And [in this meaning I] cited the example, "like two lights." This being the case, you perceive everything seated in your intellect through your own nature, *i.e.*, the transcendentally changeless, eternal, pure consciousness which is equivalent to the heat and light of fire.' (2.73a)

The student introduces a counter-example: the master and the servant, both conscious, each of whose purpose or value is determined by their mutual relation. Elsewhere Shankara responds to similar examples by pointing out that terms like "master" and "servant" pertain to finite bodies, minds and personalities, not to *Ātman*. Hence, one can only say that the body, mind and personality of the servant exist for the sake of the master, and this only to the extent that the master is conscious of them – and vice-versa. In no case does the pure consciousness of one, in and of itself, serve the purpose of the other's pure consciousness.[27]

[25] See NARASIMHAN, *Upadeśa Sāhasrī*, pp. 339-40.

[26] MAYEDA's critical edition includes only the term *prakāśa*, "light" here and in USG 2.73a; a number of variant manuscript traditions, including those adopted by JAGADĀNANDA and ALSTON, specify this further as *pradīpa-prakāśa*, "light of a lamp." See Sengaku MAYEDA (ed.), *Śaṅkara's Upadeśasāhasrī, Critically Edited with Introduction and Indices* (Tokyo: Hokuseido Press, 1973), p. 278-79nn101, 110.

[27] See BSBh 2.1.4 and 2.3.45, in GAMBHIRANANDA, *Brahma-Sūtra-Bhāṣya*, pp. 309, 509.

To extend the analogy of house and occupant: since a shed may serve the purpose of storing things that do not fit in the main residence, we may be tempted to define "residence" and "shed" primarily in terms of these mutual functions. Much more significantly, however, residence and shed both exist exclusively "for the sake of" their shared owner. They thus stand in a relation of fundamental equality relative to that owner, whose purpose they equally serve.

Shankara's model teacher makes the same point here by employing the analogy of the heat and light of two fires. Such imagery nicely illustrates how the divine self can be understood as self-revealing, self-existent, and characteristically different from everything illumined by it.[28] Light cannot be reduced to the individual lamps or torches associated with it; neither can all-pervasive consciousness be reduced to the individual bodies, minds or phenomenal experiences with which it has become confused. Moreover, just as it belongs to the very nature of fire to emit heat and light, so also the awareness of experiential objects like pleasure and pain takes place though the *Ātman*'s "own-nature" as pure consciousness. Insofar as all conscious persons share in this nature, all possess a radical equality that transcends the structured roles, such as master and servant, which ordinarily govern empirical life.

By implication, this same argument can also be extended to include the structured roles of teacher and student, as enacted in the second prose chapter. Though one teaches and the other learns, their mutual relation cannot be reduced to these roles. More fundamentally, they stand in a relationship of profound equality through the conscious awareness both equally share. This equality is not self-evident, and it does not simply elide the distinctions of their mutual relationship and particular roles. It emerges only slowly in and through that very relationship and those very roles, as teacher and student together engage in the process of inquiry. Yet, Shankara's narrative suggests, precisely by means of such sustained practices of reasoned debate, the conventional assumptions that ground pain, suffering and even social division slowly give way to a deeper sense of union in and as the self of all.

[28] See USG 55-57, 60, 64, 70-71, as well as the discussions in Paul HACKER, "Being and Spirit in Vedanta," in HALBFASS, *Philology and Confrontation*, pp. 177-85; A.G. Krishna WARRIER, *The Concept of Mukti in Advaita Vedānta*, Madras University Philosophical Series 9 (Madras: University of Madras, 1961), pp. 224-32; and J.N. MOHANTY, "Consciousness in Vedanta," in S.S. Rama Rao PAPPU (ed.), *Perspectives on Vedānta: Essays in Honor of Professor P.T. Raju* (Leiden: E.J. Brill, 1988), pp. 8-17.

A Christian Reflection: John J. Thatamanil, to whom we referred in treating the teacher's non-response to the question, "Whose is *avidyā*?", takes his analysis a step further by drawing a critical correlation between Shankara's position on this issue and the Christian theologian Paul Tillich's unwillingness to "make sin an ontological inevitability" by providing a rational account for it.[29] The Fall and Original Sin are, on this reading, transposed from literal events in a mythic past to existential realities, here and now, rooted in human freedom yet universal in human experience.[30] Christian hearers of the *Upadeśasāhasrī*, who encounter this idea in the resolutely practical and pedagogical scripts of USG 2 and who may or may not be familiar with Tillich's particular style of existentialist theology, can nevertheless gain insight from this correlation. Like Advaita teachings on *avidyā*, Christian teachings on sin acknowledge this sin's primordial and universal thrall while simultaneously placing responsibility for it squarely on the shoulders of the individual sinner. Firmly instructed to sin no more, Christian hearers can easily imagine ourselves crying out with the model disciple, "I cannot help it. I am driven to do it by another; I am not independent." For Shankara, of course, this predicament is not primarily moral but epistemological in character. Hence, there is no question of entering into communion with God and other persons through the removal of something that actually disrupts that communion, as maintained by most Christians; it is only a question of discerning that profound, ontological equality deeper than any disruption or division whatsoever – even the universal, insidious and ultimately inexplicable bondage of *avidyā*.

Changeless and Changing Knowledge (USG 2.73b-74, 76-77, 102-103, 108b-11)

In the first half of USG 2, as we have seen, Shankara's model teacher and student join together in a very particular sort of shared discernment, whereby the harsh realities of empirical life are subjected to uncompromising critical examination. One of the key points in this process of self-examination is the presumption that all objects of embodied experience differ essentially from the subject who becomes conscious of them. In the latter half of the *Upadeśasāhasrī*'s second prose chapter (2.74-111), further arguments demonstrate the same idea, showing how any attempt to objectify *Ātman* leads to an infinite regress (see esp. 2.98-101, 2.104-105). The self pervades the various states of phenomenal experience while remaining characteristically different from them (2.86-93).[31] As the sun is a source of light without itself being illumined, so also the

[29] THATAMANIL, *Immanent Divine*, pp. 56.
[30] See Ibid., pp. 54-57, 113-18.
[31] See MAYEDA, *A Thousand Teachings*, pp. 43-46, and VETTER, *Studien*, pp. 84-86.

self as pure consciousness knows all finite and transitory objects without itself being finite or transitory (2.93). Precisely as such an all-pervasive knower, it is self-established (2.97).

This is familiar terrain. What is particularly fascinating about the discussion in the latter half of the present chapter, however, is the way in which Shankara's model teacher subtly undermines even the apparent dualism between self and non-self, eternal knower and finite knowing. The doubt that governs the conversation as a whole is given in USG 2.73-74:

> [The teacher continued:] 'And if you admit that *Ātman* is always without distinctions, why did you say, "After getting relief again and again in the state of deep sleep, I perceive pain in the waking and dreaming states. Is this indeed my own nature or [is it] due to some cause?"[32] Has this delusion left [you now] or not?' (USG 2.73b)
> To this the pupil replied, 'Your Holiness, the delusion has gone thanks to your gracious assistance;[33] but I am in doubt as to how I am transcendentally changeless.' (2.74a)
> 'If I am not composite, I have pure consciousness as my nature; so I exist for my own sake. Nevertheless, I am a perceiver of notions which have the forms [of the external objects] such as blue and yellow [and] so I am indeed subject to change. [For the above reason, I am] in doubt as to how [I am] transcendentally changeless.' (2.74c)[34]

At the conclusion of the previous argument, the teacher pronounced that *Ātman*, the student's own innermost self, is "immovably firm" or, as rendered by Mayeda, "transcendentally changeless" (*kūṭastha*; USG 2.73a).

[32] USG 2.45, above.

[33] Though it is not a central theme of his teaching, Shankara speaks comfortably of "grace" (*prasāda*) in connection with instruction, with the Lord's maintenance of the world order, and even with liberation itself. See especially Bradley J. MALKOVSKY, *The Role of Divine Grace in the Soteriology of Śaṃkarācārya,* Numen Studies in the History of Religions 91 (Leiden: Brill, 2001); and Bradley J. MALKOVSKY, "Śaṃkara on Divine Grace," in B. MALKOVSKY (ed.), *New Perspectives on Advaita Vedānta: Essays in Commemoration of Professor Richard De Smet, S.J.* (Leiden, Boston and Köln: Brill, 2000), pp. 70-83.

[34] I have omitted the middle portion of this section (2.74b), which takes up and disposes of what appears to be an argument drawn from Vijñānavāda Buddhism: namely, that it is not necessary to posit an external world, or any objects independent of the perceiver, to explain the fact of perception. Chakravarthi RAM-PRASAD details this Buddhist argument and Shankara's defence of "externality" as a necessary presumption of empirical life in "Dreams and Reality: The Śaṅkarite Critique of Vijñānavāda," *Philosophy East and West* 43 (1993): pp. 405-55, which is included in a revised form in his *Advaita Epistemology and Metaphysics: An Outline of Indian Non-Realism* (London and New York: RoutledgeCurzon, 2002), pp. 38-79. See also ALSTON, *The Thousand Teachings*, p. 64n1; Hacker, *Upadeśasāhasrī*, p. 40n15; and VETTER, *Studien*, p. 81.

Although the student is now ready to admit his distinction, as pure consciousness, from pain, pleasure and all the experiences of embodied life, the additional claim of changelessness strikes a discordant note. Why? Precisely because this changeless self has, in the same section, been characterized as one who perceives these phenomena (2.73a). Such perception, as the disciple explains here, implies contact with "notions" shaped by external objects, such as colors; and this, in turn, appears to reveal the self as "one [who is] subject to change," the very opposite of "transcendentally changeless" (2.74c).[35]

A bit further along, the student further clarifies his objection:

> Then [the pupil] said, 'Perception is what is meant by the verbal root, that is, nothing but change; it is contradictory [to this fact] to say that [the nature of] the perceiver is transcendentally changeless.' (2.76)
> [The teacher said,] 'That is not right, for [the term] "perception" is used figuratively in the sense of a change which is meant by the verbal root; whatever the notion of the intellect may be, that is what is meant by the verbal root; [the notion of the intellect] has change as its nature and end, with the result that the perception of *Ātman* falsely appears [as perceiver]; thus the notion of the intellect is figuratively indicated by the term, "perception." For example, the cutting action results [in the static state] that [the object to be cut] is separated in two parts; thus [the term, "cutting," in the sense of an object to be cut being separated in two parts,] is used figuratively as [the cutting action] which is meant by the verbal root.' (2.77)

In hearing the dialogue in this section, it is important to note that the ontological status of creation, embodied life and objects of perception, in and of themselves, is not under dispute. Instead, the student focuses more narrowly on what happens in the perceiving subject in coming to know objects in this world, whatever their status may be. As the disciple explains, the very use of a word like "perception" (*upalabdhi*) implies activity and change in the self, since this nominal form is derived from the verbal root *upa+labh-*, "to perceive" (v. 76). And what is a verb other than a word indicating some action, transformation or change?

The teacher does not deny the facts of empirical perception. On the contrary, he offers a number of illustrations to show how it nevertheless coheres with the teaching. Elsewhere in the *Upadeśasāhasrī*, for example, he adverts to the simultaneity of awareness: since at any given moment

[35] For more comprehensive treatments of Shankara's theory of perception, see RAM-PRASAD, *Advaita Epistemology*, esp. pp. 31-35, 52-56; and MAYEDA, *A Thousand Teachings*, pp. 33-43.

the self perceives mental modifications all at once, such modifications can come and go without vitiating its changeless nature (2.75; 2.83).[36] In the present section, on the other hand, he instead makes use of an explanatory image already familiar from USP 5 and 18: the finite ego as a "reflection" or, in the translation above, "false appearance" of perception (*upalabdhi-ābhāsa*; v. 77; cf. USP 18.109-10).[37] In its primary and proper sense, "perception" or "apprehension" refers to consciousness itself, changeless and eternal. It is only in a figurative or secondary sense that it is used to indicate perception as the result of action or change. Such changes thus pertain to the finite intellect, not to the pure knowing reflected therein (see also USG 2.81).[38]

In essence, the teacher effects a kind of semantic reversal, which can be seen in reference to his example of "cutting." If I offer someone "cut fruit," that person automatically defines the adjective "cut" figuratively, in terms of the action by which the fruit arrived at that status: i.e., when I pulled out a knife and sliced the fruit into pieces. The verbal root – "to cut" or "to perceive" – is primary; the adjectival usage – "cut" or "perceived" – is secondary. In the case of *Ātman* as pure apprehension, this order of reasoning should be reversed, as though the action of "cutting" were a figurative usage, derived from the more fundamental state of "having been cut." The *Ātman* is, in other words, eternally apprehended by its own nature. When we *seem* to apprehend this *Ātman* through, for example, a dialogical process like that modeled in the present script, our consciousness as such does not undergo any transformation or acquire some new property. It merely comes to rest in what is already and always its own fundamental nature.

Later, Shankara's model teacher returns to this theme, introducing a second analogy:

> [The pupil objected,] 'If so, [and] if the knower is not the subject of empirical knowledge, how is it a knower?' (2.102)
> [The teacher] answered, 'Because there is no distinction in the nature of empirical knowledge, whether it is eternal or non-eternal, since empirical knowledge is apprehension. There is no distinction in the nature of this [empirical knowledge] whether it be non-eternal, preceded by remembrance, desire, and the like, or transcendentally changeless and eternal, just as there is no distinction in the nature of what is meant by verbal root such as *sthā* ["stand"], whether it is a non-eternal result preceded by "going" and

[36] See the discussion in VETTER, *Studien*, pp. 82-83.
[37] See above, ch. 3, pp. 94-95, and ch. 5, pp. 159-66.
[38] See VETTER, *Studien*, p. 81.

other [forms of actions], or an eternal result not preceded [by "going" or any other forms of actions]; so the same expression is found [in both cases]: "People stand," "The mountains stand," and so forth. Likewise, although the knower is of the nature of eternal apprehension, it is not contradictory to designate [It] as "knower," since the result is the same.' (2.103)

The student is responding here to the teacher's insistent claim, immediately prior, that the "eternal light of pure consciousness" – the primary subject of the Advaita teaching – cannot properly be said to arise through perception, remembrance and the other elements of ordinary cognition, which do not pertain to *Ātman* (USG 2.101). Against this, the student observes that the capacity to engage in perception, desire and remembrance is exactly what we intend when we describe someone as a "knower." I am a "knower," in other words, insofar as I perceive objects of knowledge, deliberately seek them out, and retain them in my memory. If none of these things can be attributed to "me," the light of consciousness within and beyond all activity whatsoever, how am I a knower at all?

The teacher answers, once again, by clarifying our ordinary use of language, at least as it pertains to *Ātman*. Before, he used the example of "cutting" to differentiate literal and figurative meanings of words like "perception." Here, he uses the example of "to stand" (*sthā*) to demonstrate the more fundamental continuity that underlies all the different meanings of such words, even in the midst of their variant usages. "Standing" refers to an activity whereby a person rises from sitting or some other posture to an upright position. But we also use the term analogically to describe what a mountain "does" by definition, without reference to any activity whatsoever: it stands on the horizon, etc. Both literal and figurative usages remain meaningful because, as the model teacher explains, they share the same result. That is, both the person and the mountain stand, one as a result of action and the other as a permanent property or eternal "result" inherent to the mountain's very existence.

From this analogy, the teacher draws a conclusion that is simultaneously obvious and radical: namely, that empirical knowledge-acquisition and the eternal knowing of the changeless *Ātman* share a single fundamental nature or result as "apprehension" (*avagati*). The two referents of the term "knowledge," though contradictory at the level of conventional reasoning, actually have "no distinction in nature." This means that the divine self can indeed be called a knower without its becoming implicated in change, just as one can truthfully say, "the mountain stands on the horizon," without insinuating that it has just gotten up from a long nap.

At a deeper level, the teacher's conclusion also implies that the very process of instruction enacted in the myriad scripts of the *Upadeśasāhasrī* represents a profound sharing in the "own-nature" (*sva-rūpa*) of *Ātman*. Earlier, in USG 2.73a, it was the mere fact of consciousness that joined servant and master, teacher and student, individually across the boundaries of their different roles. Here, at least by implication, it is the dialogue they undertake together which ultimately possesses "no distinction in nature" with the divine self. Insofar as teachers and disciples come to discern the truth of *Ātman* together – or any truth at all – their shared activity mirrors and manifests this same *Ātman*'s unchangeable, divine light.

With this insight in place, the teacher wraps up his instruction:

> 'Although [Apprehension] is transcendentally changeless and eternal, [It] appears at the end of the notion [forming process] due to sense-perception and other [means of knowledge] since [the notion-forming process] aims at It. If the notion due to sense-perception and other [means of knowledge] is non-eternal, [Apprehension, though eternal,] appears as if it were non-eternal. Therefore, [Apprehension] is figuratively called the result of the means of knowledge. (2.108b)

We have already seen in USG 2.103 that empirical knowledge and eternal knowledge share the same essential nature as "apprehension" or "awareness" (*avagati*). Here, the teacher combines this insight with the same kind of semantic reversal we witnessed in sect. 77. For the student's question in sect. 102 – "How is *Ātman* a knower?" – presumed "knowledge" as something acquired through perception and other means. But here it is the eternal and changeless apprehension of *Ātman* which is designated as the primary meaning of the term. To draw on the earlier analogy, we might say that the mountain alone stands in a true sense, since its standing is not subject to change or transformation. When I get up from my seat, on the other hand, I am standing in a figurative sense, mirroring by my activity a property that permanently inheres in the mountain. Similarly, the disciple of the *Upadeśasāhasrī* does indeed come to know *Ātman* through scriptural teaching and debate, but such knowing is said to be acquired only in a figurative sense. Once again, conventional meanings and definitions have not been simply dismissed; they have been turned inside-out and, thereby, completely transformed.

USG 2 concludes with a lengthy confession by the disciple:

> [The pupil said,] 'If so, Your Holiness, Apprehension is transcendentally changeless, eternal, indeed of the nature of the light of *Ātman*, and self-established, since It does not depend upon any means of knowledge with regard to Itself;[39] everything other than This is non-conscious and exists for another's sake, since it acts together [with others].' (2.109a)

In the first part of this confession, the student re-states leading themes of the previous discussion, drawing the analysis of embodied existence "for the sake of another" (*para-artha*) in the first half together with the deeper inquiry into *Ātman* as pure apprehension (*avagati*) in the second.

As the student continues, however, he finds himself making broader and bolder claims:

> 'And because of this nature of being apprehended as notions causing pleasure, pain, and delusion, [non-*Ātman*] exists for another's sake; on account of this very nature, non-*Ātman* exists and not on account of any other nature. It is therefore merely non-existent from the standpoint of the highest truth. Just as it is experienced in this world that a snake [superimposed] upon a rope does not exist, nor water in a mirage, and the like, unless they are apprehended [as a notion], so it is reasonable that duality in the waking and dreaming states also does not exist unless it is apprehended [as a notion]. In this manner, Your Holiness, Apprehension, *i.e.*, the light of *Ātman*, is uninterrupted; so It is transcendentally changeless, eternal and non-dual, since It is never absent from any of the various notions. But various notions are absent from Apprehension. Just as in the dreaming state the notions in different forms such as blue and yellow,[40] which are absent from that Apprehension, are said to be non-existent from the standpoint of the highest truth, so in the waking state also, the various notions such as blue and yellow, which are absent from this very Apprehension, must by nature be untrue. And there is no apprehender different from this

[39] That is, since the *Ātman* is the self-revealing precondition of all subsequent knowledge, it does not depend upon perception, inference or even to the word of scriptures to become known. These means do not, as such, make *Ātman* known; they only remove the false superimpositions which have been placed upon *Ātman*.

[40] Here the student is drawing an analogy from the dreaming state to the waking state: that is, just as one seemingly apprehend forms and colors in the dreaming state which are sublated or negated upon waking, so also the forms and colours of waking life are sublated in light of highest truth. The analogy between waking and dream was employed by Vijñānavāda Buddhists to negate the existence of the objective world; following Gauḍapāda, Shankara will use the metaphor in a similar way in some contexts, but he will also refute the Vijñānavāda Buddhists on the true externality of the world in others. See RAM-PRASAD, *Advaita Epistemology*, esp. pp. 52-56; and Richard KING, *Early Advaita Vedānta and Buddhism: The Mahāyāna Context of the Gauḍapāda-Kārikā* (Albany: State University of New York Press, 1995), pp. 153-74.

> Apprehension to apprehend It; therefore It can Itself neither be accepted nor rejected by Its own nature, since there is nothing else.' (2.109b)

It is noteworthy that, as the student re-articulates major themes of the teaching, he introduces a few ideas that appear nowhere in the dialogues of USG 2, but which are prominently featured elsewhere in the *Upadeśasāhasrī*'s teaching scripts, such as the image of a desert mirage, the rope mistaken for a snake, and the theory of two levels of truth – phenomenal experience and highest truth. Perhaps most strikingly, he repeatedly draws a conclusion which we encountered in USP 7.6 but which, again, finds no explicit place in the second prose chapter: namely, that nothing outside this highest apprehension may rightly be said to exist.

It is possible, of course, that Shankara views such ideas as the inevitable conclusion of the preceding analysis. Having undertaken such penetrating discrimination between self and non-self, the disciple necessarily judges that everything other than *Ātman* must be assigned to a level of existence that, in comparison to *Ātman*, cannot truly be said to exist at all. But it seems just as likely that these new themes function simply to re-inscribe the dialogical teaching scripts of the second prose chapter within the broader practices of teaching and learning modeled in a variety of scripts throughout the *Upadeśasāhasrī*. The present dialogue stands in intrinsic relation to the comparable dialogue of USG 1 and the various treatments of the verse portion, as fruit of a shared, layered and complex religious enterprise. Hence, the student's final conclusion can reflect a wider inquiry than that depicted in USG 2 alone.[41]

Regardless of the source of the student's conclusions, the teacher responds to them with warm approval:

> [The teacher said,] 'Exactly so it is. It is nescience that is the cause of transmigratory existence which is characterized by the waking and dreaming states. The remover of this nescience is knowledge. And so you have reached fearlessness. From now on you will not perceive any pain in the waking and dreaming states. You are released from the sufferings of transmigratory existence.' (2.110)
> [The pupil said,] 'Oṃ.' (2.111)

[41] The commentators take yet a third approach to the question, actually filling in an additional exchange between teacher and student in dialogue with the teachings of Sāṃkhya and other rivals, which they take to be implied in the disciple's remarks. See ĀNANDAGIRI, *Upadeśasāhasrī*, pp. 158-60, RĀMATĪRTHA, *Upadeśasāhasrī*, pp. 93-85, and the summary in NARASIMHAN, *Upadeśa Sāhasrī*, pp. 374-75.

One can hardly imagine a more dramatic finale. The teacher, hearing the disciple's profession, pronounces him fearless and free from all kinds of pain, here and now. In light of our previous treatments, especially in chapters 3 and 5, we have good reason to question whether the teacher is speaking primarily in terms of some new, elevated spiritual experience or existential transformation. It might be better to interpret his pronouncement as a radical reorientation of meaning and value or, again borrowing from Suthren Hirst, as an "epistemic shift."[42] On the analogy of the semantic reversal of "cutting" and "standing," the student has shifted his sense of self-worth and self-identity from his individual embodied existence, which undergoes change and experiences suffering, to that eternal awareness he now knows to be manifested and reflected therein. Ergo, he has nothing left to fear and no freedom yet to acquire. He is released.

The student replies with the single syllable, "*oṃ*." This syllable may be employed here simply to affirm the teacher's words, making it translatable as "yes, indeed," "so be it," or even "amen."[43] Yet, the *Upanishads* and other Hindu scriptures also offer this sacred combination of *a, u* and *m* as a privileged symbol of the Lord, of the world, of the breath in meditation and thus especially of the innermost self (*ātman*).[44] We might say that, from a point of view within the tradition, the entire Advaita teaching unfolds from nothing more than this sacred syllable.

Be this as it may, the disciple's invocation of *oṃ* brings the second prose chapter to a fitting conclusion. For *oṃ* is simultaneously a composite of other Sanskrit phonemes and a unitary, uninterrupted whole. It is enacted in time by the shaping of lips, exhalation of breath and vibration of vocal chords, yet it is essentially the same from one such pronouncement to the next. Like the heat and light of fire, alluded to in USG 2.73, or the "standing" of mountain and person alike in 2.103, *oṃ* beautifully captures the ultimate unity of *Ātman* even in the midst of its

[42] See Jacqueline SUTHREN HIRST, "Weaving the Strands: Cognition, Authority and Language in Śaṅkara's *Upadeśasāhasrī*," in S. RAO and G. MISHRA (eds), *Paramparā: Essays in Honour of R. Balasubramanian* (New Delhi: Indian Council of Philosophical Research, 2003), pp. 149-55.

[43] See JAGADĀNANDA, *A Thousand Teachings*, p. 70, and especially ALSTON, *The Thousand Teachings*, p. 89n1. This is also the view of the commentators, as summarised in NARASIMHAN, *Upadeśa Sāhasrī*, p. 376.

[44] Shankara provides a list of such scriptures in his introduction to the MaUBh. See the Sanskrit text and English translation in V. PANOLI (trans.) *Upanishads in Śaṅkara's Own Words*, vol. 1, rev. ed. (Calicut: Mathrubhumi Printing and Publishing Co., 1995), pp. 302-303.

diverse, changing and contingent reflections from one consciousness to the next. It is this changeless and non-dual *Ātman* which grounds and pervades the empirical apprehension shared by teacher and disciple, as they engage in reflection and debate. The second prose chapter, then, does not merely narrate a process of self-inquiry; through this narration, it illustrates how such teachers and disciples come self-consciously to embody the very reality about which they teach and learn. Together, through their mutual relation and shared discernment, they become a living manifestation of the divine *Ātman*.

III.
"Examine yourselves": A Christian *Saṃvāda* with USG 2

> Whoever, therefore, eats the bread or drinks the cup of the Lord in an unworthy manner will be answerable for the body and blood of the Lord. Examine yourselves, and only then eat of the bread and drink of the cup. For all who eat and drink without discerning the body, eat and drink judgment against themselves. For this reason many of you are weak and ill, and some have died. But if we judged ourselves, we would not be judged. But when we are judged by the Lord, we are disciplined so that we may not be condemned along with the world (1 Corinthians 11:27-32).

In our hearing of USG 2 and brief Christian reflections, we have already had recourse to the idea of communion, as both eternal reality and fruit of discernment. It thus seems natural to begin our Christian *saṃvāda* with this sacred script by turning to the apostle Paul's instructions to the Corinthians about communion in a literal sense: that is, sharing in the body and blood of Christ in the Lord's supper (1 Cor 11:17-34).

In this passage, as in the discussion of true wisdom we encountered in chapter 3 of this commentary, the apostle expresses his concern that differences in status and wealth are dividing the Corinthian community, particularly in their gatherings to share the bread and cup of the Lord (11:17-18).[45] In the course of his reproof against such divisions, he offers the earliest NT witness to this central Christian rite (11:23-26), rooted

[45] See J. Paul Sampley, "The First Letter to the Corinthians," in *The New Interpreter's Bible*, vol. 10 (Nashville: Abingdon Press, 2002), pp. 780-81, 934; Jerome Murphy-O'Connor, O.P., "The First Letter to the Corinthians," in in R. Brown, J. Fitzmyer, and R. Murphy (eds.), *The New Jerome Biblical Commentary* (Englewood Cliffs: Prentice Hall, 1990), p. 809 [49:56]; and James D.G. Dunn, *The Theology of*

in the memory of Jesus' table-fellowship and especially the last supper he shared with his disciples before his death. The liturgical form of the ritual appears to have varied considerably in the early centuries of the movement, sometimes – as in Corinth, it seems (see 1 Cor 11:21) – taking place in the context of a full supper, sometimes celebrated annually as a Passover meal, and sometimes incorporating one cup, two cups or none at all.[46] Such variety may well be read as an indirect witness to the ubiquity of the meal itself as, in one form or another, a privileged sign and means of Christians' profound union with Christ and, through Christ, with one another.

Be this as it may, Paul's emphasis on spiritual union is so strong here that the liturgical historian Paul F. Bradshaw views it as the central message of the whole passage. The motive behind Paul's narrative is, Bradshaw argues, more catechetical than ritual, and it may reveal very little about how the Eucharist was actually celebrated in Corinth.[47] On this reading, the passage functions primarily to underscore an insight already expressed earlier in the same letter, when Paul states: "The cup of blessing that we bless, is it not a sharing in the blood of Christ? The bread that we break, is it not a sharing in the body of Christ? Because there is one bread, we who are many are one body, for we all partake of the one bread" (1 Cor 10:16-17).[48] Later, the apostle will again pick up the imagery of one body to demonstrate the interrelated unity of diverse charismatic gifts, ministries and individuals in the Christian community (1 Cor 12:4-31; cf. Romans 12:3-8). And, in the present passage, Paul discusses the Lord's supper as an occasion for the Corinthians to engage in what he calls "discerning the body of the Lord" (1 Cor 11:29), which J. Paul Sampley describes as "Paul's shorthand way of talking about an individual's assessment of two distinguishable but inseparable matters: how well one's life relates to Christ and how well one's love ties one to

Paul the Apostle (Grand Rapids and Cambridge: William B. Eerdmans Publishing Company, 1998), pp. 609-13.

46 See the discussion in James D.G. DUNN, *Unity and Diversity in the New Testament: An Inquiry into the Character of Earliest Christianity*, 3d Ed. (London: SCM Press, 2006), pp. 176-83; Robert J. DALY, S.J., Eucharistic Origins: From the New Testament to the Liturgies of the Golden Age," *Theological Studies* 66.1 (2005): pp. 3-22; Gary MACY, *The Banquet's Wisdom: A Short History of the Theologies of the Lord's Supper* (New York/Mahwah: Paulist Press, 1992), pp. 15-36; and especially Paul F. BRADSHAW, *Eucharistic Origins*, Alcuin Club Collections 80 (London: SPCK, 2004).

47 BRADSHAW, *Eucharistic Origins*, pp. 13-14, 44-48.

48 See DUNN, *Unity and Diversity*, pp. 178-79, and SAMPLEY, "First Corinthians," pp. 935-36.

others who, though many, are one body in Christ."[49] Lacking such discernment, Christians reveal themselves still bound by the illness, weakness and death of the present age; with it, their celebration, their fellowship and their every action becomes a proclamation of the Lord in whose body they equally share (see 1 Cor 11:26).[50]

It is precisely due to the apostle's insistence on the close relation between discerning the body of the Lord and sharing in that body through the bread and cup of the Eucharist that this passage offers such a fruitful starting point for dialogue with USG 2. Indeed, it might be accurate to say that Paul writes less to reform the offering Christians make through their ritual *koinonia* than to reform the offering they make through their daily sharing across every aspect of their lives.[51] The focus remains resolutely on that communion with Christ which grounds both the ritual pattern and the pattern of life to which it is, or should be, intimately related. So too, in the scripted dialogue enacted in the *Upadeśasāhasrī*'s second prose chapter, the teacher continually turns the disciple back from the differences, divisions and suffering of embodied life to the divine *Ātman*, which pervades and grounds all existence. Like the master and servant of USG 2.72-73, disciples in the Advaita tradition exist not independently, but only for the sake of *Ātman*; like the heat and light, they reveal a radical equality and union far deeper than their diversity, a profound sharing in the self-illuminating consciousness of *Ātman* that comes to full realization only through the kind of rigorous discernment modeled in this chapter.

These two practices of discernment are profoundly different, of course, and they cannot be simply identified. The "discernment of the body" recommended by Paul ideally takes place before and in integral relation to the Eucharistic celebration, whereas Shankara's disciples have, at least in principle, severed their connection with any and all forms of Vedic ritual practice.[52] Even those practices which one might think would

[49] SAMPLEY, "First Corinthians," p. 936.

[50] See Ibid, pp. 935-37; DUNN, *Theology of Paul*, pp. 622-23; and J. Paul SAMPLEY, *Walking between the Times: Paul's Moral Reasoning* (Minneapolis: Fortress Press, 1991), pp. 50-56.

[51] DUNN offers an illuminating discussion of Paul's general transposition of the terms of sacrifice and cultic worship into every aspect of Christian living in his *Theology of Paul*, pp. 543-58.

[52] We recall that, although Shankara seems not to have restricted the Advaita teaching exclusively to renunciants, renunciant life can be seen as an invariable norm for those seeking self-knowledge. See above, chapter 2, pp. 59-63.

complement reception of the teaching, such as the *prasaṃkhyāna* meditation proposed in USP 18.9-18, have been ruled out as means to liberation. More deeply, as we have already noted, the two practices of discernment take place on different registers, with Paul being primarily concerned with morality and ethical deportment, and Shankara with cognition and epistemic perspective. For Paul, the illness and weakness experienced by members of the Corinthian community witnesses God's judgment against their sinful *behavior*, which they should have anticipated through their own discernment and self-reformation. The fundamental difficulty is not primordial ignorance but sin, as manifested in this case by divisions of wealth and status in the one body of Christ.

In Christian teaching and in the preaching of Paul in particular, however, the solution to the problem of sin is not to be found in ethical striving of any sort – at least, not primarily. This solution is found, by contrast, entirely outside of the efforts and empirical experience of the individual disciple: for salvation is ultimately a gift of grace. The self-giving love of God in Christ represents a fundamental gift that grounds the entire Christian life, as explored especially in the previous chapter of this commentary. Hence, it may be possible for Christian hearers of the *Upadeśasāhasrī* to reconsider the discernment commended by Paul as an ongoing, epistemic inquiry, in which disciples attempt to perceive their limited, empirical experience in the light of Christ, and thereby exercise judgment upon it. It is, no less than the epistemic shift effected tby the teacher of USG 2, an activity that achieves disciples' shared union in the life of God not by achievement of some new object, but solely in and through their shared discernment of that bond eternally achieved in Christ. In effect, Christian hearers of these scripts can close the interpretive distance between what, in Paul, seem to be two distinct activities: the practice of discernment and the sacrament of communion. In place of this division, "discerning the body" might itself be viewed as a distinctive kind of sacramental practice, which discloses, embodies and thus effects disciples' union with God and one another, a union freely given in Christ but realized in its fullness only gradually, through the assiduous work of self-examination.

To develop this idea further, we again turn to a later witness, albeit one from a position closer to the margins than the center of mainstream Christian tradition: the seventeenth-century movement founder and visionary Mary Ward (1585-1645). Born and raised in a Catholic recusant family in Protestant England, Ward was inspired by a series of illuminations between 1607 and 1611 to found the Institute of the

Blessed Virgin Mary (IBVM), a new order of women religious free from enclosure in a convent or monastery.[53] Due in no small part to the sisters' freedom of movement and their adoption of a Jesuit-inspired rule, the order was eventually suppressed by Pope Urban VIII in 1631 and Mary Ward herself imprisoned on charges of heresy.[54] Ward was soon cleared of all charges. The lifting of her Institute's suppression, on the other hand, followed only by degrees between 1703 and 1877, long after her death.[55]

Mary Ward's teaching commends itself to our attention due in no small part to her distinctive application of themes originating with Ignatius of Loyola (1491-1556) and the practices of discernment modeled in his *Spiritual Exercises.*[56] Arguably, the central governing image of Ward's spirituality is her ideal of the spiritual "estate of justice," a theme that draws deeply upon Ignatian and Augustinian precepts of freedom and spiritual indifference. In the formulation of Ignatius: since human beings are "created to praise, reverence and serve God our Lord," one ought to "use [created] things to the extent that they help me toward my end, and rid myself of them to the extent that they hinder me," even to the extent of "making myself indifferent to all created things...."[57] Ward undertook Ignatius's *Exercises* at several points in her formation and, at the conclusion of one such retreat in 1615, arrived at a critical insight. As she wrote to her retreat director Fr. Roger Lee, S.J.:

[53] See Jeanne COVER, IBVM, *Love – the Driving Force: Mary Ward's Spirituality: Its Significance for Moral Theology*, Marquette Studies in Theology 9 (Milwaukee: Marquette University Press, 1997), pp. 12-13, and Mary Ward's own description of these experiences in M. ORCHARD, IBVM (ed.), *Till God Will: Mary Ward through Her Writings* (London: Darton, Longman and Todd, 1985), pp. 23-29. The particular social and cultural forces at work in England shaped Ward's initiative, at least in part, for Catholic monasteries had been legally disbanded by Henry VIII. This left the pastoral work Ward envisioned in the hands of ordinary clergy, laypeople, and those religious orders, like the Society of Jesus, who could work outside the structures of monastic life.

[54] See COVER, *Love – the Driving Force*, pp. 13-15.

[55] Ibid, p. 16, and Gillian ORCHARD, IBVM, *Mary Ward: Once and Future Foundress*, rev. ed. (Langley: Vario Press Ltd., 1997), p. 16.

[56] For the purposes of this commentary chapter, we will glance at just a few short writings from 1612-17, excerpted in ORCHARD, *Till God Will* and cited in-text as TGW. A more extensive collection of documents from this period, in Ward's late Middle English and other original languages, is also available in U. DIRMEIER, CJ (ed.), *Mary Ward und ihre Gründung: Die Quellentexte bis 1645: Band 1*, Corpus Catholicorum 45 (Münster Westfalen: Aschendorff Verlag, 2007).

[57] *The Spiritual Exercises* #23, in G. GANSS (trans.), *Ignatius of Loyola: Spiritual Exercises and Other Works*, The Classics of Western Spirituality (Mahwah: Paulist Press, 1991), p. 130.

> It seems a clear and perfect estate to be had in this life, and such a one as [is] altogether needful for those that should well discharge the duties of this Institute… It is not like the state of the saints, whose holiness chiefly appears in that union with God, who maketh them out of themselves. The felicity of this estate, for as much as I can express, was a singular freedom from all that could make one adhere to earthly things, with an entire application and apt disposition to all good works. Something happened also discovering that freedom that such a soul should have had to refer all to God… (TGW, p. 40).

The description here clearly echoes Ignatius, particularly in Ward's ideal of freedom from worldly attachment, the better to "refer all to God."[58] Such holiness and freedom are not to be sought primarily through a form of spiritual ecstasy that "maketh [the saints] out of themselves," she suggests, but in the more ordinary union of shared work and shared mission. Later in the letter, Ward takes her argument a step further, closely identifying the estate of justice with the original state of "those in Paradise before the fall." "I have thought," she concludes, "… that perhaps this course of ours would continue to the end of the world, because it came to that in which we first began" (TGW, pp. 40-41).[59]

Unlike Shankara, Mary Ward does not seek absolute freedom from the world of means, ends and phenomenal existence, as such; merely the singular freedom to pursue the sole worthwhile such end in God. Her vision of the estate of justice aims squarely at this created world and the good works to be accomplished therein, while also pushing beyond the boundaries of present experience. Nevertheless, just as Shankara's teacher repeatedly insists that the whole range of phenomenal experience be sharply relativized and set in relation to the divine self, for whose sake alone they exist, so also Mary Ward relativizes all created things and sets them in relation to the God whose purpose they all ultimately serve. Human beings cannot choose to serve this divine purpose, or not: serve it they will, one way or the other. They can, however, discern God's purpose in any particular situation, purify themselves of those attachments that obscure their interior willingness and freedom, and thereby arrive at the estate of justice – an estate characterized by its radical, perfect willingness to embody the perfect will of God.

58 See the introduction by James WALSH, S.J., in ORCHARD, *Till God Will*, esp. pp. xxx-xxxi.

59 See also DIRMEIER, *Mary Ward und ihre Gründung*, pp. 290-91.

We can, moreover, recall how Shankara illustrates the ultimate coherence of empirical perception and acquired knowledge with that eternal apprehension of the "transcendentally changeless and non-dual Self." The former truly manifests the latter, albeit at a lower level and in a secondary sense. Along similar lines, Ward does not hesitate to identify the estate of justice with the self-giving love of Christ, as this empowers and motivates the human pursuit of justice – called "verity" – and interior freedom to "refer all to God, and to find all in God."[60] For Shankara, the reflection of the divine *Ātman* in ordinary, empirical apprehension possesses "no distinction in nature" from its transcendent ground; for Ward, this sublime estate represents a reflection, at least "in some degree," of an ontologically prior state of existence which is both origin and destiny of all humankind: namely, the state of Paradise before the fall.[61] Ignorance and sin obscure the communion of God, human persons and all creation, to be sure, but such communion nevertheless remains intrinsic to their "own-nature" and need merely to be recognized in a disciplined way to become effective in the life and mind of prospective disciples.

Mary Ward and Ādi Shankaracharya also share at least one further point in common: both push resolutely beyond abstract visions of divine perfection and its reflection in ordinary life to the sustained practice of self-examination and discernment in the very particular lives of very particular disciples. Such a practical orientation permeates Ward's writings, but for convenience we can focus on selected spiritual precepts from a list she provides for new members of her nascent Institute, probably composed in 1610 or 1611:[62]

> 1. I will endeavour that no sensible motions nor occurrent accidents change easily [my] inward composition or external carriage, because freedom of mind and calmness of passions are so necessary both for my own profit in spirit and proceedings with others.
> 2. Because I am inclined to affect and undergo more willingly such things as hath the title or outward appearance of excellency or greatness, I will henceforth endeavour to embrace and execute more simple things with a particular love, devotion and diligence, and will always be watchful... that I spend not my time and forces in seeking my own content or the praise of others.
> 9. I will never endeavour that any love me for myself, and yet will I labour to love all for God and in Him (TGW, pp. 38-39).

[60] COVER, *Love – the Driving Force*, pp. 130-31, 150-53, quotation at p. 130.

[61] See ORCHARD, *Till God Will*, p. 40, and the further discussion in COVER, *Love – the Driving Force*, pp. 119, 122, 131-34.

[62] See DIRMEIER, *Mary Ward und ihre Gründung*, p. 161.

These precepts, and the others that accompany them in Ward's original instruction, may be read, on the one hand, as distinctively Ignatian specifications of Paul's command to "discern the body of the Lord" through assiduous self-examination. In and out of our hearing of USG 2, on the other hand, Ward's instructions to cultivate interior calm, to embrace simple things above praise and excellency, and to love all others in and for the sake of God might also be heard as a distinctively Christian specification of Shankara's model teacher's injunction, *mā kārṣīs-tarhi*, "Do not do it! Do not make false superimpositions on the self."

Indeed, the instructions of Advaita teacher and Christian foundress alike might be helpfully cast in terms of what anthropologist Victor Turner referred to as the "stripping and levelling" inherent in many practices of ritual initiation, wherein new initiates lose the signs of old identities in order to be inscribed with new ones.[63] We recall that Shankara's teacher does not supply an exact philosophical answer to the question, "Whose is *avidyā*?" Neither does Mary Ward provide the sisters of her Institute with a description of the "estate of justice," its precise relation to humankind's original state, and a subsequent fall from grace.[64] Both Christian and Hindu spiritual guides eschew such etiologies. Both focus instead on encouraging their respective disciples to divest themselves, here and now, of all claims to personal status, approbation, pleasure, pain or even, on the Advaita side of the comparison, individual embodiment itself. In both cases, the ideal disciple endeavors to set aside attachment to "outward appearances" or "false superimpositions" in favor of more enduring convictions about self, God and their mutual relation, albeit to greater or lesser degrees of success. Through the proper discernment on the level of awareness, identity and intention, the Advaitin disciple, no less than the novice of Mary Ward's Institute, is gradually stripped bare and made anew.

Turner hypothesized that such practices of "stripping and levelling" culminate in "*liminal* experience" and its social correlate, a radically egalitarian mode of human relatedness he labelled "*communitas*."[65] While the idea of *communitas*, in and of itself, both supports and advances the dialogue being attempted here, it must be qualified in at least one

[63] See Victor TURNER, *The Forest of Symbols: Aspects of Ndembu Ritual* (Ithaca: Cornell University Press, 1967), pp. 93-111; and Victor TURNER, *The Ritual Process: Structure and Anti-Structure* (Ithaca: Cornell University Press, 1969), esp. pp. 95-108.

[64] It seems that Ward's insight about this estate was not, in any case, clear in her own mind by 1611.

[65] E.g. TURNER, *Ritual Process*, pp. 125-65.

respect. For neither Mary Ward nor Ādi Shankarcharya speak primarily of an ecstatic affective state, whereby – in Ward's language – God "maketh [the saints] out of themselves." Insofar as they foster new habits of thought, however, both practices do aim to supersede conventional divisions and to reveal a more profound mode of human relatedness:

The teacher said to [the student], '... A conscious being is neither dependent on another nor driven [to act] by another, for it is not reasonable that a conscious being should exist for the sake of another conscious being since they are equal like two lights.'
[The pupil objected,] 'Is it not experienced that a servant and his master, though they are equal in the sense of being conscious, exist for each other?'
[The teacher said,] 'It is not so, for what [I] meant was that you have consciousness just as fire has heat and light. And [in this meaning I] cited the example, "like two lights." This being the case, you perceive everything seated in your intellect through your own nature, *i.e.*, the transcendentally changeless, eternal, pure consciousness which is equivalent to the heat and light of fire' (USG 2.71a, 72-73a).

But to attain perfection, knowledge of verity is necessary, to love it and to effect it. That you may not err, I beseech you all to understand and note well wherefore you are to seek this knowledge. Not for the content and satisfaction it bringeth, but for the end it bringeth you to, which is God. Seek it for him, who is Verity... The other day, disputing with a father who loves you well, I could not make him think otherwise than that women are yet by nature full of fears and affections, more than men, which, with respect to him, is not so. It is true if we will not place our knowledge right, we shall be full of fears and affections... Remember then that [God] be the end of all your actions and therein you will find great satisfaction and think all things easy and possible (TGW, pp. 59-60).

Hearing these scripts together, one from USG 2 and the other from a retreat Ward gave to her sisters in December 1617,[66] it would be easy for the contemporary hearer to play the apparent liberality of either one against the other. Lest we idealize the absolute equality proclaimed by this Hindu teacher against the sexist priest alluded to by Ward, we should recall that the model disciples of the *Upadeśasāhasrī* are invariably identified as high-caste men, and that Shankara vigorously maintained traditional prohibitions against the study of Vedic texts such as the *Upanishads* by women or members of lower classes.[67] Lest we idealize the

[66] See DIRMEIER, *Mary Ward und ihre Gründung*, pp. 357-66 for the complete texts of all three addresses given by Mary Ward on this occasion.

[67] See BSBh I.3.34-38, in GAMBHIRANANDA, *Brahma-Sūtra-Bhāṣya*, pp. 229-34; Francis X. CLOONEY, S.J., *Theology after Vedānta: An Experiment in Comparative Theology* (Albany: State University of New York Press, 1993), pp. 134-41; and especially Lance

Christian visionary's protest against similar limitations in her own culture, we should keep in mind that those who would eventually react so strongly against this new women's movement and place Ward herself under arrest for heresy were not Brahmanical Hindus, but fellow Christians. There is no pure, egalitarian Christianity to play against an oppressive, elitist Hinduism, or vice-versa.

Instead of constructing caricatures on either side, then, Christian hearers do better to take note of these two teachers' respective claims, in their uniqueness, while also continuing to trace a line of comparison from one to the other. For, though the evidence suggests that Shankara was certainly no progressive in his vision of women's rights and roles, his teaching in the *Upadeśasāhasrī* may be interpreted by the Christian hearer to prefigure and possibly to radicalize the fervent exhortations of Mary Ward. Ward speaks here of the absolute "Verity" of God, authentic knowledge of whom brings "great satisfaction" and makes "all things possible" for men and women alike. What is this Verity? God the divine self, as well as communion in that perfect estate which reflects both the primordial origin of humankind and its final renewal in Christ. Through right discernment of this estate, false superimpositions – including, for example, assumptions about the inferiority of women in the service of God – simply fall away.

The temptation for many Christian hearers of Mary Ward is to hear her descriptions of the "knowledge of verity" and the estate of justice primarily within the framework of means and ends, as ideals to be achieved through moral striving. And this may be appropriate, as far as it goes. At the same time, our hearing of Shankara also encourages us to read these descriptions more sacramentally, in terms of their status as created reflections, signs and instruments of God the divine self. Proceeding by means of a kind of remotion modeled on the teacher's instruction in USG 2.76-77 and 2.108,[68] Christian hearers can reason allegorically from the practice of moral judgment to the perfect estate of justice, from the human "knowledge of verity" that arises through the practice of discernment to that transcendentally changeless, divine

E. NELSON, "Theism for the Masses, Non-Dualism for the Monastic Elite: A Fresh Look at Śaṃkara's Trans-Theistic Spirituality," in W. SHEA (ed.), *The Struggle over the Past: Fundamentalism in the Modern World* (Lanham: University Press of America, 1993), pp. 69-77.

[68] See John TABER, "Reason, Revelation and Idealism in Śaṅkara's Vedānta," *Journal of Indian Philosophy* 9 (1981): pp. 289-92; and R.V. DE SMET, "Śaṅkara and Aquinas on Creation," *Indian Philosophical Annual* 6 (1970): pp. 112-18.

"Verity" that grounds and motivates all such discernment. In each case, the analogy from *judgment* to *justice*, *verity* to *Verity* is real, at least from the inquirer's point of view. When the element of relativity and imperfection is removed from these properties by attributing them to God, however, this same inquirer reverses the order of the analogy. It is God the divine self who emerges as the true referent of terms like judgment, verity and will: human beings exercise judgment, know truly and will freely in a purely figurative, analogical sense. When Ward encourages her fellow sisters to seek knowledge of verity and to exercise freedom "not for the content and satisfaction it bringeth, but for the end it bringeth you to, which is God," therefore, she may be heard to imply that such seeking both signifies the inner reality of God and, precisely through such signification, also brings us to God as our end. We seek verity for no other purpose than Verity itself, as the sole foundation and true reality of all such seeking, knowing, judging and willing whatever.

For Shankara, of course, God's Verity would be more properly identified not primarily with one or another primordial "estate of justice" or freedom to embrace God's will, but with the discerning student's "own-nature" as the transcendentally changeless, eternal, pure consciousness of *Ātman*. Even more importantly, this same Verity reveals "no distinction in nature" from any sustained practice of discernment and self-examination and indeed any act of cognitive inquiry whatsoever. Master and servant, teacher and student, man and woman, perhaps even Hindu and Christian – all such distinctions, though never completely dissolved in practice, become ever more attenuated as critical discernment deepens and its co-participants come more clearly to embody the divine object of their shared inquiry.

In the next chapter, the universality of this vision will be sharply qualified by Shankara's narrower, far more polemical attempt to distinguish the tradition of Advaita Vedanta from false rivals on all sides. For the moment, however, Christian hearers can dwell on the beauty and challenge offered by this particular teaching script, in its integrity and in its capacity to re-frame distinctive Christian practices like those modeled by the apostle Paul and Mary Ward. The core sacramental claim, we can be reminded, is not that communion with God in Christ can be achieved through certain human actions, such as ethical striving or ritual celebration of the Lord's supper; it is, rather, that certain created realities and forms of activity may, by grace, disclose and effect a communion that is already and eternally achieved by God the divine self. In the Advaita tradition, the rigorous discernment and self-examination modeled in

USG 2 may thus be regarded as a kind of privileged, sacramental practice. So also, albeit for different reasons and in a different register, for Christians engaged in "discernment of the body" and the "labour to love all for God and in Him" (TGW, p. 39). Hearing both teachings together, such Christians may fruitfully widen the scope of our self-examination, sharpen the clarity of our discernment and thus enter more deeply into the fundamental equality of all creatures in God.

Chapter 7

A PILGRIM PEOPLE: COMMENTARY ON USP 16

I.

Upadeśasāhasrī Padyabandha 16.64-69

Therefore, assumptions concerning bondage, final release, etc., [which are] other than this are indeed confused ideas. The assumptions of the Sāṃkhyas, of the followers of Kaṇāda, and of the Buddhists are lacking in profound consideration.

As [their assumptions] contradict the scriptures and reasoning, they should never be respected. Their faults can be pointed out hundreds and thousands of times.

And since it might also involve being culpable [under the text] 'any other than this,' [they should not be respected at any time]. Therefore, having abandoned the teaching of other scriptures, a wise person should make firm his understanding of the true meaning of the *Vedānta* and also of Vyāsa's thought, with faith and devotion and without any crookedness.

Thus both the false assumptions based upon dualism and the views that *Ātman* does not exist have been rejected through reasoning; seekers after final release, being free from doubts which arise from the views of others, become firm on the path of knowledge.

If one has attained the absolutely pure and non-dual Knowledge, which is self-witnessed and contrary to false assumptions, and rightly holds a firm belief, he will go to eternal peace, unaccompanied [by anything].

II.

Steady on the Path of Knowledge: Hearing USP 16 (Selections)

Like many of the other verse chapters, USP takes its traditional title from its initial word, "consisting of earth," and the first verse makes the following, relatively undramatic assertion:

> It is said [traditionally] that the hard element in the body consists of earth and that the liquid element consists of water. Digestion, activity, and space have their origin in fire, air, and ether, respectively. (USP 16.1)

This is a far cry from the reverent salutations that opened USP 1 and 18, or the intense questioning of the disciple at the beginning of USP 2. In its first verse, USP 16 reads more like an ancient medical manual than a religious treatise. Shankara will, moreover, continue the analysis of body, senses and mind into the next several verses, in order to show the ultimate distinction of all such empirical realities from the divine self (USP 16.2-9).

More significant, however, is the way such familiar processes of interior discrimination between self and non-self open into a broader discrimination between and among different scholastic traditions with competing claims. An outline illustrates this movement:

USP 16

1-9	Differentiating Self from Non-Self
10-16	Responses to Some (Mostly Buddhist) Objections
17-22 Summary of the Teaching	
17-18	Injunction: know *Brahman* by abandoning ignorance
19-22	False identification of *Ātman* with senses, mind and intellect
23-44 Refutation of "Those Who Deny the Existence of the Self" (*nir-ātma-vāda*, v. 68)	
23-24	Summary of Buddhist positions
25-29	Refuting "momentary existence" and other Buddhist doctrines
30	A better idea: *Ātman* as locus of superimposition and its resolution
31-38	The changeless *Ātman* as the substrate of all subsequent differentiations
39-44	Summary: true liberation is giving up false self-identification
45-63 Refutation of the "Dualists" (*dvaya-vāda*, v. 68)	
45-50	Refuting Sāṃkhya doctrines of *puruṣa* and *prakṛti*
51-56	Refuting Vaiśeṣika doctrines of an inert *ātman*
57-63	A better view: liberation as mere dissolution of a false notion
64-67	Summary of the Refutations
68-74	General Conclusions

USP 16 begins with an analysis of the human constitution, to be sure, but it also begins in the middle of an animated conversation. If USG 2 turned inward, toward the disciple's consciousness and the intimate relationship between teacher and student, USP 16 opens outward onto a wider social canvas of controversy and debate, responding to objections from all sides. In the words of the commentators, it engages in a systematic "driving away of the teachings of all the philosophers," precisely in order "to make the seeker after liberation firm in his 'own-kingdom'" or even to "anoint" seekers in that divine kingdom.[1]

In our hearing of this verse chapter, we will first address the content of selected refutations and thereafter turn to the social reality they both imply and constitute: a discipleship community of those who have set aside all false teachings and become "steady on the path of knowledge." The corporate reality of the teaching tradition, as we shall hear, receives its sharpest definition at its boundaries, where potential adversaries are identified, met in debate and roundly defeated.

> **An Initial Reflection**: For Christians, the discipleship community as such represents one of the core articles of the faith: as expressed in the Nicean Creed, all Christians are called to believe in "one, holy, catholic and apostolic church." This is, at one level, radically different from Advaita Vedanta, which focuses primarily on individual consciousness and insists upon disciples' differentiation from all empirical phenomena – including, of course, the teaching tradition and the social body constituted by it. Yet, in chapter 4, we noted how Christians such as Augustine of Hippo could differentiate our final end in God very clearly from the temporal realities that carry us there – including the church and even the incarnation. So also, in the present chapter, we will discover that Shankara can be heard to insist no less strongly than most Christian hearers on the reality of a particular, sanctified community of Advaita disciples and its central place in the Advaita teaching. Not unlike *Ātman* the divine self, this community is not described positively, by enumerating its distinctive marks or prescribing its unique structure; it emerges through active engagement and differentiation from those communities that surround it... and to which it is closely, intimately, even inextricably related.

[1] See ĀNANDAGIRI's comment in S. SUBRAHMANYA SASTRI (ed.), *Shri Shankarabhagavatpada's Upadeshasahasri with the Tika of Shri Anandagiri Acharya*, Advaita Grantha Ratna Manjushi Ratna 15 (Varanasi: Mahesh Research Institute, 1978), p. 47 (line 23), and RĀMATĪRTHA's in D. GOKHALE (ed.), *Shri Shankarāchārya's Upadeśasāhasrī with the Gloss Padayôjanīkā by Shrī Rāmatīrtha* (Bombay: Gujurati Printing Press, 1917), p. 243. The term translated here as "own-kingdom" (*svā-rājya*) commonly serves as an epithet for a highest heaven or for the state of union with *Brahman*. In USP 16.74, as we shall see below, Shankara compares self-knowledge to the heavenly "kingdom" (*rājyatā*) of the god Indra. See M. MONIER-WILLIAMS, E. LEUMANN, C. CAPELLER, and others, *Sanskrit-English Dictionary, Etymologically and Philologically Arranged with Special Reference to Cognate Indo-European Languages*, rev. ed. (New Delhi: Munshiram Manoharlal Publishers, 2004), s.v. "svārājya," p. 1284.

Refuting the Other (USP 16.23-24, 30-32, 48-50, 61-62)

Spirited debate is by no means rare in Shankara's writings. A major section of his commentary on the *Brahma-Sūtras* is dedicated to dismantling other systems of thought,[2] and in his commentaries on the *Upanishads* he will periodically pause to do a sweep of major opponents.[3] This is also a significant aspect of the portrait of Shankara in the traditional hagiographies.[4] We have ourselves, earlier in this commentary, encountered refutations of two views sometimes associated with Shankara's fellow Advaitin and elder contemporary Maṇḍana Miśra: the "combination of knowledge and action" theory in USP 1 and the view of the *prasaṃkhyāna-vādin* in USP 18.

The mere presence of polemics and controversy in USP 16, therefore, does not set this chapter apart from Shankara's other writings, nor from the writings of most of his interlocutors.[5] Each such refutation nevertheless has its own distinctive structure and aims. In Shankara's *Brahma-Sūtra-Bhāṣya* 2.2, for example, opposing views are presented as a series of positions of increasing plausibility, beginning with the dualistic tradition of Sāṃkhya, finishing with the devotional tradition of Pañcarātra Vaiṣṇavism, and threaded together by intervening treatments of: Vaiśeṣika "atomism"; three schools of Buddhism; Jainism; and Maheśvara Śaivism. USP 16, by contrast, more closely resembles oral debate. Adversarial voices are initially merely implied, marked by phrases like "if [you say]" (v. 10) or "even if it is thought" (v. 11). Though these fragments likely

[2] BSBh 2.2. See Francis X. CLOONEY, S.J., *Theology after Vedānta: An Experiment in Comparative Theology* (Albany: State University of New York Press, 1993), pp. 102-13; and S.R. BHATT, "Śaṅkarācārya's Philosophy of Advaita and His Critique of Other Schools," in V. VENKATACHALAM (ed.), *Śaṅkarācārya: The Ship of Enlightenment*, (New Delhi: Sahitya Akademi, 1997), pp. 45-54.

[3] See, for example, BUBh 1.2.1, 2.1.20, and 4.3.7 in V. PANOLI (trans.), *Upanishads in Śaṅkara's Own Words*, vol. 4 (Calicut: Mathrubhumi Printing and Publishing Co. Ltd., 1994), pp. 23-40, 430-73, 864-94; KeUBh 2.4, in V. PANOLI (trans.) *Upanishads in Śaṅkara's Own Words*, vol. 1, rev. ed. (Calicut: Mathrubhumi Printing and Publishing Co., 1995), pp. 114-20; GKBh 3.4-18 in Ibid, pp. 400-24; and the more systematic survey and refutations in GKBh 4, in Ibid, pp. 450-547.

[4] See Jonathan BADER, *The Conquest of the Four Quarters: Traditional Accounts of the Life of Śaṅkara* (New Delhi: Aditya Prakashan, 2000), pp. 183-229; Mariasusai DHAVAMONY, "Śaṅkara and Rāmānuja as Hindu Reformers," *Studia Missionalia* 34 (1985): pp. 121-24; Govind Chandra PANDE, *Life and Thought of Śaṅkarācārya* (Delhi: Motilal Banarsidass Publishers, 1994), pp. 255-336; and S. ŚAṄKARANARAYANAN, *Sri Śaṅkara: His Life, Philosophy and Relevance to Man in Modern Times*, K. RAJA (ed.), Adyar Library General Series 14 (Madras: The Adyar Library and Research Centre, 1995), pp. 70-118.

[5] See Richard KING, *Indian Philosophy: An Introduction to Hindu and Buddhist Thought* (Edinburgh: Edinburgh University Press, 1999), esp. pp. 42-46, 130-37.

correspond to selected tenets of Buddhism and Jainism, the treatments are so terse as to make it difficult to know for sure.[6] Beginning in vv. 23-24, the treatment becomes more orderly, but only towards the end of the chapter, in v. 68, does Shankara introduce a fundamental division between two fundamental errors which, in retrospect, offer an organizing principle for the whole chapter: 1) "the views that *Ātman* does not exist," namely, the various forms of Buddhism addressed in vv. 23-44; and 2) "false assumptions based on dualism," including the rival Hindu traditions of Sāṃkhya and Vaiśeṣika, refuted in vv. 45-63.

Space constraints do not permit a full treatment of all of these arguments. Instead, we will focus on just a few representative exchanges from vv. 23-63, beginning with Shankara's initial statement of the fundamental Buddhist claim:

> [All] this is indeed the mere *dharma* which indeed perishes every moment and arises without intervals. [Though all this is momentary,] there arises the recognition that this [is that past one] because of similarity, just as a lamp [at this moment is recognized to be the same as it was at the previous moment on account of similarity]. The cessation of [all] this is the aim of life. (USP 16.23)
> According to some [Buddhists], there exist [the external objects] such as form-and-color, the forms of which are manifested by one other than themselves. According to other [Buddhists] nothing else exists but this [consciousness]. [Now] the improbability of the former [theory] is explained.[7] (USP 16.24)

Buddhist objections are scattered throughout this and other chapters of the *Upadeśasāhasrī*.[8] Typically, Shankara strives to distinguish among different Buddhist traditions and to recognize the internal diversity of the tradition, while also elucidating what he perceives to be their shared foundation. So also here. In v. 24, he differentiates between "some" Buddhists who grant the existence of external things, and "others" who

[6] See Sengaku MAYEDA, trans., *A Thousand Teachings: The Upadeśasāhasrī of Śaṅkara* (Albany: State University of New York Press, 1992), pp. 157-58nn6-7, 9-11, 15. The commentators read a reference to Carvaka materialism into verse 2, thereby rendering the initial verses into yet another set of refutations. See V. NARASIMHAN, *Upadeśa Sāhasrī: A Thousand Teachings of Adi Śaṅkara* (Bombay: Bharatiya Vidya Bhavan, 1996), p. 104.

[7] This last statement seems to imply that the arguments of vv. 25-29 are directed at the so-called 'realist' or *Sarva-astitva-vāda* tradition. These arguments can, however, be interpreted as a more general critique.

[8] See, for example, USG 2.57, 74-75, and USP 18.72-74, 141-58. USP 18.142 is a direct quotation of a famous verse from Dharmakīrti's *Pramāṇa Vārttika*. See MAYEDA, *A Thousand Teachings*, p. 201n104.

reduce all reality to consciousness alone.[9] At the same time, in v. 23, he identifies a common metaphysical assumption shared by both schools: namely, the "momentariness" of *dharmas*.[10]

Dharma carries a very wide range of meanings in classical Hindu and Buddhist thought. In the present context, the term appears to carry a specialized meaning, referring to "the fundamental mental and material 'micro-events' that constitute reality as we know it," as posited by mainstream Buddhist scholasticism.[11] To illustrate this idea, in v. 23 Shankara draws on a well-traveled metaphor: the flame of a lamp, which actually consists of an uninterrupted series of different flames, each one drawing its discrete existence from different oxygen molecules and different particles of oil from one moment to the next. If we perceive this flame as a single, perduring "thing," this is not due to anything inherent in the particles of oil, oxygen or even the wick. It is due only to the apparent "similarity" we impute to these different "micro-events" across time. So too for persons and perceived objects, whose existence can be reduced to successive combinations of momentary *dharmas*. Whether one recognized – with the mainstream Buddhists – the *dharmas* as real existents or viewed them – with at least some Mahāyāna critics – as mere extensions of consciousness, the systematic reduction of human experience to momentary phenomena allowed all of these diverse traditions to speak intelligibly about life and liberation without positing an ultimate, enduring self.

And this, Shankara will surmise several verses down the page, is precisely the problem:

> It is our opinion that where there is false superimposition there is [also] annihilation of it. Tell me to whom final release as the result belongs, if everything perishes. (16.30)

[9] ĀNANDAGIRI differentiates these school under the labels "external world school" (*bāhya-artha-vāda*) and "knowledge-only school" (*jnāna-mātra-vāda*). See ĀNANDAGIRI, *Upadeśasāhasrī*, p. 52, lines 12-13, and the discussion in MAYEDA, *A Thousand Teachings*, p. 158n20-21.

[10] It may be worth noting that Shankara does not use the abstract noun "momentariness" (*kṣaṇika-tva)* until v. 25; in v. 23 he merely describes the *dharmas* as "radically momentary" (*kṣaṇika ati-artha*).

[11] KING, *Indian Philosophy*, p. 116. See also the further discussion in Richard KING, *Early Advaita Vedānta and Buddhism: The Mahāyāna Context of the Gauḍapāda-kārikā* (Albany: State University of New York Press, 1995), and Peter HARVEY, *An Introduction to Buddhism: Teachings, History and Practices* (Cambridge, New York and Melbourne: Cambridge University Press, 1990), pp. 83-84. In describing the Abhidharma traditions as "mainstream," rather than as Theravāda or by the diminutive label Hīnayāna, I am following Richard KING in *Indian Philosophy*, pp. 84-91.

The commentators identify this verse as a critique of Mādhyamika Buddhism, or what Shankara elsewhere names *Sarva-śūnyatva-vāda*, according to which all things are radically "empty" (*śūnya*).[12] But the verse can also be read as an attack on the general Buddhist denial of self.

For Shankara, little may separate one interpretation from the other. Prior to classifying different Buddhist schools in the *Brahma-Sūtra* commentary, for example, he first lumps them all together as *Sarvavaināśi-karāddhānta*, "the doctrine which asserts the nihilism of everything," or, more simply, "full nihilism."[13] "This is because," Sengaku Mayeda explains, all... Buddhist schools assert "the theory of *kṣaṇabaṅga* or 'that of entities having but momentary existence' and therefore, in Śaṅkara's understanding, Buddhism as a whole is a doctrine which asserts total nihilism."[14] Along similar lines, in USP 16, having introduced momentariness in v. 23, Shankara first challenges particular elements of this teaching. He asks, for example, how one purports to speak of recognition of similarity from one moment to the next if the intellect itself is also momentary (vv. 25-26). He then goes on to illustrate an apparent contradiction between such radical reductionism and any credible theory of causation (vv. 28-29), thereby discrediting Buddhist claims to teach a true means of liberation (v. 27). Finally, in the present verse, he reaches what must be, from the Advaita perspective, the only logical conclusion: the "destruction of everything."

By adopting such a strategy, Shankara also seems implicitly to concede that most of his individual criticisms of Buddhism in vv. 25-29 could also be directed, with small modifications, at the Advaita teaching.[15] For Shankara proposes an understanding of the intellect, embodied existence and the phenomenal world that, while not reducing them to mere "momentariness," nevertheless assigns them to what he here calls "false superimposition." And this, in turn, raises many comparable problems of experience, causation and above all the means of liberation. If there

[12] See ĀNANDAGIRI, *Upadeśasāhasrī*, p. 53, lines 19-20 [*śūnya-vāda*], and RĀMATĪRTHA, *Upadeśasāhasrī*, pp. 256-57 [*śūnya-mata*].

[13] BSBh 2.2.18 in Swami GAMBHIRANANDA (trans.), *Brahma-Sūtra-Bhāṣya of Śrī Śaṅkarācārya* (Calcutta: Advaita Ashrama, 1965, 1972), p. 402, and Sengaku MAYEDA, "Śaṅkara and Buddhism," in B. MALKOVSKY (ed.), *New Perspectives on Advaita Vedānta: Essays in Commemoration of Professor Richard De Smet, S.J.* (Leiden, Boston and Köln: Brill, 2000), p. 20.

[14] MAYEDA, "Śaṅkara and Buddhism," p. 21.

[15] See, for example, the summary of the commentators in NARASIMHAN, *Upadeśa Sāhasrī*, pp. 116-17.

is no real bondage, how can there be final release? Bhāskara, among many others in Hindu tradition, would charge Shankara of being "a Buddhist in disguise" (*pracchanna-bauddha*) due to the close resemblance between these two teachings.[16]

Shankara does not deny this resemblance in v. 30. From his point of view inside the Vedanta fold, he does not need to. The two traditions may employ similar methods and mirror one another in a hundred ways, but that does not alter their ineradicable difference on the most fundamental level. On the one side, you have the removal of only those false notions we place upon *Ātman* in our ignorance; on the other, "destruction of everything," without remainder. The difference is as clear as night and day.[17]

Shankara goes on to develop this point:

> Truly [It] exists Itself; It may be called Knowledge, *Ātman*, or something else. As It is the Knower of the existence and non-existence [of things], it is not accepted that It is non-existent. (16.31)
> It is Being by which the non-existence [of things] is accepted. If It were not Being, people would not become aware of the existence and non-existence [of things]. And this is not acceptable. (16.32)

In previous chapters, we have already discussed the inaccessibility of *Ātman* to categorical language, as well as its unique status as the self-established precondition of all subsequent acts of knowledge, perception or experience. As the witness beneath and within all empirical knowledge, *Ātman* cannot become the object of such knowledge. But neither, Shankara here concludes, can it be assigned to "non-existence" (v. 31). In fact, the very judgment that all reality can be reduced to "non-existence" necessarily implies the existence of some "being" as the sole basis for each and every such judgment (v. 32). The fundamental Buddhist claim falls like a house of cards, invalidated in the very act of its own pronouncement.

Many hearers of the *Upadeśasāhasrī* may not find this refutation entirely satisfactory, with good reason. It hardly seems plausible that a few short excerpts could capture the rich diversity of Buddhist teachings correctly, much less mount an effective argument against them. For the moment, however, our primary purpose is not so much to evaluate the

[16] See MAYEDA, "Śaṅkara and Buddhism," pp. 18-19, and Daniel H.H. INGALLS, "Bhāskara the Vedantin," *Philosophy East and West* 17 (1967), p. 65.

[17] See especially Daniel H.H. INGALLS, "Śaṃkara's Arguments against the Buddhists," *Philosophy East and West* 3 (1954): pp. 304-306.

arguments themselves as to get a sense of how they function in the teaching script of USP 16.

With this limited goal in mind, we shift our attention – somewhat abruptly – to a second important rival, this one considerably closer to Shankara's Vedic home:

> Since in the Sāṃkhya system *Puruṣa* is changeless, even [there] it is not reasonable for *Pradhāna* to exist for another's sake. Even if there were changes [in It], it would still not be reasonable. (16.48)
> As no mutual relation between *Prakṛti* and *Puruṣa* is possible and as *Pradhāna* is non-intelligent, it is not reasonable for *Pradhāna* to exist for *Puruṣa*'s sake. (16.49)

In the previous chapter, we encountered the very important notion of *para-ārthya*, "existence for the sake of another," which Shankara seems to have inherited from the rival Hindu tradition of Sāṃkhya.[18] The composite of body, mind and personality exists in a dependent relation and thus "for the sake of" *Ātman*, while *Ātman* exists entirely for its own sake.

In Sāṃkhya teaching, the issue of *para-ārthya* arises when considering the relationship between two fundamental principles of existence: the principle of the "person" (*puruṣa*) as pure consciousness; and a second principle, which the pre-eminent Sāṃkhya scholar Gerald Larson calls "primordial materiality" (*mūla-prakṛti*, or simply *prakṛti*).[19] In fact, the Sāṃkhya analysis begins not with *puruṣa* but with *prakṛti*, also understood as the *Pradhāna* or "principal cause" of empirical existence. From this fundamental cause emerges, first, the intellect and "'I'-notion" and, from these, the various categories of mind, sensation, action, "subtle material" and "gross material" – twenty-four principles in all.[20] The dynamic combinations of these principles can, in turn, be traced to an interrelated triad of three *guṇa*s or fundamental "strands" of reality.[21] Manifested through the myriad relations of these *guṇa*s, the twenty-four principles give rise to the whole realm of phenomenal existence, itself further classifiable into fourteen distinct types of sentient beings, "from Brahmā to a blade of grass."[22] It is no mystery how this tradition received

[18] See above, ch. 6, pp. 187-88, 190-91.

[19] Gerald James LARSON, "The Philosophy of Sāṃkhya," in G. LARSON and R. BHATTACHARYA (eds.), *Encyclopedia of Indian Philosophies, Volume IV: Sāṃkhya, A Dualist Tradition in Indian Philosophy* (Delhi: Motilal Banarsidass, 1987), p. 49,

[20] See Ibid, pp. 49-53, and KING, *Indian Philosophy*, pp. 170-78.

[21] LARSON, "Philosophy of Sāṃkhya," p. 66.

[22] See Ibid, p. 59, and *Sāṃkhya-kārikā* 53-55, summarized in LARSON and BHATTACHARYA, *Sāṃkhya*, p. 161.

its name: for the Sanskrit word *Sāṃkhya* can be literally rendered as "enumeration."[23]

In this verse, Shankara is less concerned with the functioning of the *guṇas* than with the precise status of *puruṣa*, which Sāṃkhya posited as a twenty-fifth fundamental principle. In stark contrast to the twenty-four categories of *prakṛti*, *puruṣa* is free from the three *guṇas*, uncharacterizable and ungenerative. *Puruṣa* is conscious; *prakṛti* is not.[24] Each *puruṣa* is in essence nothing but a "witness" or "pure passive presence," the necessary precondition and ground of all possible experience without itself becoming the object of such experience. For this reason, Larson defines *puruṣa* as "contentless consciousness."[25] Bondage, and indeed the whole realm of empirical existence, results from this *puruṣa's* mis-identification with *prakṛti*, its inexplicable confusion of "consciousness" with experiential "content," including the limited body, mind and personality. The goal of the seeker after liberation can therefore be defined in terms of careful discernment between *puruṣa* and the myriad manifestations of *prakṛti*, so as to effect a cognitive return to one's natural state of pure isolation.[26]

Sound familiar? Many of these themes, of course, find echoes in Shankara's own teaching. The two systems are so closely intertwined that Larson characterises Advaita as a kind of refurbished or warmed over Sāṃkhya.[27] Like Buddhism Sāṃkhya does not represent a threat to Advaita because its teachings are so remote. Quite the opposite. It is primarily due to the relative proximity of the two systems that Shankara must demonstrate the distinctiveness of his own teaching as forcefully as possible.[28] Perhaps for this reason, not only does Sāṃkhya figure as the

[23] In modern scholarship, *prakṛti* is usually treated as a material cause and the various Sāṃkhya "enumerations" as cosmological principles. In his *Classical Sāṃkhya and Yoga: An Indian Metaphysics of Experience*, Routledge Hindu Studies Series (London and New York: Routledge, 2007), Mikel BURLEY has challenged this conventional view, arguing that Sāṃkhya would be better regarded as a distinctive form of idealism, occupied not with the existence of an external world, as such, but only with the immanent data of experience.

[24] LARSON, "Philosophy of Sāṃkhya," p. 78.

[25] Ibid, pp. 73-83.

[26] See KING, *Indian Philosophy*, pp. 173-74, 182-85, and BURLEY, *Classical Sāṃkhya*, pp. 133-55.

[27] LARSON, "Philosophy of Sāṃkhya," p. 29, and the more extensive argument in Gerald James LARSON, *Classical Sāṃkhya: An Interpretation of its History and Meaning*, 2d ed. (Santa Barbara: Ross/Erikson, 1979), pp. 209-35.

[28] See especially Hugh NICHOLSON, "Two Apologetic Moments in Śaṅkara's Concept of Brahman," *The Journal of Religion* 87 (2007): pp. 528-55.

first and purportedly least plausible opponent in BSBh 2.2, but refutations of its teaching on *puruṣa* and *prakṛti* also recur frequently throughout Shankara's other works.[29]

As they do in the present verses of the *Upadeśasāhasrī*. Specifically, Shankara here returns to the question of *prakṛti*'s existence "for the sake" of *puruṣa*. At first glance, it would seem to make good sense to conclude that, if one thing exists "for the sake of" another, then we are talking about two distinct realities. Yet, this is also where the Sāṃkhya claim overreaches itself. For the Sāṃkhyins go on to define *puruṣa* as eternally changeless (v. 48) and free of any real relation with *prakṛti* (v. 49). Otherwise one could not reach a state of eternal isolation, as desired. But these qualifications beg a further question: how can *prakṛti* serve any purpose of this changeless and relationless *puruṣa*? Shankara's answer is simple: it can't.

The opponent could respond by changing the terms of the conversation, admitting both change and relation in *puruṣa*. According to Shankara, this would create a deeper difficulty:

> If any action took place [in *Puruṣa*, It] would be perishable. If [action took place] only in knowledge [of *Puruṣa*, It would be perishable] in the same way. If [the functioning] of *Pradhāna* has no cause, it follows that there is no final release. (16.50)

For Shankara and for many of his interlocutors, the imputation of "action" or "change" in a thing implies its "perishability" of logical necessity. Anything that begins in time also ends in time. Seasons change, bodies are born and die, and thoughts rise and fall in the mind. Therefore, even if the Sāṃkhyins admit only a notional change of empirical knowledge in *puruṣa* – namely, its mis-identification with *prakṛti* – they admit its ultimate susceptibility to destruction. Conversely, if this *prakṛti* with which the *puruṣa* has become entangled is truly a fundamental principle, with no cause outside itself, then it is effectively rendered eternal. We end up with the worst of all possible worlds: a perishable *puruṣa*, and an eternal state of bondage.

But doesn't Shankara's Vedanta also view bondage and liberation in terms of ignorance and knowledge? How does its vision of final release

[29] E.g., BSBh I.1.5-12, II.1.1-12, and II.2.1-10 in GAMBHIRANANDA, *Brahma-Sūtra-Bhāṣya*, pp. 45-61, 299-324, 367-83, as well as the further discussion in CLOONEY, *Theology after Vedānta*, pp. 104-13; Natalia ISAYEVA, *Shankara and Indian Philosophy* (Albany: State University of New York Press, 1993), pp. 218-35; and esp. LARSON, *Classical Sāṃkhya*, pp. 209-22.

escape the very criticisms which have been raised against Sāṃkhya? After a brief critique of the similarly orthodox Hindu tradition of Vaiśeṣika (vv. 51-56), Shankara offers the following explanation:

> As Knowledge is the very nature of *Ātman*, It is constantly applied figuratively to the intellect. And the absence of discriminating knowledge is beginningless; this and nothing else is taken to be transmigratory existence. (16.61) Final release is its cessation and nothing else, since [every other view] is unreasonable. But final release is thought to be the destruction [of *Ātman*] by those according to whom final release is to become something else. (16.62)

In the discussion of v. 30, above, we noted that Shankara's response to Buddhism rested upon his teaching of *Ātman* as the self-evident reality behind any act of knowledge or judgment, a point more fully developed elsewhere in the *Upadeśasāhasrī*'s teaching scripts. So also here, Shankara disposes of Sāṃkhya by alluding to an idea we encountered in our treatment of USG 2.77 and 2.108: the figurative application of terms like "perception" and "knowledge," which refer primarily to the changeless apprehension of the self, to the activity of the perishable intellect. Since the state of transmigratory existence is not accepted as an independent reality, distinct from *Ātman*, final release necessitates no change or "destruction" in this same *Ātman*. It requires only that the disciple own up to *Ātman* as the sole principle, upon which the entire worldly realm depends for its relative, merely figurative and provisional existence.

In the dialogue between teacher and student in USG 2, we discerned a movement from the various distinctions of phenomenal existence, including such social distinctions as master and servant and teacher and student, toward their deeper unity in the light of pure consciousness. In the implied dialogues of the present verse chapter, by contrast, the Advaita teaching on the unity of the self provides a vantage from which to see the very clear distinction of this tradition from identifiable others. As Shankara will write at the conclusion of one of the parallel discussions in the *Brahma-Sūtra-Bhāṣya*, the Buddhist teaching "breaks down like a well sunk in sand; and we do not find any the least logic here. Hence also all behaviour based on the Buddhist scripture is unreasonable."[30] The same conclusion presumably follows in the case of Sāṃkhya and any other position that contradicts the Advaita teaching. Such positions eventually break down in the face of inquiry, pulling whole traditions and modes of life with them as they go.

[30] BSBh II.2.32, in GAMBHIRANANDA, *Brahma-Sūtra-Bhāṣya*, p. 426.

A Christian Reflection: Christian hearers of these refutations can note, first, that they are scripted primarily for insiders. One should not use the *Upadeśasāhasrī* as one's sole source for understanding Buddhism and Sāṃkhya any more than one should use the woes and curses of Matthew 23 to learn the actual teachings of Pharisaism or early Rabbinic Judaism. Such hearers can, second, appreciate the fact that – whether accurate as representations or not – the alternative positions described in these scripts are, on their own terms, no less false for Christians than for Advaitins. Early Christian teachings were clarified and developed in part through the refutation of various forms of dualism, and Christians in the modern period have contested strongly against both nihilism and materialist reductionism. So it seems reasonable that Christians and Advaitins might find common cause in defending the subsistent reality of God and soul against the momentariness of all *dharmas* or the mutual implication of *puruṣa* and *prakṛti*. Finally, and just as importantly, Christian hearers can notice how the practice of refutation itself functions to join these traditions and expose their similarities even as it differentiates them. Insofar as such refutations are essential to forming disciples in the tradition, the relationship to these refuted teachings and traditions becomes essential to the identity of the discipleship community – for the Christian hearer of Matthew 23, perhaps, no less than for the Advaitin hearer of USP 16.

A Higher Renunciation (USP 16.17-18, 44, 64-69, 74)

At this point, it may be important to recall that the commentators describe USP 16 as a "driving away of the teachings of all the philosophers" to facilitate its hearers' final release. Shankara employs philosophical reason for the sole purpose of excluding any and all teachings that contradict the revealed word of the *Śruti*, not to establish yet another philosophical view.[31] Indeed, Shankara and the commentators characterize other teachings as "philosophy" (*tarka*) not to set them in parallel with Advaita, but precisely to emphasize their utter fruitlessness as means of liberation. The refutations are scripted, in other words, for the very same hearer implied throughout the *Upadeśasāhasrī*; they function not so much to defeat a living adversary as to clarify the teaching in the mind of this hearer and to re-affirm her commitment to distinctively Advaita Vedāntin modes of reasoning and practice.[32] It becomes difficult, in this

[31] See especially CLOONEY, *Theology after Vedānta*, pp. 96-99 and 102-106, as well as J.G. SUTHREN HIRST, *Śaṃkara's Advaita Vedānta: A Way of Teaching*, RoutledgeCurzon Hindu Studies Series (London and New York: RoutledgeCurzon, 2005), pp. 64-65.

[32] In *Theology after Vedānta*, p. 109, CLOONEY similarly contends that the opponents of BSBh 2.2 "have been scripted so as to play their parts in the drama of the Advaita Text, as foils to the truth Advaita finds in the upaniṣads... The Advaitins take into account all their competitors' views, writing them up so as to confirm the view of an

context, to distinguish between interior personal discernment and exterior community formation. The errors of rival schools become live options in disciples' minds, and their effective refutation carries social consequences.

In order more clearly to see this continuity between interior and exterior, between discriminating self-inquiry and community self-definition, we turn now to a theme that recurs at several key points throughout USP 16 and which lends unity to the chapter as a whole: the theme of renunciation. Earlier, in our commentary on USP 1, we encountered formal renunciation as a preferred alternative to Vedic ritual and householder life, as well as the most suitable state of life for seeker and liberated sage alike.[33] In the present verse chapter, Shankara will reiterate this call for the abandonment of ritual as part and parcel of the Advaita teaching tradition (e.g., USP 16.43). But he also, in tandem with the refutations of Buddhism, Sāṃkhya and other errors, gives this idea a broader valence. The act of renunciation comes to encompass the whole of the Vedānta teaching, as well as to delimit its social and textual boundaries in no uncertain terms.

To trace this development, we return to the beginning of USP 16, where, after an initial sweep of objections (vv. 10-16), Shankara issues the following injunction:

> Abandoning ignorance, which is the root of false assumption and which is the impeller of transmigratory existence, one should know *Ātman* to be the highest *Brahman*, which is released and always fearless. (USP 16.17)
> One should abandon as non-existent the triad of the states of waking, dreaming, and their seed called the state of deep sleep and consisting of darkness; for when one [of them] exists, the others do not. (16.18)

These verses offer, first and foremost, a précis of the teaching and a fitting conclusion to the initial, brief refutations of USP 16.10-16. In v. 17, Shankara characterizes the hearer's innermost self as – here and now – none other than *Brahman*, the highest existent, eternally fearless and free. The false imaginings that obscure this identity, as well as transmigratory existence itself, can be traced to ignorance alone. The brief reference to deep sleep as the "seed" of waking and dream in v. 18 may be calculated to evoke other related themes: the cosmological account of USG 1.18-23, where the world of phenomenal experience emerges progressively

already convinced Advaita audience that there really is no other way to see the world than Advaita's way."

33 See above, ch. 2, pp. 59-64.

from unmanifest "name-and-form," the "seed of the universe";[34] the application USP 18's method of "agreement-and-difference," whereby the hearer discerns *Ātman* as that which is continuously present even in the absence of one or another experiential state;[35] and the wide array of similar analyses, in the *Upadeśasāhasrī* and elsewhere, including especially USP 7.4-5.[36]

What sets USP 16.17-18 apart from these other scripts is Shankara's invocation of the language of formal renunciation. In USP 1.15, for example, he has earlier stated that action "should be renounced" by the one who desires final release; in USP 16.17, he similarly describes "having renounced" as a prerequisite for self-knowledge. Echoing the injunction to renounce action and its fruits in USP 1.21a, Shankara in USP 16.18 again uses the injunctive form, "one should abandon." In USP 1, of course, such language refers to the renunciation of Vedic ritual obligations. In USP 16.17-18, Shankara takes aim at more phenomenological objects: the three states of waking, dreaming and deep sleep in one case (v. 18), ignorance in the other (v. 17).

Further along in his argument, Shankara extends this parallel:

> The attainment of *Ātman* is the supreme attainment according to the scriptures and reasoning. But the attainment of *Ātman* is not attaining something other [than *Ātman*]. Therefore one should [simply] give up [the misconception of *Ātman*] as non-*Ātman*. (16.44)

Here, at the conclusion of his extended refutation of Buddhism (USP 16.23-42), Shankara again invokes the signature phrase, "one should give up," to characterize proper reception of the teaching. What should be given up in this case? This is not entirely clear. Reading broadly, Shankara can be interpreted as commending renunciation of everything directed toward the acquisition or attainment of whatever is "other than self."[37] If so, then

[34] See above, ch. 4, pp. 124-31, and MAYEDA, *A Thousand Teachings*, pp. 22-26.

[35] See above, ch. 5, pp. 152-58, and Wilhelm HALBFASS, "Human Reason and Vedic Revelation in Advaita Vedānta," in *Tradition and Reflection: Explorations in Indian Thought* (Albany: State University of New York Press, 1991), pp. 162-80.

[36] See above, ch. 3, pp. 100-102, and the discussions of the three states of experience in MAYEDA, *A Thousand Teachings*, pp. 43-56; SUTHREN HIRST, *Śaṃkara's Avaita Vedānta*, pp. 83-85; Eliot DEUTSCH, *Advaita Vedānta: A Philosophical Reconstruction* (Honolulu: University of Hawaii Press, 1968), pp. 55-63; and especially Andrew O. FORT, *The Self and Its States: A State of Consciousness Doctrine in Advaita Vedānta* (Delhi: Motilal Banarsidass, 1990).

[37] An alternate manuscript tradition renders this attainment, to be rejected, as *an-ātma*, "not-Self." See Sengaku MAYEDA (ed.), *Śaṅkara's Upadeśasāhasrī, Critically Edited*

the "supreme attainment" known through scriptures and reasoning in the present verse can be heard in parallel with the "superior way" prescribed by the *Mahā Nārāyaṇa-Upanishad* in USP 1.20, thereby inviting close association with the formal renunciation prescribed there.[38] Reading more narrowly, however, it is actually "non-selfness" (*an-ātma-tā*) – the very notion of non-self, of personal agency, and everything that goes with them[39] – that is singled out for renunciation.

One need not choose between these possible interpretations. As we have heard at a number of points, Shankara's Advaita teaching proceeds largely by a process of negation, employing both the scriptural word and reasoned inquiry to remove from the self all that is non-self, including any sense of personal agency, attachment to the three states of experience and, at a deeper level, primordial ignorance itself. It is but a short step from "removal" to "renunciation," and no step at all to draw a further connection to the formal renunciation of the *paramahaṃsa* ascetic. Not only *can* setting aside ignorance, the three states of experience and the notion of non-self be described in terms of renunciation, but they *should* be so described. Such interior detachment and transformation constitute the proper objects of renunciation, from which and toward which alone the ascetic life acquires its full meaning.[40]

Questions linger. One can, by an act of will, break one's sacred thread. One can obviously give up ritual activity, remove one's topknot, carry a single staff and undertake a life of *saṃnyāsa*. But how precisely does one renounce the three states of waking, dreaming and deep sleep, much less primordial ignorance? In the light of the model teacher's cryptic "*mā kārṣīs-tarhi!*" in USG 2.65, Shankara might here reply in words made famous by the Nike brand: "Just do it!" More practically, in light of the discussion in USP 1, he might draw our attention to the literal, exterior renunciation of Vedic ritual as a privileged means to the deeper, interior renunciation described in USP 16. That is, one gives up limited,

with Introduction and Indices (Tokyo: Hokuseido Press, 1973), p. 240n67.

38 This interpretation is further supported by the explicit injunction to renounce Vedic rituals and their accessories immediately prior, in USP 16.43.

39 See the comment in ĀNANDAGIRI, *Upadeśasāhasrī*, p. 55, lines 29-30, and RĀMATĪRTHA, *Upadeśasāhasrī*, p. 263.

40 See especially the discussion of the internal "renunciation of all actions" (*sarva-karma-saṃnyāsa*), including especially the renunciation of doership, as distinct from mere formal "renunciation of action" (*karma-saṃnyāsa*) in Roger MARCAURELLE, *Freedom through Inner Renunciation: Śaṅkara's Philosophy in a New Light* (Albany: State University of New York Press, 2000), pp. 15-20, 65-74; as well as the discussion in Yoshitsugu SAWAI, "Śaṅkara's Theory of Saṃnyāsa," *Journal of Indian Philosophy* 14 (1986): pp. 378-79.

phenomenal experience precisely through one's physical abandonment of ritual life and retreat from ordinary society.

Either of these two options would be consistent with themes we have already encountered in the *Upadeśasāhasrī*'s sacred scripts. In and out of the refutations of the present verse chapter, however, Shankara offers another, more comprehensive and explicitly communal prescription:

> Therefore, assumptions concerning bondage, final release, etc., [which are] other than this are indeed confused ideas. The assumptions of the Sāṃkhyas, of the followers of Kaṇāda,[41] and of the Buddhists are lacking in profound consideration. (16.64)
> As [their assumptions] contradict the scriptures and reasoning, they should never be respected. Their faults can be pointed out hundreds and thousands of times. (16.65)

This passage immediately follows the final refutations of Sāṃkhya, with which we concluded the previous section. Here, at the end of these individual arguments, Shankara reduces unorthodox Buddhism, orthodox rivals like Sāṃkhya, and any "other" traditions to a single, collective "confused idea" or "error" (v. 64). Their disparate teachings on bondage and liberation are not merely dismissed as thoughtless, superficial and contradictory to the scriptures, but they themselves are characterized as "assumptions" or "false imaginings" (*kalpanā*) – the very same Sanskrit term used to describe the effects of ignorance in v. 17, above. It might not be too great a stretch to view these rival traditions, thus described, as social embodiments of ignorance, non-self and all that binds Shankara's implied hearers in the relentless wheel of *saṃsāra*.

If so, then it comes as no great surprise that Shankara offers the same prescription for these rivals as he has earlier prescribed for ignorance and *an-ātman*:

> And since it might also involve being culpable [under the text] 'any other than this,'[42] [they should not be respected at any time]. Therefore, having abandoned the teaching of other scriptures, a wise person should make firm his understanding (16.66)

[41] This term refers to the orthodox tradition of Vaiśeṣika "atomism," due to the fact that the *Vaiśeṣika-Sūtras* are traditionally attributed to Kaṇāda.

[42] RĀMATĪRTHA (*Upadeśasāhasrī*, p. 274) provides a text for this quotation, but no source; perhaps for this reason, he also offers support from other authorities. A.J. ALSTON (trans.), *The Thousand Teachings (Upadeśa Sāhasrī) of Śrī Śaṃkarācārya* (London: Shanti Sadan, 1990), p. 229n1, translates the verse as follows: "Whatever various other traditions there are to be found in the world should be regarded with suspicion by the learned ones who desire to have the purity of the true teaching."

of the true meaning of the *Vedānta* and also of Vyāsa's thought, with faith and devotion and without any crookedness. (16.67)

The key texts from this passage are, for our purposes, the absolutive phrases "having abandoned the teachings of other scriptural traditions" (v. 66) and "having given up all crookedness" (v. 67). In the previous verses, the phrase "scriptures and reasoning" was employed as a criterion of authority and judgment. But this, of course, applies only to the correct *śāstra*. All other *śāstras* should be renounced no less firmly than the topknot, sacrificial thread and ignorance itself.

The correct *śāstra*, for which the hearer should renounce all others, is specified in v. 67. It consists of "the Vedānta" – presumably referring primarily to the *Upanishads*, as well as the broader Vedanta teaching tradition – along with "what has been approved by Vyāsa," the sage to whom many popular histories, the epic *Mahābhārata* (including the *Bhagavad-Gītā*) and, at least by some later authorities, the *Brahma-Sūtras* are traditionally ascribed.[43] The boundaries of Advaita Vedanta, established logically in the preceding refutations, here receive an identifiably textual and social character. This simply reflects Shankara's religious context in part, for classical Hindu divisions between "orthodoxy" and "heterodoxy" were defined with reference to sacred texts – namely, the *Veda* – as were the major *darśanas* or schools of thought and practice, each with its own *sūtra* literature or other *śāstras*.[44] But such a textual strategy also functions to locate the Advaita tradition more securely in relation to its rivals. If the "wise person" (v. 66) must renounce other scriptural traditions and become firm in this one, then the acceptance of this tradition also sets clear boundaries on those persons who can truly be reckoned wise.

Shankara gives further depth to this portrait of the wise person by attributing "faith and devotion" to him. In USG 1.1, we have already seen Shankara characterize the prospective hearer of the *Upadeśasāhasrī* as one "possessed of faith" and "desirous."[45] At a minimum, such identifiers

[43] On the relation between Vyāsa and Bādarāyaṇa according to Śaṅkara, Sureśvara and Vācaspatimiśra, see MAYEDA, *Śaṅkara's Upadeśasāhasrī*, pp. 40-41, and 40-41n79.

[44] See Klaus K. KLOSTERMAIER, *A Survey of Hinduism*, 2d ed. (Albany: State University of New York Press, 1994), pp. 377-86; and Gavin FLOOD, *An Introduction to Hinduism* (Cambridge, New York and Melbourne: Cambridge University Press, 1996), pp. 224-25, 230-32.

[45] Here I am following the translation in Swāmi JAGADĀNANDA (trans.), *A Thousand Teachings in Two Parts – Prose and Poetry – of Srī Sankarāchārya* (Madras: Sri Ramakrishna Math, [1941]), p. 1.

suggest a personal investment in the tradition, as well as what Shankara will elsewhere specify as *āstikya-buddhi*, that is, a mind disposed to accept the Vedic revelation, mediated by the teacher and teaching tradition, as a trustworthy source of liberating knowledge.[46] More speculatively, J.G. Suthren Hirst and others have argued that the use of the specific term "devotion" (*bhakti*), here and elsewhere, may evoke a wider range of devotional connotations, whereby Shankara adapts the idiom of Vaiṣṇava temple worship to facilitate the rise of self-knowledge.[47] Just as the negation of non-self reveals the self-evident *Ātman*, then, so also here the renunciation of false scriptures, teachings and traditions reveals the Vedanta as uniquely worthy of disciples' wholehearted trust and intense devotion.

As Shankara moves into the final verses of USP 16, the nature and purpose of this discipleship community move into somewhat clearer view:

> Thus both the false assumptions based upon dualism and the views that *Ātman* does not exist have been rejected through reasoning; seekers after final release, being free from doubts which arise from the views of others, become firm on the path of knowledge. (USP 16.68)
> If one has attained the absolutely pure and non-dual Knowledge, which is self-witnessed and contrary to false assumptions, and rightly holds a firm belief, he will go to eternal peace, unaccompanied [by anything]. (16.69)

Though it may not be evident in the English translation, it is significant that the Sanskrit meter has changed. Whereas vv. 1-67 is composed in the ubiquitous 32-syllable *anuṣṭubh* metre, beginning at v. 68 Shankara switches into the 48-syllable *vaṃśastha* metre.[48] For the Sanskrit hearer,

[46] See the references in SAWAI, "Śaṅkara's Theory," pp. 374-75; Yoshitsugu SAWAI, "The Nature of the Faith in the Śaṅkaran Vedānta Tradition," *Numen* 34/1 (1987), pp. 20-21; and William CENKNER, *A Tradition of Teachers: Śaṅkara and the Jagadgurus Today* (Delhi: Motilal Banarsidass, 1983, 1995 [reprint]), pp. 51, 54.

[47] See SUTHREN HIRST, *Śaṃkara's Advaita Vedānta*, esp. pp. 129-37, and Jacqueline Gaynor SUTHREN HIRST, "The Place of *Bhakti* in Śaṅkara's Vedānta," in K. WERNER (ed.), *Love Divine: Studies in Bhakti and Devotional Mysticism*, Durham Indological Series 3 (Richmond: Curzon Press, 1993): pp. 117-45. Cf. CENKNER, *A Tradition of Teachers*, pp. 42-45, 54-55; SAWAI, "Nature of Faith," pp. 27-34; and Bradley J. MALKOVSKY, *The Role of Divine Grace in the Soteriology of Śaṃkarācārya*, Numen Studies in the History of Religions 91 (Leiden: Brill, 2001).

[48] Such a midstream change in meter is not unique to this chapter, but it does set USP 16 apart from any script we have encountered thus far in this commetnary. USP 14 switches to the *vaṃśastha* metre in vv. 41-50 and USP 15 in its final verse (v. 51). USP 8, 10 and 19 are composed entirely in the *vaṃśastha* metre. Tilmann VETTER offers

such a shift in tone, intonation and rhythm draws special attention to the present verses and signals the author's intention to conclude.[49]

Given the special attention Shankara draws to the present verses by this change, it makes sense that it is only here that he provides the ordering principle behind the preceding refutations: namely, a basic division between the "no-self tradition" of the Buddhists and the "dualist tradition" of Sāṃkhya, Vaiśeṣika and other orthodox rivals (v. 68). Between these two kinds of fundamental error, we also catch a fleeting glimpse of another, distinct community of authentic disciples, resolutely treading what Shankara calls the "path of knowledge" (v. 68).[50] Elsewhere, he will speak variously of the "path of liberation," "path of renunciation" or "road of non-activity."[51] Shankara, as we have heard, freely uses the language of both renunciation and travel to characterize various elements of the teaching, including its ongoing communication, the removal of ignorance and the rejection of rivals. It thus makes good sense to view these various expressions as different perspectives on what is, fundamentally, a single soteriological path.

Those who tread this path are characterized in at least three different ways in these verses. First, Shankara establishes a series of proximate ideals, in close connection with the argumentative purpose of USP 16: the systematic driving away of other teachings, becoming free from the doubts raised by them and firmly convinced of the truth of Advaita, and thereby remaining firmly on the path. Second, he associates such seekers closely with the object of their striving: like *Ātman*, they can be described as free of any impurity, non-dual and inherently opposed to any false alternatives.[52] Finally, he defines the members of this assembly in terms of their final end: everlasting peace and freedom from any binding connection

a chart and close analysis of the respective lengths and verse structures of these chapters in *Studien zur Lehre und Entwicklung Śaṅkaras* (Wien: Institut für Indologie der Universität Wien, 1979), pp. 93-95.

[49] As it happens, all of the remaining verses to be discussed in this commentary are in the *vamśastha* metre. So perhaps this can also be read as a signal that the volume has reached its turning point and is moving towards a conclusion. I leave this judgment to the reader.

[50] On Shankara's complex negotiation between and among rival traditions, see NICHOLSON, "Two Apologetic Moments," esp. pp. 548-554, and ISAYEVA, *Shankara and Indian Philosophy*, esp. pp. 9-18

[51] MuUBh 2.6.6 and IUBh 2 in PANOLI, *Upanishads*, vol. 1, pp. 173-74, and V. PANOLI (trans.), *The Upanishads in Śaṅkara's Own Words*, vol. 2, rev. ed. (Calicut: Mathrubhumi Printing and Publishing Co. Ltd., 1995), p. 43.

[52] I am adopting this interpretation of *vikalpanā* from ALSTON, *The Thousand Teachings*, p. 230n1.

or association – that is, primarily, freedom from the bondage of ignorance.[53] Though *Ātman* is ever-achieved, these seekers "should become" steady on the path, and the wise person is "going" onward to eternal peace. Prospective hearers are already presumed to be firm and convinced, but they are still in need of scripted refutations; already pure and non-dual, but still in need of further purification. The end is in sight and indeed already here, but the most important steps still lie ahead.

Many hearers will want to know more about the discipleship community Shankara envisions in these verses. What are its most defining features? How is it structured and organized? A number of medieval and modern Advaitins have answered such questions by tracing a line from Shankara the teacher and author of the *Upadeśasāhasrī*, through the refracted image of him as a great world conqueror in the hagiographical tradition, to the Daśanāmī monastic federation, its presiding "Shankaracharyas" and major religious centers throughout India, and the broader structures of *smārta* or Brahmanical Śaivism it fosters among householders and renunciants alike.[54] Modern historians, finding little evidence for such institutions in Shankara's indisputably authentic writings, have tended to associate him instead with various Vaiṣṇava devotional traditions.[55] We have already taken note of Suthren Hirst's hypothesis that Shankara may have adopted a Vaiṣṇava idiom to communicate his teaching. Taken a step further, this supposition would allow us to re-imagine his community of seekers not merely in terms of the individual teacher-student relationships scripted in such texts as USG 2-3 and USP 17.50-52, but also within a social and religious context that – notwithstanding profound disagreements in metaphysics and soteriology – closely resembled the *bhakti* movements of such later critics and rivals as Rāmānuja, Madhva and Vallabhācārya.

[53] See ĀNANDAGIRI, *Upadeśasāhasrī*, p. 60, line 16, and RĀMATĪRTHA, *Upadeśasāhasrī*, p. 276.

[54] See Wade Hampton DAZEY, *The Daśanāmī Order and Monastic Life*, Ph.D. Dissertation, University of California, Santa Barbara, 1987; Wade Hampton DAZEY, "Tradition and Modernization in the Organization of the Daśanāmī Saṃnyāsins," in A. CREEL and V. NARAYANAN (eds.), *Monastic Life in the Christian and Hindu Traditions* (Lewiston/Queenston/Lampeter: Edwin Mellen Press, 1990), pp. 281-321; Yoshitsugu SAWAI, *The Faith of Ascetics and Lay Smārtas: A Study of the Śaṅkaran Tradition of Śṛṅgerī*, Publications of the De Nobili Research Library 19 (Vienna: Institut für Indologie der Universitat Wien, 1992); and Matthew CLARK, *The Daśanāmī-Saṃnyāsīs: The Integration of Ascetic Lineages into an Order*. Brill's Indological Library 25 (Leiden and Boston: Brill, 2006).

[55] See the more sustained development of this thesis in CLARK, *Daśanāmī-Saṃnyāsins*, pp. 159-70.

The teaching scripts of USP 16 offer little or no help in this regard. With this brief mention, Shankara has already effectively drawn the chapter to a close. The false errors have been refuted, their exponents renounced and the hearer established within an alternative community defined, elliptically, by the content of its teachings, the collection of its authoritative texts and the nature of its final destination. In subsequent verses, he merely goes on to extol the teaching as the "highest goal" (v. 70) and "supreme purifier" (v. 71), to define the requisite characteristics of the student in terms reminiscent of USG 1 (v. 72), and to emphasize the immediacy of liberation, in this very life, for those who come to know this highest knowledge (vv. 71, 73), as treated in some detail in chapter three of this commentary. Finally, in the chapter's concluding verse, he adds a note of caution:

> Certainly in this world there is no attainment more excellent than that of one's own nature, since it comes from nothing else than this [*Vedānta*]. But the attainment of one's own nature, which is superior even to the kingdom of Indra, should not be given without examining [one's pupil] carefully. (16.74)

This verse beautifully captures the paradoxical quality of USP 16 and the whole of the Advaita teaching. On the one hand, the highest possible attainment and all-surpassing kingdom is nothing other than "one's own-nature," available in every moment of conscious awareness. On the other hand, only certain students can be admitted to instruction, and "nothing other" than this clearly delimited Vedanta teaching tradition can bring the eternal and self-evident reality of *Ātman* to light. USP 16, like all of the *Upadeśasāhasrī*'s sacred scripts, offers a portrait of this social reality by modeling, across its verses, the core practices of the tradition. But it also goes beyond other scripts by providing a glimpse of these practices' implied context and intended result: a well-defined discipleship community, steady on the path of knowledge, forged on the anvil of controversy, and constituted by its members' ongoing renunciation of all that separates them from a supreme kingdom that is, in the most important sense, already their own.

III.

"Creation Awaits the Revealing of the Children of God": A Christian *Saṃvāda* with USP 16

> For you did not receive a spirit of slavery to fall back into fear, but you have received a spirit of adoption. When we cry, 'Abba! Father!' it is that

> very Spirit bearing witness with our spirit that we are children of God, and if children, then heirs, heirs of God and joint heirs with Christ – if, in fact, we suffer with him so that we might also be glorified with him... For the creation waits with eager longing for the revealing of the children of God; for the creation was subjected to futility, not of its own will but by the one who subjected it, in hope that creation itself will be set free from its bondage to decay, and will obtain the freedom of the glory of the children of God (Romans 8:15-17, 19-21).

We began our dialogue with Shankara's *Upadeśasāhasrī* with the apostle Paul's anguished vision of historic Israel and the Christian community in Romans 9-11. There, in chapter 2, we observed that the apostle maintains a kind of double vision, whereby the otherwise legitimate referents of terms like "Israel" and "righteousness" take on new significance in the light of Christ. New meanings do not simply eclipse old ones. Rather, both levels of meaning are held in eschatological tension, suspended between the "already" and the "not yet" of salvation in the life of the individual believer and of historic Israel.

Across the various scripts of the *Upadeśasāhasrī*, Shankara nowhere speaks in the language of eschatological hope, of the beginning of a new age of salvation and its fulfillment at the end of time.[56] As we have seen repeatedly, however, there is a kind of "already-not yet" dynamic written into the individual person, into the Vedic scriptures and into the very structure of creation. From the perspective of highest truth, there is no bondage and no need for liberation. The innermost *Ātman* of each and every conscious being is already free of suffering, limitation and all the vicissitudes of ordinary life. Nevertheless, from the perspective of empirical existence, liberation comes to prospective disciples only through assiduous self-inquiry, through application of "agreement-and-difference" to the facts of experience and the words of the *mahā-vākyas*,

[56] It is perhaps worth noting that, following various scriptural accounts, Shankara does accept the periodic creation, dissolution and re-creation of the entire cosmic order. Hence, as an inferior alternative to the state of "liberation in the present life" (*jīvan-mukti*), he also accepts the idea of "gradual liberation" (*krama-mukti*) for sages who attain union with the qualified *Brahman*, waiting in a state of relative freedom with the Lord until they attain absolute freedom at the next dissolution. See BSBh IV.3.8-14 in GAMBHIRANANDA, *Brahma-Sūtra-Bhāṣya*, pp. 878-93, and the discussions in Karl H. POTTER, "Introduction to the Philosophy of Advaita Vedānta," in K. POTTER (ed.), *Encyclopedia of Indian Philosophies: Advaita Vedānta up to Śaṅkara and His Pupils* (Princeton: Princeton University Press, 1981), pp. 26-27, and A.G. Krishna WARRIER, *The Concept of Mukti in Advaita Vedānta*, Madras University Philosophical Series 9 (Madras: University of Madras, 1961), pp. 475-80.

through the reflection of *Ātman* in their own intellects, through explanatory devices employed by scriptures and teacher, and through the myriad mediations of the created world.

Now, in our hearing of USP 16, a similar tension has unfolded in more explicitly social terms. Shankara here offers a vision of a discipleship community set in sharp contrast to rival teaching traditions and straining on the way to a universal cosmic destiny: that all-surpassing kingdom or sovereignty hidden at the root of the embodied individual and of all possible experience. One of the most intriguing aspects of this vision is also in some ways its most frustrating: namely, its reticence to describe this discipleship community explicitly. The essential identity of Advaita as a corporate, social reality is not so much unfolded as unveiled by a process of successive negations and qualifications, through its members' agonistic engagement, inner renunciation and self-purification in relation to named rivals.

With this in mind, we can turn to a comparable dynamic of struggle, purification and unveiling in the apostle Paul's vision of "cosmic restorative justice" in Romans 8.[57] Just as human beings "groan inwardly" as they await the return of the Lord, the apostle insists, so also does "the whole creation" (8: 22-23). Sharing the same Spirit, both individual and world are caught in the same eschatological transformation, straining toward their fulfillment at the end of time.[58] "Creation itself will be set free from its bondage," Paul concluded, albeit along with and in inextricable relation to the "children of God" (v. 21). Such children, in fact, represent the whole creation in a unique way, as they continuously struggle to live by the Spirit and not by "the flesh" and thereby strive to renounce what one scholar calls our "present state of rebellion" against God.[59] The Spirit opens a new way of life to disciples, a way free from

[57] N.T. WRIGHT, "The Letter to the Romans," in *The New Interpreter's Bible*, vol. 10 (Nashville: Abingdon Press, 2002), p. 400.

[58] See James D.G. DUNN, "Spirit Speech: Reflections on Romans 8:12-27," in N. WRIGHT and S. SODERLUND (eds.), *Romans and the People of God: Essays in Honor of Gordon D. Fee on the Occasion of His 65th Birthday* (Grand Rapids and Cambridge: William B. Eerdmans, 1999), pp. 87-88, and WRIGHT, "Romans," pp. 596-98.

[59] WRIGHT, "Romans," p. 577. See also the discussion in Ibid, pp. 580-81; Joseph A. FITZMYER, S.J., "Pauline Theology," in R. BROWN, J. FITZMYER, and R. MURPHY (eds.), *The New Jerome Biblical Commentary* (Englewood Cliffs: Prentice Hall, 1990), pp. 1406-1407 [82:101-107]; Morna D. HOOKER, *Paul: A Short Introduction* (Oxford: Oneworld, 2003), pp. 47-48, 83, 125; and James D.G. DUNN, *The Theology of Paul the Apostle* (Grand Rapids and Cambridge: William B. Eerdmans Publishing Company, 1998), pp. 62-70.

the weakness and corruptibility of the present age and directed toward new relationships with God and with one another, as exemplified in the Spirit-filled cry, "Abba! Father!" of Romans 8:15.[60] Through baptism, such disciples have already received this divine gift, set their minds on the way of "life and peace" and entered a new state of existence.[61] Until Christ's return, however, this new state remains fragile and hidden, looking forward to its full revelation in the bodies of these disciples and in the whole creation. Only then will the tension between those who walk "according to the flesh" and those who walk "according to the Spirit" be completely resolved (see Rom 8:5-8).

James Dunn suggests that the opposing poles of this contrast are best understood as "ideal types" that compete in each believer's present experience.[62] Just as Shankara scripts refutations of Buddhism and Sāṃkhya to inculcate firm conviction in the mind of the Advaitin seeker (16.66), internal to the teaching tradition, so also Paul draws a contrast between the way of the flesh and the way of the Spirit in order to clarify the intentions and behavior of individual Christians. When the apostle goes on to speak in terms of "adoption," "inheritance," and the final revealing of God's children in subsequent verses of Romans 8, however, his idiom shifts our attention to the Christian community as such. Indeed, N.T. Wright has argued that Romans 3-8 as a whole can be read as a continuous narrative of "new exodus" and constitution of a "new people of God," modeled on the paradigmatic Jewish story of liberation from Egypt.[63] Writing to a Roman church faced with the difficult task of integrating Jewish and Gentile members into a single community, Paul narrates a story both familiar and unfamiliar to his hearers. The climax of this narrative? The inheritance or gift of the land, here re-envisioned to include the whole creation.[64] The primary categories that define this new community are no longer Jew and Gentile, Paul argues, but "Spirit"

60 See DUNN, *Theology of Paul*, pp. 477-82. DUNN recommends interpreting the "Abba" less in terms of a distinctive kind of charismatic experience than in terms of the distinctive relationships it reveals. See his *Theology of Paul*, pp. 263-64 and "Spirit Speech," pp. 83-85.

61 See WRIGHT, "Romans," pp. 582-83.

62 DUNN, *Theology of Paul*, pp. 478-79

63 WRIGHT, "Romans," pp. 510-13, 576-77, 592-93, and especially N.T. WRIGHT, "New Exodus, New Inheritance: The Narrative Structure of Romans 3-8," in SODERLUND and WRIGHT, *Romans and the People of God*, pp. 26-35. This proposal about Romans reflects WRIGHT's broader interpretative project in his *The New Testament and the People of God*, Christian Origins and the Question of God 1 (London: SPCK, 1992).

64 See WRIGHT, "Romans," pp. 596-97.

and "flesh." Those who live in the Spirit, Jew and Gentile alike, are also those who strive continuously to put aside the ways of the flesh and to look in hope toward their shared inheritance in Christ.

Wright's interpretation need not be pressed. For our purposes, it is enough to observe that internal struggle and external self-definition are rarely separable. The ideal types that define competing modes of thinking and acting in the individual also trace the boundaries of the community to which they are addressed. It is, we might say, the struggle itself that distinguishes this new people from all others, even as it also joins it to these same others in their shared, eschatological situation. The interior renunciation of the flesh and reception of the Spirit shape an external community, and, conversely, the profound division between different communities and patterns of life is written into each individual until the final glorious revelation of all God's children in and with the whole creation.

As we have heard in USP 16, Shankara also establishes the contours of his Advaita community precisely in terms of struggle and contestation. The rival traditions of Buddhism and Sāṃkhya represent far more than alternative philosophical options in this script. Shankara sets their teachings, and the embedded patterns of life that go with them, in parallel with the myriad "false assumptions," rooted in ignorance, which keep all conscious beings in bondage (USP 16.17, 64). They represent, no less than "those who live by the flesh" for the apostle Paul, ideal types of an oppressive power which continues to work in the embodied individual, in the social world and in the created order so long as the community of seekers is still on the way toward its promised goal. Neither community is defined primarily in terms of social structures, ethnic or cultural identities as Greek or Jew, or even scriptural statements like *tat-tvam-asi* – at least, not in these particular scripts. Each is, instead, defined by its soteriological orientation toward a final inheritance within and beyond the life dominated by ignorance and "false assumptions" on one side of the conversation and the rebellion of "the flesh" on the other.

Following the contemporary Christian theologian Kathryn Tanner, we might take this analysis one step further, suggesting that the identity of each community takes its specific shape less from one or another formulation of "common agreement," common leadership or even common scriptural texts than through what she calls a shared "focus of common investment and engagement."[65] What unites Christians and

[65] Kathryn TANNER, "Editorial Symposium: Roman Catholic Theology of Tradition," *Horizons* 29 (2002): p. 309.

Christian practices, according to Tanner, "is nothing internal to the practices themselves. What unites them is concern for true discipleship, proper reflection in human words and deeds of an object of worship that always exceeds by its greatness human efforts to do so."[66]

Though Tanner writes as a Christian theologian, her decision to locate religious identity in its shared focus on authentic discipleship rather than in more strictly sociological boundaries of text, doctrine or institutional structure would seem, if anything, to suit the cumulative scripts of the *Upadeśasāhasrī* even better than the letters of the apostle Paul. Whereas Paul speaks in confident, categorical language of God's redeeming action in Jesus of Nazareth, of God's Spirit bearing witness in Christian prayer, and of the eventual glorification of a specific human community as joint-heirs with Christ, Shankara points us toward that unknown knower by whose pure, uncategorical existence we judge the more conventional existence or non-existence of ordinary objects (USP 16.31-32). *Ātman* is unreachable by human concepts or language; so its acquisition is rendered less in terms of a shared content than in terms of what Tanner terms a shared "concern for true discipleship." As we have seen in this chapter, this shared concern includes not only systematic renunciation of all that is non-self, but also sustained refutations of named others whose teachings, it turns out, look uncannily similar to those of Advaita Vedanta.

The close ties that join Advaita Vedanta to its Buddhist, Sāṃkhya and other rivals may, in fact, become more intelligible in light of Tanner's cultural analysis.[67] For she argues that, if Christian identity emerges through shared engagement rather than from invariable contents or practices of faith, then Christian identity is best viewed as "essentially relational."[68] She writes:

> The boundary [between Christians and others] is... one of use, allowing Christian culture to be essentially impure and mixed, possessing the identity of a hybrid that always shares cultural forms with its wider host culture and with other religions. The distinctiveness of a Christian culture is not so much formed *by* a cultural boundary as *at* it. Christian distinctiveness is something that emerges in the very cultural processes occurring at the

[66] Kathryn TANNER, *Theories of Culture: A New Agenda for Theology*, Guides to Theological Inquiry (Minneapolis: Fortress Press, 1997), p. 152.

[67] I am indebted to Hugh NICHOLSON for initially drawing my attention to Kathryn TANNER's theoretical proposal as a resource for interpreting Shankara's refutations of other schools.

[68] See TANNER, *Theories of Culture*, pp. 110-15.

> boundary, processes that construct a Christian identity through the distinctive use of cultural materials shared with others.[69]

We have, at points, noted Shankara's willingness to adopt the Buddhist idiom of two levels of truth and to teach within an anthropological frame that presumes many of the enumerations and analyses of Sāṃkhya. Now, in and out of our dialogue with the apostle Paul and the analysis of Kathryn Tanner, we might come to see such borrowings and mutual relations as constitutive of the tradition itself. On the analogy of the mutual restriction of illustrative examples discussed in chapter 4 of this commentary,[70] the Advaita community implied in the *Upadeśasahāsrī* takes shape in and through its restriction, negation and especially qualification of those religious others it sets itself most firmly against.

Bhāskara does not go entirely astray when he characterizes Shankara as a kind of crypto-Buddhist. From one point of view, Advaita is indeed just another form of Buddhism, albeit one qualified by its insistence on the existent self – which means, of course, that it is not actually Buddhist at all. It can also be characterized as a form of Sāṃkhya, qualified by its teaching on superimposition and the merely provisional existence of the empirical world, and also as a distinctive form of Pūrva Mīmāṃsā exegesis, qualified by its understanding of liberating knowledge rather than Vedic ritual as the true end of the *Vedas*, as we heard in chapter 2. Advaitin disciples are called to renounce these other traditions, to be sure; but this renunciation proceeds by qualification, restriction and the distinctively Advaita use of themes and materials that originate in the refuted traditions themselves. Nor would this process end with Shankara or the *Upadeśasāhasrī*. The structures of the Daśanāmī Order, for example, can be interpreted as a later, distinctively Advaita adaptation of Śaiva, Śakta and even Muslim Sufi religious materials.[71]

This portrait of Advaita as a religious community that emerges through its distinctive use of other teachings may seem at first glance to distinguish it essentially from Christianity, due to the latter's claims about the church as a distinctive, well-defined and originating social reality, a people set apart from all others before the creation of the world. But of course Tanner develops her theory for the interpretation not of

[69] Kathryn TANNER, "Cultural Theory," in J. WEBSTER, K. TANNER and I. TORRANCE (eds.), *The Oxford Handbook of Systematic Theology* (Oxford and New York: Oxford University Press, 2007), p. 537.

[70] See above, ch. 4, pp. 125-27.

[71] See CLARK, *Daśanāmī Saṃnyāsīs*, pp. 214-22, 227-46.

Advaita but of Christian identity, and, if we follow Wright's interpretation, Paul's narrative across Romans 3-8 represents nothing other than a distinctively Christian use of materials with their origins in broader Jewish tradition – that is, the tropes of new Exodus, new People of God, and new inheritance. Any too-sharp distinction of the Christian community from its religious and social environment receives a further theological qualification from the apostle Paul himself, in Romans 8:18-25. Or, perhaps better, any such distinctions, including the most spirited opposition, depend upon and arise out of a deeper bond. At least until their glorious revelation at the end of time, Christian believers groan in and with the whole creation, even as Christian and creation alike look forward to a time when they shall be set free from bondage, decay and the oppressive power of the flesh.

Such a relational perspective on Christian identity and the church can draw support not only from the work of an individual theorist like Kathryn Tanner, but also from a more authoritative and pastoral document like *Lumen Gentium*, the "Dogmatic Constitution on the Church" promulgated in 1964 by Pope Paul VI and the Second Vatican Council of the Catholic Church.[72] Particularly in their depiction of the church as a pilgrim in chapter seven of this constitution, the bishops of the Council strongly underscored the intimate unity and the essential relations of the Christian community with all humankind in God's eschatological plan of salvation.[73] Drawing on the teaching of the apostle Paul, among others, they declare that:

> Already, therefore, the end of the ages has reached us (see 1 Cor 10, 11) and the renewal of the world has been irrevocably constituted and is being anticipated in this world in a real sense: for already on earth the church is adorned with a true though imperfect holiness. However, until the arrival of the new heavens and the new earth in which justice dwells (see 2 Pt 3, 13), the pilgrim church in its sacraments and institutions, which belong to this age, carries the figure of this world which is passing and it dwells among creatures who groan and till now are in the pains of childbirth and await the revelation of the children of God (see Rm 8, 19-22) (LG no. 48).

[72] Latin text and English translation in Norman P. TANNER, S.J. (ed.), *Decrees of the Ecumenical Councils, Volume Two: Trent to Vatican II* (London: Sheed and Ward, and Washington, DC: Georgetown University Press, 1990), pp. 849-99.

[73] See Richard R. GAILLARDETZ, *The Church in the Making: Lumen Gentium, Christus Dominus, Orientalium Ecclesiarum*, Rediscovering Vatican II (New York/Mahwah: Paulist Press, 2006), pp. 55-57.

This chapter both reflects and encapsulates the broader transformation of *Lumen Gentium*, over three years, from its initial focus on the institutional church as a "perfect society" to a more dynamic, eschatological and biblical understanding of Christian community.[74] In chapter one, such a shift is exemplified by the bishops' central affirmation that "the church is in Christ as a sacrament or instrumental sign of intimate union with God and the unity of all humanity" (no. 1).[75] In chapter seven, this fundamental affirmation is both affirmed and qualified by the church's "real though imperfect holiness" in the present, passing world. This pilgrim community functions as a privileged sign and means of God's salvation, to be sure, but it does so precisely by using borrowed materials: its "sacraments and institutions, which belong to this age." The bishops definitely affirm the Catholic Church as the unique if not exclusive bearer of Christ's sanctification and truth (see no. 8).[76] They also, nevertheless, firmly situate this same church as one among many fellow travelers in a sinful and groaning world, whose mark it will continue to bear until the end of time.

Such affirmations of solidarity do not preclude careful discernment between different religious traditions or strong insistence upon the unique identity of Christianity and the Catholic Church for the bishops of the Council, any more than they do for the apostle Paul, Kathryn

[74] GAILLARDETZ, *Church in the Making*, p. 100. For further discussions of the development of this document from its initial drafts to its final form, see Ibid, 8-27, and Giuseppe ALBERIGO, *A Brief History of Vatican II* (Maryknoll: Orbis Books, 2006), pp. 29-35, 45-49, 66-68, 71-76, 82-88. On its seventh chapter, which originated in discussions between Pope John XXXIII and Cardinal Larraona in 1962, was introduced into *Lumen Gentium* by Paul VI in 1964, and was subsequently rewritten by Yves Congar to shift its focus from individual Christians to the whole Church, see GAILLARDETZ, *Church in the Making*, pp. 20, 24-25; and Joseph A. KOMONCHAK, "Toward an Ecclesiology of Communion," in G. ALBERIGO (ed.), J. KOMONCHAK (ed., English version), *History of Vatican II, Vol IV: Church as Communion, Third Period and Intersession, September 1964 – September 1965* (Maryknoll: Orbis; Leuven: Peeters, 2003), pp. 49-52.

[75] See especially Francis A. SULLIVAN, *The Church We Believe In: One, Holy, Catholic and Apostolic* (New York/Mahwah, 1988), pp. 8-11, 109-51.

[76] Specifically, as is well known, the bishops elected to substitute the phrase "subsists in" (*subsistit in*) for "is" (*est*) to describe the relationship between the Church of Christ and the Catholic Church in LG 8, while also explicitly recognizing "many elements of sanctification and truth" outside its institutional bounds. See the discussion in Ibid, pp. 23-33 and GAILLARDETZ, *Church in the Making*, pp. 116-18, as well as the clarifications offered by the CONGREGATION FOR THE DOCTRINE OF THE FAITH in "Responses to Some Questions Regarding Certain Aspects of the Church," *The Holy See*, 29 June 2007, <http://www.vatican.va/roman_curia/congregations/cfaith/documents/rc_con_cfaith_doc_20070629_responsa-quaestiones_en.html>, accessed 13 June 2008.

Tanner or, in his Advaita context, Ādi Shankaracharya. Indeed, the complex interplay of solidarity, difference and uniqueness takes center stage in *Lumen Gentium*'s second chapter, entitled "The People of God." In this chapter, after a brief narrative of historic Israel, the Council develops its teaching on the church as a "new people of God," constituted by Christ as its head, by shared reception of the Spirit in its members' heart, by the law of love and by its eschatological orientation toward "the kingdom of God: inaugurated on earth by God himself and to be further extended until, at the end of time, it will be brought to its completion by the Lord when Christ will appear, our life (see Col 3, 4) and 'creation itself will be set free...' (Rm 8, 21)" (LG no. 9). Subsequent sections unfold the threefold ministry of Christ shared by all members of this Messianic and eschatological people (nos. 10-12), highlight its universality and internal diversity (no. 13) and then go on to position various religious communities and traditions relative to it (nos. 14-16). Catholics alone are "fully incorporated" into the people of God (no. 14), catechumens and members of other Christian communities are "joined" to it (nos. 14-15), and all others may be said to be "related in various ways" (no. 16).[77] At the end of the chapter, in light of this diversity, the bishops re-affirm the Christian obligation to evangelize (no. 17).

In its structure, then, *Lumen Gentium*'s account of the people of God begins with a definition of this people's essential identity and only subsequently goes on to define it in relation to various groups. From our hearing of USP 16, however, we can ask whether the chapter may also, just as fruitfully, be read in reverse. That is, we can re-imagine the church as emerging precisely through these relations, as suggested when we hear the bishops together with USP 16:

[T]hose who have not yet accepted the gospel are related to the people of God in various ways. In the first place, there is that people to whom the testaments and promises were given... But the plan of salvation also embraces those who acknowledge the Creator, and among these the Muslims are first... [T]here are others who search

As Knowledge is the very nature of *Ātman*, It is constantly applied figuratively to the intellect. And the absence of discriminating knowledge is beginningless; this and nothing else is taken to be transmigratory existence. Final release is its cessation and nothing else, since [every other view] is unreasonable... The assumptions of the

[77] See GAILLARDETZ, *Church in the Making*, pp. 69-72, and especially Jacques DUPUIS, S.J., *Toward a Christian Theology Religious Pluralism* (Maryknoll: Orbis Books, 1997), pp. 347-49.

for the unknown God in shadows and images; God is not far from people of this kind since he gives to all life and breath and everything... More often, however, deceived by the evil one, people have gone astray in their thinking and exchanged the truth about God for a lie and served the creature rather than the creator... For this reason, to promote the glory of God and the salvation of all these people, the church is mindful of the Lord's command when he said: 'Preach the gospel to the whole creation' (Mk 16, 15)... (LG no. 16).

Sāṃkhyas, of the followers of Kaṇāda, and of the Buddhists are lacking in profound consideration. As [their assumptions] contradict the scriptures and reasoning, they should never be respected. Their faults can be pointed out hundreds and thousands of times... Therefore, having abandoned the teaching of other scriptures, a wise person should make firm his understanding of the true meaning of the *Vedānta* and also of Vyāsa's thought, with faith and devotion and without any crookedness (16.61-62a, 64b-65, 66b-67).

Given common popular and scholarly understandings of Hinduism as comparatively tolerant and Christianity as comparatively intolerant, it may come as some surprise that, at least in these two passages, Shankara emerges as the less inclusive of the two voices.[78] Buddhists and Sāṃkhyins are not embraced by "God's plan of salvation," as *Lumen Gentium* declares that Jews and Muslims are; due to the fact that such teachings "contradict scriptures and reasoning," according to Shankara, they must be left resolutely behind. Yet Shankara, no less than the bishops of the Second Vatican Council, certainly recognizes the divine presence beyond the boundaries of his or any other religious community. The highest *Ātman*, whose nature is knowledge, is reflected in each and every conscious knower. Arguing on behalf of the tradition, proclaiming the truth and encouraging seekers to renounce other teachings and to embrace the path of knowledge – these flow, not from convictions about the presence or absence of the divine self, but from concerns about knowing this self rightly and participating fully in the liberation such knowledge provides.

Developing this correlation in the other direction, we can also observe that the bishops, no less than Shankara, also define the true people of God in terms of the Christian community's close relation to, and clear distinction from, named others. On the one hand, the bishops are keen to insist upon the incompleteness of other religious traditions, the deception

[78] On the rather striking difference between Śaṅkara and many of his later interpreters on this point, see Wilhelm HALBFASS, *Studies in Kumārila and Śaṅkara* (Reinbek: Verlag für Orientalistische Fachpublikationen, 1983), pp. 85-93; and Wilhem HALBFASS, *India and Europe: An Essay in Understanding* (Albany: State University of New York Press, 1988), pp. 407-14.

wrought by the evil one, and the need for Christians to continue their mission of evangelization. On the other, such a critique flows from and rests upon more basic convictions about the fundamental relatedness of all such persons and traditions to the people of God, prior to any proclamation of the word. In the 2000 declaration *Dominus Iesus*, some 36 years after the promulgation of *Lumen Gentium*, the Congregation of the Doctrine of the Faith would intensify both sides of this equation, forcefully insisting upon the uniqueness of the Catholic Church and incomparable deficiency of alternate paths while also recognizing that God's grace comes to those outside the church in a way that, in a phrase the Congregation adopts from Pope John Paul II, always "has a mysterious relationship to the church."[79] From our interpretation of USP 16, we might begin to see how, as one aspect of this mysterious relation, the full reality of the church emerges through its active engagement with, borrowing from, and refutation of those other traditions acknowledged in a text like *Lumen Gentium* no. 16.

From one point of view, in other words, the Christian community represents merely a particular type of Jewish community, qualified by the distinctive character of its Messianic consciousness – which would eventually come to mean, of course, that it is not a form of Judaism at all. It can also be seen as a distinctive form of Islam, qualified by its Christological and Trinitarian confessions, or even as a distinctive form of secular humanism, qualified by the vision of human flourishing modeled in the life and ministry of Jesus the Christ. Such relations of mutual recognition and mutual distinction with religious others are not, on this reading, somehow secondary or extrinsic to the historical reality of the church; they represent a constitutive feature of its pilgrim journey in this passing world.

In and out of our hearing of the cumulative script of the *Upadeśasāhasrī,* moreover, we might also draw one final theological conclusion. For now the church can also be seen to stand in relation, not only to Judaism, Islam, secular humanism or a generic "Hinduism," but also, significantly, to the Advaita *saṃpradāya* and the particular community of seekers depicted in USP 16. And so this same church can be reimagined as nothing other than a distinctive specification of this Advaita

[79] CONGREGATION FOR THE DOCTRINE OF THE FAITH, "'*Dominus Iesus*': On the Unicity and Salvific Universality of Jesus Christ and the Church," esp. no. 21, in S. POPE and C. HEFLING (eds.), *Sic et Non: Encountering Dominus Iesus* (Maryknoll: Orbis Books, 2002), p. 21.

tradition, a non-dualist discipleship community qualified only by its proclamation that false dualism has been overcome through the non-dual human and divine reality of Jesus, the "light of nations," who gives *Lumen Gentium* its title and the church its privileged and provisional sacramental character (see LG no. 1). From the perspective of Christian faith, of course, much – everything, in fact – depends upon this qualification. This community bears within itself the unique beginning and seed of the kingdom to come (see LG no. 5). Yet, the bishops of the Council, with the apostle Paul, recognize that the Christian community may well bear the mark of the passing world, borrow its sacraments and structures from it, and continue to groan and to struggle against the power of the flesh until the end of time.

So also does Shankara uphold the path of knowledge and community of seekers steady on this path as, here and now, uniquely oriented toward the greatest attainment possible in this or any world: the attainment of one's own nature (USP 16.74). At one level, such a claim can never be recognized as anything but a challenge and an affront to the church's preaching – yet another sign of the oppressive power of the flesh in the present age. At another level, however, the church's willingness to engage such claims might also represent a privileged moment in its own ongoing self-constitution. Until the final revealing of God's daughters and sons at Christ's return, the church and the Advaita discipleship community journey together as fierce rivals and fellow pilgrims, joined together by a mysterious relation of mutual distinction that cannot be resolved, ignored or even, possibly, completely renounced. So we boldly borrow, and we qualify, and we distinguish carefully, and we may well engage in spirited polemics[80] as we attempt to make ourselves – and each other – steadier on the path.

[80] On possibility and even the importance of interreligious polemics, see especially Paul J. GRIFFITHS, "An Apology for Apologetics," *Faith and Philosophy* 5 (1988): pp. 399-420; Paul J. GRIFFITHS, *An Apology for Apologetics: A Study in the Logic of Interreligious Dialogue*, Faith Meets Faith (Maryknoll: Orbis Books, 1991); and Paul J. GRIFFITHS, "Why We Need Interreligious Polemics," *First Things* 44 (1994): pp. 423-50.

CHAPTER 8

ANAMNESIS AND LIBERATION: COMMENTARY ON USG 3

I.

UPADEŚASĀHASRĪ GADYABANDHA 3.115

I am of the nature of Seeing, non-object, unconnected [with anything], changeless, motionless, endless, fearless, and absolutely subtle.

So sound cannot make me its object and touch me, whether as mere noise in general or as [sound] of particular qualities – pleasant [sounds] such as the first note of music or the desirable words of praise and the like, or the undesirable words of untruth, disgust, humiliation, abuse, and the like – since I am unconnected [with sound]. For this very reason neither loss nor gain is caused [in me] by sound. Therefore, what can the pleasant sound of praise, the unpleasant sound of blame, and so on do to me? Indeed a pleasant sound may produce gain, and an unpleasant one destruction, for a person lacking in discriminating knowledge, who regards sound as [connected with his] *Ātman* since he has no discriminating knowledge. But for me who am endowed with discriminating knowledge, [sound] cannot produce even a hair's breadth [of gain or loss].

In the very same manner [touch] does not produce for me any change of gain and loss, whether as touch in general or as touch in particular forms – the unpleasant [touch] of cold, heat, softness, hardness, etc., and of fever, stomachache, etc., and any pleasant [touch] either inherent in the body or caused by external and adventitious [objects] – since I am devoid of touch, just as a blow with the fist and the like [does not produce any change] in the sky.

Likewise [form-and-color] produces neither loss nor gain for me, whether as form-and-color in general or as form-and-color in particular, pleasant or unpleasant, such as the female characteristics of a woman and the like, since I am devoid of form-and-color.

Similarly, [taste] produces neither loss nor gain for me who am by nature devoid of taste, whether as taste in general or as taste in particular forms[, pleasant or unpleasant,] such as sweetness, sourness, saltiness, pungency, bitterness, astringency which are perceived by the dull-witted.

> In a like manner [odor] produces neither loss nor gain for me who am by nature devoid of odor, whether as odor in general or as odor in particular forms, pleasant or unpleasant, such as [the odor] of flowers, etc., and ointment, etc. That is because the *Śruti* says: 'That which is soundless, touchless, formless, imperishable, also tasteless, constant, odorless...'

II.
The Discipline of Recollection: Hearing USP 10 and USG 3 (Selections)

In the *Upadeśasāhasrī*'s third prose chapter, Shankara prescribes a form of meditative discipline he calls *parisaṃkhyāna*. This is an unusual choice of term, with few if any parallels elsewhere in Shankara's corpus, and its translation poses some difficulty. Translation is made even more difficult in light of his uncompromising rejection of the *prasaṃkhyāna* or *prasaṃcakṣā* meditation in the eighteenth verse chapter (USP 18.9, 12, 17).[1] In chapter 5, however, I suggested that the key difference between the practices Shankara commends and those he rejects can be found in their underlying rationales, rather than in the form of the disciplines. According to this interpretation, Shankara refutes the view of the *prasaṃkhyāna-vādin* not for prescribing reasoning and meditation, which Shankara also prescribes, but for suggesting that such reasoning and meditation provide the disciple with some kind of direct, experiential knowledge which perfects and completes the merely indirect, relational knowledge revealed in the *Upanishads*.[2]

This is not, however, the end of the issue. The question of experience (*anubhava*) and particularly of *nirvikalpa samādhi*, the highest contemplative experience and final stage of Pantañjali's Yoga, has gained special importance in contemporary scholarship, due in no small part to the interpretation of Vedanta given by such modern interpreters as Swami Vivekananda (1863-1902), Śri Ramana Maharshi (1879-1950) and the

[1] See Sengaku MAYEDA (trans.), *A Thousand Teachings: The Upadeśasāhasrī of Śaṅkara* (Albany: State University of New York Press, 1992), p. 254n1, and the discussion above, ch. 5, pp. 147-52.

[2] See also the discussion in Jonathan BADER, *Meditation in Śaṅkara's Vedanta* (New Delhi: Aditya Prkashan, 1990), 74-80. For BADER, the key difference between the two practices is the sense of personal agency implied in the injunction to perform *prasaṃkhyāna*, which Shankara attempts to avoid by introducing a similar practice under a different name.

former President of India, Sarvepalli Radhakrishnan (1888-1975). In his famous work *Rājayoga*, for example, Vivekananda came very close to identifying such pure contemplation with liberating knowledge itself. "The highest grade of *samādhi*," he writes, "is when we see the real thing, when we see the material out of which the whole of these grades of beings are composed, and that one lump of clay being known, we know all the clay in the universe."[3] From this conviction, he goes on to generalize:

> From the lowest animal to the highest angel, some time or other, each one will have to come to that state, and then, and then alone, will real religion begin for him. Until then we only struggle towards that stage. There is no difference now between us and those who have no religion, because we have no experience. What is concentration good for, save to bring us to this experience? Each one of the steps to attain *samādhi* has been reasoned out, properly adjusted, scientifically organized, and when faithfully practised, will surely lead us to the desired end. Then will all sorrows cease, all miseries vanish; the seeds of action will be burnt, and the soul will be free forever.[4]

The Advaita teaching on liberation-in-life is here transposed seamlessly into the terms of spiritual practice and mystical experience. Authentic religion commences only with the aspirant's arrival at *samādhi*, and the way to that pure experiential state is through refined and scientifically organized yogic concentration.

Vivekananda was a sophisticated thinker, and two isolated quotations cannot do justice to his views. I simply wish to note that, while this modern position reveals affinity with some early Advaita teachers and texts – notably, the *Vivekacūḍāmaṇi* – it is very difficult to square with Shankara's teaching if we restrict our attention to his indisputably authentic writings.[5] In the *Upadeśasāhasrī*, the term *samādhi* appears in only three verses, and it can be read in every case as an evanescent property of the mind, distinct from the eternal *Ātman* (USP 13.14; 13.17;

[3] *The Complete Works of Vivekananda,* Mayavati Memorial Edition, vol. 1 (Calcutta: Advaita Ashrama, 1964), p. 164, quoted in Anantanand RAMBACHAN, *The Limits of Scripture: Vivekananda's Reinterpretation of the Vedas* (Honolulu: University of Hawaii Press, 1994), pp. 104-5.

[4] *Complete Works*, vol. 1, p. 188, quoted in RAMBACHAN, *Limits of Scripture*, p. 98.

[5] See especially RAMBACHAN, *The Limits of Scripture*, pp. 113-25; Anantanand RAMBACHAN, "Śaṅkara's Rationale for *Śruti* as the Definitive Source of *Brahmajñāna*: A Refutation of Some Contemporary Views," *Philosophy East and West* 36 (1986): pp. 25-40; and Michael COMANS, "The Question of the Importance of *Samādhi* in Modern and Classical Advaita Vedanta," *Philosophy East and West* 43 (1993): pp. 19-38.

14.35).[6] This also seems to be the thrust of Shankara's comment on *Brahma-Sūtra* 2.1.9, where the state of *samādhi* is equated with deep sleep.[7] There are other places, to be sure, where Shankara is more appreciative of yogic practices as a secondary means for purifying the mind.[8] Nevertheless, even in light of these more favorable remarks, it does not seem proper to privilege *samādhi* as either the highest means or final end of liberation. It is telling that recent defenses of experientialist approaches to Advaita by Arvind Sharma and Thomas A. Forsthoefel have tended to distinguish such positions from Shankara's own teaching.[9] As Sharma puts the matter, "Ramana [Maharshi] may be said to be the chief spokesman of *experiential* Advaita just as the philosopher Śaṅkara... is looked upon as the leading expositor of *doctrinal* Advaita."[10]

But this, again, is not the end of the issue, either for Shankara or for this commentary project. For, if the third prose chapter can be admitted as a reliable witness, this path of knowledge does ordinarily include some form of disciplined contemplation. Hence, in the present chapter we shift our attention from negative refutation to positive prescription, from those practices, understandings and whole traditions which must be set aside by authentic seekers to the single moment when the whole teaching is brought to bear on such seekers' present experience, here and now, through *parisaṃkhyāna* and related disciplines. We begin our inquiry not directly with USG 3, but with selected verses of USP 10, in which Shankara speaks in the first-person discourse of the liberated self-knower – or, more precisely, from the perspective of such a person's unblemished "perception of the highest truth" (*paramārtha-darśana*) – in order to provide a model for self-conscious imitation (USP 10.14).[11] Only then, after first hearing this other, closely related meditative discipline, we will return to the specific practice of *parisaṃkhyāna* and its intended result, as both are described in USG 3.

[6] COMANS, "Importance of *Samādhi*," p. 30.

[7] In Swami GAMBHIRANANDA (trans.), *Brahma-Sūtra-Bhāṣya of Śrī Śaṅkarācārya* (Calcutta: Advaita Ashrama, 1965, 1972), pp. 317-19, and the discussion in COMANS, "Importance of *Samādhi*," pp. 23-24.

[8] See COMANS, "Importance of *Samādhi*," pp. 24-29, and especially BADER, *Meditation*, pp. 102-105.

[9] Arvind SHARMA, *The Experiential Dimension of Advaita Vedanta* (Delhi: Motilal Banarsidass, 1993); Thomas A. FORSTHOEFEL, *Knowing Beyond Knowledge: Epistemologies of Religious Experience in Classical and Modern Advaita*, Ashgate World Philosophies (Hants and Burlington: Ashgate Publishing, 2002).

[10] SHARMA, *Experiential Dimension*, p. xiv.

[11] My translation.

An Initial Reflection: Despite its uncertain roots in Shankara's teaching, the experientialist interpretation given by Vivekananda and Radhakrishnan has decisively shaped many if not most Christian approaches to Advaita. Perhaps the most dramatic example is that of the Benedictine monk Henri Le Saux (1910-73), who took up the ocher robe and renunciant name Swami Abhishiktananda to pursue the "advaitic experience" of the *Upanishads*.[12] More recently, Michael von Brück has attempted to bring the Trinitarian theologies of Luther and Hegel into constructive dialogue with the meditative "non-dual experience" of *Brahman* as "knowledge, consciousness and bliss" (*sat-chit-ānanda*).[13] Through a careful and contextual hearing of these scripts, however, I hope to demonstrate that the categories of "remembrance" or "*anamnesis*" provide a more fruitful lens than "spiritual experience" to interpret the practices of repetition they prescribe. This does not in any way diminish the radicality of the Advaita claim. For, understood as *anamnesis,* such practices do not merely bring the teaching to mind; they ideally function to re-shape disciples' habitual patterns of thought and behavior at the most fundamental level. The disciple's own self is continually re-membered, and she herself is, thereby, gradually but inexorably re-made.

Rehearsing the Truth of the Self (USP 10.1-3, 7-8, 12-13)

In his discourses, the contemporary Advaita teacher Swami Paramarthananda Saraswati introduces USP 10 by drawing attention to the chapter's singular lack of originality. This chapter, he suggests, merely reiterates many topics already treated in USP 1-9 and throughout the *Upadeśasāhasrī*. But it does this in a very distinctive way: for Shankara has composed these particular verses in the form of *nididhyāsana*.[14]

[12] See the discussion in Jacques DUPUIS, S.J., *Jesus Christ and the Encounter of World Religions*, R. BARR (trans.), Faith Meets Faith (Maryknoll: Orbis Books, 1991), pp. 67-90; Edward T. ULRICH, "Swami Abhishiktananda and Comparative Theology," *Horizons* 31 (2004): pp. 40-63; Peter C. PHAN, "Multiple Religious Belonging: Opportunities and Challenges for Theology and Church," in *Being Religious Interreligiously: Asian Perspectives on Interfaith Dialogue* (Maryknoll: Orbis Books, 2004), esp. pp. 74-76; and Judson TRAPNELL, "Two Models of Dialogue with Hinduism: Bede Griffiths and Abhishiktananda," *Vidyajyoti* 60 (1996): pp. 101-10, 183-91, 243-54.

[13] Michael von BRÜCK, *The Unity of Reality: God, God-Experience, and Meditation in the Hindu-Christian Dialogue*, J. ZEITZ (trans.) (New York/Mahwah: Paulist Press, 1986 [German original], 1991 [Eng. Trans.]). Such efforts might be characterized, following ULRICH ("Swami Abhishiktananda," p. 52), as different forms of "experiential inclusivism," which views "the convergence of religions in terms of spiritual experience rather than in terms of belief and practice." ULRICH draws significant support for this contention from Michael F. STOEBER, *Theo-Monistic Mysticism: A Hindu-Christian Comparison* (New York: St. Martin's Press, 1994).

[14] Swami PARAMARTHANANDA Saraswati, *UPADEŚA SĀHASRĪ*, audio cassettes, Vedānta Vidyārthi Sangha, n.d., cassette #10-1.

We have already encountered this term as the final element of the so-called threefold method of Advaita Vedanta. According to this schema, *nididhyāsana* follows the hearing of the *Upanishads* (*śravana*) and reflection under the guidance of a teacher (*manana*). It is normally glossed as "contemplation" or "meditation." For his part, Paramarthananda concedes that this term, like the word *dhyāna* with which it is etymologically related, does indeed refer to a form of contemplative practice.[15] But he insists that it should also be understood, more importantly, as a systematic "dwelling upon what has been heard in *śravanam* and *mananam*" or, as he comments later and more pointedly, "remembering the *already established* ideas of the teaching."[16] This practice simply helps the hearer overcome habitual attitudes that obscure full assimilation of what has been previously heard and understood in dialogue with the teacher. Though disciples initially practice it in quiet, withdrawn places and with considerable effort, it can eventually become a spontaneous feature of one's whole existence, continually flowing in and through every activity of embodied life.[17] If one lives in accord with true knowledge, in fact, life itself becomes a form of *nididhyāsana*.[18]

Thus described, *nididhyāsana* reveals great affinity with what the fourteenth-century teacher Swami Vidyāraṇya – citing USP 10.1-3 as an example – describes as the "mental flow" that should be fixed resolutely on *Ātman* by the committed disciple.[19] And Shankara himself, elsewhere

[15] *Dhyāna* and *upāsanā* are two common Sanskrit terms accepted by Shankara to describe meditation. The key difference seems to be that, while the latter retains a sense of devotion and aims to inculcate a profound connection and correspondence between the practitioner and the divine object of meditation, the former is more frequently associated with yoga and the successive stages of mental discipline it prescribes. See BADER, *Meditation*, pp. 32-44.

[16] PARAMARTHANANDA, *UPADEŚA SĀHASRĪ*, #10-1 and #10-2 (emphasis added).

[17] Ibid, cassette #10-1.

[18] Ibid, cassette #10-5.

[19] Sanskrit text and English translation in Swāmī MOKṢADĀNANDA (trans.), *Jīvanmukti-Viveka of Swāmī Vidyāraṇya* (Kolkata: Advaita Ashrama, 1996), pp. 214-16. In translating *pravāha* as "mental flow," I am following Andrew O. FORT, "On Destroying the Mind: The *Yogasūtras* in Vidyāraṇya's *Jīvanmuktiviveka*, " *Journal of Indian Philosophy* 27 (1999): p. 383. VIDYĀRAṆYA includes this citation of USP 10 in his account of *samādhi* and other methods for "annihilating the mind" (*manas-nāśa*) in the third chapter of the *Jīvan-mukti-viveka*, which draws heavily on the *Yoga-Sūtras* and thereby serves as an important link between Shankara's own teaching and the interpretations of Swami Vivekananda, Ramana Maharishi and other modern interpreters. See Ibid, esp. pp. 384-85; Andrew O. FORT, "Liberation While Living in the *Jivanmuktiviveka*: Vidyāraṇya's 'Yogic Advaita,'" in A. FORT and P. MUMME (eds.), *Living Liberation in Hindu Thought* (Albany: State University of New York Press, 1996), pp. 135-55; and Andrew O. FORT,

in his writings, gives an account of a meditative discipline he characterizes with the term *smṛti-saṃtati*, the "continual flow of recollection" of liberating self-knowledge.[20]

We will explore the place and function of such recollection, and Shankara's ambivalent defense of it, in the next section. For the moment, we turn to the practice itself, as modeled in selected verses of USP 10, beginning with a brief statement of the chapter's essential message:

> The highest [*Brahman*] – which is of the nature of Seeing, like the sky, ever-shining, unborn, one alone, imperishable, stainless, all-pervading, and non-dual – That am I and I am forever released. Oṃ. (USP 10.1)

Perhaps the most noticeable feature of this initial thesis, at least on first hearing, is its final syllable, *oṃ*. The commentators suggest that the inclusion of the sacred syllable in USP 10.1 draws attention to its special status as a means to apprehend the true nature of the self, as well as an indication of the disciple's conscious assent to the teaching.[21]

In content, the verse offers a fairly straightforward list of teachings associated with *Brahman,* "the Highest," none of which would come as a surprise to the seasoned Vedantin disciple. *Brahman* is described as self-established "seeing" and "eternal illumination," all-pervading and expansive like the sky, one and non-dual, untainted, and free from birth, destruction and, by implication, all the modifications of empirical existence.[22] To this familiar list is added the equally familiar response on the part of the disciple, who would hear this verse, repeat it, and affirm the

Jīvanmukti in Transformation: Embodied Liberation in Advaita and Neo-Vedānta (Albany: State University of New York Press, 1998), esp. pp. 77-125.

[20] See BUBh 1.4.7, in V. PANOLI (trans.), *Upanishads in Śaṅkara's Own Words*, vol. 4 (Calicut: Mathrubhumi Printing and Publishing Co. Ltd., 1994), p. 194 (my translation). The term is introduced by an adversarial voice (*pūrva-pakṣin*), but Shankara accepts the term and uses it, with variations, throughout the subsequent discussion.

[21] See V. NARASIMHAN, *Upadeśa Sāhasrī: A Thousand Teachings of Adi Śaṅkara* (Bombay: Bharatiya Vidya Bhavan, 1996), p. 24, as well as the full comment of ĀNANDAGIRI in S. SUBRAHMANYA SASTRI (ed.), *Shri Shankarabhagavatpada's Upadeshasahasri with the Tika of Shri Anandagiri Acharya*, Advaita Grantha Ratna Manjushi Ratna 15 (Varanasi: Mahesh Research Institute, 1978), p. 17, lines 25-26, and of RĀMATĪRTHA in D. GOKHALE (ed.), *Shri Shankarāchārya's Upadeśasāhasrī with the Gloss Padayôjanīkā by Shrī Rāmatīrtha* (Bombay: Gujurati Printing Press, 1917), p. 255. Only RAMATĪRTHA includes the second of these two interpretations.

[22] PARAMARTHANANDA, *UPADEŚA SĀHASRĪ*, cassette #10-1, points out that mentioning two of the six modifications of transient life implies all of them. John GRIMES, *A Concise Dictionary of Indian Philosophy: Sanskrit Terms Defined in English*, rev. ed. (Albany: State University of New York Press, 1996), s.v. "*Ṣaḍvikāra*", lists these modifications as "origination or birth, growth, maturity, decline, death and dissolution" (p. 264).

truth of its claim: "I" am none other than "that" all-pervasive, expansive, non-dual, changeless Seeing. I am completely liberated, now and eternally.

This is well-traveled terrain. What Shankara adds in this verse chapter is not new content, but a distinctive pattern of repetition:

> I am Seeing, pure and by nature changeless. There is by nature no object for me. Being the Infinite, completely filled in front, across, up, down, and in every direction, I am unborn, abiding in Myself. (10.2)
> I am unborn, deathless, free from old age, immortal, self-effulgent, all-pervading, non-dual; I am neither cause nor effect, altogether stainless, always satisfied and therefore [constantly] released. Oṃ. (10.3)

The recapitulation of themes from verse 1 in these two verses, already evident in the English translation, is even more striking in Sanskrit. Several terms are repeated verbatim: "seeing" (vv. 1 & 2), "non-dual" (vv. 1 & 3), "all-pervading" (vv. 1 & 3) "completely liberated" (vv. 1 & 3), the twice-repeated "unborn" (vv. 1-3), and above all the crucial "I [am]" (vv. 1 & 2).[23] Other important themes, such as purity, all-pervasiveness and freedom from change or modification, have been restated under slightly different idioms. Treated as a unit, these two verses also echo verse 1 by concluding with the same sacred syllable, *oṃ*.

Within this solid frame of repeated terms and shared themes, Shankara also further elaborates several ideas which have already been very briefly stated. In v. 1, the implied disciple affirmed that *Brahman* shines; in v. 3, this is specified in terms of self-effulgence or illumination. Having asserted that "I" am one alone and changeless (vv. 1-2), this disciple goes on to proclaim her freedom from objects of perception (v. 2), causes or effects (v.3) in the world. In verse 2, finally, Shankara expands on the all-pervading, immanent nature of *Brahman*, emphasized in all three verses, in language reminiscent of *Muṇḍaka Upanishad* 2.2.11:

> *Brahman* alone here extends to the east; // *brahman,* to the west;
> *brahman,* to the south, to the north, // *brahman* extends above and below;
> It is *brahman* alone that extends // over this whole universe, // up to its widest extent.[24]

[23] Some manuscript traditions also repeat "one" (*eka*) in v. 3. See Sengaku MAYEDA (ed.), *Śaṅkara's Upadeśasāhasrī, Critically Edited with Introduction and Indices* (Tokyo: Hokuseido Press, 1973), p. 224.

[24] MuU 2.2.11. Sanskrit text and English translation in Patrick OLIVELLE, *The Early Upaniṣads: Annotated Text and Translation*, South Asia Research Series (New York and Oxford: Oxford University Press, 1998), pp. 448-49.

The *Muṇḍaka* passage attributes omnipresence to "*Brahman* alone." In USP 10.2, it is attributed by the speaker to *aham,* "I," the one who is changeless its own nature, the one who rests or has become established in my own self and also, paradoxically, the limited mind, body and personality who repeats these words and affirms them as her own. By mindfully repeating such words, Swami Paramarthananda suggests, the disciple does not merely affirm the unity between *Brahman* and the individual soul as the teaching of the scriptures and a compelling idea; she actually enacts this very truth, as she speaks from both points of view at once.[25] Only an embodied being can recite, but only *Brahman* can truthfully make these claims. In the performance of the verses, these two become one.

Up to this point, the two referents of "I" – the individual disciple and highest *Brahman* – have simply been juxtaposed in the act of repetition. After several verses of further reiteration and expansion (vv. 4-6), Shankara goes on to clarify their mutual relation:

> Since I am beginningless and attributeless, I have neither action nor result [of action]. Therefore I am the highest [*Ātman*], non-dual. Just as the ether, though all-pervading, is not stained, so am I not either, though abiding in the body, since I am subtle. (10.7)
> And I am always the same to [all] beings, the Lord, for I am superior to, and higher than, the perishable and the imperishable. Though I have the highest *Ātman* as my true nature and am non-dual, I am nevertheless covered with wrong knowledge which is nescience. (10.8)

The seventeenth-century commentator Ramatīrtha discerns in these verses a clear echo of the *Bhagavad-Gītā*.[26] First, the analogy between the very subtle ether and the still subtler *Ātman* in v. 7 seems to depend upon Krishna's teaching in BG 13.[27] Verse 8, then, selectively consolidates several further ideas and images from BG 15:

> In the world there are these two persons, – perishable the one, Imperishable the other: the 'perishable' is all contingent beings, the 'Imperishable' they call the 'sublime, aloof.'

[25] See PARAMARTHANANDA, *UPADEŚA SĀHASRĪ*, cassette #10-3.

[26] See RĀMATĪRTHA, *Upadeśasāhasrī*, pp. 260-62; Swāmi JAGADĀNANDA (trans.), *A Thousand Teachings in Two Parts – Prose and Poetry – of Srī Sankarāchārya* (Madras: Sri Ramakrishna Math, [1941]), p. 113Nn1-2,4; and MAYEDA, *A Thousand Teachings*, p. 125nn6,8.

[27] BG 13.31-32. Romanised Sanskrit text and English translation in R.C. ZAEHNER, *The Bhagavad-Gītā, with a Commentary Based on the Original Sources* (London, Oxford and New York: Oxford University Press, 1969), p. 349.

> But there is [yet] another Person, the [All-]Sublime, surnamed 'All-Highest Self': the three worlds He enters-and-pervades, sustaining them, – the Lord who passes not away.
> Since I transcend the perishable and am more exalted than the Imperishable itself, so am I exalted in Vedic as in common speech as the 'Person [All-] Sublime.[28]

The "I" in this *Gītā* passage is Lord Krishna, addressing himself to Arjuna. In the disciple's recitation of vv. 7-8, this "I" of the Lord becomes the disciple's own "I," mindfully repeated in each of these verses, again following the model set in verse 1. Like the "supreme person" which gives BG 15 its traditional title, "I" stand above and apart from the "perishable" and "imperishable" realities that constitute the earthly and heavenly worlds. Finally, again rehearsing the fundamental claim that "I" am non-dual, the disciple gives an explanation for the apparent misapprehension of this highest self as a limited, embodied being: namely, "nescience" or primordial ignorance – which cause of bondage will itself be negated as ultimately unreal and unrelated to *Ātman* in the very next verse (USP 10.9).

Unlike the model teacher's frequent scriptural citations in USG 1, or the brief references we have encountered in other verse chapters of the *Upadeśasāhasrī*, Shankara does not appear to evoke images from the *Upanishads* and the *Gītā* in these verses in order to convince hearers of the truth of the teaching. This truth has already been established, from the scriptures themselves. Instead, in the present verse chapter, Shankara encourages the disciple to recall these same scriptures as mnemonic tropes, which re-iterate, amplify and deepen the disciple's well-rehearsed self-identification as "Seeing," "the Highest," *Brahman* the divine self. Like the waves of the rising tide, the verses of USP 10 draw in previously established teachings and scriptural imagery even as they draw the disciple, with each repetition, just a few steps further up the shore – that shore where she can say, without a trace of doubt or slightest hesitation, "I am always the same to all beings, the Lord" (v. 8).

Beginning at USP 10.10, Shankara shifts his attention from providing a model for the actual practice of *nididhyāsana* to extolling the desired effect of such repetition on the part of the Advaitin disciple. Towards the end of this eulogy, he proclaims:

> When there is completely non-dual and stainless knowledge, then the great-souled experiences neither sorrow nor delusion. In the absence of

[28] BG 15.16-18, in Ibid, pp. 366-68.

> both there is neither action nor birth. This is the firm belief of those who know the *Veda*. (10.12)
> He who, in the waking state, like a person in the state of deep sleep, does not see duality, though [actually] seeing, because of his non-duality, and similarly he who, though [in fact] acting, is actionless – he [only] is the knower of *Ātman*, and nobody else. This is the firm conclusion here [in the Vedanta]. (10.13)

From one point of view, the key terms of these verses are *niścaya*, translated above as "firm conclusion" (v. 13), and the more intensive form *viniścaya*: the "firm belief," "settled conviction" or even "fixed resolve" of those who know the *Vedas* (v. 12).[29] Just a few verses earlier, at the beginning of the eulogy, Shankara similarly speaks of the "sure conviction" (*viniścaya*) of the one who knows *Brahman* as oneself (v. 10), and the final, concluding verse of the chapter extols both the liberating knowledge which is "ascertained" (*viniścita*) in the Vedanta and the final liberation of the person who becomes "perfectly convinced" of it (*niścita;* v. 14).[30]

Shankara's emphasis on *niścaya* and *viniścaya* in USP 10.10-14 and elsewhere in his writings shifts our attention from the elevated experience of meditation to a more practical, concrete focus on firm conviction as such meditation's stated goal. In this respect, the practice of *nididhyāsana* does not differ greatly from the other stages of the triple method or other teaching scripts of the *Upadeśasāhasrī*. We recall, for example, that one of the goals of the argumentation in USP 16 was precisely for seekers on the path to become "firmly convinced" of the Vedanta teaching (*niścita;* USP 16.68). Such settled conviction arises, first and foremost, from the word of the scriptures and reasoning with the authorized teacher – this we have seen over and over again in our hearing of the *Upadeśasāhasrī*.

But there is also an important place, Shankara suggests across the stanzas of the tenth verse chapter, for deliberately remembering and rehearsing the truth of *Ātman*, in confident expectation that, precisely through such disciplined practices of recollection, our perspective on the present world and our spontaneous activity in it may be thoroughly transformed.

29 See M. Monier-Williams, E. Leumann, C. Capeller, and others, *Sanskrit-English Dictionary, Etymologically and Philologically Arranged with Special Reference to Cognate Indo-European Languages*, rev. ed. (New Delhi: Munshiram Manoharlal Publishers, 2004), s.v. "vi-niścaya," p. 971.

30 Here, I am following the translation in Jagadānanda, *A Thousand Teachings*, p. 115.

A Christian Reflection: Not a few interpreters of Advaita Vedanta draw a sharp contrast between the firm knowledge promised by Advaitic study and the mere, unverifiable faith offered by Christianity and other religious traditions. Usually, in these contexts, the Sanskrit term glossed as "faith" is *śraddhā*, that is, the confidence or trust in the word of the scriptures and the teacher which is stipulated in USG 1.1 and other scripts as a preliminary qualification for the teaching. Christian hearers of USP 10 can, however, recognize in the use of *niścaya* and *viniścaya* a stronger correlate to Christian faith as a fundamental conviction or orientation to one's whole life, grounded in personal trust in Christ and refined through repeated participation in scriptural study, reasoned argument and regular prayer and worship. Just as some scholastics distinguished between "unformed" faith and a faith "formed" or "living" by self-giving love,[31] so also Christian hearers of the *Upadeśasāhasrī* might distinguish between a preliminary assent to the gospel proclamation (*śraddhā*) and the firm conviction (*viniścaya*) that arises in and through the life of discipleship. The former is the precondition for the latter; the latter is the *telos* of the former. Both are intended by the single phrase, "faith in Christ."

A Method of Recollection (USG 3.112, 114-15)

We began the commentary in this chapter with USP 10 rather than USG 3 in order to avoid being misled by Shankara's choice of the idiosyncratic term *parisaṃkhyāna* to describe the method of repetition prescribed in the latter text.[32] Repetitive, contemplative practice is not the unique province of the third prose chapter. Patterns of repetition emerge at several points in the scripts of the *Upadeśasāhasrī*, whether as the central theme of a chapter, such as we have just seen, or as a secondary motif in other treatments that also adopt the literary form of first-person address, such as USP 7, which we took up early in this volume, and USP 19, with which we will conclude.[33] Even the method of "agreement and difference" underscored so strongly in USP 18 or the tightly choreographed arguments of USG 2 could conceivably be interpreted along the lines of *nididhyāsana* – that is, as systematic intra- and intersubjective meditations aiming, through repeated application, to call the teaching to

[31] See, for example, Johann Adam MÖHLER, *Symbolism: Exposition of the Doctrinal Differences between Catholics and Protestants as Evidenced by Their Symbolical Writings*, Milestones in Catholic Theology (New York: Crossroad Publishing Company, 1997), pp. 118-24.

[32] Even the term *parisaṃkhyāna* itself, though very unusual, does not seem to be entirely unique. MAYEDA (*A Thousand Teachings*, pp. 88, 96n1) notes that the *Padabhāṣya* on the *Kena Upanishad*, attributed to Shankara, prescribes *parisaṃkhyāna* for the wise person.

[33] Other examples include USP 8-9, 11 and 13, as well as individual verses and sections of other chapters.

mind, to overcome habitual patterns and to generate firm conviction on the part of the qualified student.[34] Not unlike the all-pervasive *Ātman*, in other words, repetition and remembrance might be said to pervade the whole of the *Upadeśasāhasrī* in its final form.

To clarify the dialectic between the acquisition of self-knowledge and its self-conscious recollection, implied across all these practices, we can have recourse to the concept of *anamnesis.* According to a Platonic understanding, *anamnesis* describes the process by which the seeker turns inward and upward to recover a divine truth known in a previous life or prior to the descent of the soul. In the *nididhyāsana* modeled in USP 10, on the other hand, the practice focuses on the more exterior word of the teaching, as revealed in the *Upanishads* and as received from the teacher. Since what the student has learned in this hearing and reflection is so persistently neglected or forgotten in her ordinary transactions, Shankara seems to imply, she must engage in its deliberate recollection.

Two key texts from Shankara's other writings illustrate the fundamentally anamnestic character of the contemplative practices he prescribes here. The first of these, *Brahma-Sūtra-Bhāṣya* 4.1.1-2, defends repetition in general – the kind of repeated exposure to the teaching revealed in the multiple, interrelated teaching scripts of the *Upadeśasāhasrī* – as a useful way to remove "false ideas" and to clarify the teaching in the mind of the disciple.[35] In his commentary on *Bṛhadāraṇyaka Upanishad* 1.4.7, on the other hand, Shankara addresses himself more directly to the meditative practice modeled in USP 10 and parallels.

At issue in this argument is the statement that "one should indeed remain intent upon '[my own] self'" (BU 1.4.7), which an opponent interprets as an injunction to engage in meditation or, as it will later be specified, in the cultivation of a "continual flow of recollection of self-knowledge" (*ātma-jñāna-smṛti-saṃtati*).[36] Shankara's strong refusal to grant such an injunction, as well as his rejection of the mental restraint prescribed by Yoga as a means of liberation, has led some interpreters to

[34] See MAYEDA, *A Thousand Teachings*, p. 50-56; and Jacqueline SUTHREN HIRST, "Strategies of Interpretation: Śaṃkara's Commentary on Brhadāraṇyakopaniṣad," *Journal of the American Oriental Society* 116 (1996): p. 65.

[35] BSBh 4.1.1-2, in Swami GAMBHIRANANDA (trans.), *Brahma-Sūtra-Bhāṣya of Śrī Śaṅkarācārya* (Calcutta: Advaita Ashrama, 1965, 1972), pp. 644-757, and the further discussion in Francis X. CLOONEY, S.J., *Theology after Vedānta: An Experiment in Comparative Theology* (Albany: State University of New York Press, 1993), pp. 124-26.

[36] BUBh 1.4.7, in PANOLI, *Upanishads*, vol. 4, pp. 187-209 (my translation).

invoke this text as evidence of his wholesale rejection of meditation in the pursuit of liberation.[37]

In fact, Shankara's response to yogic practice and to the "continual flow of recollection" in this text is quite nuanced.[38] First of all, though he does deny the force of a firm injunction to meditate – as he denies all such injunctions as means to liberation, due to their connection with the "I-notion" and sense of personal agency – he grants such practices as a possible option that can support the acquisition of knowledge. Second, just as we saw him do with reference to renunciant life in chapter 2 of this commentary, so also in BUBh 1.4.7 he argues from the distinguishing marks or characteristics of the liberated state to the means that can be employed to achieve it. He first speaks of the "flow of recollection" (*smṛti-saṃtati*) that arises spontaneously in the mind of the person who has come to know *Ātman* from the *Upanishads*, arguing that "when the false notions about the Self are removed, the memories naturally arising from them and relating to the duality of non-Self [also] cease to exist."[39] From this spontaneous characteristic of the self-knower, he infers that such a mental flow can also function as a means to acquire liberating self-knowledge, albeit one strictly subordinate to knowledge itself.[40]

Most remarkably, in his comment on BU 1.4.7 Shankara seems to suggest that *smṛti-saṃtati* may function as a helpful means not only for the seeker, but even for the liberated sage:

> ... inasmuch as that [past] action, on account of which this body has come into being, is bound to produce a definite result, even when the right knowledge is attained, the activities connected with speech, mind and body continue, for [stored] action which has begun to bear fruit is powerful like the motion of an arrow already shot. Hence the operation of knowledge which is weaker than that of action is bound to be interrupted by the latter... Therefore this necessitates the regulation of the flow of recollection of self-knowledge by resorting to means such as renunciation and detachment.[41]

[37] See Paul HACKER, "Śaṅkara the Yogin and Śaṅkara the Advaitin," in Wilhelm HALBFASS (ed.), *Philology and Confrontation: Paul Hacker on Traditional and Modern Vedanta* (Albany: State University of New York Press, 1995),p. 107, and John A. TABER, *Transformative Philosophy: A Study of Śaṅkara, Fichte, and Heidegger* (Honolulu: University of Hawaii Press, 1983), pp. 8-9.

[38] Throughout the discussion in this paragraph, I am indebted to the analysis in BADER, *Meditation*, esp. pp. 88-92.

[39] BUBh 1.4.7, in PANOLI, *Upanishads*, p. 195 (modified).

[40] Ibid, p. 197.

[41] Ibid, pp. 201-202 (modified).

Here Shankara is referring to *prārabdha-karma*, those past actions bearing immediate fruit in the present life. This idea, as we have already seen briefly in chapter 3, is invoked by Shankara and further developed in subsequent Advaita tradition to explain the continued embodiment of the liberated sage.[42] In this passage, however, it also seems to pose a persistent risk to self-knowledge. Lest such knowledge become overwhelmed or confused by the momentum of past actions – from this or past lives – Shankara recommends the cultivation of renunciation, detachment and a continual, anamnestic discipline of recollection.[43]

From BSBh 4.1.1-2 and especially BUBh 1.4.7, then, we see that Shankara places considerable emphasis upon repetition, meditation and mental discipline. The "continual flow of recollection" discussed in BUBh 1.4.7 and modeled in such texts as USP 10 is, according to Shankara, something to be cultivated by the seeker, sustained even after the teaching has been fully assimilated, and ultimately recognized as a spontaneous consequence of liberation. The Advaita teaching, we can speculate, does not culminate in *nididhyāsana* because *śravana* and *manana* are somehow incomplete without it. Rather, as a form of *anamnesis*, it recapitulates and crystallizes the essential vision they themselves aim to foster. It stands in a strictly supporting role to these other practices, while also bringing their various teachings to living expression in the mind, heart and embodied performance of the disciple.

With these considerations in mind, it may come as no surprise that the *Upadeśasāhasrī*'s third prose chapter, which follows the lengthy scriptural instruction and spirited disputations of USG 1-2, does not make any reference to these previous chapters, or even to the teacher and student who dominated their pages. Instead, Shankara speaks directly to the prospective hearer:

> This *parisaṃkhyāna* meditation is described for seekers after final release, who are devoting themselves to destroying their acquired merit and demerit and do not wish to accumulate new ones. Nescience causes faults; they cause the activities of speech, mind, and body; and from these activities are accumulated [further] actions[44] of which [in turn] the results are desirable, undesirable, and mixed. For the sake of final release from those actions [this *parisaṃkhyāna* meditation is described] (USG 3.112)

[42] See above, ch. 3, p. 84-85.

[43] See the discussion in BADER, *Meditation*, pp. 73-74, and TABER, *Transformative Philosophy*, pp. 16-17.

[44] MAYEDA's original rendering leaves this untranslated as *karmans*.

Given the traditional identification of the three prose chapters of the *Upadeśasāhasrī* with the threefold method of Advaita Vedanta, it is mildly puzzling that neither Shankara nor the commentators explicitly identify the discipline prescribed in this chapter as *nididhyāsana*. Shankara uses the term *parisaṃkhyāna*, which Jagadānanda renders as "method of repetition," Narasimhan as "method of recollection," Alston as "recapitulation," Hacker as "recapitulating contemplation" and Mayeda, above, simply as "*parisaṃkhyāna* meditation."[45] The commentators gloss this term as *anucintaṇa*, which connotes focused consideration, recollection or even, in its broader usage, anxiety or preoccupation.[46] Given our treatments above, we might add "flow of recollection" (*smṛti-saṃtati*), Vidyāraṇya's "mental flow" (*pravāha*), or even "*anamnesis*" to this list of possible equivalents.

More significant than the name of this practice is its intended purpose. The commentators indicate that it is prescribed for "those who are not absolutely clear about what was told earlier" in the previous prose chapters.[47] Shankara himself makes no such reference to previous teaching, simply commending this practice for those who desire to escape the cycle of transmigratory existence, described here in terms that echo USP 1.3-5.[48] In the section that follows (USP 3.113), moreover, he will extend this analysis from soteriology to phenomenology, reducing "objects of sense," constituted as they are by organs of knowledge such as ears, to the realm of evolving name-and-form or non-self – again echoing treatments from elsewhere in the *Upadeśasāhasrī* and in Shankara's other writings.[49]

All this is, once more, familiar terrain. Along lines already familiar from USP 10, what Shankara adds in USG 3 is not new content, but a distinctive pattern of repetition:

45 JAGADĀNANDA, *A Thousand Teachings*, p. 71; NARASIMHAN, *Upadeśa Sāhasrī*, p. 377; A.J. ALSTON (trans.), *The Thousand Teachings (Upadeśa Sāhasrī) of Śrī Śaṃkarācārya* (London: Shanti Sadan, 1990), p. 90; and Paul HACKER (trans.), *Upadeśasāhasrī: Unterweisung in der All-Einheits-Lehre der Inder, von Meister Shankara: Gadyabandha oder das Buch in Prosa*, Religionsgeschichtliche Texts Herausgegeben von Gustav Mensching 2 (Bonn: Ludwig Röhrscheid Verlag, 1949), p. 53.

46 See ĀNANDAGIRI, *Upadeśasāhasrī*, p. 161, lines 13-14, and RĀMATĪRTHA, *Upadeśasāhasrī*, p. 96.

47 NARASIMHAN, *Upadeśa Sāhasrī*, p. 377. See also the original comment in ĀNANDAGIRI, *Upadeśasāhasrī*, p. 161, lines 11-13, and RĀMATĪRTHA, *Upadeśasāhasrī*, p. 96.

48 See above, ch. 2, pp. 51-52.

49 See especially USG 1.18-23, 33-35; USG 2.70-75; BSBh 2.4.6-19, in GAMBHIRANANDA, *Brahma-Sūtra-Bhāṣya*, pp. 527-47; and the discussion in MAYEDA, *A Thousand Teachings*, pp. 28-37.

> So the wise person who is tormented by sound and the other [objects of the senses] which are being perceived should perform *parisaṃkhyāna* meditation as follows (3.114):
> I am of the nature of Seeing, non-object, unconnected [with anything], changeless, motionless, endless, fearless, and absolutely subtle. So sound cannot make me its object and touch me, whether as mere noise in general or as [sound] of particular qualities – pleasant [sounds] such as the first note of music or the desirable words of praise and the like, or the undesirable words of untruth, disgust, humiliation, abuse, and the like – since I am unconnected [with sound]. (3.115a)

In the English translation, this practice of repetition begins with the assertion that "I" am of "the nature of seeing," which very closely resembles the repeated refrain of USP 10.1-2.[50] Though this captures the essential thrust of the passage, it somewhat betrays the practitioner's actual movement in the Sanskrit text, starting with "sound" (*śabda*), continuing through a classification of different types and examples of such sounds, and only then arriving at the "witness," motionless, changeless, extremely subtle and, by definition, not itself an object of perception.

This witness has also, however, been described as being "without fear." Why? The disciple goes on to rehearse and to reflect more deeply:

> For this very reason neither loss nor gain is caused [in me] by sound. Therefore, what can the pleasant sound of praise, the unpleasant sound of blame, and so on do to me? Indeed a pleasant sound may produce gain, and an unpleasant one destruction, for a person lacking in discriminating knowledge, who regards sound as [connected with his] *Ātman* since he has no discriminating knowledge. But for me who am endowed with discriminating knowledge, [sound] cannot produce even a hair's breadth [of gain or loss] (3.115b)

In the first section of this prose chapter, the one undertaking this meditation was described as a "seeker after liberation" and as one who desires to become released from merit, demerit and their continued accumulation (3.112). In prescribing the actual *parisaṃkhyāna* meditation, Shankara instead describes this same practitioner as a *vid-vant*, a wise person or self-knower (3.114).[51] Now, in the process of repetition, the disciple describes himself as a *vivekin*, a "person of discrimination." In light of the discussion in BUBh 1.4.7 above, such variations are reconciled easily

[50] In the case of 3.115, the first person pronoun is rendered in the accusative case as *māṃ*, rather than the nominative *aham* – so the echo works only on the level of semantics, not of sound.

[51] JAGADĀNANDA (*A Thousand Teachings*, p. 73) translates it as "knower of *Brahman*."

enough: this practice of repetition, like the "continual flow of recollection" described in that text, can in fact serve as a supporting means at various points along the path of knowledge.

In the present context, however, Shankara introduces the "person of discrimination" primarily to draw a contrast to its opposite, the one who lacks such discrimination (*a-vivekin*). Only the latter, due to his identification with the limited body, mind and personality, will profit from the sound of praise or suffer from the sound of blame. The former, fully identified with *Ātman*, has no cause to fear either becoming swollen by commendation or diminished by criticism. From this very fact of self-identification, we can infer, such a person becomes free to act in the world in a transformed way, no longer driven by the twin forces of praise and blame.

He is not completely free, however – at least not yet; for he has thus far addressed only words and sound. To complete the meditation, he must continue the exercise:

> In the very same manner [touch] does not produce for me any change of gain and loss, whether as touch in general or as touch in particular forms – the unpleasant [touch] of cold, heat, softness, hardness, etc., and of fever, stomachache, etc., and any pleasant [touch] either inherent in the body or caused by external and adventitious [objects] – since I am devoid of touch, just as a blow with the fist and the like [does not produce any change] in the sky.
> Likewise [form-and-color] produces neither loss nor gain for me, whether as form-and-color in general or as form-and-color in particular, pleasant or unpleasant, such as the female characteristics of a woman and the like, since I am devoid of form-and-color.
> Similarly, [taste] produces neither loss nor gain for me who am by nature devoid of taste, whether as taste in general or as taste in particular forms[pleasant or unpleasant,] such as sweetness, sourness, saltiness, pungency, bitterness, astringency which are perceived by the dull-witted (3.115c-e)

USP 10, as we saw above, began with a simple repetition of the identity of the "I" with Seeing (vv. 1-3), moved on to explain the merely apparent relation of *Ātman* to the embodied individual (vv. 7-8), and eventually declared that the truly wise person ceases to see duality even in the midst of ordinary phenomenal experiences (v. 13). The present meditation builds on the same fundamental idea, but does so in a more sustained, systematic and explicitly embodied way. Instead of negating experience in general, or even touch, sight and taste in general, Shankara has the disciple move through a litany of bodily experiences, from the overwhelming heat of a deadly fever to a mild sweetness on the tip of the tongue, from a stomach ache to the sight of a beautiful woman. These are experiences specific to a particular, embodied person – specifically, we can infer, the human, male and heterosexual kind of embodied person. Yet, none of these experiences has the power to affect the self, and so none are "perceived" or acknowledged as ultimately real by the liberated self-knower.

Having proceeded through the senses of hearing, touch, sight and taste, the disciple draws this part of the repetition to a close:

> In a like manner [odor] produces neither loss nor gain for me who am by nature devoid of odor, whether as odor in general or as odor in particular forms, pleasant or unpleasant, such as [the odor] of flowers, etc., and ointment, etc. That is because the *Śruti* says: 'That which is soundless, touchless, formless, imperishable, also tasteless, constant, odorless...' [KaU 3.15] (3.115f)

The manner in which the disciple moves through the senses does not reveal any obvious ordering principle. One might suppose that the movement from sound, sight and touch to taste and smell follows a progressive pattern of interiorization and increasing subtlety.[52] At the conclusion of the section, however, it is revealed that Shankara, in starting with the "word" of sound (*śabda*), is also following an example set by the verbal testimony (*śabda-pramāṇa*) of the *Vedas*.

These two explanations are not contradictory, for Shankara has not chosen this concluding text arbitrarily. It lies at the end of what the great teacher himself describes, in his commentary on *Kaṭha Upanishad*, as a process of "successively seeing what is more subtle."[53] And, reading selectively in this Upanishad, we do indeed discover a familiar pattern:

> Higher than the senses are their objects;// Higher than sense objects is the mind;
> Higher than the mind is the intellect;// Higher than the intellect is the immense self;
> Higher than the immense self is the unmanifest;// Higher than the unmanifest is the person;
> Higher than the person there's nothing at all,// that is the goal, that's the highest state;

[52] On such methods of interiorization, which Shankara employs often in his teaching, see SUTHREN HIRST, *Śaṃkara's Advaita Vedānta*, pp. 83-85; and J.G. SUTHREN HIRST, "The Place of Teaching Techniques in Śaṃkara's Theology," *Journal of Indian Philosophy* 18 (1990): pp. 134-39.

[53] KaUBh 1.3.12 [3.12], following the translatation in SUTHREN HIRST, "Place of Teaching Techniques," p. 136. The full comment is available in PANOLI, *Upanishads in Śaṅkara's Own Words,* vol. 1, pp. 227-28.

Hidden in all the beings,// this self is not visibly displayed.
Yet, people of keen vision see him,// with eminent and sharp minds.

It has no sound or touch,// no appearance, taste or smell;
It is without beginning or end,// undecaying and eternal;
When a person perceives it,// fixed and beyond the immense,
He is freed from the jaws of death.[54]

In summing up his own repetition with a citation of KaU 3.15, the disciple not only recalls the scriptural text itself but also rehearses its message and movement in the embodied performance of the repetition. The *Upanishad* begins with the senses and moves, by measured progression, to the "person" at its root; the disciple begins with hearing and, from one sense to another, recalls both the embodied experiences revealed by those senses and the pure seeing in whose illuminating presence they are thus revealed. He systematically re-imagines and remembers himself as the "person of keen vision" described in the Upanishad and, through such systematic recollection, endeavors ever more fully to become the very person he recalls.

A Christian Reflection: Many Christian hearers will be struck forcefully – and rightly – by the contrast between Christian and Advaita attitudes toward the human body and physical embodiment. Faith in Christ, as we shall explore below, is also faith in the bodily resurrection of Christ and, at the end of time, of all humankind. In USG 10.2-3, by contrast, the implied disciple pronounces herself infinite, "unborn," incapable of change or transformation and distinct from any object of embodied experience. And the bulk of the *parisaṃkhyāna* meditation prescribed in USG 3 systematically negates such objects and thereby, to all appearances, drives a firm wedge between final liberation and any connection to a physical body – even a transformed one. The *jīvan-mukta* may well achieve liberation in this life and in this body, as argued in chapter 3 of this commentary, but such embodied existence never becomes directly implicated in liberation itself.

A Vision of Transformation (USG 3.116)

Our hearing in this chapter started with a question of meditative experience in general and yogic *samādhi* in particular, both of which have been strongly emphasized in certain strands of ancient and contemporary Advaita. In neither the *nididhyāsana* implied in USP 10 nor the *parisaṃkhyāna* prescribed in USG 3, however, have we witnessed a

[54] KaU 3.10-12, 15, in OLIVELLE, *Early Upaniṣads*, pp. 388-91 (modified).

strong emphasis upon *nirvikalpa samādhi*, the cessation of mental activity or exceptional yogic discipline. Reception of the teaching has experiential implications, to be sure: the one who ceases in some sense to see duality (USP 10.13), who is no longer affected by the sensations of praise, blame, saltiness or raging fever (USG 1.116), who maintains a "continual flow of recollection" of the fundamental teaching, "I am Seeing," *Brahman* the divine self, cannot reasonably be said to understand or even to perceive the world in a conventional way. But this transformed experience cannot logically be traced to yet another experience. It is the result of repeatedly hearing, reflecting and recollecting the word of the teaching, as communicated and embodied in its various scripts.

In the previous discussion, I suggested the concept of *anamnesis* as a way to capture the fundamental orientation of the contemplative practices Shankara prescribes in the *Upadeśasāhasrī*. So too here, we might approach the transformation such practices presume and intend by means of an Aristotelian understanding of *habitus*, particularly as this category has been adapted by such modern theorists as Marcel Mauss, Pierre Bourdieu, Talal Asad and Saba Mahmood.[55] Bourdieu in particular proposed that the interplay between social structures and individuals could be mediated with recourse to this idea, understood in practical terms as "a system of lasting, transposable dispositions which, integrating past experiences, functions at every moment as a *matrix of perceptions, appreciations, and actions* and makes possible the achievement of infinitely diversified tasks...."[56] A *habitus*, thus described, comprises far more than mere habits, conventionally understood; it comprehends a complex pattern of reflexive behaviors and unconscious dispositions which, though inculcated by means of imitation, codes of conduct, traditional maxims and the like, is not reducible to them. Precisely as a

[55] See Pierre BOURDIEU, *Outline of the Theory of Practice*, R. NICE (trans.) (Cambridge: Cambridge University Press, 1977), esp. pp. 72-95; Talal ASAD, "Toward a Genealogy of the Concept of Ritual," in *Genealogies of Religion: Discipline and Reasons of Power in Christianity and Islam* (Baltimore and London: Johns Hopkins University Press, 1993), pp. 74-77; Talal ASAD, *Formations of the Secular: Christianity, Islam, Modernity*, Cultural Memory in the Present (Stanford: Stanford University Press, 2003), pp. 92-99, 248-52; and Saba MAHMOOD, *Politics of Piety: The Islamic Revival and the Feminist Subject* (Princeton and Oxford: Princeton University Press, 2005), pp. 134-39.

[56] BOURDIEU, *Outline of the Theory of Practice*, pp. 82-83 (emphasis by BOURDIEU). See also the discussion in Catherine BELL, *Ritual Theory, Ritual Practice* (New York and Oxford: Oxford University Press, 1992), 79-81; and David SWARTZ, *Culture and Power: The Sociology of Pierre Bourdieu* (Chicago and London: University of Chicago Press, 1997), pp. 95-116.

matrix of internal dispositions, one's *habitus* shapes one's expectations and even experience and thus sets limits on one's sphere of action. Within that sphere and even pressing its boundaries, however, Bourdieu also saw room for the genuine exercise of individual and collective human agency.

Understood in quite broad terms, this notion of *habitus* offers a helpful interpretative tool for our hearing of scripts like USP 10 and USG 3. As a crystallization of the many teaching scripts of the *Upanishads,* the *Bhagavad-Gītā,* and the *Upadeśasāhasrī* itself, disciplined repetition not only responds to deeply engrained patterns of thought and practice on the part of its disciples; it also attempts to generate a new *habitus,* a distinctive "*matrix of perceptions, appreciations, and actions*" conditioned, not on praise or blame, pleasure or pain, but solely on liberating self-knowledge.[57] Experience does not generate some new knowledge. Experience is ideally re-shaped by knowledge and, most importantly for our present purposes, by its repeated, habituating and thoroughly embodied recollection.

In USP 10, as we have seen, Shankara encapsulates the transformed *habitus* intended by its meditative discipline in cryptic formulas like "I am the same to all beings" (v. 8), "the one who does not see duality, though seeing" and "the one who, though acting, is actionless" (v. 13). At the conclusion of USG 3, Shankara has his model disciple offer a more ample account:

> Moreover, whatever sound and the other external [objects of the senses] may be, they are changed into the form of the body, and into the form of the ear and the other [senses] which perceive them, and into the form of the two internal organs[58] and their objects [such as pleasure and pain], since they are mutually connected and composite in all cases of actions. This being the case, to me, a person of knowledge, nobody is foe, friend or neutral (USG 3.116a)

Drawing on his prior repetition, the disciple reflects that sense-objects undergo transformation and are composite. From this, he draws a possibly

[57] For BOURDIEU, though *habitus* is definitely learned, there seem to be significant limits upon the possibility of its intentional cultivation. In their appropriations of the category, ASAD and MAHMOOD place much greater emphasis on the self-conscious formation of an interior *habitus* through external, performative practice. See especially the discussion in MAHMOOD, *Politics of Piety,* pp. 138-39.

[58] Most commentators identify these as the mind (*manas*) and the discriminating faculty of the intellect (*buddhi*), though HACKER (*Upadeśasāhasrī,* p. 55n4) and MAYEDA (*A Thousand Teachings,* pp. 30-31) point out that Shankara does not consistently distinguish between the two.

unexpected consequence: namely, that other persons can no longer be regarded as friends, as foes or even as neutral or indifferent.

Why would such a conclusion follow? The meditation continues:

> In this context, if [anybody] through a misconception [about *Ātman*] due to false knowledge, were to wish to connect [me] with [anything], pleasant or unpleasant, which is characteristic of the result of action, he wishes in vain to connect [me] with it, since I am not its object according to the *Smṛti* passage: 'Unmanifest he, unthinkable he...' [BG 2.25]. Likewise, I am not to be changed by [any of] the five elements,[59] since I am not their object according to the *Smṛti* passage: 'Not to be cut is he, not to be burnt is he...' [BG 2.24] (3.116b)

If no sounds of praise or blame, no sensation pleasant or unpleasant, and no injury or transformation from any material thing can touch the self pronouncing these words, then it stands to reason that the same follows in the case of all other persons, as well. Such persons may well, due to *their* false knowledge or ignorance, wish to influence or even to harm me; yet from the perspective or *habitus* of the person of knowledge, there is absolutely nothing to fear.

As in the first prose chapter and many of the verse chapters, the discourse once again includes explicit citations of the scriptures to authorize the disciple's repeated affirmations – in this case, drawn from the *Bhagavad-Gītā*. As the chapter draws to a close, moreover, the *anamnesis* shifts toward still firmer epistemological ground:

> Furthermore, paying attention only to the aggregate of the body and the senses, [people, both] devoted and adverse to me, have the desire to connect [me] with things, pleasant, unpleasant, etc., and therefrom results the acquisition of merit, demerit, and the like. It belongs only to them and does not occur in me who am free from old age, death, and fear, since the *Śrutis* and the *Smṛtis* say: 'Neither what has been done nor what has been left undone affects It' [BU 4.4.22]; '... he does not increase nor become less by action' [BU 4.4.23]; '... without and within, unborn' [MuU 2.1.2]; '... not afflicted with the suffering of the world, being outside of it' [KaU 5.11]; etc. This is because anything other than *Ātman* does not exist, – this is the highest reason (3.116c)

The teaching, which begins with the *Upanishads*, also concludes with the *Upanishads*, in this case the *Bṛhadāraṇyaka*, *Muṇḍaka* and *Kaṭha Upanishads*. In the present context, the citations from these scriptures function

[59] On the role of the five elements in the generation of empirical existence, see above, ch. 4, pp. 127-30.

to clarify the fact that what pertains to those without knowledge – namely, body, mind and personality; merit and demerit; old age, death and, of course, fear – does not pertain to "me," since the *Upanishads* proclaim me to be unaffected by action, suffering and origination. The reverence of the one who loves me and the aversion of the one who dislikes me remain real from the perspective of ignorance, and that alone. From the point of view of highest knowledge, nothing besides the self can properly be said to exist at all.

We first encountered this claim, stated in such unequivocal terms, at the conclusion of our hearing of USP 2-7 in chapter 3. There, we treated the teaching of non-duality as a kind of scandal, which upsets conventional assumptions and provokes rejection on the part of those who "fear that action may be destroyed" (USP 5.1). Here, it emerges in more positive terms as the firm conviction and embodied *habitus* of those who have already come to know the self, as well as those who are in the process of cultivating such conviction through disciplined *anamnesis*. In both cases, the claim "nothing but *Ātman* exists" does not stand on its own, as an apodictic assertion. It arises only at the end of well-choreographed processes of self-inquiry, self-discovery and repeated self-cultivation.

For this reason, perhaps, the third prose chapter does not conclude with the simple pronouncement of non-duality. Instead, Shankara turns its hearers back to the process itself:

> As duality does not exist, all the sentences of the *Upaniṣads* concerning the non-duality of *Ātman* should be fully contemplated, should be contemplated (3.116d)

It may initially seem odd that a prose chapter dedicated to the third and final phase of the threefold method should close with an injunction to contemplate or, perhaps better, thoroughly to investigate the revealed word of the *Upanishads*. Shankara seems to suggest that, at the end of this meditation, the disciple should return again to his hearing and reflection on the scriptures.

In support of this interpretation, we recall that many of Shankara's defenses of repetition address repeated hearing and reflection, rather than *parisaṃkhyāna* or any other meditative discipline as such. The repeated affirmations of USP 10 and USG 3 represent culminating moments or, with a more literal rendering of *parisaṃkhyāna* in mind, anamnestic recapitulations of what should be happening across all of the scripts of the *Upadeśasāhasrī* and the Vedic scriptures themselves. In and through their repeated application, a transformed vision and way of life opens for seeker and self-knower alike.

What is the content of this transformation? It is difficult to say for sure. Shankara's strong insistence that the self-knower cannot be connected to any action and stands unaffected by devotee and adversary alike suggests a kind of cool, passive indifference. But, in fact, indifference (*udāsa*) too has been firmly negated (USG 3.116a). The envisioned way of life cannot therefore be reduced to a mere negation of old dispositions and possibilities. It also implies the opening of new ones, of a radically non-conventional *habitus* that takes its stand entirely outside and beyond the realm of means and ends, pleasure and pain, amity and enmity, and even placid disengagement. No longer will worldly activity be driven by commendation, censure or any form of external incentive. It will instead flow spontaneously from its disciples' continual, disciplined and transformative recollection.

III.
"Lest you have come to believe in vain": A Christian *Saṃvāda* with USG 3

> Now I would remind you, brothers and sisters, of the good news that I proclaimed to you, which you in turn received, in which also you stand, through which you are being saved, if you hold firmly to the message that I proclaimed to you – unless you have come to believe in vain.
>
> For I handed on to you as of first importance what I in turn had received: that Christ died for our sins in accordance with the scriptures, and that he was buried, and that he was raised on the third day in accordance with the scriptures, and that he appeared to Cephas, then to the twelve... For since death came through a human being, the resurrection of the dead has also come through a human being; for as all die in Adam, so all will be made alive in Christ. But each in his own order: Christ the first fruits, then at his coming those who belong to Christ. Then comes the end, when he hands over the kingdom to God the Father, after he has destroyed every ruler and every authority and power. For he must reign until he has put all his enemies under his feet. The last enemy to be destroyed is death (1 Cor 15:1-5, 21-26)

Having arrived at the last of our experiments in dialogue, we begin with what may be one of the most significant passages of the entire New Testament: the apostle Paul's spirited defense of the resurrection of the dead (1 Cor 15). The apostle speaks here of the *parousia* or arrival of

Christ at the end of time and, with this triumphant arrival, of the decisive establishment of God's reign on earth, "so that God may be all in all" (v. 28). Though eschatological hope runs as a consistent thread throughout all of Paul's writings, it is only in 1 Corinthians and the Thessalonian correspondence that he strikes such an explicitly apocalyptic tone of imminent expectation.[60] The placement of these reflections at the end of the letter, moreover, suggests that they offer more than a sketch of Christians' future hope. They also provide a template for the whole Christian life. No less than the scandal of "Christ crucified," with which Paul began this letter and with which we began our *saṃvāda* in chapter 3 of this commentary (1 Cor 1:18-25), resurrection faith touches the heart of the gospel message, in present and future alike.[61]

Despite its broad importance, Paul's teaching here, as elsewhere, also addresses issues specific to its intended recipients. Some members of the Christian community in Corinth, it seems, may have overly "spiritualized" Paul's message about sharing in the death and resurrection of Christ in the present moment, emphasizing the gift of the Holy Spirit here and now to the exclusion of its final consummation in a bodily resurrection at the end of time.[62] The problem did not stem from rejection of the resurrection of Jesus the Christ, as such; it stemmed from a misunderstanding or distortion of the consequences of this resurrection in the embodied life of the Christian believer.[63]

Paul responds to this misunderstanding on several levels. At one such level, late in his exposition (1 Cor 15:35-58), the apostle draws an analogy between seeds and plants to elucidate the difference between believers' present bodies and the resurrection bodies they will inherit at the end of time: the former body is "physical" or "soulish," whereas the latter is "spiritual," possessed of what N.T. Wright characterizes as a kind of "noncorruptible physicality."[64] On this point, as we have seen

[60] See especially James D.G. DUNN, *The Theology of Paul the Apostle* (Grand Rapids and Cambridge: William B. Eerdmans Publishing Company, 1998), pp. 294-315.

[61] See Ibid, pp. 235-40; Morna D. HOOKER, *Paul: A Short Introduction* (Oxford: Oneworld, 2003), pp. 39-43; and J. Paul SAMPLEY, "The First Letter to the Corinthians," in *The New Interpreter's Bible*, vol. 10 (Nashville: Abingdon Press, 2002), pp. 973-74.

[62] See the discussion in SAMPLEY, "First Corinthians," pp. 980-82, and Jerome MURPHY-O'CONNOR, O.P., "The First Letter to the Corinthians," in R. BROWN, J. FITZMYER, and R. MURPHY (eds.), *The New Jerome Biblical Commentary* (Englewood Cliffs: Prentice Hall, 1990), p. 812 [49:65].

[63] See especially SAMPLEY, "First Corinthians," pp. 979-80.

[64] N.T. WRIGHT, "The Resurrection of the Messiah," *Sewanee Theological Review* 41 (1998): esp. pp. 125-31, quotation at p. 129. See also the further discussion in HOOKER,

on several occasions, the teaching of Paul and of mainstream Christian tradition stands in sharp contrast not only to that of the Corinthian spiritualists, but also to Shankara's Advaita.[65] But this, once again, is not the end of the issue. For the apostle also responds to the Corinthians' objections by drawing out the universal consequences of Christ as the representative of all humankind, on the analogy of Adam (vv. 12-34): "as all die in Adam, so all will be made alive in Christ," beginning with Jesus' own death and resurrection in the past and continuing on to include all who belong to him, in present and future alike (v. 22-23). The emphasis here, as in Philippians 2, is that Christians can look to Christ as the model and image after which they are re-made, the paradigm of their moral striving and their final destiny.[66]

To function effectively, of course, this model depends upon disciples' clear memory of those decisive events upon which it has been founded. So it comes as no surprise that Paul begins his defense of resurrection faith with a rehearsal of what some scholars consider an early creedal formula: a brief account of Jesus' death "for our sins," his burial, his resurrection on the third day "according to the scriptures," and the witness to this resurrection by Peter and the other disciples (1 Cor 15:3b-5). To this basic proclamation Paul adds the evidence of other witnesses, including himself as "the least of the apostles" (vv. 6-10).[67] He does not offer any of this as new information. He offers it as a reminder of a truth his hearers already know and to which they must "hold firmly," lest they "have come to believe in vain" (v. 2). At the end of the chapter, the apostle echoes this same idea, exhorting the Corinthians to "be steadfast, immovable, always excelling in the work of the Lord, because you know

Paul, pp. 134-37; MURPHY-O'CONNOR, "First Corinthians," pp. 813-14 [49:72-75]; SAMPLEY, "First Corinthians," pp. 986-89; and, more broadly, N.T. WRIGHT, *The Resurrection of the Son of God*, Christian Origins and the Question of God 3 (London: SPCK, 2003).

65 This should not be read, however, to mean that there may not be alternative Christian interpretations of resurrection, nor that resurrection itself is incapable of an Advaita re-interpretation. On this point, see especially Anantanand RAMBACHAN, "Advaita Vedanta and Marcus Borg: Opportunities for Hindu-Christian Dialogue," *Hindu-Christian Studies Bulletin* 16 (2003): pp. 30-36; and Ravi RAVINDRA, *Christ the Yogi: A Hindu Reflection on the Gospel of John* (Rochester: Inner Traditions, 1990, 1998), pp. 215-25.

66 Morna D. HOOKER characterizes this relationship as "interchange in Christ" and regards it as one of the most central, controlling ideas of Paul's theology. See Hooker, *Paul*, pp. 80-89, and especially chapters 1-4 of Morna D. HOOKER, *From Adam to Christ: Essays on Paul* (Cambridge: Cambridge University press, 1990).

67 See MURPHY-O'CONNOR, "First Corinthians," p. 812 [49:66], and SAMPLEY, "First Corinthians," pp. 976-77.

that in the Lord your labor is not in vain" (v. 58).[68] As in his teaching on the Lord's supper in the same letter, then, Paul's teaching here can be seen as commending a form of *anamnesis* not unlike that modeled in USP 10 and prescribed in USG 3, whereby the continual recollection of Christ's death and resurrection in the past shapes Christian commitment in the present, "until he comes again" (see 1 Cor 11:26).[69] Perhaps more accurately, in 1 Corinthians 15 Paul calls believers to recall *both* past suffering and future promise, so as radically to transform the way they perceive and evaluate present existence.

If we adopt *anamnesis* as our point of correspondence between the teaching scripts of USG 3 and 1 Cor 15, as I have briefly suggested, then our attention necessarily shifts from the discursive contents of the teaching in these two traditions, which are irreconcilably different, to the more readily comparable function of repetition and memory in their respective pursuits. Our emphasis also shifts, more importantly, from *samādhi* or mystical experience as a desired end for the individual disciple to self-cultivation and mystical practice as constitutive, ongoing features of discipleship itself. In our hearing of USP 10, for example, we noted that Shankara describes the goal of *nididhyāsana* not in terms of one or another elevated experiential state, but in terms of conviction (*niścaya*), fixed resolve (*viniścaya*) and profound transformation on the level of understanding and commitment (10.12-14). In so doing, we can now observe, this great Hindu teacher also echoes a core theme of the apostle Paul's Corinthian correspondence. In both cases, disciples are cautioned to recall a teaching they have received in the past, when they first became hearers, lest it fail to bear its intended fruit. In both cases, the content and consequences of this *anamnesis* well exceed the limitations of a scriptural text, a past event or a line of argument. They cannot be "remembered" in any ordinary sense of the term, as though they could be filed away, summarized in an encyclopedia article or cataloged as an incidental product of history or culture. *That* form of "remembering," as the contemporary political theologian Johann Baptist Metz has argued forcefully, is actually more appropriately characterized as a form

[68] See SAMPLEY, "First Corinthians," pp. 990-91.

[69] On the connection between liturgical practice and other anamnestic practices in Paul and elsewhere in the New Testament, see the discussions in DUNN, *Theology of Paul*, pp. 620-23; J. Paul SAMPLEY, *Walking between the Times: Paul's Moral Reasoning* (Minneapolis: Fortress Press, 1991), pp. 11-17; and especially Bruce T. MORRILL, S.J., *Anamnesis as Dangerous Memory: Political and Liturgical Theology in Dialogue* (Collegeville: Liturgical Press, 2000), pp. 139-88.

of amnesia, for it consigns these memories to the irrelevance of a specialized discipline or a distant past.[70]

Instead, according to Metz, the liberating memory of Christ – and perhaps also, by extension, the liberating memory of *Ātman* – require continual, deliberate and self-conscious practices of "remembrancing" modeled on and intimately connected with the liturgical *anamnesis* in the Eucharist.[71] Indeed, among post-Vatican II theologians, few have made memory and *anamnesis* as central to their theology as Metz has done. In his major work *Faith in History and Society*, he writes that, "Christian faith can be understood as an attitude according to which man [*sic*] remembers promises that have been made and hopes that are experienced as a result of those promises and commits himself to those memories."[72] Taken only thus far, this compact definition echoes not only Paul's exhortation in 1 Cor 15, but also the picture of *parisaṃkhyāna* we have discerned in our hearing of USG 3, in which seekers self-consciously take on the perspective of the liberated sage, commit themselves to a "continual flow of recollection" of self-knowledge, and thereby cultivate a new *habitus* or pattern of dispositions and perceptions shaped by the very liberation they seek.

Metz goes on, however, more precisely to delimit the kind of memory he intends:

> What is meant here is... not the memory that sees the past in a transfiguring light, nor the memory that sets a seal on the past by being reconciled with all that is dangerous and challenging in that past. It is also not the memory in which past happiness and salvation are applied merely individually. What is meant in this context is that dangerous memory that threatens the present and calls it into question because it remembers a future that is still outstanding.[73]

[70] See especially Johann Baptist METZ, "Anamnestic Reason: A Theologian's Remarks on the Crisis in the *Geisteswissenschaften*," in A. HONNETH, T. MCCARTHY, C. OFFE and A. WELLMER (eds.), *Cultural-Political Interventions in the Unfinished Project of Enlightenment,* B. FULTNER (trans.) (Cambridge and London: MIT Press, 1992), pp. 190-92.

[71] See ibid, p. 190; Johann Baptist METZ, *A Passion for God: The Mystical-Political Dimension of Christianity*, J. ASHLEY (trans.) (New York/Mahwah: Paulist Press, 1998), pp. 130-32; and the further discussion in MORRILL, *Anamnesis as Dangerous Memory*, pp. 69-70; and James Matthew ASHLEY, *Interruptions: Mysticism, Politics, and Theology in the Work of Johann Baptist Metz* (Notre Dame: University of Notre Dame Press, 1998), pp. 116-22, 132-33, 161-62.

[72] Johann Baptist METZ, *Faith in History and Society*, D. SMITH (ed.) (New York: Seabury Press, 1980), p. 200.

[73] Ibid.

Unlike Platonic *anamnesis*, which is "exempt from time and history," this more Hebraic and Biblical notion of *anamnesis* attends carefully to the particulars of history and especially to narratives of suffering and freedom, which establish solidarity with the victims of this history and lay the ground for future hope, as well as for political struggle in the present.[74]

The central narrative of suffering, for Metz and for the Christian tradition more generally, is the *memoria passionis* of the crucified Christ.[75] Metz and those indebted to him develop this insight, moreover, by establishing clear connections between the memory of Christ's suffering and so many others like it throughout history – thereby setting this mystical practice of *anamnesis* dramatically apart from that prescribed by Shankara in the *Upadeśasāhasrī*'s third prose chapter. For Metz himself, the grim memory of Auschwitz is absolutely decisive in this regard.[76] Bruce T. Morrill reaches further afield to narratives of oppression from Latin America, as conveyed in a "text of terror" like the *testimonio* of Rogoberta Menchú, whereas Johann M. Vento calls attention to the similarly brutal history of pornography, rape and violence against women in modern and contemporary North America.[77] M. Shawn Copeland identifies race slavery, the slave trade and the subsequent narrative of institutionalised racism as a primary, and too often forgotten, *memoria passionis* for any theologian living and working in the United States.[78] In each case, the comfortable, conventional assumptions of the present are called into question not by the teaching of a changeless self within

[74] METZ, "Anamnestic Reason," p. 190. See also METZ, *Faith in History and Society*, pp. 186-89; ASHLEY, *Interruptions*, pp. 148-54; and MORRILL, *Anamnesis as Dangerous Memory*, pp. 165-70.

[75] See METZ, *Faith in History and Society*, esp. pp. 109-15; and MORRILL, *Anamnesis as Dangerous Memory*, pp. 30-33.

[76] See METZ, *Passion for God*, pp. 39-42, 121-32; ASHLEY, *Interruptions*, pp. 122-29; and Steven T. OSTOVICH, "Melancholy History," in J. DOWNEY, J. MANEMANN, and S. OSTOVICH (eds.), *Missing God? Cultural Amnesia and Political Theology*, Religion – Geschichte – Gesellschaft Fundamentaltheologische Studien 30 (Berlin: LIT Verlag, 2006), esp. pp. 98-101.

[77] See Bruce T. MORRILL, "Reading Texts of Terror: Mystical Imagination and Political Conviction," in DOWNEY, MANEMANN and OSTOVICH, *Missing God?*, pp. 36-58; and Johann M. Vento, "Not in Vain: Memoria Passionis and Violence against Women," in DOWNEY, MANEMANN and OSTOVICH, *Missing God?*, pp. 79-92.

[78] See M. Shawn COPELAND, "Knowing Christ Crucified: Dark Wisdom from the Slaves," in DOWNEY, MANEMANN and OSTOVICH, *Missing God?*, pp. 59-78; and M. Shawn COPELAND, "Memory, Emancipation, and Hope: Political Theology in the 'Land of the Free,'" *The Santa Clara Lectures* 4.1 (9 November 1997): pp. 1-20.

and beyond all empirical experience, but by the very particular, very empirical narratives of very specific victims of horrendous violence.

To soften this point of contrast between these two traditions, however, we can observe that the sustained remembrancing of suffering, prescribed by Metz and other political theologians, can never be severed from an equally sustained remembrancing of Christ's resurrection and the eschatological future of humankind, so powerfully articulated by Paul in 1 Cor 15. Such "resurrection faith," argues Metz, "acts 'contra-factually' in making us free to bear in mind the sufferings and hopes of the past and the challenge of the dead."[79] And this, in turn, opens new possibilities for dialogue. For the Advaitin disciple's repetitive pronouncements that "I am Seeing" or "I am the same to all beings, the Lord" are nothing if not "contra-factual."

When Shankara prescribes *parisaṃkhyāna* meditation in USG 3, he has the disciple distinguish himself firmly and systematically from any "loss or gain" associated with the objects of sound, sight, touch, taste and smell (USG 3.115). Yet, it is of central importance that such objects are never entirely excluded from view. Quite to the contrary: the disciple deliberately summons very particular sensual experiences to mind and, at one and the same moment of repetition, denies such experiences the final word on his true nature, life and liberation. The mystical practice of repetition thus draws together both the specific, embodied memories of pleasure and pain and the no less specific, scriptural memories that call all such pleasure and pain radically into question – and neither apart from the other. Hence, we can at least imagine that such disciples, who proclaim themselves to be *Brahman*, the highest self, the same in and to all conscious beings throughout history, past and present, dead or alive, might also summon up the dark memories of Auschwitz, of Menchú's *testimonio*, of slavery, of pornography and rape, and of Jesus of Nazareth's brutal execution, while at one and the same moment refusing to give such *memoriae passionis* the final word on selfhood and salvation.[80]

Building on Metz's theology, Shawn Copeland has drawn attention to traditional Spirituals as embodying a similar "dark wisdom" and mystical

[79] METZ, *Faith in History and Society*, p. 113.

[80] The Advaitin theologian RAMBACHAN comes very close to recommending precisely such a practice of self-conscious meditation on the history of suffering in his "Marcus Borg and Advaita Vedanta," esp. pp. 35-36, and *The Advaita Worldview: God, World, Humanity* (Albany: State University of New York Press, 2006), pp. 109-11.

discipline, allowing black slaves both to recognize their intense suffering and to refuse to grant such suffering the final word on their individual or collective lives.[81] Such Spirituals also commend themselves to our attention for reasons of genre; for they, unlike the scholarly treatises of systematicians like Metz or Copeland herself, enact their *anamnesis* of Christ's suffering by means of embodied recollection, repetition and performative practice. It might therefore be fruitful, following the pattern set in previous chapters, to hear such a Spiritual alongside the meditative discipline of USG 3:[82]

... to me, a person of knowledge, nobody is foe, friend or neutral. In this context, if [anybody] through a misconception due to false knowledge, were to wish to connect [me] with [anything], pleasant or unpleasant, which is characteristic of the result of action, he wishes in vain to connect [me] with it, since I am not its object according to the *Smṛti* passage: 'Unmanifest he, unthinkable he...' (USG 3.116).	Dey crucified my Lord/ An' He never said a mumblin' word. Not a word – not a word – not a word. Dey nailed him to a tree... /Dey pierced him in de side. De blood came twinklin' down... /He bowed his head and died. An' He never said a mumblin' word. Not a word – not a word – not a word.

In tone and content, it would seem that these two meditations could not be more different. One offers a series of declarative statements, rooted in the *Bhagavad Gītā*, about the immutability of *Ātman* and, by extension, of the person who knows this *Ātman* to be non-different from himself. The other narrates a step-by-step *memoria passionis* of Christ on the cross, including the nails, the piercing of his side, the flow of blood and the drooping of his head as he breathes his last.

Once juxtaposed, however, the repetitive refrain, "An' he never said a mumblin' word//not a word – not a word – not a word," might be heard to strike a resonate chord with a statement like "no one is foe, friend or neutral." Both could be read in terms of pure passivity or indifference, of course, encouraging those who identify with these words to bear suffering without protest or to withdraw from relations of any kind. But a better interpretation would almost certainly take them as affirmations of the serene transcendence of Christ, and of the divine *Ātman*, not apart from opposition, suffering and the vicissitudes of this life, but in the midst of or even – to borrow an expression used by Swami Paramarthananda to

[81] See COPELAND, "Knowing Christ Crucified," pp. 71-75.
[82] Spiritual quoted in Ibid, p. 74.

describe the liberated self-knower[83] – *in spite of* such travails. Repeating such memories of transcendence in song or in meditation, disciples in both traditions acknowledge their historical, embodied existence while, at one and the same moment, denying its power to define them. The enslaved women and men who sang this Spiritual, Copeland writes, "were sustained by a dark wisdom: the story of Jesus is their story, the suffering of Jesus is their suffering, the vindication of Jesus is their vindication."[84] So also, though in a very different context and for very different reasons, for the disciple who repeatedly enacts and identifies with *Ātman* through *parisaṃkhyāna* meditation.

This comparison raises at least one further question, particularly in light of Metz and the political theology project: that is, do such mystical and meditative practices conduce to the more practical – but no less mystical – praxis of solidarity and struggle for those who are oppressed? Do they empower disciples to strive for political and social justice, here and now? Copeland certainly argues for just such a connection, drawing in one article upon the writings of Catherine of Siena, further Spirituals and particularly the example of the freed slave Josiah Henson, who, in and out of his meditation on the crucified and resurrected Christ, eventually "confronted a slave-holding society and church with a demand for justice and transformation."[85]

Such a case would be considerably more difficult to make on behalf of Shankara's Advaita. Though there are notable exceptions in the modern and contemporary eras, it can hardly be doubted that the overall influence of this tradition has been to reinforce the status quo, rather than to challenge it.[86] Shankara himself admitted only Brahmins into renunciant life and upheld traditional restrictions of the Vedic teaching to upper caste males, and the institutionalization of his tradition in the Daśanāmī Order and *smārta Śaivism* has served primarily to support

[83] PARAMARTHANANDA, *UPADEŚA SĀHASRĪ*, cassette #10-5.

[84] Ibid, p. 71.

[85] M. Shawn COPELAND, "To Live at the Disposal of the Cross: Mystical-Political Discipleship as Christological Locus," in A. CLIFFORD and A. GODZIEBA (eds.), *Christology: Memory, Inquiry, Practice*, College Theology Society Annual Volume 48 (Maryknoll: Orbis Books, 2003), pp. 188-91, quotation at p. 191.

[86] It should be clearly acknowledged, of course, that such support of the status quo does not differentiate Advaita Vedanta from Christianity, as such. The perpetrators of race slavery were also Christians, who presumably identified strongly with the suffering and resurrection of Christ while also, in the early period of the slave trade, refusing to baptise African slaves on the grounds that they were not recognised as full persons. See the discussion in COPELAND, "Memory, Emancipation and Hope," pp. 8-9; and COPELAND, "Knowing Christ Crucified," pp. 63-64.

patterns of Brahmanical privilege.[87] Perhaps more importantly, Shankara's repeated and uncompromising insistence that the "way of non-action," characteristic of his Advaita teaching, stands inherently opposed to the "way of action" would seem to exclude any form of striving or struggle – political or otherwise – on the path of discipleship.[88]

Among the many possible responses to this objection, two commend themselves for our special attention.[89] First of all, we recall that the scope of "non-action" comprehends not merely the interior renunciation cultivated in such meditative practices as those described in USP 10 and USG 3, but also the more literal and physical renunciation of ritual activity and householder life, which we discussed in chapter two of this commentary. And, as Aloysius Pieris has argued, the voluntary poverty exemplified in such Hindu and Buddhist monastic traditions pose a significant challenge to the status quo and can thereby become a "seed of liberation."[90] Though *saṃnyāsa* was eventually domesticated within the Brahmanical system of castes and stages of life, not least by Shankara himself, it seems to have originated as a radical repudiation of conventional norms.[91] It thus represents a significant resource for articulating

[87] See N. SUBRAHMANIAN, "Śaṅkara and the Vedāntist Movement," in S. SEN (ed.), *Social Contents of Indian Religious Reform Movements* (Calcutta: Institute of Historical Studies, 1978), pp. 30-42; Jacqueline SUTHREN HIRST, "Images of Śaṃkara: Understanding the Other," *International Journal of Hindu Studies* 8 (2004): pp. 168-70; and especially the exchange between George SOARES-PRABHU, Sara GRANT and Swami AMALRAJ in Vandana Mataji (ed.), *Christian Ashrams: A Movement with a Future?* (Delhi: ISPCK, 1993), pp. 153-60.

[88] See especially R.C. PANDEYA, "Jīvan-Mukti and Social Concern," *Indian Philosophical Annual* 2 (1966): pp. 119-24; Karl H. POTTER, "Śaṃkarācārya: The Myth and the Man," *Journal of the American Academy of Religion Thematic Studies* 48/3-4 (1982): pp. 117-23; and the further discussion in Andrew O. FORT, *Jīvanmukti in Transformation: Embodied Liberation in Advaita and Neo-Vedānta* (Albany: State University of New York Press, 1998), pp. 173-78.

[89] See also FORT, *Jīvan-Mukti in Transformation*, pp. 176-84; Wilhelm HALBFASS, *India and Europe: An Essay in Understanding* (Albany: State University of New York Press, 1988), esp. pp. 238-42; and S.L. MALHOTRA, *Social and Political Orientations of Neo-Vedāntism: Study of the Social Philosophy of Vivekananda, Aurobindo, Bipin Chandra Pal, Tagore, Gandhi, Vinoba, and Radhakrishnan* (New Delhi: S. Chand and Company, 1970).

[90] Aloysius PIERIS, S.J., *An Asian Theology of Liberation*, Faith Meets Faith (Maryknoll: Orbis Books, 1988), pp. 15-23, 38-45, quotation on p. 20.

[91] See especially J. Patrick OLIVELLE, "Village vs. Wilderness: Ascetic Ideals and the Hindu World," in A. CREEL and V. NARAYANAN (eds.), *Monastic Life in the Christian and Hindu Traditions: A Comparative Study*, Studies in Comparative Religion, vol. 3 (Lewiston: Edwin Mellen Press, 1990), pp. 125-60, and the fuller historical survey in Patrick OLIVELLE, *The Āśrama System: History and Hermeneutics of a Religious Institution* (New York: Oxford University Press, 1993).

an authentically Advaita vision of social justice and political engagement.[92]

In the context of the present discussion, however, a more valuable insight might emerge from the nature and function of *anamnesis* itself. We have been reminded in USG 3.112 that, for Shankara, "action" invariably implicates the actor in a sense of personal agency and desire for some result. In the *Bhagavad-Gītā*, Lord Krishna recommends action without attachment to the fruits, but Shankara ultimately interprets this injunction less in terms of absolute detachment than in terms of a displacement of desire from the pursuit of temporal pleasures or rewards to a more subtle purification of the mind.[93] Ergo, such detached action too possesses only preliminary, preparatory value. Still, in USG 3.112 Shankara in fact goes on to prescribe a definite form of action precisely for the destruction of *karma* and the achievement of final release: namely, *parisaṃkhyāna* meditation. This empirical activity appears, paradoxically, to effect something only attributable to the transcendent "non-activity" of *Ātman*. Why?

From our hearing of previous scripts of the *Upadeśasāhasrī*, perhaps especially USG 2, we might venture a number of possible responses to this question, each drawing in various ways upon the ultimate non-difference between empirical knowing and the pure knowledge of *Ātman*. From our hearing of USP 10 and USG 3, however, we might venture a slightly different hypothesis: namely, that the practice of *anamnesis* modeled in these texts posits a form of action and intentionality that is, at its furthest extent, beyond the scope of even the most subtle desire.[94] Specifically, these teaching scripts imagine and intend a field of continued activity that flows spontaneously from habituated practice and is

[92] See Reid B. LOCKLIN, "Integral *Saṃnyāsa*? Adi Shankaracharya and Liberation Hermeneutics," *Journal of Hindu-Christian Studies* 20 (2007): pp. 43-51; and especially Kapil N. TIWARI, *Dimensions of Renunciation in Advaita Vedānta* (Delhi: Motilal Banarsidass, 1977).

[93] See BGBh 3.19-20, in A.G. Krishna WARRIER (trans.), *Śrīmad Bhagavad Gītā Bhāṣya of Sri Śaṃkarācārya, with Text in Devanagiri & English Rendering, and Index of First Lines of Verses* (Madras: Sri Ramakrishna Math, 1983), pp. 116-17, and the discussion in Roger MARCAURELLE, *Freedom through Inner Renunciation: Śaṅkara's Philosophy in a New Light* (Albany: State University of New York Press, 2000), pp. 105-30.

[94] For the background of this discussion, albeit with some important differences in emphasis, see Eliot DEUTSCH, *Advaita Vedānta: A Philosophical Reconstruction* (Honolulu: University of Hawaii Press, 1968), pp. 99-102; and especially Karl H. POTTER, "Introduction to the Philosophy of Advaita Vedānta," in K. POTTER (ed.), *Encyclopedia of Indian Philosophies: Advaita Vedānta up to Śaṅkara and His Pupils* (Princeton: Princeton University Press, 1981), pp. 34-38.

motivated entirely by memory, rather than by the pursuit of means and ends. Such activity includes, at the very least, the "continual flow of recollection of self-knowledge" itself. As outlined in BUBh 1.4.7 and in the *Upadeśasāhasrī*'s third prose chapter, to be sure, such meditative disciplines are described in strictly phenomenological and individualistic terms. There would seem to be no logical reason, however, to exclude the possibility that these same mystical practices could be broadened to include the historical memory of suffering, as suggested above, perhaps including especially the suffering of outcaste communities and others oppressed by the structures of Shankara's own Brahmanical Hinduism.[95] If so, then the transformed *habitus* intended, modeled and cultivated by such practice could be re-imagined to include a continual, anamnestic striving on behalf of these and indeed all conscious beings. Though liberative political engagement does not seem to have been a priority for Shankara or for the tradition that followed him, in other words, this need not mean that such engagement is necessarily incompatible with the Advaita teaching.

Be this as it may, it remains true that political struggle, or any kind of worldly action, does not and cannot stand at the center of Shankara's Advaita tradition – as it does not stand at the centre of the resurrection faith of the apostle Paul nor, presumably, at the center of the hope that prompts the Spiritual's refrain, "An' he never said a mumblin' word// not a word – not a word – not a word."[96] What does stand at this center

[95] This process of *anamnesis* with regard to caste is already an important dimension of certain strands of contemporary Advaita, at least on a discursive level. See, for example, the discussions in Sengaku MAYEDA, "Śaṅkara and Nārāyaṇa Guru," in G. LARSON and E. DEUTSCH (eds.), *Interpreting across Boundaries* (Princeton: Princeton University Press, 1988), pp. 184-202; Anantanand RAMBACHAN, "Evangelization and Conversion Reconsidered in Light of the Contemporary Controversy in India – A Hindu Assessment," *Hindu-Christian Studies Bulletin* 15 (2002): esp. pp. 24-25; and Anantanand RAMBACHAN, "Is Caste Intrinsic to Hinduism?" *Tikkun*, January/February 2008, pp. 59-61. It should also be recognized, in this connection, that this proposal, particularly in connection to issues of race and class, should not be considered a Christian norm against which Advaita could be easily measured and found wanting. Though the many calls for a "purification of memory" by Pope John Paul II and his frequent acts of repentance represent a significant step in this direction, contemporary church practices arguably still fall short of the penetrating *anamnesis* commended by Metz and his disciples.

[96] This is also well-recognized in political and liberation theologies, of course. COPELAND, for example, writes that "the reign of God is no utopian project, it is a very different kind of reality. Over time and in time, the disciples (we as well) learn that they (and we) can and must prepare a context for its advent, but it is most fundamentally God's gift" ("To Live at the Disposal of the Cross," p. 187).

is a liberating, dangerous memory beyond the boundaries of 'past' history and 'reasonable' expectation, a memory that calls the entire cycle of worldly oppression, struggle and victory radically into question. The apostle proclaims the defeat of every authority and power, including even death, at the moment of Christ's glorious return. The Advaitin disciple recites, "I am of the nature of Seeing, non-object, unconnected, changeless, motionless, endless, fearless, and absolutely subtle." Liberation, in these quite disparate visions, is not something that can be achieved through any human effort. Through one's manner of living and one's performative practice, however, it can *be remembered*, with consequences no authority and no power – not even, perhaps, Paul or Shankara themselves – might reasonably be able to calculate.

PART III:

THE LITURGY OF LIBERATION

Chapter 9

CONCLUSION: SHANKARA'S *UPADEŚASĀHASRĪ* – ALL THINGS RECONCILED?

I.

"God was pleased to reconcile all things": Christ the Divine *Saṃvāda*

> [Christ] is the image of the invisible God, the firstborn of all creation; for in him all things in heaven and on earth were created, things visible and invisible, whether thrones or dominions or rulers or powers – all things have been created through him and for him. He himself is before all things, and in him all things hold together. He is the head of the body, the church; he is the beginning, the firstborn from the dead, so that he might come to have first place in everything. For in him all the fullness of God was pleased to dwell, and through him God was pleased to reconcile to himself all things, whether on earth or in heaven, by making peace through the blood of his cross. (Colossians 1:15-20)

In chapter one of this study, we explored the notion of *saṃvāda* – dialogue or conversation – as the central practice of the Advaita teaching and as a primary goal of interreligious hearing, interpretation and commentary on the *Upadeśāhasrī*'s sacred scripts. In chapter two, we added to this general notion of *saṃvāda* the mystery of mutual priority and reconciliation that joins the church to historic Israel, as well as, by analogy, Shankara's Uttara Mīmāṃsā to its Pūrva Mīmāṃsā forebear. It is this latter, controverted, textual and social practice of dialogue and reconciliation that has guided the individual experiments in *saṃvāda*, in the intervening chapters of Part II. Now, having attempted these experiments with little concern for their mutual coherence, we can perhaps consider the broader significance of the *Upadeśasāhasrī*, as a cumulative whole, for the Christian hearer who has carefully, patiently allowed herself to become inscribed within the sacred scripts it offers.

We begin this more global and synthetic project of reconciliation not with the *Upadeśasāhasrī*, but with the profound vision of reconciliation and the cosmic Christ offered in the letter to the Colossians. As a first observation, we can note how the particular – and disputed – place of this letter in the Pauline corpus makes it a very suitable starting-place for the task of broader dialogue and synthesis. The apostle Paul's indisputably authentic letters, as we have repeatedly witnessed, are invariably addressed to the particular concerns of particular communities; when the apostle speaks of "church" in these letters, he nearly always intends a specific, local community of faith.[1] Though the letter to the Colossians is certainly addressed to the concerns of a local Christian community in Colossae, it nevertheless adopts a stand at some remove from the local and the particular. The church emerges in this letter as a truly universal body, with Christ at its head, and the intense eschatological expectation so characteristic of Paul's letters seems to have somewhat faded.

In 1 Corinthians 15, as we have just seen in the previous chapter, Paul looks forward to the final victory of Christ, the establishment of God's reign and the glorious resurrection of the dead, "so that God may be all in all" (1 Cor 15:28). In the letter to the Colossians, the author views all things as already reconciled to God through the cross of Christ, here and now, just as all things were created in and for Christ at the dawn of time (Col 1:16, 20). In 1 Corinthians, Jesus returns to destroy the authorities, rulers and powers who oppose him and his followers (1 Cor 15:24); in Colossians, he is depicted as such authorities and powers' transcendent origin and ultimate fulfillment (Col 1:16). The language is still to a very large extent that of Paul, but it has also risen to a higher, more universalizing and more cosmological level.[2]

Whatever the position one takes on the authorship of Colossians – whether one ascribes it to one of Paul's fellow workers or to Paul himself, late in his career – it can hardly be doubted that the hymn of Col 1:15-20 represents one of the most exalted visions of Jesus the Christ in the entire NT. In this hymn, Jesus is unambiguously proclaimed as the "image of the invisible God," the "firstborn of creation," "before all things," and the universal savior of all humankind and, indeed, the entire created order (1:15-16, 20). For this reason, according to some interpreters, it

[1] See Maurya P. HORGAN, "The Letter to the Colossians," in R. BROWN, J. FITZMYER, and R. MURPHY (eds.), *The New Jerome Biblical Commentary* (Englewood Cliffs: Prentice Hall, 1990), p. 877 [54:6].

[2] See the discussion in Andrew T. LINCOLN and A.J.M. WEDDERBURN, *New Testament Theology* (Cambridge: Cambridge University Press, 1993), pp. 58-63; and Andrew T. LINCOLN, "The Letter to the Colossians," in *The New Interpreter's Bible*, vol. 11 (Nashville: Abingdon Press, 2000), pp. 577-83.

both poses great difficulty to ongoing relations between Christianity and other religions and provides important support for those Christians who wish to find value in sacred texts and traditions outside the Christian fold.[3] As Pheme Perkins explains:

> In the early Christian hymnic traditions, one has sought out those symbols and concepts that express God's creative and saving relationship with the world of humanity. From there, the Christian confession takes the further difficult and controversial step of seeing those realities as embodied and personalized in Christ.[4]

According to this vision, the world and its many traditions possess inalienable value; yet, this value stems from an intrinsic orientation toward Christ as their source, end and final perfection.

Obviously, such a conviction would not be controversial if members of other religions consistently judged that their traditions were indeed completed by the Christian proclamation. This is far from self-evident in the history of interreligious relations, of course, or even in the hearing of the *Upadeśāhasrī* that has been attempted in this commentary. Yet, we have still been bold to maintain the possibility and practice of Christian conversation with this Advaita text. How? What have we expected to learn? To discern these issues more fully – after the fact, as it were – we can draw comparisons to two significant precedents.

First of all, we can look to the example of the Jesuit Pierre Johanns' *To Christ through the Vedānta*.[5] Originally published as a series of articles in the periodical *Light of the East* between 1922 and 1934 in Calcutta, this ambitious work attempts to do exactly what its title indicates: namely, to offer a Christian appropriation of the various Vedanta schools, especially the major systems of Shankara, Rāmānuja and Vallabha. Taken as a whole, with each of its major thinkers correcting errors in the others, the Vedanta represents for Johanns an instance of the "perennial philosophy" or natural dispensation that, like Plato and Aristotle, can be synthesised and brought to fulfillment in the Christian

[3] See, for example, the discussions in Jacques DUPUIS, S.J., *Toward a Christian Theology of Religious Pluralism* (Maryknoll: Orbis Books, 1997), pp. 284-92; and Jacques DUPUIS, S.J., *Christianity and the Religions: From Confrontation to Dialogue*, P. BERRYMAN (trans.) (Maryknoll: Orbis Books, 2002), pp. 169-72.

[4] Pheme PERKINS, "Christianity and World Religions," *Interpretation* 40 (1986): p. 377.

[5] Rev. P. JOHANNS, S.J., *To Christ through the Vedānta,* T. DE GREEF (ed.), 2 vols. (Bangalore: The United Theological College, 1996).

philosophy of Neo-Thomism.[6] Hinduism is merely natural, not supernatural, but there is no need for the Christian revelation to abrogate what it finds therein. After his treatment of Vallabha, for example, Johanns writes:

> The Hindus... have not got the real thing. They know nothing of a God becoming a *real* man, who is *really* born, *really* suffers and dies, and the mystery of *transubstantiation* is unknown to them. But the wonder is that they did seek out a substitute, and did so by their reflections on the law of love! *To Christ*, therefore, *through the Vedānta*! Only Catholicism can offer to the Indians the realities of which they possess but the shadow.[7]

At one level, this is straightforward Christian fulfillment theology. What is remarkable is Johanns' impressive attention to the details of the Vedanta systems.[8] If in fact Christianity does complete the Vedanta, as he declares, then this should be demonstrable through painstaking study of these Hindu traditions on their own terms.

Similar in its close attention to the particulars of texts and traditions, but quite different in its theological perspective, Raimon Panikkar's now classic study *The Unknown Christ of Hinduism* offers another important benchmark for evaluating what we have attempted in these pages.[9] Summarizing this text is no easy task, and it is made more difficult by the fact that Panikkar's thought undergoes a significant shift from the book's first edition in 1964 to a revised and enlarged edition some 15 years later.[10]

One consistent thread that does run through *Unknown Christ*, in both editions, is Panikkar's conviction that "Christ is the point of encounter" between Christianity and Hinduism – or, better, that this point of encounter is "in a reality which partakes of both the Divine and the Human, i.e. in what Christians cannot but call Christ."[11] This means that, *contra* the fulfillment theories of such great lights as Johanns, Christ

[6] See Ibid, vol. 1, esp. pp. 2-6, 186-200; as well as the very helpful treatment in Sean DOYLE, *Synthesizing the Vedanta: The Theology of Pierre Johanns, S.J.*, Religions and Discourse 32 (Oxford, Bern, Berlin, Bruxelles, Frankfurt am Main, and Wien: Peter Lang, 2006).

[7] JOHANNS, *To Christ through the Vedānta*, vol. 1, p. 353.

[8] On this point, JOHANNS' fulfillment theology compares favorably to those of Brahmabāndab Upādhyāy and John Nicol Farquhar. See DOYLE, *Synthesizing the Vedanta*, pp. 324-31.

[9] Raimundo PANIKKAR, *The Unknown Christ of Hinduism: Toward an Ecumenical Christophany*, Rev. Ed. (Maryknoll: Orbis Books, 1981).

[10] See DUPUIS, *Toward a Christian Theology*, pp. 149-53.

[11] PANIKKAR, *Unknown Christ*, p. 37.

does not arrive from outside to complete Hinduism. The reality which Christians name as Christ is already operative in the tradition, albeit in a way that can be transformed through contact with Christianity:

> ... there is within Hinduism itself a dynamism that leads it toward that peculiar movement of death and resurrection in which we detect the work of the *antaryāmin*, the inner guide, which Christians call Christ. The individual must die to himself, to his previous limiting beliefs concerning the nature of Man [*sic*], and be 'resurrected' in true knowledge of the cosmotheandric reality.[12]

This inner guide and "unknown" Christ Panikkar identifies in the Advaita commentarial tradition on *Brahma-Sūtra* 1.1.2 and in the figure of Īśvara, the Lord, as a principle of "pure relation" between *Brahman* and the world.[13] The reconciliation thus effected is perhaps better rendered as a discovery or recognition of that one "undivided Mystery" that discloses the true "cosmotheandric," Trinitarian and Advaitic structure of reality and of human experience.[14] In this respect, the name "Christ" and the narrative of his death and resurrection represent distinctively Christian mediations of a more fundamental, existential and transcendental "faith" shared by all humankind and unfolded by Panikkar in broadly mystical terms.[15] Hinduism will not, therefore, be the only one transformed by its encounter with Christianity. Both traditions will be reshaped by their mutual encounter and by the very nature of the Mystery they share.[16]

Both Panikkar and Johanns attempt to bring Vedanta and Christianity into conversation through close attention to key texts, as we have also done in this commentary, and both can claim support for their projects

[12] Ibid, pp. 93-94.

[13] See Ibid, pp. 148-62.

[14] Ibid., pp. 23-30 (from the expanded, 1979 introduction). See also Raimundo Panikkar, "Religious Pluralism: The Metaphysical Challenge," in L. ROUNER (ed.), *Religious Pluralism* (Notre Dame: University of Notre Dame Press, 1984), pp. 97-115; Raimon PANIKKAR, *Christophany: The Fullness of Man,* A. DILASCA (trans.), Faith Meets Faith (Maryknoll: Orbis Books, 2004); and Joseph PRABHU (ed.), *The Intercultural Challenge of Raimon Panikkar,* Faith Meets Faith (Maryknoll: Orbis Books, 1996), especially essays by Gerald T. CARNEY (pp. 131-44) and Daniel P. SHERIDAN (pp. 145-61).

[15] See PANIKKAR, *Unknown Christ,* pp. 22-23, 82-83; Raimon PANIKKAR, *The Intra-Religious Dialogue,* rev. ed. (New York/Mahwah: Paulist Press, 1999), esp. pp. 41-59; Raimon PANIKKAR, *The Experience of God: Icons of the Mystery,* J. CUNNEEN (trans.) (Minneapolis: Fortress Press, 2006); and Raimon PANIKKAR, "The Methodic of Hindu-Christian Studies," *Journal of Hindu-Christian Studies* 20 (2007): pp. 52-54.

[16] On this point, see especially PANIKKAR, *Unknown Christ,* pp. 94-96.

from the vision of cosmic reconciliation in Colossians 1:15-20 – in fact, Panikkar's *Unknown Christ* concludes with a citation from this very hymn (1:17).[17] Both also reveal some affinities with and differences from the *saṃvādas* attempted in previous chapters of this volume. Like Johanns but unlike Panikkar, for example, I have been reluctant to identify the presence of Christ *in* the *Upadeśasāhasrī* scripts, much less in a fundamental mystical experience or orientation anterior to text, teacher or tradition. Following the example of the Pontifical Biblical Commission, among others, I have instead adopted the more tentative language of "prefiguration and dissimilarity," correspondence and analogy. In a way parallel to Johanns' treatment of "the Vedanta" as a single reality constituted by its various discordant voices, moreover, so also on a smaller scale have we treated the *Upadeśasāhasrī* as a collection of self-enclosed and interrelated fragments, each of which reflects the whole teaching in a limited and pedagogically specific way. Ultimately, the coherence of these teaching scripts cannot be discovered in the scripts themselves; their coherence arises only in their mutual relation and in a broader performative reality which lies beyond these verses and sections, but which they themselves presume, prefigure and anticipate.

Unlike Johanns, however, I have again found myself reluctant to identify this broader reality unambiguously with Christ, much less with a particular Christian script – even one as glorious as the Neo-Thomistic synthesis. We have identified lines of correspondence and even of fulfillment from the *Upadeśasāhasrī* to such particular Christian scripts, but these have been deliberately plural in character, drawn synchronically from the letters of Paul and diachronically from subsequent Christian tradition, beginning with Irenaeus of Lyons in the second century and continuing to Johann Baptist Metz and his disciples in the contemporary era. Some of these scripts, such as those of Augustine of Hippo or the Dogmatic Constitution *Lumen Gentium*, come from the solid mainstream of Catholic tradition. Others, such as Mary Ward's spiritual vision or Peter Lombard's controversial teaching on the Holy Spirit, stand nearer to its boundaries. Yet, all witness to the broader reality of the one body of Christ in its intractably diverse realizations, across the local Christian communities of Paul's correspondence and across the long history of the Church. Insofar as possible through a commentary volume that is, at the end of the day, merely another such Christian

[17] Ibid, p. 16.

script, it is this whole reality that has to be brought into relation with the whole reality presumed and anticipated by Shankara's *Upadeśasāsrī*.

In attempting to employ the scripts of the *Upadeśasāhasrī* to relate Advaita and Christianity as living wholes, rather than primarily as systems of thought, the strategy attempted in this volume bears a closer resemblance to Panikkar's *Unknown Christ* than to Johanns' *To Christ through the Vedānta*.[18] In addition, these comparisons and conversations have presumed – perhaps, by this point, even demonstrated – that the *Upadeśasāhasrī*, the letters of Paul and also, by extension, the work of later thinkers and spiritual writers, reveal what Panikkar calls "a *sensus semper plenior*, an ever fuller meaning of sacred texts."[19]

Peter Ochs and David F. Ford, two founders of the contemporary Scriptural Reasoning project, refer to a similar idea under the rubric of the "superabundance of meaning" of the Jewish, Christian and Muslim scriptures. They have also, further, connected this idea to the Rabbinic tradition of *midrash*.[20] As Ochs explains:

> ... individual Hebrew words of Scripture are generative not of single meanings but of broad fields of meaning and... if we want to retrieve a single meaning from out of those fields, we cannot sit idly by the text and wait for disclosure but must bring ourselves openly to the text, declaring who and where we are and then searching actively for the meaning that seeks *us* out in this time and space... we read each word of scripture as generative of broad fields of meaning, from which we are led to encounter certain deeper meanings appropriate to this given day.[21]

As Ochs and Ford describe it, the interreligious dimension of this encounter with the fuller meaning of scripture takes place through a living exchange, in a spirit of warm friendship and by means of sustained, shared reading of one another's sacred texts.[22] On this count, the various attempts at conversation and re-interpretation in this commentary diverge rather profoundly from the ideal. Yet, in our hearing of the *Upadeśasāhasrī*, we have started with the plain sense of each individual

[18] See, for example, the discussion in PANIKKAR, *Unknown Christ*, pp. 100-102; and PANIKKAR, *Intrareligious Dialogue*, pp. 67-70.

[19] PANIKKAR, *Unknown Christ*, p. 163.

[20] See David F. FORD, "An Interfaith Wisdom: Scriptural Reasoning between Jews, Christians and Muslims," *Modern Theology* 22 (2006): esp. pp. 357-59; and Peter OCHS, "Reading Scripture Together in Sight of Our Open Doors," *Princeton Seminary Bulletin* 26 (2005): pp. 36-47.

[21] OCHS, "Reading Scripture Together," p. 43.

[22] Ibid, pp. 40-42; and FORD, "Interfaith Wisdom," pp. 348-51.

script, drawing selectively on traditional sources and historical scholarship to inform our understanding. From this, in a subsequent moment of *midrash* interpretation, we have attempted to specify what this sacred text might mean for Christian hearers, in light of our own primary sacred texts and in the *kairos*, the present moment in time and space.[23] In this work of interpretation, moreover, we have found ourselves discerning fuller meanings not merely for the Hindu text, but also for the Christian inter-texts with which it has been set into provisional, mutually implicating relation.

Here again we can draw strength, in a rather different way, from the example of Colossians 1:15-20. Some scholars hypothesize that this hymn owes its origin neither to Paul nor to the early Jesus movement, but to the syncretic formulae of particular Hellenistic Jewish traditions about the relation of God and God's *logos* to the created world.[24] In the *kairos* of a specific moment in space and time, and in response to the "philosophy" or cosmic speculation that threatens to lead members of the Colossian community astray (Col 2:8), this author offered a kind of Christian *midrash* on these traditions: a fuller, Christological and Pauline re-signification of a borrowed text.[25] In so doing, she or he also uncovered a fuller meaning of Christ himself – freshly disclosed as the firstborn, origin and end of all creation, by whose blood all things have been reconciled to God. In the very act of bringing these formulae into conversation with the teaching of Paul, in other words, the face of the Reconciler himself became more fully manifest.

This is also the hope that has underlain the present commentary project: namely, that the Christ, in whom and by whom God has reconciled all things, can become more fully revealed through our various attempts at personal, social and textual *saṃvāda*, including even those attempts that may ultimately fall short (cf. 2 Cor 5:11 – 6:10). To borrow Shankara's idiom, there is "no distinction in nature" (USG 2.103) between the eternal *saṃvāda*, accomplished once for all in the life, death and resurrection of Christ, and the temporal, assiduous and self-consciously provisional work of bringing a sacred text like the *Upadeśasāhasrī* into critical conversation with the ever fuller meanings of this same Christ in Christian tradition.

[23] On *kairos*, see especially OCHS, "Reading Scripture Together," pp. 42-44.

[24] See LINCOLN and WEDDERBURN, *The Theology of the Later Pauline Letters*, pp. 13-20.

[25] Ibid, pp. 4-13.

Thus far, we have undertaken this work bit by bit, in a fragmentary manner. But if, as maintained throughout the commentary, these teaching scripts do genuinely cohere in the *Upadeśasāhasrī*'s final form, then broader, more synthetic questions should also be amenable to a similarly temporal, assiduous and self-consciously provisional attempt at conversation. This is the specific task of section II of this chapter, wherein we gather the fragments from previous chapters in a freer dialogue with selected verses from Shankara's own synthesis in the text's nineteenth verse chapter (USP 19). Finally, in section III, we will dwell at some leisure upon the salutation which concludes this verse chapter and, at least in some manuscript traditions, the *Upadeśasāhasrī* as a whole.

II.
Therapy of Knowledge, Liturgy of Liberation: USP 19 after Commentary

> Having taken the treatment by the medicines of knowledge and dispassion, which brings about the annihilation of the fever of desires, one does not [again] come to suffer pain from the delirium of that fever of desires and the connection with the series of hundreds of bodies. (USP 19.1)

The first question that a synthesis of the *Upadeśasāhasrī* must face is: how do we *name* the principle of coherence that underlies its teaching scripts? This is an issue that I have already taken up, in a preliminary way, at the outset of this study,[26] but it is worth returning to it here, in and out of our more sustained hearing of the text. At one end of the interpretative spectrum, the obvious choice is simply "teaching" (*upadeśa*), or possibly "knowledge" (*jñāna*), as embodied in these pluriform scripts. Though we have used these terms throughout this commentary, they nevertheless risk reducing the tradition to a determinate content or doctrine. That it *has* such contents and doctrines can hardly be doubted; but the tradition is not, as such, reducible to them. At another, more metaphysical extreme, it is "*Ātman*," the divine self, or "*a-dvaita*," the non-duality of self, world and *Brahman,* that alone suffice to designate the truly ultimate coherence of the tradition. Yet, characterizing Advaita in terms of its transcendent goal also carries a risk: specifically, the risk of obscuring the well-defined social, textual and performative

[26] See above, ch. 1, pp. 31-35.

elements that disclose this divine *Ātman* in actual practice. And so, along the way, we have also encountered phrases that delimit the tradition in more social terms, while also setting it in dynamic relation to its liberating source and end. These include: a "verbal means of knowledge" (*śabda-pramāṇa*), "scripture and the teacher" (*śāstra-ācārya*), a uniquely efficacious "means of liberation" (USG 1.1), the "boat of the knowledge of *Brahman*" (USP 17.53), the ongoing "continuity" or "spreading out of knowledge" from one generation to the next (USG 1.3), the "path of knowledge" tread by authentic seekers (USP 16.68), the "continual flow of recollection" of self-knowledge (BUBh 1.4.7) and, most conspicuously, the "end of the *Vedas*," i.e. "the Vedanta."

In the introductory verse of USP 19, Shankara offers a further, more synthetic characterization of the teaching tradition. This can be discerned most clearly, perhaps, in reference to the chapter's title in three different manuscript traditions.[27] The first of these titles is taken, as per the usual practice, from the first line of the Sanskrit text: "Annihilation of Fever." This title characterizes the chapter, and the Advaita tradition as a whole, in terms of its soteriological objective, as briefly summarized in the verse itself. As we are suffering from a "fever of desires," which keeps us bound in the cycle of birth, death and rebirth, we desire some treatment or therapy for its removal.

The primary ingredient of this therapy is specified in a second traditional title: "Spiritual Medicine."[28] In the verse, Shankara enumerates this medicine – unsurprisingly, by this point – as "knowledge and detachment." Finally, some manuscript traditions adopt a title drawn not from USP 19.1 but from what immediately follows, beginning in verse 2: "A Conversation [*saṃvāda*] between the Self and the Mind."[29] *Saṃvāda* is the integral and invariable means by which the Advaitin "medicine of knowledge and detachment" is, in practice, administered to its patients. If so, then we have arrived at a concise, synthetic definition of Shankara's Advaita Vedanta: it can be described as a distinctive "therapy," aimed toward the annihilation of the "fever of desire" that keeps humankind

[27] See Sengaku MAYEDA (ed.), *Śaṅkara's Upadeśasāhasrī, Critically Edited with Introduction and Indices* (Tokyo: Hokuseido Press, 1973), pp. 189, 261n47.

[28] In Sanskrit: *Bheṣaja-prayoga.* Here I am following the translation in A.J. ALSTON (trans.), *The Thousand Teachings (Upadeśa Sāhasrī) of Śrī Śaṃkarācārya* (London: Shanti Sadan, 1990), p. 382.

[29] In Sanskrit: *Atha-ātma-manas-saṃvāda*, this time following Swāmi JAGADĀNANDA (trans.), *A Thousand Teachings in Two Parts – Prose and Poetry – of Srī Sankarāchārya* (Madras: Sri Ramakrishna Math, [1941]), p. 288.

in bondage, constituted by the ongoing cultivation of knowledge and detachment, and concretely enacted through various forms of conversation or dialogue.[30]

But, the Christian hearer may wish to ask, would it be proper to call it *religion*?

This is a difficult question, not least due to the colonialist freight carried by this term, which has tended to re-fashion other traditions according to a Western Christian mold.[31] Modern Vedantins have frequently refused the label "religion" to describe their tradition. Sometimes, the preferred label is "philosophy." Other times, the denial itself functions as part and parcel of an apologetic strategy to demonstrate the superiority of the Advaita claim – thereby, in the process, ironically replicating many of the features that defined such "religion" in the first place.[32] Sensitive to its historical origins and ideological misuse, some secular scholars have suggested that the category can still function descriptively, in a pluralist and less prescriptive vein, to account for such disparate social realities as Advaita, Buddhism and Islam.[33] Others, within the Christian tradition, re-assert normative definitions in chastened forms, precisely to bring out the theological value of other traditions. So, Nicholas Lash suggests that

> ... we have lost sight of the extent to which the ancient traditions of devotion and reflection, of worship and enquiry, have seen themselves as *schools*. Christianity and Vedantic Hinduism, Jainism and Buddhism and Islam are

[30] The therapeutic language of USP 19.1 is by no means unique to Advaita; it may well represent yet another trope that the tradition inherits from Buddhism. See the helpful discussion in John J. THATAMANIL, *The Immanent Divine: God, Creation, and the Human Predicament* (Minneapolis: Fortress Press, 2006), pp. 16-18.

[31] See, for example, Nicholas LASH, *The Beginning and the End of 'Religion'* (Cambridge: Cambridge University Press, 1996), pp. 10-17, 108-9; Richard KING, *Orientalism and Religion: Postcolonial Theory, India and 'The Mystic East'* (London and New York: Routledge, 1999), esp. pp. 35-52; Tomoko MASUZAWA, *The Invention of World Religions: Or, How European Universalism Was Preserved in the Language of Pluralism* (Chicago and London: University of Chicago Press, 2005); and the summary of recent scholarship on this question in Daniel DUBUISSON, "Exporting the Local: Recent Perspectives on 'Religion' as a Cultural Category," *Religion Compass* 1 (2007): pp. 787-800.

[32] See KING, *Orientalism and Religion*, pp. 135-42; Wilhelm HALBFASS, *Studies in Kumārila and Śaṅkara* (Reinbek: Verlag für Orientalistische Fachpublikationen, 1983), pp. 85-88; and Wilhem HALBFASS, *India and Europe: An Essay in Understanding* (Albany: State University of New York Press, 1988), esp. pp. 408-9.

[33] E.g. KING, *Orientalism and Religion*, pp. 53-61; and Jonathan Z. SMITH, "Religion, Religions, Religious," in M. TAYLOR (ed.), *Critical Terms for Religious Studies* (Chicago and London: University of Chicago Press, 1998), pp. 269-84.

> schools… whose pedagogy has the twofold purpose – however differently conceived and executed in the different traditions – of weaning us from our idolatry and purifying our desire.[34]

Or, again, further along in the same argument: "… the great religions can be seen as contexts in which human beings may learn, however slowly, partially, imperfectly, some freedom from the destructive bondage which the worship of the creature brings."[35]

At one level, Lash's definition of religion as a school or context for weaning human beings from idolatry fits quite comfortably with the portrait of Advaita we have discerned in USP 19's opening verse. "Therapy" itself, left relatively uninterpreted, might also function reasonably well to describe Advaita and also to create room for further comparison and conversation.[36] Throughout this commentary, however, we have preferred yet another category, which is both more self-consciously Christian and, at least arguably, more authentically descriptive of the *Upadeśasāhasrī*'s sacred scripts: namely, the category of liturgy and ritual performance. That is, from the point of view of the Christian hearer, the therapy of knowledge modeled in the *Upadeśasāhasrī* is best characterised as a liturgy of liberation, a coordinated cluster of performative practices with carefully scripted parts and players, reflective of a transformed vision of the world and of humankind, and oriented toward final release.

Of course, labelling the Advaitin therapy as "liturgy" does not do one thing that Lash's definition of "religion" is specifically designed to do: it does not offer the Christian hearer a straightforward rubric for positive valuation and critical evaluation of the tradition. What it does provide is a more general re-attunement, shifting our attention from the content of the scripts, *per se*, to the specific ways this content is scripted to disclose and to shape patterns of intention, disposition and social life. If we discern a fuller meaning of Christ by attempting to bring Christian texts and traditions into critical conversation with the *Upadeśasāhasrī*, as I have attempted to do in previous chapters and discussed more fully above, we have done so by engaging directly with the performative practices themselves.

[34] LASH, *Beginning and End,* p. 21.

[35] Ibid, pp. 21-22.

[36] See, for example, GREGORY OF NYSSA, *An Address on Religious Instruction* Introduction, #8, and #15, in E. Hardy (ed.), *Christology of the Later Fathers*, ed. (Philadelphia: Westminster Press, 1954), pp. 268-69, 284-85, 292-93, and AUGUSTINE OF HIPPO, *Instructing Beginners in the Faith* 4.8, in R. CANNING (trans.), B. RAMSEY (ed.), The Augustine Series 5 (Hyde Park: New City Press, 2006), pp. 71-72.

In the context of USP 19, this means that the Christian hearer must now do more than merely hear the text. She must be drawn into yet another, engaged conversation.

Striving against Striving: The Means of Grace (USP 19.2-3)

> You [O My Mind] seek to obtain valueless things, such as the notions of 'I'- and 'my'-notions. Other people realize that your effort is for the sake of one other than yourself.[37] You indeed have no knowledge of the objects, and I [who have it] have no desire to possess them. Therefore, it is proper for you to be calm, O Mind! (19.2)
> As I am none other than the supreme and eternal One I am always satisfied [and] I have no desire. And being always released, I do not wish [My] welfare. O Mind, make more efforts for your tranquilization! (19.3)

We have already observed on a number of occasions that the Advaita teaching scripts, understood in broadly liturgical terms, reveal a complex dialectic between scripted performance and the broader "liturgy of life" such performances may be understood to imply. More fundamentally, this therapy also entails a similarly complex, paradoxical dialectic between human and divine initiative in the work of liberative performance itself. As the divine *Ātman* insists in USP 19.2-3, above, there is no effort to be made, no objects to pursue and in fact no liberation to achieve: the self, the supreme one, is eternally released[38] and therefore free from any desire for its own welfare (v. 3). The embodied mind of the disciple seeks to acquire liberation as though it were yet another object, to say "I" am liberated or it is "mine" (v. 2), but such liberation is absolutely beyond the sphere of human achievement. Given this fact, it may seem strange that the divine self addresses the situation by commanding still further effort, enjoining the mind to become "quiet" (v. 2) and to "make further efforts for your tranquilization" (v. 3). We are called to strive mightily precisely to renounce any and all such striving, to trust that what we seek has already been achieved, apart from our efforts, and thereby to be consoled, even in the midst of our profound limitations.

In practice, as we have seen throughout the commentary, this striving to renounce striving takes place in a variety of different ways, specific to each

[37] The commentators infer that the discussion of existence "for the sake of another" (*para-artha*) in this verse implies a further refutation of Sāṃkhya. See V. NARASIMHAN, *Upadeśa Sāhasrī: A Thousand Teachings of Adi Śaṅkara* (Bombay: Bharatiya Vidya Bhavan, 1996), p. 264, and the discussion above, ch. 6, pp. 189-92.

[38] An alternative manuscript tradition reads "eternally content" (*sadā tṛpta*) rather than "eternally released" (*sadā mukta*). See MAYEDA, *Śaṅkara's Upadeśasāhasrī*, p. 259n2.

teaching script. Nevertheless, we could quite easily adopt it as a controlling theme of the whole *Upadeśasāhasrī*, allowing us to line up our previous commentary chapters in terms of what has been, step by step, given up:

- Vedic rituals and their accessories (ch. 2);
- Everything about which one can say, *idam-ātman*, "this self" (ch. 3);
- Identification with body, caste or purifying ceremonies (ch. 4);
- The apparent difference between *tat* and *tvam*, *Brahman* and the innermost self (ch. 5);
- False superimpositions on this self (ch. 6);
- The erroneous texts and traditions of Buddhists, Sāṃkhyas and other rivals (ch. 7);
- The objects of hearing, seeing, touch, taste and smell (ch. 8).

Since *Ātman* is ever-released, the unknown Knower and unseen Seer at the base of all possible experience, the *Upadeśasāhasrī*'s cumulative script can be heard to consist entirely in setting aside one's own efforts, assumptions and attachments to let the light of this *Ātman* shine through.

On the other hand, we can also, just as easily, organise these same chapters by the various social, institutional and empirical means Shankara prescribes to Advaitin disciples for achieving identification with that very *Ātman*:

- The institution of formal renunciation (ch. 2);
- Application of such Upanishadic sentences as "Not thus! Not so!" (ch. 3);
- The progressive accommodation of the *Veda*s, the teacher and the created order (ch. 4);
- The method of "agreement and difference" (ch. 5);
- The authorized teacher and practice of shared discernment (ch. 6);
- Firm adherence to the social, scriptural and interpretative tradition of Vedanta (ch. 7);
- *Nididhyāsana* and *parisaṃkhyāna* meditation (ch. 8).

Liturgy implies performance, and performances we have seen aplenty in the *Upadeśasāhasrī*'s scripts. To exert the proper effort on this path of non-action, to achieve what is beyond all human achievement – for this, Shankara has offered both specific rubrics and well-choreographed models for emulation.

How do we hold these two aspects together? How can one negate striving with one hand and re-institute it with the other? One strategy, following Thomas Forsthoefel, might involve differentiating "internalist" from "externalist" epistemologies, and the pure interior experience that is *Brahman* from the exterior "culture of liberation" prescribed to foster this experience and bring it to light.[39] Another strategy might, drawing a spatial metaphor from Bernard Lonergan, speak instead of development "from below upwards," by which one gains wisdom and sheds false notions through one's own maturation, and also of the handing on of development "from above downwards," whereby the insights of a previous generation are transmitted, assumed and become one's own.[40] According to either schema, we are encouraged to see liberation primarily in terms of personal experience or progressive illumination, which may be helped or even shaped by these exterior structures but must nevertheless be clearly distinguished from them.

Elsewhere, however, Lonergan himself strikes a rather different chord with regard to the development that reaches to human beings from above:

> ... there also is development from above downwards. There is the transformation of falling in love; the domestic love of the family; the human love of one's tribe, one's city, one's country, mankind [*sic*]; the divine love that orientates man in his cosmos and expresses itself in his worship... [this] love breaks the bond of psychological and social determinisms with the conviction of faith and the power of hope.[41]

The language of this passage echoes what Lonergan describes, in a number of his later writings, as "religious conversion," that is, "being-in-love" in an unrestricted manner,[42] and we will indeed take up the question of love, below. For the moment, I simply wish to observe that this particular exposition of development "from above" clearly views it, at least in part, as something that follows from God's initiative. It is a power of divine healing, which breaks psychological and social bonds and empowers new

[39] Thomas A. FORSTHOEFEL, *Knowing Beyond Knowledge: Epistemologies of Religious Experience in Classical and Modern Advaita*, Ashgate World Philosophies (Hants and Burlington: Ashgate Publishing, 2002).

[40] See Bernard J.F. LONERGAN, S.J., "Natural Right and Historical Mindedness," in F. CROWE (ed.), *A Third Collection: Papers by Bernard J.F. Lonergan* (New York/Mahwah: Paulist Press; London: Geoffrey Chapman, 1985), pp. 180-81. I am grateful to Joseph Ogbonnaya for drawing my attention to this discussion.

[41] Bernard J.F. LONERGAN, S.J., "Healing and Creating in History," in CROWE, *Third Collection*, p. 106.

[42] See, for example, Bernard J.F. LONERGAN, S.J., "Religious Experience," in CROWE, *Third Collection*, pp. 115-28; and Bernard J.F. LONERGAN, S.J., *Method in Theology* (Toronto: University of Toronto Press, 1971, 1996 [reprint]), pp. 104-109, 242-44, 267-69.

forms of commitment, all the while working through ordinary institutions of family, tribe, city, country and worship. Reading this account of development "from above downwards" in parallel with the previous one, moreover, we might infer that one encounters God's initiative precisely in and through the transmission and reception of such traditional structures as family, culture and especially worship.[43]

So too for the *Upadeśasāhasrī*'s sacred scripts. From one point of view, there is nothing but *Ātman*, ever liberated and self-evident, which becomes manifest by its own nature. From another, there is nothing but the repeated, performative practice of these scripts, along with the various structures and institutions they model and prescribe. Reading *these* two statements in parallel, then, these practices, structures and institutions become seamlessly identified with the liberating self-revelation of *Ātman* the divine self. They disclose this self and thereby adduce an eternal "result" that reaches to the hearer from outside the closed, relentless cycle of cause and effect. Thus Shankara describes them, in this secondary and paradoxical sense, as means of liberation (USG 1.1).

Working from a slightly variant manuscript tradition, Swāmi Jagadānanda offers a translation of USP 19.3 with a nuance rather different from that of Mayeda, above:

> As I am none other than the Supreme Eternal One, I am always contented and have no desires. Always contented, I do not desire my own welfare, but I desire your welfare. Try to make yourself quiet.[44]

Interpreting this verse as a statement about the entire *Upadeśasāhasrī*, the Christian hearer discovers a distinctive idiom of grace, and of the means of grace, embodied therein.[45] Liberation is not achieved through any human effort, but *given*, in the most profound sense one can imagine. Yet, this givenness – this grace – is something that is realized only through a discipline of continual, carefully scripted performance. And this suggests, in turn, that the scripts themselves are also a gift of grace. They are offered by the self who desires nothing at all… or who, at least

43 For a development of the social and historical dimensions of LONERGAN's theology, see especially Joseph A. KOMONCHAK, *Foundations in Ecclesiology*, Supplementary Issue of the *Lonergan Workshop* Journal 11 (Chestnut Hill, MA: Boston College, 1995).

44 JAGADĀNANDA, *A Thousand Teachings*, p. 289 (modified).

45 Cf. LASH, *Beginning and End*, pp. 32-33; Bradley J. MALKOVSKY, *The Role of Divine Grace in the Soteriology of Śaṃkarācārya*, Numen Studies in the History of Religions 91 (Leiden: Brill, 2001); and Bradley J. MALKOVSKY, "Śaṃkara on Divine Grace," in B. MALKOVSKY (ed.), *New Perspectives on Advaita Vedānta: Essays in Commemoration of Professor Richard De Smet, S.J.* (Leiden, Boston and Köln: Brill, 2000), pp. 70-83.

in some manuscript traditions of the nineteenth verse chapter, desires nothing save the good of the hearer with whom this same self has initiated a sacred conversation.

How is the Christian hearer to respond to this offer? This is not, of course, determined by the scripts. But the offer has been made, and, insofar as one accepts it, entering into this sacred conversation by means of these scripts, one cannot exclude the risk that they may come to be regarded as genuine means of grace and divine quietude – if not, perhaps, strictly means of liberation – even for that Christian hearer.

Telling the Truth: The Difficulty of Difference (USP 19.4-5)

> According to the *Śruti* it is the *Ātman* of both the world and us that transcends a series of the six waves of existence; it is also known by Me from the [other] means of knowledge as well. Therefore, O Mind, you make useless efforts. (19.4)
> When you have been calmed there is indeed no notion of difference, on account of which people fall into delusion through illusion, since the perception [of difference] is the cause of the rise of illusion; at the time of release from the perception [of difference], nobody has any illusion at all. (19.5)

One of the major themes of this commentary has been the interplay between embodied experience and the Vedic scriptures as the privileged, verbal means of knowledge (*śabda-pramāṇa*) for knowing *Ātman*. We first encountered the notion of "pure experience" (*anubhava*) in chapter 3, where it served to conclude the process of scriptural negation enacted across the verses of USP 2-5. Then, in chapters 4 and 5, we encountered two different defenses of the *śabda-pramāṇa* as the sole, sufficient and efficacious means of liberating self-knowledge: first, the theory of accommodation offered by the teacher of USG 1, according to which the apparent contradictions of *Śruti* are ascribed to different stages of its recipients' understanding; and, second, Shankara's refutation of the *Prasaṃkhyāna-vāda* by recourse to the theory of *ābhāsa* – the reflection of the eternal *Ātman* in the limited, embodied mind – in USP 18. Finally, in chapter 8, I directly addressed some modern accounts, Hindu and Christian, which place special emphasis upon the practice of Yogic meditation and the pure contemplative experience of *nirvikalpa samādhi*. At each point, the interpretation has weighed against framing these teaching scripts in terms of elevated spiritual experience; in chapter 8, in particular, I recommended the idea of mystical *practice* as an alternative to mystical *experience* in order to account for the transformative effect of the teaching scripts and of their self-conscious, continual recollection.

The present verses raise several of these issues again, albeit on a more cosmic and explicitly communal level than we have witnessed thus far in our hearing of the *Upadeśasāhasrī*. The common thread between the two verses is not, in this case, the embodied individual but *jagat*, the universe, translated above as "the world" in verse 4 and all "people" in verse 5. On the one hand, *Ātman* is described as the eternal self of this world and, therefore, of "us [all]" (v. 4), beyond the "six waves" of hunger, thirst, pain, delusion, old age and death.[46] On the other, the perception or apprehension of difference binds this universal body in the chains of illusion (v. 5). Liberating knowledge proceeds from the *Śruti,* as well as other unspecified "means of knowledge."[47] The idiom, whether of bondage or liberation, is here transposed from the individual to the universal level. Intriguingly, the final portion of verse 5 hints at a moment of release when anyone, or perhaps everyone, ceases to perceive difference at all.

The key difficulty, for this Advaita script and for its Christian hearer, is precisely this negation of difference: difference between self and God, difference across the states of waking, dreaming and deep sleep, difference among various traditions and teaching scripts. Part of the attraction of appealing to a distinctive *advaitic* or non-dual mystical experience to understand the tradition stems from this very difficulty; for, if the differences between these scripts and those of Christian tradition can be ascribed to different formulations of a common experience, or even to different kinds of experience, then it becomes possible to relativize and to reconcile the conflicting claims of their respective scripts more easily.[48]

If, on the other hand, one maintains that experience is primarily shaped by mystical practice and scripted performance rather than the

[46] See ALSTON, *The Thousand Teachings,* p. 393n1.

[47] RĀMATĪRTHA glosses this alternative means of knowledge as the experience or vision of the liberated sage (*vidvat-anubhava*); it might also refer to the *Gītā* or another textual authority, or to perception, inference and other standard *pramāṇas.* See ibid, pp. 393-94n2, and the full comment in D. GOKHALE (ed.), *Shri Shankarāchārya's Upadeśasāhasrī with the Gloss Padayôjanīkā by Shrī Rāmatīrtha* (Bombay: Gujurati Printing Press, 1917), p. 422.

[48] See, for example, DUPUIS, *Toward a Christian Theology*, pp. 268-78; Michael F. STOEBER, *Theo-Monistic Mysticism: A Hindu-Christian Comparison* (New York: St. Martin's Press, 1994); and Vernon GREGSON, *Lonergan, Spirituality, and the Meeting of Religions*, College Theology Society Studies in Religion 2 (Lanham and London: University Press of America, 1985).

other way around, as I have tried to suggest at several points in this commentary, this would seem actually to intensify the difficulty. As Francis X. Clooney has argued in reference to the *Brahma-Sūtra* commentary, the truth of the Advaita tradition, while firmly maintained *as true*, arises only in and out of the *Upanishads* and the commentarial tradition, and it is not easily assessed apart from thorough immersion in those texts and exegetical practices.[49] Terrence Tilley has made a similar claim with regard to Christian practices as a whole, advancing a "consequential realist" approach to religious truth. The truths of Christian faith, while again maintained *as true*, depend for their recognition upon appraisal by reliable and skilful practitioners in the tradition.[50] In this situation, it becomes very difficult to tell the truth, or to tell *what* is true, across the boundaries of performative practice.[51]

In this task of telling the truth, however, such a practice-oriented approach offers an oblique way out of the dilemma. For, though one may not be able to adduce any universal criterion of truth independent of the *Śruti*, the Bible and the implicated practices of both traditions, these practices can nevertheless become mutually implicating through the further practice of comparative inquiry.[52] For example, in chapter four I introduced Augustine of Hippo's *Teaching Christianity* to draw a parallel from the pedagogical cosmology and "continuity of knowledge"

[49] See Francis X. CLOONEY, S.J., *Theology after Vedānta: An Experiment in Comparative Theology* (Albany: State University of New York Press, 1993), pp. 77-118.

[50] Terrence TILLEY, *Inventing Catholic Tradition* (Maryknoll: Orbis Books, 2000), esp. pp. 156-70, and Terrence W. TILLEY, *History, Theology and Faith: Dissolving the Modern Problematic* (Maryknoll: Orbis Books, 2004), pp. 67-85. In the background of both CLOONEY and TILLEY's proposals is the cultural-linguistic model advanced by George LINDBECK in *The Nature of Doctrine* (Philadelphia: Westminster Press, 1984).

[51] See especially TILLEY, *History, Theology and Faith*, pp. 81-82. It is worth noting that, unlike some proponents of a cultural-linguistic model, TILLEY does not abdicate the task of adjudicating different religious claims. In *Inventing Tradition* (pp. 164-67), he offers five rules for judging the truth of such claims, namely: 1. the claim must represent "the world in which we live, or a part of it, in a revealing way"; 2. it must fit "with other facts we recognize can be appraised as true"; 3. it must enable "communities or individuals to be 'true to themselves'"; 4. it must enable its adherents "to 'be true to' others and to the tradition carried on in practice"; and 5. it must enable its participants "to live in ways that propel them to develop revelatory insight."

[52] See especially Francis X. CLOONEY, S.J., "Reading the World in Christ: From Comparison to Inclusivism," in G. D'COSTA (ed.), *Christian Uniqueness Reconsidered: The Myth of a Pluralistic Theology of Religions* (Maryknoll: Orbis Books, 1990), pp. 63-80; James L. FREDERICKS, *Faith among Faiths: Christian Theology and Non-Christian Religions* (Mahwah, NJ: Paulist Press, 1999); and Hugh NICHOLSON, "A Correlational Model of Comparative Theology," *The Journal of Religion* 85 (2005): pp. 191-213.

in USG 1 to Augustine's own account of "Christ the Way" (*Christus via*), including his body, the church of Christ. Then, in chapter 7, beginning with the apostle Paul's eschatological vision of groaning creation and the final revealing of the children of God, I placed the Vatican II teaching on the church as a pilgrim people into conversation with the vision of community, boundary definition and the path of knowledge in USP 16. In neither case could we say that the visions of community in the two scripts are the same, much less that they refer to the same realities or core experience. But, for some hearers at least, the *Upadeśasāhasrī* scripts may now possess permanent *resonance* with the various scripts by which Christians talk about the church. The difference between the Advaita and Christian scripts are neither overcome nor denied in these cases; instead, these specific differences become internal to the Christian tradition, and to the various ways in which its practitioners strive to tell the truth in our contemporary, pluralistic environment.

Questions remain. Above all, what of the *jagat*, the universe, the liberation of all people and the end of all difference, as hinted at in USP 19.5? On the Advaita side of this question, such differences retain their force only from the empirical point of view, not from the highest vision of the *Śruti*, of the enlightened sage, and ultimately of *Ātman* the divine self. For their part, Christian hearers can recall the eschatological *mysterion* of Romans 11:25, with which we began our *saṃvāda* in chapter 2 of this commentary. As Jacques Dupuis has written:

> The tension between the "already" and the "not yet" is reflected in the Church's evangelizing mission and, markedly so, in the relationship within it between interreligious dialogue and proclamation: insofar as the Church remains on her pilgrimage, together with "others," towards the fullness of the Kingdom, she engages with them in dialogue, insofar as she is the sacrament of the reality of the Kingdom already present and operative in history, she proclaims to them Jesus Christ in whom the Kingdom of God has been established by God.[53]

The church proclaims an ultimate, universal vision of present and future redemption, no less than Shankara upholds an ultimate, universal vision of the eternal self in all beings and indeed throughout the cosmos. Both are

[53] Jacques DUPUIS, "A Theological Commentary: Dialogue and Proclamation," in W. Burrows (ed.), *Redemption and Dialogue* (Maryknoll: Orbis Books, 1993), p. 155, cited in DUPUIS, *Christianity and the Religions*, pp. 225-26. See also the helpful discussion of different kinds of appeals to mystery in interreligious dialogue, in Edward T. Ulrich, "Religious Pluralism and Catholic Theology in the Greco-Roman World and India Today," *Studies in Interreligious Dialogue* 18 (2008): 1-10.

bound to tell the truth, as it has been disclosed to them. Short of the *eschaton* or the *pāramārthika* vision of non-dual truth, however, both traditions may also find themselves obliged to seek what sociologist Nira Yuval-Davis has called penultimate "transversal" values, worked out through shared conversation and articulated in terms specific to each tradition.[54] And this, like the pursuit of liberation itself, requires continued practice.

Interrupting the Intellect: A More and Other God (USP 19.6)

> I am not deluded by your activity since I am by true nature enlightened, unfettered, and changeless. There is indeed no difference in our nature at an earlier and later time. Therefore, O Mind, your effort is useless. (19.6)

One of the most difficult points of difference between Christianity and Advaita strikes at the heart of both traditions: their fundamental conceptions of God and of the created world's relation to this God. Our hearing of the *Upadeśasāhasrī* commenced with Shankara's salutation to *Ātman* in USP 1.1, in chapter two, and the two subsequent commentary chapters explored in some detail the identification of this *Ātman*, the Lord, with the innermost self of the hearer, as well as *Ātman*'s sharp dissociation from phenomenal experience and from the progressive manifestation of name and form. Though I have not hesitated to call this *Ātman* "God," and even to build tentative associations with Irenaeus of Lyons' Christology, Peter Lombard's theology of the Holy Spirit and Mary Ward's vision of "Verity," it remains apparent that this conception of God diverges radically from common Christian belief. As stated in the present verse, God the divine self is possessed of absolute knowledge, free from bondage, changeless, and non-different in nature from the hearer's innermost self. This is not a God who enters into human life and history in order to transform it. This is a God who is ultimately indifferent to the workings and the petitions of the embodied hearer, a God who remains serenely unaffected, even before or after the rise of liberating knowledge. How can such contradictory notions be reconciled?

[54] See Nira YUVAL-DAVIS, "Women, Ethnicity and Empowerment," in A. OAKLEY and J. MITCHELL, *Who's Afraid of Feminism? Seeing through the Backlash* (London: Hamish Hamilton, 1997), pp. 77-98. This ideal of "transversalism," rather than universalism, emerged from the efforts of feminist activists to collaborate across boundaries of religious, ethnic and other forms of difference without abstracting a single, monolithic "community." I am conscious of introducing some distortion into the concept by using it to characterise the dialogue between "Hinduism" and "Christianity," understood here in perhaps too monolithic terms.

This is not a new question, either in the encounter between Christianity and Advaita or in the broader intellectual history of Christianity itself. Not infrequently, theologians have distinguished between at least two fundamental conceptions of the divine, under several different typologies: impersonal or personal, mystical or monotheistic, monist or theist.[55] Though the Advaita tradition certainly retains personalist conceptions of *Brahman* – *Brahman* "with qualities" – for the purposes of meditation and worship, these have usually been assigned to lower levels of understanding. It is *Brahman* "without qualities" that represents the fullest expression of divinity.[56] Christian theologians have tended to respond in kind, recognizing a provisional validity in such impersonal notions and connecting them to apophatic traditions of Christian mysticism, while also privileging traditional Jewish, Christian and Muslim monotheism, either as a point of contrast,[57] or as Advaita's complementary term of convergence,[58] or in a higher "theo-monistic" synthesis.[59] On both sides of this conversation, there is a sense of broadly inclusivistic accommodation, in which each recognizes value in the other by assigning it to a lower level in the interpretive hierarchy.[60]

[55] E.g., DUPUIS, *Christianity and the Religions,* pp. 117-29; STOEBER, *Theo-Monistic Mysticism,* esp. pp. 23-31; Joseph Cardinal RATZINGER, *Many Religions, One Covenant: Israel, the Church and the World,* G. HARRISON (trans.) (San Francisco: Ignatius Press, 1998), pp. 96-102; Joseph Cardinal RATZINGER, *Truth and Tolerance: Christian Belief and World Religions,* H. TAYLOR (trans.) (San Francisco: Ignatius Press, 2003), pp. 15-42.

[56] See CLOONEY, *Theology after Vedānta,* pp. 81-85; STOEBER, *Theo-Monistic Mysticism,* pp. 41-49; Anantanand RAMBACHAN, "Hierarchies in the Nature of God? Questioning the *Saguna-Nirguna Brahman* Distinction in Advaita Vedanta," *Hindu-Christian Studies Bulletin* 14 (2001): pp. 13-14; and especially the treatment in A.G. Krishna WARRIER, *God in Advaita* (Simla: Indian Institute of Advanced Study, 1977).

[57] E.g. RATZINGER, *Many Religions,* pp. 96-109; and RATZINGER, *Truth and Tolerance,* pp. 32-44.

[58] DUPUIS, *Toward a Christian Theology,* pp. 278-79. DUPUIS develops his position in explicit conversation with the Benedictine inculturationists Bede Griffiths and Swami Abhishiktananda; though he cites the latter's earlier work in support of his position, his own views actually seem closer to that of Griffiths. See Judson TRAPNELL, "Two Models of Dialogue with Hinduism: Bede Griffiths and Abhishiktananda," *Vidyajyoti* 60 (1996): esp. pp. 101-10; and Judson TRAPNELL, *Bede Griffiths: A Life in Dialogue* (Albany: State University of New York Press, 2001).

[59] STOEBER, *Theo-Monistic Mysticism,* esp. pp. 50-60. STOEBER also invokes Abhishiktananda in support of his argument, again drawing on the latter's earlier synthesis. See the further discussion in TRAPNELL, "Two Models of Dialogue," pp. 183-91, 243-54.

[60] On this point, see especially Bradley MALKOVSKY, "Swami Vivekananda and Bede Griffiths on Religious Pluralism: Hindu and Christian Approaches to Truth," *Horizons* 25 (1998): pp. 217-37.

Another line of interpretation presses beyond this comfortable stalemate, querying whether it is really proper to view the Advaita conception of God as "impersonal" in the first place. Thus, drawing on the historical scholarship of Paul Hacker and Richard DeSmet, among others, Bradley Malkovsky distinguishes Shankara from his later interpreters with regard to the great teacher's realist ontology and his "transpersonal," rather than impersonal, teaching on *Brahman*.[61] In a more self-consciously constructive vein, the contemporary Advaitin Anantanand Rambachan has questioned the traditional hierarchy between *sa-guṇa* and *nir-guṇa Brahman* on the grounds of *advaita* itself, arguing that a truly non-dualist reading of the *Upanishads* necessarily includes both impersonal and personal understandings of God in dynamic relation with one another and with the created world.[62] Finally, John J. Thatamanil has challenged both Shankara's Advaita and the Christian theology of Paul Tillich on a still deeper level: their "substantialist conceptions" of the divine, which invariably implicate each tradition, for different reasons, in new forms of dualism.[63] "The solution," he writes, "is to repudiate the notion that Brahman is an unchanging substance and embrace the alternative notion that Brahman is infinite, ontological creativity apart from which nothing would be."[64] The problem, on this reading, does not arise from what differentiates Advaitin and Christian understandings of God. The true difficulty arises from what *unites* them: a fundamental misconception about divinity itself, prior to any considerations of personhood, mysticism or creation.

Malkovsky, Rambachan and Thatamanil's proposals are cogent and persuasive, and all three have significantly shaped the exposition in previous chapters of this commentary. Nevertheless, from the perspective of the scripted performances of the *Upadeśasāhasrī*, such systematic resolutions risk softening and domesticating the radicality of these scripts. In the present verse of USP 19, for example, the divine *Ātman* scolds the embodied mind quite roundly, refusing to be deluded by its activity and

[61] Bradley MALKOVSKY, "The Personhood of Śaṃkara's *Para Brahman*," *Journal of Religion* 77 (1997): pp. 541-62. This argument has been sharply critiqued on historical and philological grounds by T.S. RUKMANI in her article, "Dr. Richard De Smet and Sankara's Advaita Vedanta," *Hindu-Christian Studies Bulletin* 16 (2003): pp. 12-21.

[62] RAMBACHAN, "Hierarchies in the Nature of God?" pp. 14-18; and Anantanand RAMBACHAN, *The Advaita Worldview: God, World, Humanity* (Albany: State University of New York Press, 2006), pp. 67-97.

[63] THATAMANIL, *Immanent Divine*, pp. 184-201.

[64] Ibid, p. 195.

insisting that it exerts itself in vain. In some respects, this rebuke strongly echoes the model teacher's injunction in USG 2.65, *mā kārṣīs-tarhi*, "Do not do it! Do not make false superimpositions on the self." In the commentary on that passage, we noted that, according to Thatamanil, Shankara refuses either to dismiss the reality of ignorance and suffering or to give a rational account for them. This conclusion would seem to apply even more strongly to the precise ontological status of *Ātman,* and indeed to liberation itself. Over and over again, the *Upadeśasāhasrī*'s teaching scripts deny the ability of the embodied intellect to make *Ātman* its object or to resolve a question like, "Whose is *avidyā*?" We can also recall, from chapter 3, the deeply paradoxical character of *jīvan-mukti*, "liberation-in life." Neither the embodied intellect nor the innermost *Ātman* ever become liberated, properly speaking. The individual body, mind and personality of the hearer can never shake their limitations, and *Ātman* can never be touched or constrained by them. For this reason, at least in part, Shankara compares the Advaita teaching with urine, from which any conventionally reasonable person would certainly recoil (USP 5.1).

Is this a form of apophaticism? Surely, if viewed primarily as a doctrine or theory about how to name – or not to name – God.[65] When viewed through the lens of liturgy, of performative practice, however, it may more closely resemble what Johann Baptist Metz refers to as an "interruption." When discussing the power of suffering to unsettle any comfortable, systematic understanding of God, for example, Metz writes of Jesus that

> … His cry from the cross is the cry of one forsaken by God, who for his part had never forsaken God. It is this that points inexorably into Jesus' God-mysticism: he holds firmly to the Godhead. In the God-forsakenness of the cross, he affirms a God who is still other and different from the echo of our wishes, however ardent; who is ever more and other than the answer to our questions, even the strongest and most fervent – as with Job, and finally with Jesus himself.[66]

As discussed in the previous chapter, many themes of Metz's political theology are missing in Advaita, and it seems unlikely that he would see in the serene, unaffected *Ātman* of USP 19.6 anything but an echo of

[65] See the discussion in THATAMANIL, *Immanent Divine*, pp. 90-94; and Madeleine BIARDEAU, "Quelques Réflections sur L'Apophatisme de Śaṅkara," *Indo-Iranian Journal* 3 (1959): pp. 81-101.

[66] Johann Baptist METZ, *A Passion for God: The Mystical-Political Dimension of Christianity*, J. ASHLEY (trans.) (New York/Mahwah: Paulist Press, 1998), p. 67.

Plato's a-historical Ideal.[67] We can nevertheless remember that the most pressing of the student's questions to the teacher across the scripts of the *Upadeśasāhasrī* are precisely questions of pain and suffering, which neither Shankara nor the *Ātman* of USP 19 permit to be systematically resolved. The God disclosed in these scripts is "more and other" than its disciples' most ardent desires, "more and other" than their most fervent questions, "more and other" than even the finest rational system would allow.

So these scripts take an entirely different approach. They interrupt our desires, interrupt our questioning, interrupt our conceptions of God, and interrupt any systematic resolution that might domesticate or contain the teaching's disruptive power. The *jīvan-mukta*, then, need not and perhaps should not be interpreted in terms of the divine perfection of human consciousness. Instead, she represents a different kind of ideal altogether: the ideal of the person who has, through assiduous practice, allowed herself to be continually and irrevocably interrupted.

Right Relations (USP 19.12)

> Nobody belongs to me and I do not belong to anybody, for I am non-dual and nothing that is falsely constructed exists. And I am not that which is falsely constructed but am established before the false construction. It is only duality that is falsely constructed. (19.12)

In an important 1985 article, Peggy Starkey asked the question, "What constitutes truth in a religion?"[68] After a review of the New Testament evidence, particularly the gospels and the Johannine correspondence, she finds her answer in *agape*, the self-giving love modeled in Christ:

> *Agape*... is a valid criterion by which, from a Christian perspective, the scriptures and traditions of other religions can be examined to see whether or not they contain revelation that requires the practice of love toward other human beings. Christians, therefore, can affirm that wherever the

[67] On this point, however, METZ actually stands closer to classical Christian tradition, and thus to Shankara, than do some of his contemporaries. In distinction from Jürgen Moltmann or Hans Urs von Balthasar, for example, METZ believes that it only exacerbates the problem to implicate God directly in suffering. He writes (*Passion for God*, pp. 69-70): "What I see in these worthy attempts is *too much* of a response, soothing the eschatological questioning of God. Is there not in them still too much of a speculative, almost gnostic reconciliation with God behind the back of the human history of suffering? And do not these ways of responding underestimate the negative memory of humans suffering that will not allow itself to be harmonized under any other name?"

[68] Peggy STARKEY, "Agape: A Christian Criterion for Truth in the Other World Religions," *International Review of Mission* 74 (1985): pp. 425-63, quotation on p. 426.

> scriptures and traditions of other religions call for a response of *agape* toward other people, there religion that contains truth is found.[69]

Some 15 years later, in his magisterial – and controversial – works *Toward a Christian Theology of Religious Pluralism* and *Christianity and the Religions*, Jacques Dupuis adopted the main conclusions of Starkey's argument, together with recent papal teachings on the possibility of "participated mediations" of Christ and the universal gift of the Holy Spirit. How can Christians discern the hidden work of Christ and the Spirit in other traditions? Through the careful discernment of "saving values," Dupuis argues, and, above all, the central value of agapic love.[70]

But this, of course, begs the further question: how does one discern the presence or absence of *agape* in another tradition? While conceding the limitations of such an approach, Starkey attempts to discern the leading ideals of each tradition as revealed in its sacred texts and major modern exponents. In the case of Hinduism, she finds traces of *agape* in the ideal of perfect *dharma* in the great epics, as well as in Krishna's teaching in the *Gītā* that "one's own self or soul is identical to the self or soul of all other creatures."[71] This so-called "*Tat-tvam-asi* ethic" represents a standard feature of much modern Advaita moral theology, and it is, along with a few other key ideas – notably, the nature of *Ātman* as self-diffusive bliss (*ānanda*) – often correlated with Christian teachings on love.[72]

The *Tat-tvam-asi* ethic has also, however, come under serious criticism as a suitable foundation for any moral action, much less as a motive for agapic love.[73] The fundamental basis of such a critique can be readily inferred from USP 19.12, above. For this verse denies relationship of any kind in the divine *Ātman*. Since any difference represents a "false construction" or mere superimposition on this self, there is no authentic recognition of other persons in their distinctiveness, much less of

[69] Ibid, p. 434.

[70] DUPUIS, *Toward a Christian Theology*, pp. 316-29; and DUPUIS, *Christianity and the Religions*, pp. 185-94.

[71] STARKEY, "Agape," pp. 446-51, quotation on p. 450.

[72] For the former, see the discussion in Paul HACKER, "Schopenhauer and Hindu Ethics," in W. HALBFASS (ed.), *Philology and Confrontation: Paul Hacker on Traditional and Modern Vedānta* (Albany: State University of New York Press, 1995), pp. 273-318; for an indirect example of the latter, derived from the Trinitarian Advaita of Upadhyāy, see LASH, *Beginning and End*, pp. 68-69.

[73] See especially HACKER, "Schopenhauer and Hindu Ethics," esp. pp. 275-79, 305-6, and Karl H. POTTER, "Introduction to the Philosophy of Advaita Vedānta," in K. POTTER (ed.), *Encyclopedia of Indian Philosophies: Advaita Vedānta up to Śaṃkara and His Pupils* (Princeton: Princeton University Press, 1981), pp. 36-38.

non-conscious elements of the natural world. Hearing this verse, we may be excused if we discern what very much appears to be an ethic of complete withdrawal, the sublation of all desires and disdain for corporeality – what Lance Nelson refers to as "the dualism of non-dualism."[74] There can be no true love and care for others, in other words, where there are no true others to love.

Some of these concerns have already occupied us in previous chapters of this commentary. In the context of the present discussion, we can first observe that comparable criticisms have been raised against some Christian understandings of *agape* itself. In particular, such understandings have sometimes been characterized by critics as too "otherwordly" and, particularly through the tradition's radical universalism and its tendency to deny any and all preference in love, prone to become "strangely inattentive to concrete human needs."[75] *Agape*, no less than Advaita, is not without a degree of ambiguity, and the ambiguity becomes more profound if one looks at the actual practices of Christians throughout the tradition's long history.

On the Advaita side of the conversation, we can also ask whether relationality, as such, can really be dismissed as an integral aspect of the teaching. In his study of the the Daśanāmī monastic federation, for example, Matthew Clark has highlighted a somewhat paradoxical combination of individualist, asocial ideals and highly complex communal practices in this and other traditions of Indian renunciant life.[76] "Whether as a [married, semi-secularised] *gosain* or as a celibate *saṃnyāsī*," he writes, "the initiate is a member of a community which has complex relations with the rest of society, which in many respects defy the archetype of the 'lone' *saṃnyāsī* that is presented in ancient Brahmanical texts."[77] One searches in vain for references to the Daśanāmī Order in the *Upadeśasāhasrī* scripts, but we have certainly encountered relationships

[74] Lance E. NELSON, "The Dualism of Nondualism: Advaita Vedānta and the Irrelevance of Nature," in L. NELSON (ed.), *Purifying the Earthly Body of God: Religion and Ecology in Hindu India*, SUNY Studies in Religious Studies (Albany: State University of New York Press, 1998), pp. 61-88.

[75] William SCHWEIKER, "Distinctive Love: Gratitude for Life and Theological Humanism," in W. SCHWEIKER, M. JOHNSON and K. JUNG (eds.), *Humanity before God: Contemporary Faces of Jewish, Christian, and Islamic Ethics* (Minneapolis: Fortress Press, 2006), pp. 99-100, 106-7, quotation on p. 106. SCHWEIKER is referring here primarily to the criticisms of Martha Nussbaum and Tzvetan Todorov, though he also cites the "similar worries" of Iris Murdoch, Raimond Gaita, Irving Singer and Darlene Weaver.

[76] See Matthew CLARK, *The Daśanāmī-Saṃnyāsīs: The Integration of Ascetic Lineages into an Order*. Brill's Indological Library 25 (Leiden and Boston: Brill, 2006), pp. 3-22.

[77] Ibid, p. 22.

aplenty. These include relationships between teacher and student throughout the first two prose chapters; between Vedantins and Pūrva Mīmāṃsākas in USP 1; between the *Veda* and its variously qualified hearers in USG 1; between and among seekers on the path of knowledge, as well as their primary rivals, in USP 16; between master and servant in USG 2.72-74; between the recollecting disciple and the various objects of sense in USG 3; between Shankara and the rival Advaitins of the *samuccaya-vāda* and *prasaṃkhyāna-vāda* in USP 1 and 18, respectively; between Shankara, his teacher and the "teacher of his teacher" in the salutation of USP 18.2 and others like it; between Shankara and the implied hearers of all these scripts; and even – particularly in the present verse chapter – between the divine *Ātman* and the embodied mind. As we have recently heard, *Ātman* will go so far as to speak of a fundamental nature shared by "us" (USP 19.6), that is, both by *Ātman* and the one whom this *Ātman* addresses as "thou." In theory, and from the highest point of view, Shankara's Advaita radically negates the value of all relationships; in *practice*, it no less radically affirms them.

Now, valorizing certain highly scripted, privileged relationships in one's rhetorical and performative practice is not quite the same thing as embodying the "saving value" of agapic love. But, I contend, it offers a far more secure point of departure than the simple assertion of *tat-tvam-asi*, the same self in all living beings, as a theoretical basis for moral action. In particular, this highly relational orientation provides the necessary framework for revealing the various ways that *tat-tvam-asi* or any great saying actually functions to shape distinctive patterns of life and behavior. The question of a reshaped intention and intentionality has already recurred at several points, and it represents a significant sub-theme of the commentary. The line of inquiry began, in chapter 4, with very ordinary virtues like personal purity, mental acumen and compassion, which defined teacher and student alike in the scripted dialogue of USG 1. In the fifth and sixth chapters, we then explored the innate reflection of *Ātman* in the human consciousness, as well as its power, once disclosed, radically to relativize the structures and power relationships that define ordinary life. Finally, in chapter 8, I tried to adduce a connection from such transformations on the level of intention and conviction to the broader *habitus* of the enlightened sage. Along the way, of course, we also established parallels with comparable Christian scripts, beginning with the model of righteous living offered by Paul and his fellow workers, continuing through the transforming social visions of Mary Ward, Johann Baptist Metz and the Spirituals of African slaves, and punctuated in chapter 5 by Peter Lombard's beautiful, contested meditation on divine *caritas* or agapic love as the personal presence of the Holy Spirit in the embodied existence of the Christian disciple.

On both sides of this conversation, the fundamental values of *agape* or *advaita* acquire their actual significance in the life and mind of the disciple only dialectically, through a complex interplay between the content of the teachings themselves and a universe of relationships – intra- and intersubjective, human and divine – posited by these same teachings. It is therefore important to articulate these fundamental values in a way that remains attentive to this complex dynamic. This is, for example, exactly what we find in the work of the Christian ethicist William Schweiker, who has attempted to understand *agape* not as an isolated ideal, but against a rich interpretive context of "ancient humanisms," the Sermon on the Mount and the various different kinds of love commands offered therein.[78] From this more contextual reading he concludes that

> The love commands are a prism through which a vision of life must be factored if any love is to attain fullness. The command of love locates human life within a space defined by God's action to respect and enhance creation in the face of threats to life... Christian love thereby lends its voice to reclaiming 'ancient humanism' about how to treat others by grounding that command not in aspirations to virtue or the demands of justice but gratitude for creation.[79]

In associating *agape* less with a distinctive kind of love than with a distinctive "prism" or "vision" of gratitude that reorients all other loves, Schweiker echoes major elements of our treatment of the Advaita scripts in this commentary. In place of gratitude, we might perhaps identify "fearlessness" (*abhayatva*; see USG 2.110; 3.115) as the relevant, distinctively Advaita prism. Through this prism, as well as through all of the manifold values and relationships that lead the disciple to it, the whole of life emerges in sharper, transformed relief.

Can we then conclude, with Starkey and Dupuis, that "the Hindu scriptures meet the criterion of *agape*"?[80] Such a conclusion overreaches the evidence. It may, in any case, be quite beside the point to search for this Christian teaching in these Advaita scripts. To paraphrase USP 19.12,

[78] See SCHWEIKER, "Distinctive Love," pp. 107-17, as well as William SCHWEIKER, *Theological Ethics and Global Dynamics: In the Time of Many Worlds* (Malden, Oxford and Victoria: Blackwell Publishing, 2004).

[79] SCHWEIKER, "Distinctive Love," pp. 113-14.

[80] STARKEY, "Agape," p. 351.

above, the final truth of these scripts does not belong to the Christian interpreter, nor do the comparable Christian scripts belong to Advaita. By identifying points of resonance around the notion of *agape,* we are attempting something more modest: namely, to assist in the ongoing articulation of merely one of many bases for ongoing conversations about human rights, social justice and one's fundamental moral disposition in the world – albeit a basis that has come to claim special importance in contemporary conversations.[81] *Agape* may not represent a common ground, in other words, but the ground it does provide can and has become *shared ground.* On the basis of such shared ground, it becomes possible to offer "friendly amendments" and loving correction, as attempted especially in the previous chapter of this commentary. It also becomes possible, perhaps more importantly, to receive such corrections in kind.

Through such relationships of mutual correction, moreover, we may find that we have stumbled once again across what Panikkar describes as the "ever greater meaning" (*sensus semper plenior*) of the Christian scriptures and indeed of God's love in Christ. More than this, we will have discovered a fuller meaning this same Christ himself, if not precisely in the scripted performances of the *Upadeśasāhasrī,* then in the continuing work of transformation and reconciliation these scripts can nevertheless be heard to empower.

III.

Namaḥ: The *Upadeśasāhasrī* and the Possibility of a Christian Salutation

> Salutation to the teachers who churned out from the ocean of the *Veda* what they held to be supreme, this knowledge, as the gods, the great souls, [churned] out from the great ocean the elixir of immortality. (19.28)

This chapter set out to gather the fragments of the previous chapters into a cohesive whole, and to facilitate a more direct encounter between

[81] E.g., SCHWEIKER, *Theological Ethics,* pp. 153-71; Arvind SHARMA, *Religious Studies and Comparative Methodology: The Case for Reciprocal Illumination* (Albany: State University of New York Press, 2005), pp. 161-79; Arvind SHARMA, *Hinduism and Human Rights* (New Delhi: Oxford University Press, 2003); and particularly the recent public letter from 138 scholars to the Vatican initiating Muslim-Christian dialogue around the topic of love of God and love of neighbour: "A Common Word between Us (Summary and Abridgement," 13 October 2007, *A Common Word,* < http://www.acommonword.com/index.php?lang=en&page=option1>, accessed 25 June 2008.

Christianity and Advaita. These realities are complex, of course, so the actual results remain modest. Instead of a grand synthesis, we have identified four or possibly five further, more comprehensive fragments, each of which draws together significant elements of previous discussions while also raising questions for still deeper conversation.

Given the tentative and still fragmentary character of our synthetic efforts, it is particularly suitable that Shankara concludes the *Upadeśasāhasrī*'s nineteenth verse chapter – and, with it, the verse portion as a whole – by directing our attention to a quite different vision of profound synthesis, of the "churning" of a great ocean to extract its essence, at the very source of the teaching tradition. "Supreme knowledge," like the legendary elixir of immortality, comes to the hearer only because it has been previously churned out of the revealed *Śruti* and handed on by eminent teachers. So eminent are these teachers, in fact, that they compare favorably with divine beings. For this reason, as well as to signal the end of the present verse chapter, Shankara offers reverent salutations.

We thus conclude this commentary project with a question about such reverence: that is, what about the Christian hearer of the *Upadeśasāhasrī*? Is it possible for such a hearer to join Shankara in these salutations?

Shankara has not made this judgment easy for us. Were he to reverence an individual teacher, as he does in USP 18.2, many Christian hearers might have no particular difficulty following suit. Regardless of tradition or beliefs, such a teacher would still be a full human being, a bearer of God's image, an object of God's reconciling love and therefore worthy of great reverence. Similarly, had Shankara offered salutations to *Ātman* the divine self, as in USP 1.1, with which we began this commentary, a perhaps smaller but not insignificant number of Christians might judge that, notwithstanding major differences, this *Ātman* is nevertheless recognizable as a legitimate, if limited expression of God the divine self and therefore a suitable object of devotion. But in this verse Shankara reserves his reverent salutations for the ancient teachers as a group[82] and, through them, for the sacred teaching tradition.

This poses far greater difficulties for the Christian hearer, and rightly so – for it asks us to make a performative judgment about the sacredness

[82] It is possible that Shankara has adopted the plural form of *guru* to express his honor for an outstanding individual teacher such as his predecessor Gauḍapāda. Given the parallel he draws to the gods, however, retaining the plural form in translation seems preferable. This judgment is also supported by the commentators. See the discussion in NARASIMHAN, *Upadeśa Sāhasrī*, pp. 278-79, and ALSTON, *The Thousand Teachings*, p. 406n1.

of the tradition, in light of God's revelation in Christ. One can certainly imagine many such hearers who would simply decline the offer, thanking Shankara and the tradition for the enlightening dialogue, but reluctant to stand, to place their palms together and to make reverent submission. Others might, however, find themselves more inclined to accept the offer, to join Shankara in his reverence for the tradition. Though the motives for such a decision would surely vary quite widely, person to person, three possibilities commend themselves for our special attention.

Following a recent proposal by Jeannine Hill Fletcher, we can first imagine a hearer who offers salutations out of pure astonishment and wonder at this strange, unfamiliar and perhaps even offensive teaching.[83] Relating a story of her sister's startled, "I don't get it," when confronted with an image of the god Krishna, Hill Fletcher suggests that such moments of disorientation can be highly fruitful, reminding us of the true difference of the other and the ultimate incomprehensibility of God. "The experience of unknowing," she writes, "in the encounter with otherness offers an immediate theological wellspring because, prior to the endeavor to learn from other faiths, there can be a moment of profound wonder, a moment that comes *before* understanding."[84] So we might imagine a highly disoriented hearer of the *Upadeśasāhasrī*, to whom these teaching scripts appear to contradict all that is good and familiar from previous experience and religious upbringing, who searches in vain for an appropriate, measured response. Finding none, this Christian hearer pleadingly places her palms together and lowers her head in exhaustion, in frustration and, just possibly, also in reverent wonder.

One can also imagine a different situation, however, where the move to reverence is more self-conscious and deliberate. For example, in his commentary on the three sacred Mantras of the Śrīvaiṣṇava tradition, Francis Clooney concludes with the question, "Can we pray simply with the Mantras?"[85] He answers with a carefully nuanced affirmative:

> ... we pray as Christians who pray with a widened understanding and possibly with hearts moving in two directions at once. With our deepened and enhanced dispositions, we can certainly utter the Mantras with a certain reverence and understanding, even if incompletely and with reservations...

[83] Jeannine HILL FLETCHER, "As Long as We Wonder: Possibilities in the Impossibility of Interreligious Dialogue," *Theological Studies* 68 (2007): pp. 531-54.

[84] Ibid, p. 549.

[85] Francis X. CLOONEY, S.J., *The Truth, the Way, the Life: Christian Commentary on the Three Holy Mantras of the Śrīvaiṣṇavas,* Christian Commentaries on Non-Christian Sacred Texts (Leuven, Paris, and Dudley, MA: Peeters and W.B. Eerdmans, 2008), p. 191.

> Our repetition of the Mantras may then be something more than reading, even if not fully prayer in a fully Christian sense – our limit resting not on the Mantras, but rather on the truth of who we ourselves are and what we can do. In this new situation, we read and repeat the Mantras as if our own prayers, the meaning of this practice neither more nor less than appears appropriate to us.[86]

What Clooney describes in this passage somewhat resembles Catholic and Eastern Orthodox distinctions between *latria*, the adoration that belongs to God alone, and *dulia*, the service or reverence that is appropriately directed toward icons, saints and other created realities in reference to God.[87] So, again, we can imagine a different kind of Christian hearer of the *Upadeśasāhasrī*, one who has understood its teaching scripts, has found them insightful and perhaps has even recognized in them a means of God's grace, as discussed above. So she bows. Unlike our first hearer, she does this in a way that is highly self-aware, specific about the limitations of such a gesture and serious about the importance of maintaining continual, conscious reference to Christ and to the Trinity, who alone are worthy of full, true adoration.

Finally, somewhere between these two positions – and perhaps many others that have escaped my attention – we can imagine a third hearer: the one who has become personally implicated in the *Upadeśasāhasrī*'s sacred scripts, who has become something like a true hearer, as these scripts themselves intend. She may find the teaching extraordinarily difficult and even offensive, like our first example, or she may find it insightful, like our second example, or possibly both at the same time. Less important than her judgment *on* the tradition, in this case, is her implication *in* it, her willingness to become vulnerable on the model of Christ and to allow herself to be interrupted by what these scripts have to say about God, about liberation and about many other issues of central human concern. Here again there are sharp limits upon what the Christian hearer can be willing to affirm and to do, but this hearer per-

86 Ibid., pp. 191-92.

87 See, for example, JOHN OF DAMASCUS, *On the Divine Images: Three Apologies Against Those Who Attack the Divine Images*, D. ANDERSON (trans.) (Crestwood: St. Vladimir's Seminary Press, 1980); and the Definition on Sacred Images of the Second Council of Nicaea (787 CE), in Norman P. TANNER, S.J. (ed.), *Decrees of the Ecumenical Councils, Volume One: Nicaea I to Lateran V* (London: Sheed and Ward, and Washington, DC: Georgetown University Press, 1990), pp. 133-37. Cf. Daniel P. SHERIDAN, *Loving God: Kṛṣṇa and Christ: A Christian Commentary on the* Nārada Sūtras, Christian Commentaries on Non-Christian Sacred Texts (Leuven, Paris and Dudley, MA: Peeters and W.B. Eerdmans, 2007), pp. 54-56.

ceives such limits as an expression of weakness, rather than as a privileged position from which she can pass judgment.

So this hearer also bows. She is not, perhaps, possessed of a sure conviction in the truth of the tradition. She may have serious reservations about *jīvan-mukti* and other controversial points of these sacred scripts. She will certainly insist upon combining her reception of the teaching with worship in one or another Christian setting, thus flirting with the *samuccaya-vāda* that Shankara so roundly rejects. But she may nevertheless find herself persuaded that, through her willingness to offer reverent salutations, through continued hearing, and perhaps also through devoted service to these teachers and the liturgy of liberation they have churned, she may yet come ever more clearly to reflect and to know the perfect love of Christ.

Namaḥ.

INDEX OF SCRIPTURAL CITATIONS

Bṛhadāraṇyaka Upanishad
1.4.7 261
1.4.10 86, 132, 163n
2.3.6 47, 60, 86
2.4.5 165
2.4.12 124
2.4.14 132, 132n
2.5.19 124, 134, 143
2.6 24n
3.4.1 124
3.7.23 124, 130
3.8.8 90
3.9.26 60n
4.1.1-2 261
4.2.4 60n
4.3.7 94
4.3.31 132
4.4.22 60n, 62, 271
4.4.23 271
4.4.19 132
4.5.13 132, 134, 143
4.5.15 60n, 61-62
4.6 24n
6.5 24n

Chāndogya Upanishad
6.1.4 87n, 132, 153
6.2.1 124, 132, 153n, 158n
6.8-16 153
6.8.7ff 145, 163
6.12 153n
6.13.3 148
6.14.1-2 89
6.14.2 20
6.16.3 153
7.24.1 132

Iśa Upanishad
7 132, 132n

Kaṭha Upanishad
3.10-12 268n
3.15 267, 268, 268n
5.11 271

Mahā Nārāyaṇa Upanishad
505-17 63, 63n, 230

Muṇḍaka Upanishad
1.2.12-13 117
1.2.12 117, 121
2.1.2 91, 132, 134, 143, 271
2.2.11 256-57, 256n

Mahābhārata Aswamedha Parvan
92

Bhagavad-Gītā
2.24 271
2.25 271
4.34 20
13 257
13.8-11 117n
13.31-32 257n
15 257-258
15.16-18 258n

Code of Manu
11.44 55

Yoga-Sūtras
2.30 119n
2.32 119n
2.35-39 119n

Genesis
15:6 137

Wisdom of Solomon
1:7 108

Gospel of Matthew
23 227

Gospel of Mark
16:15 246

Gospel of Luke
10:27 176
24:44 76
24:45 75
24:27 76

Gospel of John
1:10 108
1:11 108
1:14 108
14:6 143

Letter of Paul to the Romans
3-8 239, 243
5 169
8:15 239
8:15-17 237
8:18-25 243
8:19-21 237
8:19-22 243
8:21 245
8:22-23 238
9-11 69, 71, 75, 103, 237
9:3 71
9:6–10:21 69
11:1 69
11:1-36 69
11:25 308
11:25-32 67-68
11:25-26 69
11:28 69
12:3-8 203
12:3 110

First Letter of Paul to the Corinthians
1:18 107
1:18-25 103-104, 274
10:11 243
10:16-17 203
11:17-18 202
11:17-34 202
11:21 203
11:23-26 202
11:26 275
11:27-32 202
15 169, 273, 275, 277, 279, 290
15:1-5 273
15:2 275
15:3b-5 275
15:6-10 275
15:21-26 273
15:24 290
15:28 290
15:35-58 274

Second Letter of Paul to the Corinthians
5:11–6:10 296
11:21–12:10 105

Letter of Paul to the Philippians
1:27–2:18 168
2 170, 172, 275
2:5-13 167
2:6-11 168, 170
3:9 72

Letter of Paul to the Colossians
1:15-20 289, 294, 296
1:16 290
1:17 294
1:20 290
2:8 296
3:4 245

First Letter of Paul to the Thessalonians
1:5 136
1:6-10 137
2:13 168
2:14-16 137
2:9-13 135

Second Letter of Peter
3:13 243

INDEX OF NAMES

Peter Abelard, 172
Abhināvagupta, 35
Swami Abhishiktananda (Henri Le Saux), 253, 310n
Adam, 108, 273, 275
Ānandagiri, 3, 8, 28, 30, 116n, 147n, 220n
Akhaṇḍadhāman, 28
Alston, A.J., 87n, 147n, 162, 164, 191n, 231n
Anderson, E.B., 32
Antarkar, W.D., 7n
Thomas Aquinas, 172, 175, 176n
Uddālaka Āruṇi, 87n, 89, 153, 155, 156
Asad, T., 33-34, 269, 270n
Augustine of Hippo, 139-144, 172, 181, 217, 294, 307-308

Bader, J., 7, 7n, 17n, 250n
Venerable Bede, 142
Bell, C., 58n
Bhāskara, 35, 35n, 93, 106, 110, 242
Biardeau, M., 10
Bodhanidhi, 28
Bonaventure, 172
Bourdieu, P., 269, 270n
Bradshaw, P.F., 203
Brahmadatta, 54
Brereton, J., 153n
von Brück, M., 253
Burley, M., 224n
Byrne, B., 168n

Calvin, J., 4
Swami Chinmayananda, XIII, XVII, 28
Clark, M., 315
Clooney, F.X., 12n, 32, 38-40, 41-42, 227n, 307, 320-321
Colish, M., 172n, 175
Comans, M., 12n, 163, 164
Congar, Y., 244n
Congregation for the Doctrine of the Faith, 78n, 247
Copeland, S.M., 278, 279-281, 284n
Cornille, C., 37-38, 78

Swami Dayananda, 121n
De Smet, R., 9, 176n, 311
Deussen, P., 9
Deutsch, E., 9, 133
Dunn, J.D.G., 43, 71, 136, 169, 170, 204n, 239, 239n
Dupuis, J., 308, 310n, 314, 317

Farquhar, J.N., 292n
Flood, G., 123n
Ford, D.F., 295
Forsthoefel, T., 96, 252, 303
Fort, A.O., 254n

Gauḍapāda, 8, 24, 27, 93, 101n, 146n, 199n, 319
Govinda, 8, 24, 146n
Griffiths, B., 310n
Griffiths, P., 22
Grimes, J., 255n

Hacker, P., 10, 21, 88, 101, 118n, 182n, 189, 270n, 311
Hagner, D., 71n
Halbfass, W., 11, 154, 182-183
Henry VIII, 206n
Hill Fletcher, J., 320
Hooker, M.D., 168n, 169, 275n
Hugh of St. Victor, 172

Ignatius of Loyola, 206, 207

Indra, 93, 145, 145n, 146n, 217n, 236
Ingalls, D.H.H., XVIII, 35n, 93, 189
Irenaeus of Lyons, 42, 107-112, 175, 181, 294, 309

Swami Jagadānanda, 87n, 147n, 162, 191n, 264, 304
Jaimini, 51
Jesus of Nazareth, Jesus the Christ, 44, 70-73, 75-79 86, 103-112, 121, 136-137, 143-144, 147, 152, 167-172, 181, 202-205, 237, 240, 241, 245, 247, 268, 273-276, 277, 285, 289-292-296, 300, 308, 313-314, 318, 320-322
Johanns, J.P., 291-295
Pope John XXIII, 244n
Pope John Paul II, 247, 284n

Kaṇāda, 215, 231, 231n, 246
King, R., 15n, 220n
Krishna, 37, 111, 257-258, 283, 314, 320
Kumārila Bhaṭṭa, 8, 51

Larraona, A., 244n
Larson, G., 223-224
Lash, N., 299-300
Lee, R., 206
Lipner, J., 153n, 156n
Peter Lombard, 171-178, 181, 294, 309, 317
Lonergan, B., 303
Lorenzen, D., 8

Mādhava, 7, 7n, 235
Mahadevan, T.M.P., 27n
Mahmood, S., 269, 270n
Maitreyī, 165
Malkovsky, B., 6, 12n, 311
Maṇḍana Miśra, 8, 54, 148, 151, 218
Marcaurelle, R., 12n
Marcion of Pontus, 64
Mauss, M., 269
Mayeda, S., XVII, 12n, 21, 23n, 28, 30n, 31, 61n, 87n, 94n, 101n, 127n, 147, 147n, 154, 162, 164, 180n, 191n, 194, 221, 260n, 263n, 270n, 304
Metz, J.B., 276-281, 284n, 294, 312, 313n, 316
Moltmann, J., 313n
Morill, B.T., 278

Nakamura, H., 6n
Narasimhan, V., 28n, 87n, 264
Nelson, L., 84, 111, 160, 315
Nicholson, H., 241n

Ochs, P., 295
Olivelle, P., 50, 59n, 66n, 132n
O'Neil, L.T., 138

Padmapāda, 8, 94n
Panikkar, R., 38, 292-295, 318
Pāṇini, 66n
Swami Paramarthananda, 28-30, 31, 31n, 56, 88, 95, 99, 121n, 147n, 154, 157n, 161, 162, 164, 190, 253-254, 255n, 257, 279
Patañjali, 27, 35, 250
Patton, L.L., 36-38
Paul the Apostle, 42, 43-44, 68-73, 75-77, 103-107, 109, 135-139, 142, 144, 152, 159, 167-170, 181, 202-205, 209, 237, 238-243, 244, 248, 273-276, 279, 284, 285, 290, 294-295, 296, 308, 316
Pope Paul VI, 243, 244n
Perkins, P., 291
Pieris, A., 33, 282
Pontifical Biblical Commission, 75-77, 75n, 294
Pseudo-Dionysius, 160

Radhakrishnan, S., 251, 253
Ramana Maharshi, 28, 250, 252
Rāmānuja, 33, 83n, 235, 291
Ramatīrtha, 3, 28, 29, 30, 32, 56n, 119n, 146n, 147n, 231n, 257, 306n

Rambachan, A., 9, 96, 311
Ram-Prasad, C., 36-38, 126n, 194n
Renou, L., 66n
Rosemann, P.W., 173, 175, 176n
Rukmani, T.S., 311n
Rüping, K., 35n
Rydstrøm-Poulsen, A., 175

Śabara, 51
Sadānanda, 27
Sampley, J.P., 203
Sanders E.P., 69, 72
Swami Satchidanandendra, 10
Schweiker, W., 315n, 317
Second Vatican Council of the Catholic Church, 33, 70-71, 78-79, 243-48, 244n
Shankara, XIV, XV, XVII, XVIII, 8n, 1-12, 13, 24, 48, 50, 59, 66, 84n, 85, 93, 119, 120n-121n, 126, 128n, 166, 182, 184, 189, 218, 225, 226, 232n, 234, 243n, 251, 254n, 261-263, 267
Sharma, A., 252
Sheridan, D.P., 38-40, 42, 73-74n
Starkey, P., 313, 317
Stoeber, M., 310n
Sundaresan, V., 8n
Sureśvara, 8, 25-27, 30, 32, 94n, 150-151, 154, 158, 232n
Suthren Hirst, J.G., 9, 11, 96n, 126, 138, 152n, 156, 182-183, 201, 233, 235

Śvetaketu, 87n, 89, 153

Tanner, K., 240-243, 244-245
Swami Tejomayananda, XIII
Tertullian of Carthage, 92
Thatamanil, J., 160, 161, 189, 193, 311, 312
Tilley, T., 307, 307n
Tillich, P., 193, 311
Turner, V., 209

Udaṅka, 92-93, 112
Ulrich, E.T., 253n
Upadhyay, B., 292n
Pope Urban VIII, 206
Urs von Balthasar, H., 313n

Vācaspati Miśra, 36, 232n
Vallabha, 235, 291-292
Vento, J.M., 278
Vetter, T., 6n, 10,182, 233n-234n
Vidyāraṅya, 27, 30, 32, 35, 84, 119n, 254, 254n, 264
Vishnu, 92-93
Swami Vivekananda, 250-251, 253

Ward, M., 42, 205-211, 294, 309, 316
Wright, N.T., 239, 243, 274

Yājñavalkya, 165
Yuval-Davis, N., 309